CANADIAN ENERGY POLICY AND THE STRUGGLE FOR SUSTAINABLE DEVELOPMENT

In recent years, energy policy has been increasingly linked to concepts of sustainable development. In this timely collection, editor G. Bruce Doern presents an overview of Canadian energy policy, gathering together the top Canadian scholars in the field in an examination of the twenty-year period broadly benchmarked by energy liberalization and free trade in the mid-1980s, and by Canada's ratification of the Kyoto Protocol in 2002.

The contributors examine issues including electricity restructuring in the wake of the August 2003 blackout, the implications of the Bush administration's energy policies, energy security, northern pipelines and Aboriginal energy issues, provincial changes in energy policy, and overall federal-provincial changes in regulatory governance. They also demonstrate that, since per capita energy usage has actually increased in the past several years, sustainable development remains very much a struggle rather than an achievement. When the Kyoto Protocol and its requirements for reductions in greenhouse gas emissions are factored in, the Canadian record is especially dubious in basic energy terms. *Canadian Energy Policy and the Struggle for Sustainable Development* is key to understanding many of the issues in Canada's endeavour to live up to its many energy-related environmental responsibilities.

G. BRUCE DOERN is a professor in the School of Public Policy and Administration at Carleton University, and the Politics Department at the University of Exeter.

Canadian Energy Policy and the Struggle for Sustainable Development

Edited by G. Bruce Doern

UNIVERSITY OF TORONTO PRESS
Toronto Buffalo London

© University of Toronto Press Incorporated 2005
Toronto Buffalo London
Printed in Canada

ISBN 0-8020-8758-2 (cloth)
ISBN 0-8020-8561-X (paper)

Printed on acid-free paper

Library and Archives Canada Cataloguing in Publication

Canadian energy policy and the struggle for sustainable development /
edited by G. Bruce Doern.

Essays from a conference held Oct. 2002.
Includes bibliographical references.
ISBN 0-8020-8758-2 (bound)   ISBN 0-8020-8561-X (pbk.)

1. Energy policy – Canada – Congresses.   2. Sustainable development – Canada – Congresses.—3. Energy industries – Environmental
aspects – Canada – Congresses.   4. Power resources – Environmental aspects – Canada – Congresses.   I. Doern, G. Bruce, 1942–

HD9502.C32C347 2005   333.79'0971   C2004-903623-8

University of Toronto Press acknowledges the financial assistance to its
publishing program of the Canada Council for the Arts and the Ontario Arts
Council.

University of Toronto Press acknowledges the financial support for its
publishing activities of the Government of Canada through the Book
Publishing Industry Development Program (BPIDP).

Contents

Preface

This book is the product of a collaborative effort by the editor and the contributing authors initiated through the work of the Carleton Research Unit on Innovation, Science, and Environment (CRUISE) in the School of Public Policy and Administration at Carleton University. It builds on other energy regulation and governance publications at CRUISE and in the school.

Initial drafts of the chapters, along with other commentaries, were presented at the CRUISE Conference on Canadian Energy Policy held in Ottawa on 17 and 18 October 2002. Besides the authors represented in this book, we were fortunate in securing the involvement of leading energy and environmental policy practitioners and academics, including John Lowe of Natural Resources Canada, Bob Slater of Environment Canada, Karen Wristen of the Canadian Arctic Resources Committee, Ken Ogilvie of Pollution Probe, Takis Plagiannakos of the Ontario Department of Energy, Science, and Technology, Government of Ontario, Bonnie Gray of the National Energy Board, and Professor Glen Toner of CRUISE. There was also insightful input from many others who attended the conference or who commented on draft chapters after the conference.

Many thanks are due to all these individuals, who gave unstintingly of their time. The book also benefited greatly from the very constructive comments and suggestions of two of the University of Toronto Press's anonymous assessors. All of these individuals helped make the book a better product.

Special thanks are also due for the research funding for this book and related energy policy research, which has come from a variety of sources, including the Social Science and Humanities Research Council of Canada, the Carleton Research Unit on Innovation, Science and Environment (CRUISE) at the School of Public Policy and Administration, the Politics Department, University of Exeter, Natural Resources Canada, Environment Canada, Industry Canada, the Department of Indian Affairs and Northern Development, the Canadian Electricity Association, and the Canadian Association of Petroleum Producers.

Abbreviations

ADR	Alternative dispute resolution
AE	Alberta Environment
AECL	Atomic Energy of Canada Ltd.
AEP	Alberta Environment Protection
AEUB	Alberta Energy Utilities Board
AGS	Alberta Geological Survey
AGTL	Alberta Gas Trunk Line
AHP	Alaska Highway Pipeline
AIT	Agreement on Internal Trade
ANWR	Alaska Natural Wildlife Refuge
ATC	average total cost
BP	British Petroleum
CAGPL	Canadian Arctic Gas Pipeline
CANDU	Canada deuterium uranium (reactor)
CAPP	Canadian Association of Petroleum Producers
CASA	Clean Air Strategic Alliance
CCAP	Climate Change Action Fund
CCGT	combined cycle gas turbine
CDM	clean development mechanism
CEA	Canadian Electricity Association
CEAA	Canadian Environmental Assessment Agency
CEC	Commission for Environmental Cooperation
CEPA	Canadian Environmental Protection Act
CNSC	Canadian Nuclear Safety Commission
COP	conference of the parties
CSR	corporate social responsibility
DFAIT	Department of Foreign Affairs and International Trade

DIAND	Department of Indian Affairs and Northern Development
DIR	director of investigation and research
DFO	Department of Fisheries and Oceans
DSM	demand-side management
EC	Environment Canada
EMR	Energy, Mines and Resources
ENGOs	environmental non-governmental organizations
ERCB	Energy Resources Conservation Board (Alberta)
EU	European Union
FERC	Federal Energy Regulatory Commission (US)
FTA	Free Trade Agreement (between Canada and the US)
GHG	greenhouse gases
JI	joint implementation
IAEA	International Atomic Energy Agency
IEA	International Energy Agency
IMO	independent market operator
IOU	investor-owned utility
IPCC	Intergovernmental Panel on Climate Change
ISO	Independent System Operator (US)
LCA	life cycle assessment
LDC	local distribution company
MMT	methycyclopentadienyl manganese tricarbonyl (gasoline additive)
MOU	memoranda of understanding
MPMA	market power mitigation agreement
MVP	Mackenzie Valley Pipeline
NAERO	North American Electricity Reliability Organization
NAERC	North American Electricity Reliability Council
NAEWG	North American Energy Working Group
NAFTA	North American Free Trade Agreement
NEB	National Energy Board
NEP	National Energy Program (1980)
NGOs	non-governmental organizations
NOP	national oil policy
NOX-VOCS	nitrogen oxides and volatile organic compounds
NPM	new public management
NRCan	Natural Resources Canada
NRC	National Research Council
NSPI	Nova Scotia Power Inc.

NTFOSS	National Task Force on Oil Sands Technology
NUGs	non utility generators
OEB	Ontario Energy Board
OECD	Organization of Economic Cooperation and Development
OPEC	Organization of Petroleum Exporting Countries
OPG	Ontario Power Generation Inc.
PEMEX	Petroleos Mexicanos
PERD	Program on Energy Research and Development
PCO	Privy Council Office
PUB	Public Utilities Board (Alberta)
PUCs	Public Utility Commissions (U.S.)
PURPA	A Public Utility Regulation Policies Act (U.S.)
PX	power exchange
QF	qualifying facilities
RPS	renewable portfolio standard
RRO	regulated rate options
RTG	regional transmission grids
RTOs	regional transmission organizations
SDTF	Sustainable Development Technology Fund
TCPL	TransCanada Pipelines Ltd.
TEAM	technology early action measures
TOU	time of use
UARB	Utilities and Review Board (Nova Scotia)
UNFCCC	United Nations Framework Convention on Climate Change
US NEP	US National Energy Policy (2001)
WTO	World Trade Organization
WTI	West Texas Intermediate

CANADIAN ENERGY POLICY AND THE STRUGGLE
FOR SUSTAINABLE DEVELOPMENT

Chapter 1

Canadian Energy Policy and the Struggle for Sustainable Development: Political-Economic Context

G. BRUCE DOERN

This book examines selected key energy policy issues and challenges that have confronted Canadians over the past twenty years, the period during which the struggle for sustainable development began. Its purpose is to provide a broad political-economic analysis of how energy policy has evolved over the last twenty years and also of how and why energy policy ideas, interests, and governance approaches have changed. It also examines key energy policy and political issues facing Canada in the short-term future. This book, which draws on authors whose academic and practitioner backgrounds include political science, economics, law, and science, is the first in many years to examine broadly the changing nature of Canadian energy policy and overall energy governance.[1]

This book presents an overview of Canadian energy policy during a period in which energy policy is being linked more and more closely to concepts of sustainable development in addition to more traditional notions of environmental policy, which focus more narrowly on pollution control. This broad task necessarily requires that the book also canvas the underlying political economy of institutional change in the national, North American, and global contexts. The twenty years on which the book focuses are roughly bracketed by energy liberalization and free trade in the mid-1980s and by Canada's signing of the Kyoto Protocol in 2003–4. But these are by no means the only manifestations of Canadian energy policy, and hence this book seeks to cover other selected but important aspects of energy policy, including the following: electricity restructuring, including the implications of the August 2003 electricity blackout; the implications of the George W. Bush's energy policies; energy security; northern pipelines and Aboriginal energy issues; changes in provincial energy policy and overall federal–provincial changes in regulatory governance; and energy in relation to federal innovation and science/technology policy. All of these policy and political challenges will test Paul Martin's new Liberal government and provincial governments as well.

Energy policy as a whole refers to policies aimed at influencing and shaping the supply of energy sources and fuels, the demand for these by various users of energy, and – ever more importantly – the environmental impacts of energy use. Energy policy thus covers sources and fuels such as oil and natural gas, coal, hydroelectricity, nuclear energy, and a host of alternative or complementary sources such as fuel cells, solar energy, wind power, and biomass. Energy policy is also about national and regional politics, in the sense that past conflicts influence present views of what policy should and should not be. Energy policy seeks to influence behaviour at many various stages of production and consumption, from initial extraction, to processing and transportation, to use in homes, public institutions, and commercial establishments, to the disposal and remediation of wastes. It involves the use of all of the main policy instruments: regulation, persuasion or voluntary approaches, spending (mainly on science, technology, and innovation), and taxation. This book examines the first three of these instruments; however, only limited attention is paid to energy taxation.

Sustainable development policy refers to policies intended to ensure that in any number of areas of governance, the environment and its ecosystems will be left in at least as good a state for the next generation as they were for the current generation (Lafferty and Meadowcroft, 2000). Cast somewhat more loosely, these policies are often defined by governments as those which take into balanced consideration the economic, social, and environmental effects of policies – the so-called 'triple bottom line' (Toner, 2000; Toner and Frey, 2003). In more specific energy policy terms, sustainable development is also initially tested against the basic question of whether Canada has made progress in even reducing energy use on a per capita basis over the past twenty years. This per capita usage has actually increased marginally; clearly, then, there is much more to do. This book shows that as a whole, sustainable development in energy terms remains very much a struggle rather than an achievement. When we apply the Kyoto Protocol and its requirements for reductions in greenhouse gas emissions as a core test of sustainable development, we must conclude that Canada's record is still dubious in basic energy terms.

It is true that the issues of sustainable development have been debated for longer than twenty years. It is also true that in some federal departments, sustainable development criteria have been implanted in policy and decision processes and in some reporting activities (VanNijnatten, 2002). As well, some conservation measures have had a positive impact in that per capita energy consumption would have been higher without them. But while some policies and processes have been changed, there have been no fundamental changes in policy outputs and outcomes, and certainly not in energy policy overall (see more below).

This book's structure reflects its broad purposes. Chapters 2, 3, and 4 cover major developments in energy policy, nationally, in North America, and globally. André Plourde in chapter 2 examines key changes in Canadian and North American energy markets in three sectors – oil, natural gas, and electricity – and shows that promarket energy policies and ideas are being practised in the first two sectors but not as clearly in the third. In contrast to Plourde's more retrospective focus, Robert Morrison in chapter 3 considers the central issues of future energy supply, demand, and impacts in the context of sustainable development ideas at the global and national levels. In this complex global context, sustainable development can actually require *more* energy use, especially in poorer countries, in addition to stronger energy and environmental conservation measures. As a practitioner of federal environment policy, Bill Jarvis in chapter 4 asks key questions relating to the conceptual approaches to energy and environment – approaches that are sometimes still quite polarized. Jarvis's focus is on the crucial practical issues for policy, including these two: the still very great need for core systems for gathering information about ecosystem impacts; and the difficult task of ensuring that the prices of the environmental and health costs of environmental impacts will be internalized as they relate to energy supply and use. He considers this in the context of governmental data and information (and the lack thereof), but also in terms of corporations' environmental reporting.

Chapters 5 to 7 focus on the electricity sector, although from different analytical perspectives. Electricity requires a careful look because of its status as the most recent frontier for experimenting with more market-centred approaches to policy, especially over the past decade. Don Dewees in chapter 5 deals with Canadian electricity restructuring developments from the perspective of an economist who has contributed directly to design discussions and debates in Ontario. Chapter 6 by Scott Vaughan, Chantal Line Carpentier, Zachary Patterson, and

Paul Miller examines the electricity sector in a North American context, with a particular focus on environmental impacts and the management of regional grids in North America. In chapter 7, Stephan Schott returns the focus to Ontario (but with global references as well), and offers a generally very critical view of electricity restructuring in Ontario. His framework for analysis centres on both social efficiency and sustainable development.

Chapters 8 to 12 examine other selected regional and provincial realms; they focus more on petroleum development and on related regulatory changes and approaches to energy governance. In chapter 8, Keith Brownsey zeroes in on Alberta, this country's key oil-and-gas province; he looks at its historical policies on energy, at how oil patch interests are being transformed, and at the province's battles with federal governments, including the ones over the Kyoto Protocol. In chapter 9, Frances Abele explores key energy issues in the context of northern development and Aboriginal peoples as well as the crucial and vastly changed systems of governance and democracy in the North. Chapter 10 by Nigel Bankes and Michael Wenig examines issues surrounding the regulation and building of a northern pipeline in the wake of the Americans' renewed interest in both Alaskan and Canadian natural gas. These authors explore the current debate about pipelines in relation to the debates and regulatory processes that surfaced initially in the mid-1970s, which was the last time a pipeline debate arose. One of the core outcomes of that era was the Berger Commission, which considered the issue of sustainable development long before that concept was articulated at the global level by the 1987 Brundtland Commission. Chapter 11 by Monica Gattinger focuses on the growing use of dispute resolution approaches to regulation by the National Energy Board and also by energy regulatory bodies in Alberta and British Columbia. Then, in chapter 12, Alastair Lucas considers Alberta's preference for, and use of, voluntary approaches to regulation, not only in terms of energy regulation but also in the context of approaches promised by the Alberta government to reduce greenhouse gas emissions by taking a 'made in Alberta' approach to climate change.

While this book is wide-ranging, two limitations to its analysis must be noted. First, it focuses strongly on oil-and-gas and electricity policy and pays much less attention to other aspects of energy policy such as nuclear and hydroelectric energy, alternative energy technologies, and hydrogen fuel cells (Flavin, 1998; Hoffman, 2001; Morrison, Layell, and McLean, 2001; Doern, Dorman, and Morrison, 2001; Toner, 2004).

Second, although the book deals with many key aspects of federal and overall Canadian energy policy over the past twenty years, it does not deal with all of the provinces' and territories' approaches and changes. A sample profile of some provinces is presented in this chapter, as are key federal–provincial issues relating to regulatory development and the Kyoto Protocol process; however, this book as a whole pays much more detailed attention to developments in Alberta, Ontario, and the North. This reflects the fact that for oil and gas, Alberta is still the main producer province and Ontario the main consuming province; it also reflects the fact that these two provinces have experimented the most with electricity restructuring, with all the resultant problems. Attention to the North is clearly necessary given the issues of future supply, links with American energy policy, and sustainability.

This introductory chapter provides the political-economic and institutional context for Canadian energy policy development and for the contributing authors' analyses. It has six sections and draws both on the chapters that follow and on other relevant Canadian and comparative literature. The first section provides a brief historical background for Canadian energy policy and profiles current overall federal energy policy in the context of key developments in international trade and climate change policy prior to the Bush administration's 2001–2 energy policies. The second section examines the current sources of energy supply and current energy use, as well as the core barriers and opportunities for conservation and for movement toward a low-carbon economy in Canada and globally. The third section sets out the Bush administration's National Energy Policy and the alternative it offers to the Kyoto Protocol – policies that will have a crucial effect on Canada's energy and sustainable development approaches. The fourth section discusses global climate change, with a focus on the federal–provincial debate in Canada on approaches to implementing (or not) the Kyoto Protocol. The fifth section then offers a brief account of how the basic federal–provincial energy regulatory system has evolved. Finally, the sixth section profiles broad changes in the configuration of energy interests, including industry interests and those of non-governmental organizations (NGOs), the scientific and technological community, and Aboriginal peoples.

Historical and International Contexts and Federal Energy Policy

Current energy policy issues, pressures, and developments need to be placed – albeit very briefly – in the context of recent Canadian energy policy history, including key international developments in trade and climate change policy, as well as in the context of stated federal energy and sustainable development policy. Chapters 2, 3, and 4 will flesh out key aspects of this history. In terms of recent history, this introduction emphasizes two main features: deregulation, free trade, and relative promarket policy stability since the mid-1980s (but set against the political memory of the energy policy wars of the early 1980s); and the emergence of the sustainable development policy paradigm and the climate change debate.

Deregulation, Free Trade, and Promarket–Energy Policy Stability

The first recent historical reference point is the strong trend toward energy deregulation and free trade and considerable promarket policy stability in federal policy between 1984 and 2000. When Brian Mulroney's Conservatives were elected in 1984 with a massive majority, the energy agenda changed drastically from that of the Trudeau Liberals. Ideologically, the Conservatives favoured a return to strongly promarket policies on energy and the economy (Toner, 1986; Watkins, 1991; Canada, 1988). Politically, especially regarding relations with western Canada, the new government sought national reconciliation and an end to the energy wars fought over the Liberal National Energy Program (NEP) of 1980 and the formation of Petro-Canada in the 1970s. Internationally, the government sought closer relations with the United States; this would lead to the Canada–U.S. Free Trade Agreement.

The Mulroney Conservatives moved swiftly on the energy front; it saw its primary task as to dismantle the NEP. The federal government's conciliatory approach toward the provinces and its promarket slant were reflected in four initiatives; the net result of these was an oil-and-gas market even freer than the one that existed before 1973, when the prodevelopment National Oil Policy was in operation (McDougall, 1982; Economic Council of Canada, 1985; Doern and Toner, 1985).

The first initiative was the signing of the Western Accord between Ottawa and the western producer provinces. This accord deregulated oil and restored continental oil markets. Second, the Atlantic Accord between Ottawa and (mainly) Newfoundland settled a long-festering issue: Which level of government had jurisdictional control over off-shore resources? This accord was not especially promarket in its content, but it certainly reflected a commitment to national reconciliation.

Third, the Western Accord was followed by an agreement to phase in the deregulation of gas. This would allow more direct buy–sell relationships between gas producers and gas users, with a consequent weakening of some of the previous monopoly powers of pipelines and distribution companies. As Plourde's analysis in chapter 2 shows, long-term contracts made this gas policy more difficult to implement than oil deregulation; nevertheless, a significant promarket change came about fairly quickly. Gas deregulation eventually brought an end to the past policy, which had required surplus reserve tests for exports of natural gas. These had required a twenty-five-year domestic supply cushion before exports were allowed.

Fourth, the Mulroney government negotiated a free trade agreement (FTA) with the United States, which came into effect 1 January 1989 (Doern and Tomlin, 1991). The FTA further dissolved the continental boundaries, mainly by preventing the future use of two-price systems and by restraining the Americans from applying many of the restrictive measures they had resorted to in the postwar era regarding Canadian oil and gas (and uranium) exports. The quid pro quo for this long-sought agreement – more secure access to the massive American market – was the so-called proportionality clause, which provided that Canada could not arbitrarily cut off contracted American buyers of Canadian oil and gas. If shortages arose, Canada could only reduce supply in proportion over an agreed three-year base period. The FTA did protect Canada's existing foreign ownership laws regarding energy investments; however, for the most part the FTA constituted the capstone for the Mulroney government's promarket energy policies, in effect quasi-'constitutionalizing' them. As Plourde's analysis in chapter 2 shows, the later North American Free Trade Agreement (NAFTA) did not change the Canada–U.S. energy policy relationship, although it did allow Mexico to retain most of its state-controlled energy policies.

Though the promarket policies of the Mulroney era still dominate, they continue to be couched in the context of the political legacy of the earlier NEP. In its budget in the fall of 1980, Trudeau's Liberal government announced the National Energy Program (NEP). Coming in the wake of the 1979 global energy crisis (the second in six years) and soaring world oil prices, the NEP was a massive act of federal intervention premised on the Liberals' campaign promise of fair, 'made in Canada' prices; 50 per cent Canadian ownership of the oil-and-gas industry; and a promise to promote energy security, including self-

sufficiency in oil by 1990. The NEP was premised on absolutely bullish expectations regarding rising future energy prices and rising energy tax revenues for governments; both, however, failed to materialize (Doern and Toner, 1985; Canada, 1988).

With the NEP, the federal Liberals had thrown down the gauntlet.
That program precipitated angry negotiations and acts of political
brinkmanship that seriously threatened national unity. Nonetheless, a
pricing agreement was eventually reached in September 1981, in part
because both Alberta and the federal government believed their own
forecasts of ever-increasing prices and hence thought they were sharing a very large revenue pie. The NEP also angered the newly elected,
free enterprise–oriented Reagan administration in the United States,
as well as large parts of the energy industry and the Canadian business community as a whole. It was, however, initially popular in
Ontario and Quebec, the home of the largest portion of energy consumers (and voters).

Politically, the NEP left a bitter taste, especially regarding relations
between central and western Canada. Especially in western Canada, it
became the quintessential example of how not to make policy. It was
seen as a combative and unilateral act by an unsympathetic and east-
ern-dominated government. This lesson was a major contributing factor in later discussions in 1987–8, when energy free trade was secured
through the FTA. From the perspective of western Canada, the FTA
ensured that there could never again be 'another NEP.' Debates in the
early 2000s over the Kyoto Protocol on greenhouse gas reductions
resonate with the view in Alberta that federal policy on Kyoto is or
could be cast as 'another NEP.'

*The Global and National Emergence of the Sustainable Development
Paradigm*

The second recent historical point to be emphasized centres on the
growing interactions between energy policy and environmental policy
– especially the emergence of the paradigm of sustainable development. Robert Morrison's analysis in chapter 3 and key elements of the
Bill Jarvis's analysis in chapter 4 examine sustainable development in
more detail and show its contested nature. Historically, there is no
doubt that with the political emergence of the environmental movement in the late 1960s, the linkages between energy and environment
have intensified and have also become both more complex and more

specific. The increased political visibility of the moral case advanced by Aboriginal peoples for their land claims in energy-rich areas of Canada has only strengthened these links.

Environmental–energy issues first peaked on the national political-economic agenda in the mid-1970s, when a major inquiry, the Berger Commission, examined the desirability of building a controversial mega-project, the Mackenzie Valley gas pipeline. Because of that commission's hearings and the sensitivities they raised, the project was put on hold. In chapter 11, Bankes and Wenig compare the Berger hearings with the current debate over northern pipelines. They conclude that sustainable development is no more a reality now than it was at the time of the Berger Commission. There is still much more talk than action.

In the 1980s, there was a gradual strengthening of regulatory requirements at both the federal and provincial levels to protect the environment (VanNijnatten and Boardman, 2002). In the late 1980s, the federal government along with other G-7 countries formally committed itself to adopting 'sustainable development' – a concept advocated by the prestigious Brundtland World Commission on the Environment (Toner, 2000). In the past decade, policies on climate change have become increasingly contentious; they have also helped rekindle East–West suspicions in Canada and have complicated relations between traditional energy sectors and resource sectors such as forestry, mining, and fisheries and oceans (Natural Resources Canada, 2000). As we will discuss later on, most provincial energy policies have embraced sustainable development at least rhetorically, but also in some areas of energy policy and practice. However, like the federal policy, the provincial ones have embraced the much looser 'triple bottom-line' notions of sustainable development rather than an ecosystem notion of sustainability.

The Chrétien Government's Energy-Sustainable Development Policies

The Chrétien Liberal government stated in 2000 that since 1993, federal energy policy has been 'guided by the principles of sustainable development' and consists of three main objectives:

- to develop a competitive and innovative energy sector – by implementing a framework that promotes the long term development of Canadian energy resources, encourages wise use of energy re-

sources, and maximizes economic opportunity in the energy sector for Canadians (which reflects the government's goal of promoting jobs and growth).
• to encourage environmental stewardship – by addressing the environmental impacts of energy development, transportation, and use and by integrating environmental objectives into all policies and programs.
• to establish secure access – by ensuring that current and future generations of Canadians have enough competitively priced energy and by taking measures that make efficient use of existing resources and provide reliable energy services to Canadians. (Natural Resources Canada, 2000, 9)

As indicated earlier, this commitment pays homage to the very broad 'triple bottom-line' notion of sustainable development. The Liberal government also described its approach as being 'driven by the same global trends–globalization, deregulation, increased environmental awareness, and the overall theme of reliance on markets' (ibid., 137). Federal energy policy sees energy regulation as quintessentially federal and provincial in nature – and increasingly continental and global as well – and holds, furthermore, that managing energy markets means 'more markets–less government.' But having established this principle of market reliance, the same statement goes on to say in the very next breath that 'environmental concerns are growing' and that 'contrary to the trend towards trusting markets and competition, environmental concerns, particularly those related to energy, often call for more regulation' (ibid., 138).

The federal view also emphasizes that energy commodities are 'no longer considered "unique" or "special"' and that energy regulation today must be contrasted with that of the 1970s and early 1980s, when it was driven by several different precepts:

• A perception of scarcity – The world's energy resources were finite, while demand for energy would inevitably rise. The demand for energy needed to be regulated.
• An emphasis on security – Western countries were susceptible to disruptions in their supply.
• An emphasis on self-sufficiency – Canada sought to reduce its vulnerability by protecting and increasing its domestic supply of energy.
• An expectation of rising prices – With scarcity came the belief that prices for energy would rise.

- A perception of market inadequacy – Oil markets, in particular, were distorted and concentrated which led to oligopoly control. (ibid., 137)

As we will see, some of these supposedly discarded notions are being at least partly challenged by recent energy policy developments and pressures.

In the early years of the twenty-first century, the federal government sees the core of federal energy policy and regulation as consisting of several key regulatory elements and treaties (Natural Resources Canada, 2000, 139 and Appendix I):

- The National Energy Board and the National Energy Board Act.
- The Canadian Environmental Assessment Act
- The North American Free Trade Agreement (NAFTA) – Energy Chapter
- Agreement on Internal Trade – Energy Chapter
- Energy Supplies Emergency Act
- Energy Efficiency Regulations and the Energy Efficiency Act
- the Canadian Nuclear Safety Commission

Add to this the ongoing issues surrounding the 1997 Kyoto Protocol and the related National Implementation Strategy, including the early 2000s processes for discussing climate change options and commitments. Prime Minister Chrétien's announcement in Johannesburg that Canada would ratify the Kyoto pact by the end of 2002 was a decisive decision point; however, the decision to ratify merely begs a series of questions that in federal and provincial energy policy are only beginning to be dealt with and that will be a central challenge for Paul Martin's Liberal government.

Clearly, federal energy policy is complex. But even the above list of federal policy and regulatory elements does not do justice to the nature of contemporary Canadian energy policy and regulation for the country as a whole. A sampling of provincial energy policies is presented later in this chapter.

Energy Supply and Barriers and Opportunities for Conservation and a Low-Carbon Economy

The history of Canada's energy policy testifies to the social, political, and economic importance of this resource, to a vast continental country with a relatively small population. This history also shows how Canada has relied on various fuel sources over time: wood and coal gradually gave way over the decades to hydroelectric power and oil, and then nuclear power and natural gas. Most recently, alternative sources such as wind, the tides, biomass, and fuel cells have been tapped, albeit in small quantities. Of growing importance are the huge oil sands of northern Alberta. By the 1980s Canada was in a position to practise a high degree of interfuel substitution. Throughout its history, Canada has seen itself and been seen by others as an energy-rich country.

As Bob Morrison's analysis in chapter 3 shows, Canada's sources of energy supply in 2000 were oil (37%), natural gas (29%), coal (11%), hydro (10%), nuclear (8%), and other (5%). Chapter 3 shows that Canada's carbon emissions are double those of European countries owing to this country's high overall per capita use of energy. Canada and the United States are among the world's most energy-wasteful countries. By this test, sustainable development, defined as basic conservation of energy per capita, is on this continent more rhetoric than reality.

Since well before the Kyoto Protocol and the climate change debate, there has been a general debate in Canada about how to reduce energy use. This was certainly a central concern at the time of the 1973 and 1979 oil crises. In fact, the high prices for oil during those two crises promoted conservation, although they also, of course, created macroeconomic havoc. Energy conservation was also a central part of the 'limits to growth' arguments of the 1960s and 1970s, when some important activists argued that the world was running out of oil (Doern and Toner, 1985; Economic Council of Canada, 1985). The Liberals' NEP of 1980 included some key incentive programs to encourage conservation and to get Canadians 'off oil' and on to other fuels, especially natural gas.

But from the mid-1980s on, many conservation policies waned, in part because of pressure from dominant producer groups and regions in oil and gas, but also simply because of a booming economy and the success of promarket energy policies and what was to become a decade or more of low and stable oil and gas prices. The climate change debate of the 1990s and the politics of the Kyoto Protocol eventually brought the conservation debate to the fore again, this time in the sharpened context of greenhouse gas emissions. Indeed, key supporters of the Kyoto Protocol saw it – even if implemented successfully –

as merely the first in a series of necessary steps for tackling climate change in the decades ahead (Grubb et al., 1999; Houghton, 1997).

Current and near-term energy policies are clearly being influenced by the climate change debate. However, such policies are always partly premised as well on long-term energy projections and scenarios, both national and global. These are discussed further by Morrison in chapter 3 and also by Brownsey in chapter 8 in his analysis of Alberta's energy policy goals and its desire to exploit its massive oil sands reserves. A central question in these scenarios is whether Canada is planning for, or moving toward, a low-carbon economy. Questions of what *low carbon* means and whether it can be achieved are of course themselves contentious. Some argue that past patterns of change in fuel use have reflected steady progress toward a *lower*-carbon economy, in that the shift from wood to coal to oil to gas and so on has been a shift away from high-carbon toward lower-carbon emissions per unit of energy (Dunn, 2001). But of course, economic and population growth means that carbon emissions have been growing to the point that climate change has become a serious global and Canadian issue. A low-carbon economy is also a term centred on time and on how fast such a shift or progression might occur. This in turn is driven by the power of various producer interests, by their alliances with governments, and by the counterpressure exerted by environmental lobbies and their alliances with governments.

There is little doubt that Canada needs an explicit debate about its energy future and about whether it is simply drifting toward or away from a lower-carbon economy. Climate change and the Kyoto Protocol are very important facets of this question, but questions about a low- or lower-carbon future track are ultimately far broader than the current politics and economics of the Kyoto Protocol. Bob Morrison in chapter 3 provides a basic account of global and Canadian projections in the context of what sustainable development might variously mean for rich and poor countries.

Some initial reference points about the craft, science, and politics of energy forecasting are a necessary starting point for projections about the energy future, low-carbon or otherwise (Mommer, 2002). For example, a 1998 study reviewed six possible scenarios and thus a range of possible energy developments extending out to 2050 and beyond (Nakicenovic, Grubler, and McDonald, 1998). The study covered scenarios ranging from 'a tremendous expansion of coal production to strict limits, from a phase-out of nuclear energy to a substantial increase, from carbon emissions in 2100 that are only one-third of today's levels to increases by more than a factor of three' (ibid., xi). Some of the highlights of this analysis follow:

- It is easier to anticipate the forms in which energy will be demanded by consumers in the future than to estimate the absolute level of demand, or which energy sources will supply that demand.
- With increasing per capita incomes around the world, people will demand higher levels of more efficient, cleaner, and environmentally less obtrusive energy services ...
- The question of what kind of companies will supply energy services, and how, is wide open ...
- At least through 2020, the world will have to rely largely upon fossil fuels, with relatively few opportunities for alternatives.
- But after 2020 the six scenarios start to diverge and depend in part on policy choices and development strategies; ... two scenarios lead to less fossil fuel use ...
- Most of the post 2020 divergence will depend on technological developments, industrial strategies, and consumer choice ...
- The answers to those questions will be determined between now and 2020 ... The choice of the world's energy systems may be open now. It will be a lot narrower by 2020. (Ibid., xi–xii)

Analyses of global forecasts also contain some debate and speculation about whether OPEC and Saudi Arabian dominance of long-term oil supplies might be challenged by current and eventual Russian supplies. However, the conclusions seem to fall back onto the old but important constant that Saudi Arabian and Middle East supply is and will continue to be pivotal (Morse and Richard, 2002; National Post Business, 2001). Uncertainty about postwar Iraq and about possible further conflict in the Middle East inevitably qualifies these findings. Clearly, the Americans with their energy plan (see more below) are seeking ways to reduce their own pivotal dependence on Middle Eastern and OPEC supplies.

Another recent forecast was by the *Economist* (*Economist*, 2002). It explicitly linked energy and environment choices and scenarios but focused its analysis and conclusions on the inevitable economic importance of coal and hence on the key importance of fostering clean coal or cleaner coal technologies. Its reasoning: 'There is so much cheap coal, distributed all over the world that poor countries are bound to want to burn it' (ibid., 11).

A further recent example of energy forecasting and planning is Britain's recently published study (Cabinet Office, 2002). Interestingly, this study was not sponsored by the British energy ministry; rather, it came out of the Cabinet Office's Performance and Innovation Unit. It focused on the period until 2020, and it developed scenarios that reflected the interaction between energy and the environment. Importantly as well, this study focused strongly on the issue of energy security for Britain, largely because Britain's new sources of energy mainly involve natural gas supplied by pipelines from eastern Europe and the former Soviet republics. This cannot but raise British concerns about political instability in those regions. This British study also traced the virtual elimination of the coal industry in Britain over the past twenty years. This, in concert with the reduction of North Sea oil reserves, prompted the report to warn Britain not to abandon nuclear power as a source, even though the nuclear industry faced serious economic problems and even though there are profound concerns about the long-term storage of nuclear wastes (ibid., 2002; Helm, 2003; Connor, 2002).

In a Canadian context, the Canadian Association of Petroleum Producers (CAPP) has recently drawn on Shell International's scenarios and forecasts (Canadian Association of Petroleum Producers, 2002). The basic Shell scenario cited by CAPP is one in which:

- the world will continue to use increasing amounts of energy, and oil and gas will continue to be the dominant forms of primary energy for many decades.
- new renewables and clean coal could come to supply an increasing amount of global primary energy, but given rising population and the rise in standards of living projected for developing countries, increasing amounts of natural gas will be required to meet rising global energy demand for the next five decades. (In CAPP, 2002, 3)

Other projections are equally bullish about Canada's oil-and-gas supply situation, in part because of more recent confirmations of the oil sand reserves (Sweet, 2004). These analyses also point to the growing presence of a global rather than just continental natural gas market through expanded trade in liquified natural gas (LNG).

Morrison in chapter 3 explores forecasts in more detail, and what those forecasts (if accurate) mean for energy growth and use. He also discusses the environmental impact of those forecast results both for Canada and for Canada's positions on global energy policy. For example, he discusses the need for developing countries to vastly increase their energy use. In the latter context, sustainable development – when defined as balanced economic, social, and environmental development – often does mean *increased* energy use – and increased GHG emissions as well. Brownsey (chapter 8) shows the crucial importance, both immediate and long-term, of the Alberta oil sands. Canada is already dependent on this vast petroleum reserve.

There are clearly important but also complex aspects to these energy forecasts. No forecast is perfect or foolproof. Generally, though, forecasts do raise the issue of whether Canada needs a more public and even formal process of looking at and debating these crucial energy alternatives. Some form of low(er)-carbon economy may be drifting into view, but it is doubtful whether in Canada this and other aspects of energy-sustainable development policy have received a proper public review. The debate in Canada in the early 2000s over climate change and the Kyoto Protocol does not even come close to meeting this test. Some other aspects of this issue are discussed further in chapter 13, in which aspects of the NEB's role are examined regarding how to assess and monitor long-term energy supply and demand.

The Bush Administration's NEP and Alternative to Kyoto

Current and prospective Canadian energy policy and the possibilities for a low-carbon economy must be placed in the crucial context of the Bush administration's National Energy Policy (NEP) of 2001–2, and its alternative to the Kyoto Protocol. Nothing could be more ironic than an American 'NEP' bringing energy policy back in Canada with a prominence not seen since the demise of Canada's NEP twenty years earlier. The interplay of issues arising from the Bush NEP, the American alternative to Kyoto, the Enron scandal and related ones, the stockmarket collapse, the California electricity crisis, and the electricity blackout in August 2003 has brought energy issues into the North American media and public eye in the early 2000s in a way that has not been seen for two decades (Duane, 2002).

The trauma of the 11 September 2001 terrorist attacks on New York and Washington, D.C., added a further crucial dimension to American policy in general, including energy security (security of supply) and the physical security of energy pipelines and nuclear power plants (see further discussion in chapter 13). This was followed in February 2002 with the Bush administration's announcement of its unilateral alternative to Kyoto, which centred on voluntary approaches for American energy producers and on incentives for developing alternative energy technologies (Victor, 2001; Schelling, 2002).

But undoubtedly it is the Bush NEP that has the broadest implications for pan-Canadian energy policy. The NEP was drafted by Vice-President Dick Cheney for an administration whose Cabinet contains several ex–energy industry executives. As a policy, it is unabashedly driven and dominated by the supply mantra (Government of the United States, 2001). It was crafted in the midst of rapidly rising gas prices, both at the pump and in home heating fuel; it was forged in the midst of the electricity crisis in California, during which electricity prices in that state were soaring and blackouts were frequent in a booming, Internet-driven knowledge economy (Jaccard, 2002). The central features of the Bush NEP are as follows:

- Ease restrictions on oil and gas development on public lands.
- Open part of the Arctic National Wildlife Refuge in Alaska for drilling.
- Reconsider requirements for 'boutique' gasoline blends that contribute to supply shortages.
- Streamline the approval process for siting power plants.
- Allow government to take over private property for power lines.
- Provide tax breaks for developing clean coal technologies.
- Ease regulatory barriers, including clean-air rules, to speed up expansion or build new plants.
- Speed up nuclear safety reviews in the relicensing of reactors and the licensing of new plants.
- Limit industry liability from a nuclear accident.

The Bush NEP also includes tax breaks for renewable energy and conservation, but these are decidedly secondary in the plan as a whole.

These plans will have a major influence on Canada simply because of their great impact on the North American energy industry overall. But the Bush plan also speaks of energy security for the United States in terms of North American energy supply, and thus Canada's oil and gas reserves – along with those of Mexico – are a key part of the

Americans' continental plan. Following furious partisan debate in the U.S. Congress, a compromise but still strong energy bill was on the verge of approval by late 2003; the political logjam had largely been broken by the electricity blackout of August 2003 (McKenna, 2003). The bill does not include opening up for exploration the Arctic Natural Wildlife Refuge, but it does include over $20 billion in incentives for increasing domestic American production of natural gas, clean coal, and nuclear energy, and for fostering the development of hydrogen fuel cells and wind power. It also includes mandatory reliability standards for electricity transmission companies, backed up with penalties. Furthermore, there are generous tax incentives and loan guarantees for the Alaska pipeline. The Bush administration's energy agenda is clearly the one to which everyone is now reacting. Of consequence for Canada, the U.S. House of Congress and the Senate seem to concur on the construction and route for a northern gas pipeline; they are trying to encourage the construction of a pipeline from the northern slope of Alaska, while specifying a route through Alaska rather than mainly through Canada. The new American energy policy will undoubtedly affect Canada in other ways, although in general and in policy and regulatory terms, exactly how remains to be seen.

Underlying all of these developments has been the need to keep in mind the basic patterns and growth of the energy trade in the context of NAFTA. As Plourde shows in chapter 2, the trade in North American energy has been growing rapidly over the past decade. The broadest overall implication of the Bush energy plan is that Canada will have enormous opportunities to sell more oil and gas. However, these American plans and pressures are also raising issues and challenges centred on the Canadian approach to the Kyoto Protocol, to which we now turn.

Climate Change and Canada's Federal-Provincial Kyoto Protocol Politics and Process

The Kyoto Protocol on the United Nations Framework Convention on Climate Change (UNFCCC) was agreed to by 178 nations in December 1997. Canada undertook to reduce its greenhouse gas emissions by 6 per cent below its 1990 levels, averaged over the 2008 to 2012 period (Canada, 2002b; Schwanen, 2000). But owing to a lag in action, that commitment now amounts to a required 26 per cent reduction. This is one among many factors that are making it difficult for the federal government to honour this commitment with reasonable federal–provincial consensus behind it (Canada, 2002a, b). Prime Minister Chrétien's long goodbye from power between 2002 and 2004 included the crucial decision in September 2002 to announce that Canada would ratify the Kyoto Protocol – a process completed late in 2002. There are serious national unity issues at stake here, as well as of course energy and environmental ones. In real terms, the real and practical decisions, both economic and technological, are only now being seriously and publicly debated, although they have been discussed semiprivately in policymaking circles for several years (VanNijnatten and Macdonald, 2003; Jaccard, Nyboer, and Sadownik, 2002). As Daniel Schwanen has emphasized, the core problem is how to achieve the reductions:

> Unfortunately, the Kyoto targets were set without reference to the cost of meeting them (or of their potential benefits relative to those of following alternative scenarios of emissions reductions and time frames). Considering how far Canada is from reaching its Kyoto target, and how closely the emissions of the principal GHGs (green house gasses) resulting from human activity are linked with the growth and type of economic activity the country has typically enjoyed, a serious attempt at meeting the commitment within a given timetable would likely involve significant changes in the economy and even in Canadian lifestyles. (Schwanen, 2000, p. 1)

For many, dealing with climate change through the Kyoto Protocol and commitments to reduce greenhouse gas emissions is the ultimate acid test of whether sustainable development policies, rules, and processes can be made real and operational (Houghton, 1997; Dunn, 2001; Rowlands, 1995). So it is important to have a capsule view of the Kyoto Protocol process up to the present – a process that brought most key developed countries on board, the dominant exception being the United States. In February 2002, the Bush administration announced its alternative to Kyoto. We also look at the core institutional processes applied at the national, federal–provincial, and stakeholder levels and at why important national-unity and economic concerns lie at the heart of the issue.

The negotiation of the Kyoto Protocol followed years of policy and economic analysis and decades of scientific research to determine whether human emissions of greenhouse gases were causing climate change, and if so, how (Grubb et al., 1999; Houghton, 1997; Dotto, 1999). The 1979 World Climate Conference created the World Climate

Research Programme to help stimulate research. Then in 1988 the Intergovernmental Panel on Climate Change (IPCC) was established. The IPCC's successive reports provided the scientific underpinning first for the UN Framework Convention on Climate Change and then for the 1997 Kyoto Protocol. The IPCC's first assessment report was published in 1990, its second in 1996, and its third in July 2001. With input from several hundred scientists from around the globe, the IPCC's assessments resulted in an ever stronger scientific consensus that more and more governments began to accept, although they were not yet ready to make firm commitments to act. In short, even though the Kyoto Protocol had been adopted in 1997 with commitments for greenhouse gas reductions, these commitments were not yet truly regulatory or rule-based; rather, they were target-based and reflected only good intentions. But future rule making (and thus some vital command and control activity) was clearly at the core of Kyoto, and some institutions and interests were therefore already beginning to change their behaviour in anticipation of eventual regulatory commitments. However, policy solutions as a whole and the character of the policy mix – including its regulatory provisions – would only emerge after prolonged and protracted negotiations among (eventually) 178 countries, with enormous pressure being exerted by national and international NGOs and scientists (Hoffman, 2001; Calamai, 2001; 2001a; 2001b).

The IPCC and Kyoto processes also identified all the other possible actions that countries and stakeholders could take, some combination of which would be necessary both to deal with the problem and, equally important, to forge a consensus around which a negotiated and enforceable global agreement could emerge. This was because the final complex package had to do more than meet the core test of reducing greenhouse emissions; it also had to do so in a way that was economically efficient (hence the need for flexible, incentive-based regulation and other measures). The package also had to be equitable, especially in terms of the gap between developing and developed countries (Rowlands, 1995) but also in terms of disparities *within* countries such as Canada. Quite early on, an IPCC policymakers' working group had identified the portfolio of actions that countries could consider

- Implementing energy efficiency measures, including removing institutional barriers.

- Phasing out distorting policies such as some subsidies and regulations, non-internalizing of environmental costs, and distortions in transport pricing.
- Cost-effective fuel-switching measures such as renewables.
- Enhance sinks or reservoirs such as improving forest management and land use practices.
- Implementing measures and developing new techniques for reducing other greenhouse gas emissions.
- Encouraging forms of international cooperation such as coordinated carbon/energy taxes, actions implemented jointly, and tradeable permits.
- Promoting national and international energy efficiency standards.
- Planning and implementation measures to adapt (to climate change).
- Research aimed at better understanding the causes and impacts of, and adaptation to, climate change.
- Conduct technology research minimizing emissions and developing commercial non-fossil energy sources.
- Improved institutional arrangements, such as improved insurance arrangements to share the risks of damages.
- Promoting voluntary actions to reduce greenhouse gas emissions.
- Education and training, information and advisory measures for sustainable development and consumption patterns. (Adapted from Grubb et al., 1999, 16)

Many of these kinds of actions were both significant and difficult; others were often referred to as 'no regrets' actions because they would be beneficial and relatively costless no matter what future negotiations might hold.

While such action portfolios were being thought through and pushed globally, Canada's strategies were proceeding in tandem through newly established domestic institutional processes. After the 1997 Kyoto Protocol was negotiated, Chrétien and the premiers and other first ministers directed the federal, provincial, and territorial ministers of energy and environment jointly 'to examine the impacts, costs and benefits of implementing the Kyoto Protocol, as well as the options for addressing climate change' (National Climate Change Process, 2000, 2). They were to do so under 'a guiding principle that no region should bear an unreasonable burden from implementing the Protocol' (ibid., 2000, 2).

In this way, the central importance of rules and policies regarding equity considerations among Canada's regions, analogous to the broader 'equity' debate in global negotiations among countries, was implanted at the political level.

Such a guideline was undoubtedly necessary in an overall national unity sense, but it was especially imperative for accommodating Alberta. Alberta, as already noted, was already beginning to rhetorically cast federal policy on Kyoto as 'another NEP,' and of course it knew that it was the province at the heart of the carbon-producing part – albeit not the carbon-*using* part – of the Canadian economy. Central Canadian industries were major carbon emitters, and of course Canadians as consumers are also energy 'polluters' in a fundamental sense as well (see chapter 13 for further discussion).

This directive from the first ministers resulted in the establishment in 1998 of the National Climate Change Process (hereafter the National Process). A National Implementation Strategy (among other initiatives) resulted from an elaborate multigovernmental, multistakeholder process involving sixteen issue tables or working groups comprising about 450 experts from industry, government, academia, and NGOs. The issue tables reviewed seven key sectors of the economy and eight cross-cutting strategies. An analysis and modelling group then integrated the results into a comprehensive preliminary analysis.

The resulting National Implementation Strategy has been summed up as follows:

- Taking action to reduce risks and to improving our understanding of risks associated with climate change, as well as the costs and consequences of reducing emissions and adapting to a changing environment (see First National Business Plan).
- Instituting a national framework that includes individual and joint action, and that recognizes jurisdictional flexibility in responding to unique needs, circumstances and opportunities.
- Adopting a phased approach, which schedules future decisions and allows progressive action in response to changing domestic and international circumstances and improved knowledge.
- Improving our understanding of the functioning of the climate system and the national and regional climate change impacts as they affect Canada, in order to take actions to reduce emissions and adapt to a changing environment.
- Understanding the necessary relationship between international and national strategies.

• Developing our understanding of the implications of emission reduction targets and major options, including cross-cutting policy approaches such as emissions trading and allocation of responsibility for reducing emissions, before making decisions about targets or moving to the next phase of the strategy. (National Climate Change Process, 2000, 3)

These elements reflect the complexity of the mix of regulatory and non-regulatory actions necessary to eventually reduce GHG emissions. Other statements about Kyoto by the federal government emphasize more overtly that climate change is providing *opportunities* for Canada in that it is already driving the development of innovative products and services. One such initiative cited often is the Ballard hydrogen-powered fuel cell (*Scientific American*, 1999). Federal policy also draws attention to a number of federal programs for funding and promoting new technologies and approaches (Natural Resources Canada, 2000, 164). These include the $150 million Climate Change Action Fund (CCAP) introduced in 1998, the Sustainable Development Technology Fund (SDTF) announced in the 2000 federal budget, and other initiatives cited earlier (see further discussion in chapter 13).

A further element in Canada's approach to the Kyoto Protocol negotiations and implementation, nationally and internationally, was the issue of carbon sinks (Brown, 1998). Canada sought – and at Bonn in 2001 eventually obtained – agreement that such sinks would be credited for removing carbon dioxide from the environment. This was based on the fact that plants and trees 'breathe in' and store CO_2 from the atmosphere; thus, forests and agricultural soils that absorb and store CO_2 are known as 'carbon sinks' under the Kyoto Protocol. Canada wanted credit for enhancing sinks (Canada, 2001a; 2001b). Credits for carbon sinks became a key negotiating issue at several levels – moral, political, and economic. The EU and many NGOs sought to exclude sinks on the grounds that these were not real greenhouse emission reductions and that indeed they were based (according to some) on dubious science. Canada and other countries with extensive forests supported the inclusion of carbon sinks. In the end, the Bonn 2001 agreement included them under certain conditions.

The carbon sinks element of the Kyoto Accord is of course complex in its own right. It is also of some import to the domestic regulatory and practical politics of the eventual national position and of the core political bargain on Kyoto. This is that a forest sinks provision simply had to be a part of the package or else Canada would have had to impose fairly draconian direct emission controls in a way that would seriously harm national unity in general (as defined by the federal and provincial governments) and that would violate federal–provincial principles such as the one about not imposing undue burdens on any one region.

In 2002 and 2003, the broader politics, symbolism, and practical realities of the Kyoto commitments became more starkly revealed as the Chrétien government and the provinces faced the then looming deadline of Canada actually ratifying the Kyoto Protocol to reduce GHG emissions. Several past and current positions converged and collided. The first was that Canada's initial Kyoto commitments had always been partly based at a high political level on symbolism – that is, on a desire to simply *look* better than the United States and thus to convey green foreign policy virtue to the rest of the world. When the Bush administration abandoned Kyoto in June 2001 and announced its own largely market- and incentive-based alternatives in February 2002 (Bush, 2001, 2002) the Chrétien government was in a sense hoisted on its own petard. Not only was the Bush administration saying that it did not really care much about how it *appeared* to the rest of the world, but as well, Canada's Kyoto position now had to be crafted in light of the fact that its oil and gas industry (mainly Alberta's oil and gas exports, but also new Atlantic Canadian sources of supply), and Canadian industry generally (mainly in central Canada), could be placed at a comparative disadvantage in its main market, the United States, and that all Canadian industries might face similar disadvantages if they had to pay higher energy costs than their American competitors. Moreover, the United States was now keenly interested in longer-term Canadian oil and gas supplies (Cordon, 2001). Hence, selling oil and natural gas – especially the latter – was a key imperative, all the more so because Chrétien in early 2001 was determined to woo Alberta for the next political-electoral round of Canadian politics (Tupper, 2002), especially in the context of the weakened political standing of the Canadian Alliance during the brief Stockwell Day era.

The other imperative was that as real decisions were required in 2002 and 2003, the specifics of exactly what kinds of reductions in emissions, and what kinds of credit arrangements, had to be determined through some sort of more focused cost–benefit analysis of regulatory, tax, and other policy alternatives and instruments (Jaccard, Nyboer, and Sadownik, 2002). During 2002 this resulted in a flurry of studies and leaked reports of what the costs and benefits (but mainly the costs) of action and inaction would be. Competing studies and projections by business lobby groups – both general and petroleum lobby groups – and by Alberta and other producing provinces showed such costs to be very high; Alberta was claiming at times that such costs would decimate the Alberta and Western Canadian economies. In turn, the federal government and some NGOs claimed that these and earlier cost projections were highly exaggerated and that they often ignored the costs of not taking action.

There is little doubt that both sides were playing the tactical game of analytical exaggeration; this often happens when serious policy/regulatory battles reach their point of no return or of actual decision making and compliance (Jaccard, Nyboer, and Sadownik, 2002). For example, similar tactical analytical gamesmanship had occurred in the great free trade debate of 1987–8 (Doern and Tomlin, 1991). There is also little doubt that neither side had perfect information or could say or know with certainty what kind of final bargain it was actually dealing with, and around which it could model and estimate costs and benefits.

These dynamics, coupled with the demonstratable effects of the Bush administration's alternative to Kyoto, helped sow the seeds of a 'made in Canada' alternative to Kyoto. Alberta's Conservative government began seeking support among the provinces and in Ottawa for a package of initiatives that would focus on energy efficiency – that would reduce and lower emissions, but at a slower pace, until 2020. Different calculations would be used that would rely more on the development of alternative technologies and that would be calibrated to keep Canadian energy competitive in American markets (Alberta, 2002; Moore, 2002). Splits began to develop in the Chrétien Cabinet over the wisdom of Canada signing an agreement, given the new North American energy and environmental context propelled by the strongly aggressive and determined Bush administration (Mertl, 2002). The race to succeed Prime Minister Chrétien as Liberal leader made these splits more apparent – all the more so because the winner, Paul Martin, will have to deal with the fallout from a detailed national plan, whose contours and details are still largely unknown to most Canadians as voters, as citizens, and as energy consumers (see chapter 13).

Bush's anti-Kyoto policy prompted Canada to add a further caveat to its eventual signing on. This came in the form of a Canadian requirement that this country be extended 'clean energy' credits for energy it exported to the United States such as natural gas and hydroelectric power, when that energy replaced dirtier American sources, such as coal and oil (Canada, 2002a, b). Whether the world will agree to this further condition remains to be seen.

Nonetheless, by November 2002 the Chrétien government had published its Climate Change Plan for Canada (Canada, 2002a). This plan
was built on and was a partial response to reactions to its earlier
consultation paper (Canada, 2002b). It also reflected some of the heated
reactions from Alberta and some other provinces and from the Canadian business community – that is, from the provinces and groups
that were against ratifying the Kyoto Protocol. Accordingly, the plan
called for a more complex of set of principles listed under 'our Canadian approach':

- a made-in-Canada approach based on collaboration, partnerships
  and respect for jurisdiction;
- no region bearing unreasonable burden;
- taking a step-by-step approach that is transparent and evergreen;
- minimizing mitigation costs while maximizing benefits;
- promoting innovation;
- limiting uncertainties and risks. (Canada, 2002a, 2)

The plan also proposed the use of five key instruments:

- Emissions reductions targets for large industrial emitters established through covenants with a regulatory or financial backstop ...
  (linked to flexibility measures for these emitters) through emissions
  trading and access to domestic offsets and international permits;
- A Partnership fund;
- Strategic Infrastructure Investments;
- A Coordinated Innovation Strategy;
- Targeted measures including information, incentives, regulations
  and tax measures. (Canada, 2002a, 2)

The resort to such multiple principles (with contested views about
their meaning and ranking) linked to multiple instruments (which,
though cast as policy *means*, are also highly contested because of different values placed on them and into them by different interests)
means that any plan will be fraught with implementation difficulties.
To get a flavour of some of these principles-instruments battles, we
need to discuss provincial energy policies next, and then federal–provincial energy regulatory governance and the changing structure of
energy interests.

Provincial Energy and Sustainable Development Policies: Selected Profiles

As we have already seen, Canadian energy policy has always been a quintessentially federal–provincial matter. Increasingly, it is also becoming an even more complex interregional matter in terms of energy infrastructure, electricity grids, and actual ecosystems. So it is crucial to look at general directions of change at the provincial level. The following discussion does not cover each province in detail; rather, it briefly profiles developments in selected provinces as they have separately and collectively responded to some of the same factors and contexts sketched above.

In one sense, the baseline for this discussion is inevitably the bitterly contested and still remembered federal–provincial battle over the NEP. As emphasized in chapter 8's account of Alberta energy policy, the Mulroney government's promarket energy policies did much to defuse the 1980–4 energy wars. Thus, as we have seen, for most of the past fifteen to twenty years there has been relative energy peace and relatively stable oil and gas prices and, in most provinces, quite low or stable electricity prices. But each province has also had to conduct its own domestic debate over sustainable development and provincial energy–environment issues, a debate that includes the general one over how each province might be effected by climate change commitments, given local–regional energy sources and industries and given local and regional climate change impacts or feared impacts.

At the provincial level, one initial change has obviously been in the electricity sector. As chapters 5, 6, and 7 show, Alberta and Ontario have adopted major policies of electricity market reform to allow for greater competitive forces both in sources of supply and at the retail level (Dewees, 2001; Jaccard, 2002). Many other provinces have been reviewing their electricity policies (in concert with overall provincial energy policy), in part because neighbouring provinces are, or because American states have. These changes then affect the cost structures of markets in which provincial firms must compete. The electricity restructuring processes in Alberta and Ontario have been carried out against the backdrop of the California energy and electricity crisis (Jaccard, 2002) and also, since August 2003, against the shock effects of the North American electricity blackout. Dewees shows in chapter 4 that in the two provincial contexts, the systems eventually adopted were quite different from the California case. The progress of the Canadian provincial reforms has also been influenced by a debate over energy networks and grids. How can these, which are quasi-competitive, be managed with regard to environmental policy and reliable and appropriate power supplies? The August 2003 blackout and the later defeat of the Eves Conservative government in the October 2003 Ontario election starkly highlighted the weaknesses in Ontario's grid and in its regulatory regime. Jaccard's account of the two provincial experiments notes their different origins and political-economic contexts:

> Alberta has a conservative tradition of minimizing the role of central planners and favouring markets and private ownership where possible; before the 1990s it was the only province dominated by privately owned utilities. Indeed Alberta stands out as a region interested in electricity reform despite having some of the lowest electricity prices in North America. In contrast, Ontario's electricity sector reform had been motivated primarily by high costs, although ideology played a role. (Jaccard, 2002, 19)

Alberta and Ontario have launched their changes. However, as we see in later chapters, both these provinces' new programs have encountered considerable opposition relating to energy price fluctuations and peak-time shortages, and both have brought into public view the links between domestic sources of supply and the need to import supply.

The general debate over electricity restructuring has inevitably brought out differences in provincial situations. Each province's current prices and current mix of energy types for generating electricity is different; for this reason their approaches to restructuring vary, though on the whole they are quite cautious. For example, British Columbia's generation is 89 per cent hydro, 5 per cent natural gas, and 5 per cent 'other' sources, whereas Nova Scotia's is 66 per cent coal, 23 per cent oil, and 9 per cent hydro (ibid., 20). Residential electricity prices in B.C. are 6.1 cents per kilowatt hour versus 9.4 in Nova Scotia.

Almost all provincial governments have taken into account the same energy and environment factors examined in this book. However, they have also folded into the mix their own specific provincial realities, and they have looked at their energy issues through the political lenses of their governing political parties. Next we briefly sample the policy statements and postures of several specific provinces.

Quebec

A major change in Quebec energy policy occurred in 1996 (Quebec, 1996). The Parti Québécois government's policy document *Energy at the Service of Quebec: A Sustainable Development Perspective* was still anchored to the central role played by Hydro-Québec in the province's political economy. But the policy also acknowledged the need to establish a new relationship with native peoples (a key issue in large-scale hydro projects); the need to promote new ways of developing the economy, including fostering industries that would depend less heavily on large supplies of hydro power; and the need to ensure more equity and transparency (ibid., 10–11). Changes in Quebec also included the establishment of an energy board as an arm's-length regulator. That the province did not yet have a fully independent regulator indicates the extent to which Quebec energy policy had long been equated with a tight relationship between Hydro-Québec and successive Quebec governments. Quebec policy also firmly endorses the concept of sustainable development as a policy goal; the province has been strongly supportive of Canada's basic climate change policy and the federal approach to the Kyoto Protocol. But at the same time, Quebec, through Hydro-Québec, is also investing significantly in the exploration of natural gas reserves in the Gulf of St Lawrence (Seguin, 2002). The Liberals under Jean Charest won the 2003 provincial election after a decade of Parti Québécois rule, and this may well turn Quebec's energy policy in a more market-oriented direction and somewhat reduce the political power of Hydro-Québec. These possibilities arise because of the early indications that under the Charest Liberals, industrial subsidies will be greatly reduced.

Ontario

Energy policy in Ontario over the past decade has been centred around electricity restructuring policies and processes (Ontario, 1996; Ontario Ministry of Energy, Science and Technology, 2001). Ontario is Canada's largest energy user, yet there were no serious Ontario energy concerns about oil and gas supply as long as prices were stable and relatively low, which they were for most of the 1990s. Because of its focus on electricity and on rising electricity costs, Ontario policy was essentially a frontal challenge – politically and economically – to the power of Ontario Hydro and to the role of nuclear power. The province not only broke up Ontario Hydro but also created in 1998, for the first time, a full-fledged energy regulator. The Ontario Energy Board (OEB) had existed for some time but had been largely a regulator of natural gas (Doern and Gattinger, 2003). The entire energy sector was now its domain.

It is also important to note that Ontario's changes did not involve massive privatization in the sense of private ownership. The Harris Conservative government, with its strong ideological bent, was keen to emphasize the promarket aspects of its electricity restructuring, but it also knew that Ontario Hydro, in particular the local, municipally run hydros, had deep populist roots. The Harris Conservatives were remarkably successful in shepherding their changes through without huge controversy. However, the ownership issue did re-emerge in 2002 and 2003 when the possible sale of Hydro One, the distribution company, and the precise institutional form it would take, became a high-profile policy issue. The new Conservative government headed by Ernie Eves backtracked quickly on the Hydro One issue as it sought to distance several of its policies from those of the Harris years and more toward a more centrist role for government. Early in 2003 it announced that it would keep Hydro One entirely as a government-owned enterprise (Gray, 2003). As the chapters by Dewees and Schott show, it also backtracked on its electricity policy by placing a four-year ceiling on electricity prices. The Liberals under Dalton McGuinty won the October 2003 provincial election, and announced soon after that they would let electricity prices rise. Even so, overall it can be said that Ontario's energy policy has become more promarket over the past decade. This has been complemented, however, by more transparent *energy* regulation than had been the case. The emphasis here must be on *energy* regulation, because in the overall realm of *environmental* regulation, the Harris ideology undoubtedly resulted in the province severely cutting resources in the environmental field. The McGuinty government must now address the ensuing problems.

Alberta

In the past decade, Alberta energy policy has included the previously mentioned electricity restructuring. But of course it is the oil and gas industry itself – including the huge and crucial oil sands resource – that is at the core of its ongoing provincial energy policy. As Keith

Brownsey's analysis in chapter 8 shows, the makers of Alberta's energy policy still have bitter memories of the NEP of the 1980s. Yet in other ways they have moved on to deal with two unavoidable issues: how to develop the energy industry, and how to regulate it on a sustainable basis. And Alberta itself is a different place than it was twenty years ago, in that it is more urbanized, has a somewhat more diverse economy, and has environmental groups and interests that are exerting pressure to reform such basic systems of regulation as the AEUB. Furthermore, the Alberta Department of Energy has become a broader resource development department; this means that integrated resource management and sustainable development are a larger part of its mandate than was once the case (Alberta, 2000).

However, there is little doubt about the promarket and developmental ethos of Alberta energy policy over the past decade. The analyses by Monica Gattinger in chapter 11 and Alastair Lucas in chapter 12 show the extent to which ingrained market-based regulation and voluntary approaches are central to Alberta's political culture. The degree to which this is true can be seen even in the ways in which the province takes in its crude oil royalties from producers. Crude oil royalties are taken in kind (as product), not in cash, and since 1996 the royalty on conventional crude has been 'sold through marketing agents ... and the average price realized by the private sector agents ... exceeded all established benchmark prices' (Alberta, 2000, 16). But much more importantly, the Alberta government has worked to expand its pipeline capacity to feed into growing Canadian and American markets. The province has also worked with industry and with federal NRCan S&T agencies such as the CANMET Western Research Centre to develop Alberta's rich oil sands. New technologies of production and higher oil prices have combined to greatly improve the economics of the oil sands. About $25 billion in investment was approved in 1999–2000 alone, and higher amounts are anticipated over the next few years (ibid., 16). A new tenure regulation for the oil sands was also completed in 2000, following extensive consultations.

The current business plan of the Alberta Department of Energy is even more strongly oriented to development, especially given the new opportunities arising from the Bush agenda and from growing energy needs. The stated goals of the department are as follows:

• Optimize Albertans' resource revenue share and benefits from the development of their resources over the long term;

- Advocate for the removal of barriers to the development of energy and mineral resources in Alberta;
- Advance the competitiveness of Alberta's energy and mineral resources;
- Provide strategic research direction to achieve long term energy and mineral development goals;
- Prepare a long term energy outlook for Alberta that secures supply and benefits and positions Alberta within a broader North American energy marketplace;
- Inform Albertans about the opportunities for a continuing supply of Alberta's energy and mineral resources from conventional and non-conventional sources;
- Establish a customer choice framework for providing stable, affordable energy for Albertans;
- Build an organizational environment for success. (Alberta Ministry of Energy, 2001, 119–22)

The 'removal of barriers' goal actually contains a number of strategies that are nominally in keeping with sustainable development, environmental protection, and consulting with native communities. Lucas's analysis in chapter 12 shows that Alberta does have a developed regime for the environmental regulation of the energy industry, both through its Department of Environmental Protection and through the Alberta Energy and Utilities Board (AEUB). The AEUB was restructured in the 1990s to absorb the previously separate Energy Resources Conservation Board, whose history goes back to the very earliest concerns among Albertans about conserving the resource (Breen, 1993; Doern and Gattinger, 2003).

As Brownsey's analysis shows, regulatory change in the 1990s extended beyond general sustainable development issues; it also addressed individual landowner rights vis-à-vis energy companies. Indeed, in the AEUB's portion of the Alberta Energy Ministry's 2001–4 business plan, its first listed goal is the 'prompt and satisfactory resolution of landowner and industry conflicts' (Alberta Ministry of Energy, 2001, 124).

Alberta energy policy has thus sought to maintain its overall developmental goals for energy. But increasingly in the early 2000s, Alberta policy has focused on the Kyoto debate in the context of the Bush Administration's NEP. The Bush NEP constitutes a huge developmental opportunity for Alberta's energy industry. The Americans' anti-

Kyoto stance is a potential competitive threat, given that American industry will enjoy lower costs. That said, the Bush anti-Kyoto stance is also philosophically compatible with Alberta's own preference for a slower pace of adjustment (e.g., meeting GHG emission reductions by 2020 rather than 2012) and for an approach to change that relies more on energy S&T and innovation than on precipitous regulation. This is why Premier Ralph Klein and the Alberta environment minister, Lorne Taylor, pushed for an Alberta alternative to the Chrétien government's climate change options in the 2002–3 federal–provincial consultation process (Alberta, 2002; Gillis, 2002). Alberta has sometimes deployed the rhetoric that federal Kyoto policy is 'another federal NEP,' but it has adopted some conciliatory approaches as well. In part this is due to a desire to cooperate nationally, and in part this is because Albertans are concerned about climate change. As Brownsey notes, the autumn 2002 campaign by the Klein government did turn Alberta public opinion against the Kyoto Protocol, but only up to a point. The Alberta Conservatives have realized that some programs are necessary to respond to Canadians' environmental concerns. This is why Alberta has partially financed a public–private partnership group called Climate Change Central, whose mandate is to help cut GHGs through conservation measures (Jang, 2002). And Alberta has been advocating its own alternative to the federal climate change program.

Nova Scotia

Early in 2001, Nova Scotia reviewed its energy policy, initially through a discussion paper, *Powering Nova Scotia's Economy* (Nova Scotia, 2001), and later through an energy strategy paper (Nova Scotia, 2001b). Among the key issues examined was increased competition. At present, the province's main utility, Nova Scotia Power Inc (NSPI), is a vertically integrated monopoly that owns and operates 97 per cent of the generation, 99 per cent of transmission, and 95 per cent of the distribution systems in Nova Scotia. It is regulated by the Nova Scotia Utility and Review Board (UARB). The relatively recent introduction of natural gas into Nova Scotia is the main source of competitive pressure on NSPI.

The potential for competition policy issues to arise had already emerged in the NSPI's reaction within the province to competition from natural gas. NSPI sought the ability to 'provide Load Retention Rates (LLR's) to industrial customers, and to seek approval from the

UARB for a process for rapid approval of Energy Solutions Packages (ESPs) [and] a key focus of these options would be to prevent customers from switching to gas for space and water heating purposes' (Competition Bureau, 2001, 3).

In Ontario, rapidly increasing electricity prices in the early 1990s helped trigger pressure from the industry sector, and this led to competitive restructuring. In contrast, Nova Scotia's prices were stable and competitive for most of the 1990s. Nova Scotia's review process was thus inclined to ask an obvious question: Why should more competition be contemplated? The first reason given for restructuring was to maximize the benefits of natural gas for consumers and businesses in the province. The second reason was that neighbouring jurisdictions were restructuring. New Brunswick intends to introduce wholesale electricity competition and is exploring the changes it will have to make to give NB Power greater access to American markets. This is important in itself, but it ultimately becomes a third reason: for Nova Scotia to attract investment from globally and continentally mobile firms, it must be able to supply competitive and innovative energy. The federal Competition Bureau's advice to the Nova Scotia review was that the province should adopt an 'evolutionary approach.' The language the bureau chose for Nova Scotia's case was somewhat more cautious than it had been for Ontario. In part this was because Nova Scotia's situation in terms of energy markets was different; in addition to this, Alberta's and Ontario's experiences with electricity restructuring, and the California electricity crisis, had taught the bureau to show more caution.

The focus of Nova Scotia's energy policy review was on offshore oil and gas development. In this, it shared concerns with other Atlantic provinces such as Newfoundland and New Brunswick about how this emerging sector would fit into overall regional, national, and continental energy policy and sustainable development policy. Thus, Nova Scotia has been lobbying provincial premiers, especially Alberta's Ralph Klein, to help it make the case that federal–provincial fiscal arrangements regarding oil revenues should be revised so as to ensure that the now-operational oil and gas sector will help Nova Scotia become a 'have' province – in short, potentially another Alberta.

The maturation of the oil and gas industry in Atlantic Canada has also prompted Nova Scotia to announce its new energy strategy, which is to create a Nova Scotia Offshore Heritage Trust for the benefit of future generations. This kind of 'rainy day' investment fund is clearly modelled on Alberta's trust fund. Nova Scotia has also created a Department of Energy with a full-time minister. The new minister will have to keep a careful sustainable-development eye on the Nova Scotia and Atlantic Canada marine environment and fishing industry (Nova Scotia, 2001a).

New Brunswick

For its part, New Brunswick in its energy policy has had to steer a course which reflects the fact that it is not an offshore oil and gas supplier although it is clearly embedded in the new North American energy market. Its 2000 *White Paper on New Brunswick Energy Policy* pulled no punches; in its introduction it stated that 'there is little option but to become part of what is developing into a fully integrated North American electricity supply and marketing grid. In order to participate and to continue to capture the benefits of a competitive market, New Brunswick must operate by rules and procedures compatible with those established by FERC' (New Brunswick, 2001, 1). Policies of the Federal Energy Regulatory Commission (FERC) in the 1990s had been largely driving the electricity restructuring process in North America (Doern and Gattinger, 2003).

British Columbia

Meanwhile on the West Coast, British Columbia's energy policy was responding to new political and economic forces. B.C. had thrived on hydro power. Its energy policy had also been influenced by a very strong green lobby, which had compelled the province to place a moratorium on the development of offshore oil and gas resources. A lot of this seems to be changing under the new Liberal government, which came to power in 2001 after a decade of economic doldrums and has taken very strong steps to reduce the province's public spending, in the hope that this will generate stronger economic growth. Higher deficits have been the early result. In the longer term, the B.C. government is carefully considering developing its offshore oil and gas reserves as an economic engine – that is, as a source of revenues for the province, especially from sales to the United States.

A provincial task force on energy policy published an interim report in late 2001. In keeping with the mandate given to it by Premier Gordon Campbell, this report called for an energy policy 'consistent with exemplary environmental practices'; however, the focus of the final report will undoubtedly be on energy development (British Columbia, 2001, i).

Its first three elements of suggested strategic direction are *growth*, *diversification*, and *competitiveness*. The task force notes that 'if the past can serve as a guide, a comprehensive energy policy can be the early-21st century equivalent of the two-river policy of the latter half of the 20th century' (ibid., iii). The two-river policy refers to key hydroelectric investments made on the Peace and Columbia rivers, especially in the W.A.C. Bennett era in B.C. politics.

In November 2002, the province's energy minister announced a policy that on the electricity side was highly cognizant of the electricity restructuring problems and controversies in Ontario and Alberta (Jang, 2002). He announced that B.C. would not privatize the British Columbia Hydro and Power Authority; rather, it would be split into two provincially owned firms. The province would also allow expanded room for new independent power producers. Regarding oil and gas, the minister announced that a new committee would be formed to proceed with proposals to develop offshore oil and gas reserves.

B.C.'s emerging energy policy cannot focus solely on offshore oil and gas and diversification from the 'two-river' hydroelectric policy. The task force has noted that fuel cells are a potential alternative energy source (and industry). In Canada, fuel cell development is being driven by B.C.-based Ballard Power Systems and other related B.C. and Alberta (and national) firms.

This survey has not included all provinces, but it does show the variety of changes in provincial energy policy. The greater recognition of regional grid–centred North American electricity markets is a central feature of change. There are strong indications of promarket approaches overall, but at the same time there are growing concerns about sustainable development and about exactly how to practise such precepts. Central to this on the national stage is the national debate over Canada's Kyoto commitments, but crucially, there are also many provincial and interregional aspects to these challenges.

Overall Federal–Provincial Energy Regulatory Governance

Although energy policy utilizes all of the key instruments of policy – spending, persuasion, taxation, and regulation – an appreciation of the regulatory governance aspects is essential as a backdrop for the chapters that follow. Several strands of change relating to overall energy regulatory governance are evident in the chapters as a whole and in those which focus more explicitly on regulation, such as chapters 10, 11, and 12.

First, there is certainly evidence over the two-decade period as a whole of extensive deregulation. As Plourde shows in chapter 2, this was the essence of the oil and gas story during the Mulroney era, and for most of its decade in power, the Chrétien government also had a high comfort level with such policies.

Second, there is little doubt that more flexible and incentive-based regulatory approaches have emerged. Gattinger in chapter 11 shows that there is increasing use of alternative dispute resolution (ADR) by federal and some provincial energy regulators. She casts this type of change as a part of broader notions of economic or flexible regulation and of a movement away from so-called 'command and control' regulation. Lucas in chapter 12 considers the Alberta system of voluntary approaches. As a legal scholar, he links this approach to the theory of 'reflective law.' In other regulatory literature, these approaches are cast more basically as voluntary codes, albeit with state action looming in the background, to be resorted to as necessary (Webb, 2003). Although there are undoubtedly some positive features to these approaches, both Gattinger and Lucas ask whether such regulatory reforms downplay or shunt aside the broader public interest or third-party interest.

A third theme about regulatory governance to emerge is, not surprisingly, the greater presence of international and North American regulation of energy. International regulatory features have always been a key part of nuclear energy. The Saudi-centred oil cartel, OPEC, continues to be of central importance. For some time, OPEC has been moderating and controlling oil prices in a fundamental way. But a crucial change in the past decade or more has been the growing role of FERC, the Americans' leading energy regulator. The three chapters on electricity regulation all bring out FERC's crucial influence on new electricity grids and (even earlier) on natural gas. The electricity chapters also point to other areas of expanded regulation and rule making; this is why it is more accurate to cast recent changes as electricity *restructuring* rather than simply as *deregulation* (Duane, 2002; Joskow, 2000). As shown in the preceding provincial survey, electricity restructuring has involved important new forms of regulation, including expanded mandates and capacities for core provincial energy boards.

The debate over the Kyoto Protocol, in Canada and elsewhere, shows that in the end, there will have to be a blend of highly diverse rules in order for the world to meet its bedrock commitment to reduce 1990-level GHG emissions by 6 per cent. The rest of the necessary steps (still being negotiated) will undoubtedly be found in a myriad of incentive-based, S&T- or innovation-based, and voluntary actions. The key for the Kyoto Protocol as an implemented agreement is that it will require both 'commands' and incentives (Doern and Gattinger, 2003).

What does not emerge as clearly in the chapters in this book, is the emergence of what are in effect larger complex *regimes* of energy regulation involving numerous old and new sets of regulatory bodies. Abele in chapter 9 and Bankes and Wenig in chapter 10 partly capture this dense and complex array of regulators in the North. Other recent research (Doern and Gattinger, 2003) points to the need to visualize and understand the emergence of broader energy regulatory *regimes* in Canada, composed of different sets of well over thirty regulators structured into sectoral and horizontal regimes of rule making that increasingly watch and police but also collide with one another.

The *sectoral energy regime* refers to a set of regulatory laws, agencies, values, interests, and processes that govern energy as a vertical industrial sector. In the framework offered by Doern and Gattinger, the various federal and provincial energy boards are at the core of this system of rules. At the federal level, the NEB would be joined also by the Canadian Nuclear Safety Commission and by the other federal agencies.

The *horizontal regulatory regime* refers to the laws, agencies, values, interests, and processes that apply across the economy and society, regardless of sector. A proper institutional mapping of this regime would necessarily have to include not only particular regulatory bodies (such as the Competition Bureau and the federal and provincial environmental regulatory bodies and departments), but also those industry and environment ministers who have some rule-making powers in these realms. In the sectoral energy regulatory regime described above, considerable *deregulation* has been underway; in contrast, the horizontal regulatory regime has exhibited an *expanded realm of overall rule-making* and is facing pressure to undertake yet more rule making.

Changing Energy Interests

A final but crucial contextual backdrop for the chapters that follow centres on how core energy interests have changed. The term *interests* is used here because it is important to appreciate changes not only in interest groups but also in the strategies and lobbying activities of key firms (e.g., individual corporations), players (e.g., scientists), and groups (e.g., native peoples, who constitute more than just an NGO because as peoples they have constitutional rights and are owners of energy resources and land).

A starting point for this kind of summary historical treatment is that there is still much conflict between energy industries and environmental NGOs as a whole; but until the Kyoto Protocol ratification debate of late 2002, this conflict was not as great or as intense as in the earlier years of energy policy – for example, during the Berger Commission era of the mid-1970s. A key feature of interests is that they are highly complex and diverse. There are key divisions or subelements *within* and also *across* the two overarching categories of interests: 'energy businesses' and 'environmental NGOs.'

In the early 2000s, energy business interests certainly encompass firms that are polluters and GHG emitters, but they also include key firms that are known to be environmentally progressive and that see economic opportunities in the new green technologies as alternatives to the carbon economy (Macdonald, 2002). This partly explains why British Petroleum (BP), a huge global firm, has changed its logo to mean 'beyond petroleum' and has generally been pursuing strategies quite different from those of, say, Exxon (Rowlands, 2000). In Canada, companies such as TransAlta have been developing strategies to profit from emission reductions and alternative technologies. There are many similar examples besides these (Toner, 2004; Macdonald, 2002; Corporate Knights, 2002).

Energy associations offer yet another illustration of the complexity and diversity of contemporary energy interests. Key Canadian lobbies such as the Canadian Electricity Association (CEA) used to consist of a small handful of big utilities, most of them provincially owned; the CEA now counts among its members many dozens of smaller firms that are entering the newly restructured electricity markets. These smaller players bring to the table diverse views about energy–environment trade-offs and linkages and how to profit from them. In a similar vein, core energy lobbies such as the Canadian Petroleum Producers Association (CAPP) are finding that they must now lobby in ways which recognize that they now represent both small and large energy players. Some of their members actually see themselves as part of the environmental industry sector. CAPP is having to recast its approaches to environmental policy to take this into account.

On the environmental NGO side of the equation of interests, there are more NGOs than there used to be, reflecting more diverse interests (Parson, 2001; VanNijnatten and Boardman, 2002). NGOs still seek to mobilize global pressure to ensure that Canada's environmental policy relating to energy and other policy fields will be progressive; however, the strategies of groups such as Greenpeace, Energy Probe, Pollution Probe, the Sierra Club, the Pembina Institute, the Canadian Arctic Resources Committee, and the David Suzuki Foundation vary enormously. Environmental advocates also serve on, or conduct their activities through, advisory bodies such as the National Roundtable on the Environment and the Economy as well as in many local and provincial–regional settings. Compared to even a decade ago, these interests – while still maintaining overall pressure – are much more literate about and experienced with, and prepared to consider, various ways of dealing with energy–environmental problems (from direct regulation to incentives and tradeable emission systems).

The interests surrounding native peoples and other groups such as consumers have also changed in the energy regulatory context. Self-governance in the North has conferred direct powers on native peoples. It has also resulted in a quite different set of views regarding energy and resource development relative to the Berger era. Today, by and large, native peoples tend to favour development provided there is local control over employment, benefits, and investment (Poelzer, 2002; Doyle-Bedwell and Cohen, 2001). But with regard to other aspects of energy policy such as climate change, there are major concerns among the North's native peoples because they are already experiencing some adverse climate change effects.

The issue of consumer interests and citizen-consumers is also germane to this brief survey of reconfigured interests. A key point to make is that there are now more arenas for expressing consumer interests, precisely because the market system has gained a greater hold in the energy sector. Consumer-citizens are constantly mounting challenges regarding not just *what* products are made but *how* they are made (Webb, 2003; Princen, Maniates, and Comca, 2002). The growth of business user groups as an organized class of consumers is another significant change in the profile of interest groups over the past twenty years.

Last but not least – and probably the hardest to pin down – is the role of scientists (inside and outside of government, and internationally). Both individual scientist-advocates such as David Suzuki and those who are members of environmental roundtables and panels, or who have strong university-based reputations, are exerting considerable influence, certainly in the identification of environmental hazards and sustainable development requirements. Moreover, federal scientists in NRCan and Environment Canada and in the global bodies that form around particular environmental agreements are also exerting influence (Doern and Reed, 2000).

This brief portrait of energy policy interests is by no means intended to suggest that there are no core conflicts between core business lobbies and NGOs. Arguably, raw political conflict rose in the fall of 2002 to a height and intensity not seen since the 1970s. Business interests formed a strong coalition to try and defeat or significantly delay the ratification of the Kyoto Protocol; this effort was countered, successfully, by a coalition of NGOs, backed by public opinion. In the end, Chrétien belatedly decided to ratify the protocol (Macdonald, 2003; Environmental Studies Program, 2002).

Last but not least, it is important to link the role of energy interests to how these interests have recently been represented in and mediated through core federal decision-making bodies. Over the past decade, energy interests have found their most sympathetic voices through Natural Resources Canada and environmental interests through Environment Canada (Doern and Gattinger, 2003). These basic alignments are understandable, given the two departments' rationales and histories; but even these overall arenas of interest must be qualified somewhat, because both departments have sustainable development mandates and both are part of a larger government whose ministers are concerned about both energy production and wealth creation as well as about climate change (VanNijnatten and MacDonald, 2003).

Some of this institutionalized ambivalence, with its inherent contradictions, was evident in the formation of new Cabinet groups and committees as energy issues re-emerged in 2001–2 following the announcement of the Bush energy plan in the United States. Initially, a Cabinet reference group on energy was formed, largely because Bush's initial energy plan was seen as a great economic opportunity. But key federal players also felt that the Cabinet – which had not had to deal with overall energy policy for many years – required a more concerted review and learning process in order to reassure itself that the overall promarket policy of the previous fifteen years still made sense, but also to see if other issues were being dealt with in the new circumstances. Broadly speaking, this initial reference committee process satisfied key people in the energy file that the largely promarket policies did make sense. At the same time, however, a second Cabinet reference group committee was formed, this one with climate change as its mandate, to review the ongoing issues already apparent in the run-up to the 2002 signing of the Kyoto Protocol. This committee focused on intervention actions, and as we have seen, it used the full policy tool kit. This committee later evolved into a standing committee; within it, the key trade-offs and actual Kyoto Protocol implementation decisions will be brokered and made.

Conclusions

This chapter has provided the political-economic and institutional context and setting for the changes and developments in Canadian energy policy that are examined in the book as a whole. In it, I have contrasted the largely promarket era of federal energy policy since the mid-1980s with the earlier combative politics of the early 1980s. Its discussion of current sources of energy supply and of past efforts at, and barriers against, energy conservation serves as an important backdrop for later discussions of the actual or potential movement toward a low-carbon economy in Canada and globally. George W. Bush's NEP and his alternative to the Kyoto Protocol will crucially affect Canada's energy and sustainable development approaches and challenges; it will generate both opportunities and difficulties and hence partial policy contradictions.

This chapter has traced Canada's internal federal–provincial politics and processes for dealing with the Kyoto Protocol as a further central feature of recent energy policy evolution. But these changes in turn must be juxtaposed against our initial, albeit brief, account of a sample of provincial energy and sustainable development policies and changes in recent years and also against our initial profile of how the basic federal–provincial energy regulatory system has evolved. Finally, further analyses by the chapter authors must be couched against the broad changes in the configuration of energy interests, including those of industry sectors and NGOs as well as user groups and consumers and the S&T community.

The discussion in this chapter represents the editor's views on some of the key contextual features and factors in Canadian energy policy over the past two decades. However, the authors whose analyses follow have much more to say in the specific context of the areas they examine, and of course, each has individual views about Canadian federal and provincial energy policy in the sustainable development era. Chapter 13, which follows their contributions, considers some further related analytical issues and concerns about Canadian energy policy and governance: (a) Kyoto Protocol implementation challenges, now that Canada has signed; (b) energy security; (c) northern pipelines, native peoples, and sustainable northern development; (d) electricity restructuring and the limits of market and regulatory design; (e) energy S&T and innovation policy links; and (f) the prospects for the greater institutionalization of sustainable development within energy policy and institutional mandates.

NOTES

1 This book complements a co-authored analysis that focused explicitly on Canadian energy regulatory institutions (Doern and Gattinger, 2003) and an earlier volume on nuclear energy policy in Canada (Doern, Dorman, and Morrison, 2001).

REFERENCES

Alberta. 2000. Ministry of Resource Development. *Annual Report 1999–2000*. Alberta Ministry of Resource Development.
– 'Proposed Plan on Climate Change Balances Environmental Action with Economic Prosperity.' Alberta government website www.gov.ab.ca/home/news/dsp_feature.cfm. (accessed 14 July).
Alberta Ministry of Energy. 2001. *Energy Business Plan*. Alberta Ministry of Energy, 10 April.
Breen, David. 1993. *Alberta's Petroleum Industry and the Conservation Board*. Edmonton: University of Alberta Press.
British Columbia. 2001. *Strategic Considerations for a New British Columbia Energy Policy*. Interim Report of the Task Force on Energy Policy. Government of British Columbia.
Brown, Paige. 1998. *Climate, Biodiversity, and Forests*. Washington, D.C.: World Resources Institute.
Bush, President George W. 2001. 'Climate Change Policy Options.' White House Statement, 11 June. Washington: The White House.
– 2002. 'Climate Change Initiatives.' White House Statement, 14 February. Washington: The White House.

Cabinet Office. 2002. *The Energy Review: A Performance and Innovation Unit Report*. London: UK Cabinet Office.

Calamai, Peter. 2001. 'Forecast Hazy.' *Toronto Star*. 7 April, A3.

– 2001a. 'Doubters Struggle to Make Voices Heard.' *Toronto Star*. 7 April, A3.

– 2001b. 'Burying the Problem.' *Toronto Star*. 8 April, A5.

Canada. 1988. *Energy and Canadians into the 21st Century*. Ottawa: Minister of Supply and Services.

– 2001a. *Canada and the Kyoto Protocol*. 'Removing Carbon Dioxide: Credit for Enhancing Sinks' and 'Why Canada Wants Carbon Sinks.' climatechange.gc.ca (accessed 24 July).

– 2001b. *Canada's Position on Forests and Agriculture Sinks*. Ottawa: Minister of Supply and Services.

– 2002a. *Climate Change Plan for Canada*. Ottawa: Public Works and Government Services Canada.

– 2002b. *A Discussion Paper on Canada's Contribution to Addressing Climate Change*. Ottawa: Public Works and Government Services Canada.

Canadian Electricity Association. 2000. 'Canadian Electricity Association Brief to Energy Ministers.' September.

CAPP (Canadian Association of Petroleum Producers). 2002. 'Understanding Emission Trading, Global Emissions and Canadian Competitiveness.' Presentation by Rick Hyndman to Greenhouse Gas Emissions Conference. Toronto, 6 February.

Chase, Steven. 2002. 'Ottawa Slams Alberta over Kyoto Estimates.' *Globe and Mail*, 15 March, A1.

Competition Bureau. 2001. *Realizing the Benefits of Competition in the Nova Scotia Electricity System: An Evolutionary Approach*. Submission to the Nova Scotia Energy Strategy Review, Department of Natural Resources, 31 May.

Connor, Steve. 2002. 'Coal Has Gone, Gas Is Low, So Is Britain Running on Empty?' *The Independent*. 17 July, A13.

Cordon, Sandra. 2001. 'US Wants Canadian Gas, Oil, Electricity More Than Ever, Says Ambassador.' *National Post*. 19 December, A5.

Corporate Knights. 2002. 'Green Machines.' *Corporate Knights* 1, no. 2: 20–4.

David Suzuki Foundation. 2000. *Negotiating Climate Change*. Vancouver, November, www.davidsuzuki.org.

Doern, G. Bruce, Arslan Dorman, and Robert Morrison, eds. 2001. *Canadian Nuclear Policies: Changing Ideas, Institutions, and Interests*. Toronto: University of Toronto Press.

Doern, G. Bruce, and Monica Gattinger. 2003. *Power Switch: Energy Regulatory Governance in the 21st Century*. Toronto: University of Toronto Press.

Doern, G. Bruce, and Ted Reed, eds. 2000. *Risky Business: Canada's Changing Science-Based Policy and Regulatory Regime.* Toronto: University of Toronto Press.

Doern, G. Bruce, and Brian W. Tomlin. 1991. *Faith and Fear: The Free Trade Story.* Toronto: Stoddart.

Doern, G. Bruce, and Glen Toner. 1985. *The Politics of Energy.* Toronto: Methuen.

Dotto, Lydia. 1999. *Storm Warning: Gambling with the Climate of Our Planet.* Toronto: Doubleday Canada.

Doyle-Bedwell, Patricia, and Fay G. Cohen. 2001. 'Aboriginal Peoples in Canada: Their Role in Shaping Environmental Trends in the Twenty-first Century.' Pp. 169–206 in Edward A. Parson, ed., *Governing the Environment.* Toronto: University of Toronto Press.

Duane, Timothy P. 2002. 'Regulation's Rationale: Learning from the California Energy Crisis.' *Yale Journal on Regulation* 19, no. 2: 471–540.

Dunn, Seth. 2001. 'Decarbonizing the Energy Economy.' Pp. 83–101 in Lester Brown, ed., *State of the World.* New York: Norton.

Economic Council of Canada. 1985. *Connections: An Energy Strategy for the Future.* Ottawa: Minister of Supply and Services.

Economist. 2002. 'How Many Planets? A Survey of the Global Environment.' *Economist,* 6 July, 1–16.

Environmental Studies Program. 2003. *Ratification of the Kyoto Protocol: A Citizen's Guide to the Canadian Climate Change Policy Process.* Environmental Studies Program, University of Toronto.

Flavin, Christopher. 1998. 'The Next Energy Revolution.' Pp. 56–76 in Lester Brown and Ed Ayres, eds., *The World Watch Reader on Global Environmental Issues: 1998 Edition.* New York: Norton.

Gilles, Charlie. 2002. 'Alberta Pushes the Merits of Its Kyoto Alternative.' *National Post.* 29 May, A8.

Gray, Jeff. 2003. 'Eves Scraps Sale of Hydro One Stake.' *Globe and Mail.* 20 January, B1.

Government of the United States. 2001. *Reliable, Affordable and Environmentally Sound Energy for America's Future.* Washington: U.S. Government Printing Office.

Grubb, Michael, with Christiaan Vrolijk and Duncan Brack. 1999. *The Kyoto Protocol: A Guide and Assessment.* London: Royal Institute of International Affairs.

Helm, Dieter. 2003. *Energy, the State and the Market: British Energy Policy since 1979.* Oxford: Oxford University Press.

Hoffman, Peter. 2001. *Tomorrow's Energy.* Cambridge, MA: MIT Press.

Houghton, John. 1997. *Global Warming: The Complete Briefing*, 2nd ed. Cambridge: Cambridge University Press.

Jaccard, Mark. 2002. *California Shorts a Circuit: Should Canadians Trust the Wiring Diagram?* C.D. Howe Institute Commentary, no. 159, February.

Jaccard, Mark, John Nyboer, and Bryn Sadownik. 2002. *The Cost of Climate Change*. Vancouver: UBC Press.

Jang, Brent. 2002. 'No Privatization for B.C. Hydro, Province Says.' *Globe and Mail*. 26 November, B7.

Joskow, Paul. 2000. 'Deregulation and Regulatory Reform in the US Electric Power Sector.' Pp. 113–88 in Sam Pelzman and Clifford Winston, eds. *Deregulation of Network Industries: What's Next?* Washington, DC: Brookings Institution.

Lafferty, William M., and James Meadowcroft, eds. 2000. *Implementing Sustainable Development*. Oxford: Oxford University Press, 2000.

Macdonald, Douglas. 2002. 'The Business Response to Environmentalism.' Pp. 66–86 in Debora VanNijnatten and Robert Boardman, eds., *Canadian Environmental Policy: Context and Cases*, 2nd ed. Oxford, UK: Oxford University Press.

– 2003. 'The Business Campaign to Prevent Kyoto Ratification.' Paper presented to the Canadian Political Science Association Meeting, Dalhousie University. 31 May.

McDougall, John N. 1982. *Fuels and the National Policy*. Toronto: McClelland and Stewart.

McKenna, Barrie. 2003. 'U.S. to Unveil Massive Energy Bill.' *Globe and Mail*. 15 November, B1.

Mertl, Steve. 2002. 'Canada May Not Ratify Climate-Change Agreement, Dhaliwell Suggests.' *National Post*. 14 March, A2.

Mommer, Bernard. 2002. *Global Oil and the Nation State*. Oxford: Oxford University Press.

Moore, Oliver. 2002. 'Klein, Hamm Voice Support for Kyoto Alternative.' *Globe and Mail*. 3 May, A1.

Morrison, Robert, David Layell, and Ged McLean. 2001. 'Technology and Climate Change.' Paper presented at Climate Change 2: Canadian Technology Development Conference, 3–5 October, Toronto.

Morse, Edward, and James Richard. 2002. 'The Battle for Energy Dominance.' *Foreign Affairs*. March–April: 16–31.

Nakicenovic, N., A. Gruber, and A. McDonald. 1998. *Global Energy Perspectives*. Cambridge; International Institute for Applied Systems Analysis and World Energy Council.

National Climate Change Process. 2000. *Canada's National Implementation Strategy on Climate Change*. Ottawa: Minister of Supply and Services.

National Post Business. 2001. 'Energy: Are We Running Out.' *National Post Business*, Special Issue. October.

Natural Resources Canada. 2000. *Energy in Canada 2000*. Ottawa: Natural Resources Canada.

New Brunswick. 2001. *White Paper on New Brunswick Energy Policy*. Fredericton: New Brunswick Department of Natural Resources and Energy.

Nova Scotia. 2001a. *Powering Nova Scotia's Economy*. Halifax: Government of Nova Scotia.

– 2001b. *Seizing the Opportunity: Nova Scotia's Energy Strategy*. Halifax: Government of Nova Scotia.

Ontario. 1996. *A Framework For Competition*. Report of the Advisory Committee on Competition in the Ontario Electricity System to the Ontario Ministry of Environment and Energy. Toronto: Queen's Printer.

Ontario Ministry of Energy, Science and Technology. 2001. 'Ontario's New Electricity Market: Safeguarding Ontario's Electricity Future.' Toronto: Ministry of Energy, Science and Technology.

Parson, Edward A., ed. 2001. *Governing the Environment*. Toronto: University of Toronto Press.

Poelzer, Greg. 2002. 'Aboriginal Peoples and Environmental Policy in Canada: No Longer at the Margins.' Pp. 87–106 in Debora L. Van Nijnatten and Robert Boardman, eds., *Canadian Environmental Policy: Context and Cases*, 2nd ed. Toronto: Oxford University Press.

Princen, Thomas, Michael Maniates, and Ken Comca. 2002. *Confronting Consumption*. Cambridge, MA: MIT Press.

Quebec. 1996. *Energy at the Service of Quebec*. Quebec City: Government of Quebec.

Rowlands, Ian H. 1995. *The Politics of Global Atmospheric Change*. Manchester: Manchester University Press.

– 2000. 'Beauty and the Beast? BP's and Exxon's Position on Global Climate Change.' *Government and Policy* 18: 339–54.

Schelling, Thomas C. 2002. 'What Makes Greenhouse Sense?' *Foreign Affairs* 81, no. 3: 1–9.

Schwanen, Daniel. 2000. *A Cooler Approach: Tackling Canada's Commitments on Greenhouse Gas Emissions*. Toronto: C.D. Howe Institute.

Seguin, Rheal. 2002. 'Hydro-Quebec Planning Offshore Exploration.' *Globe and Mail*. 28 November, B9.

Seskus, Tony, and Claudia Cattaneo. 2002. 'Gas Giants Applaud NEB Ruling.' *Financial Post*. 20 September, A6.

Scientific American. 1999. 'The Future of Fuel Cells.' *Scientific American* (July), 72–93.

Sweet, Earl. 2004. 'Energy Markets in Transition: 21st Century Challenges.' Presentation to Conference on Canadian Foreign Policy, Canadian Institute of International Affairs, Calgary, March 27, 2004.

Toner, Glen. 1986. 'Stardust: The Tory Energy Program.' In Michael Prince, ed., *How Ottawa Spends, 1986–87*. Toronto: Methuen.

– 2000. 'Canada: From Early Frontrunner to Plodding Anchorman.' Pp. xx–xx in William M. Lafferty and James Meadowcroft, eds., *Implementing Sustainable Development*. Toronto: Oxford University Press.

– 2004. *Building Canadian Capacity: Sustainable Development and the Knowledge Economy*. Vancouver: UBC Press.

Toner, Glen, and Carey Frey. 2003. 'Governance for Sustainable Development: Next Steps and Policy Innovations.' Paper prepared for the Conference 'New Prime Minister ... New Era.' School of Public Policy and Administration, Carleton University, Ottawa. 29–30 October.

Tupper, Allan. 2002. 'Toward a New Beginning? The Chrétien Liberals and Western Canada.' Pp. 88–101 in Bruce Doern, ed., *How Ottawa Spends 2002–2003: The Security Aftermath and National Priorities*. Toronto: Oxford University Press.

VanNijnatten, Debora. 2002. 'Getting Greener in the Third Mandate?' Pp. 216–33 in Bruce Doern, ed., *How Ottawa Spends 2002–2003: The Security Aftermath and National Priorities*. Toronto: Oxford University Press.

VanNijnatten, Debora, and Robert Boardman, eds. 2002. *Canadian Environmental Policy: Context and Cases*, 2nd ed. Toronto: Oxford University Press.

VanNijnatten, Debora, and Douglas Macdonald. 2003. 'Reconciling Energy and Climate Change Policies: How Ottawa Blends.' Pp. xx–xx in Bruce Doern, ed., *How Ottawa Spends 2003–2004: Regime Change and Policy Shift*. Toronto: Oxford University Press.

Victor, David G. 2001. *The Collapse of the Kyoto Protocol and the Struggle to Slow Global Warming*. Princeton: Princeton University Press.

Watkins, G. Campbell. 1991. 'Deregulation and the Canadian Petroleum Industry: Adolescence or Maturity.' Pp. 215–52 in Walter Block and George Lermer, eds., *Breaking the Shackles: Deregulating Canadian Industry*. Vancouver: Fraser Institute.

Webb, Kernaghan, eds. 2003. *Voluntary Codes: Private Governance, the Public Interest and Innovation*. Ottawa: Carleton Research Unit on Innovation, Science and Environment.

Chapter 2

The Changing Nature of National and Continental Energy Markets

ANDRÉ PLOURDE

The past twenty-five years in Canada and the United States have witnessed a wholesale move away from direct state intervention in the terms and conditions of contracts between buyers and sellers of energy. In the mid-1970s, governments in these two countries, and in Mexico, were heavily involved in determining the conditions under which both international and intranational trade in energy products would be allowed to occur. By the end of the 1970s, however, the first steps toward energy market deregulation had been taken. By the time the Canada–U.S. Free Trade Agreement (FTA) was signed in 1988, the role of the state in energy markets had changed dramatically. That agreement amounted to a commitment mechanism through which the governments of these two countries expressed their intention to allow market forces to play a stronger role in determining energy trade patterns.

The North American Free Trade Agreement (NAFTA) of 1993 was designed to broaden the scope of the FTA between the two original partners (e.g., by including additional provisions on the treatment of investment), and to extend the free trade zone to include Mexico. However, the net effect of NAFTA's energy provisions was limited by the fact that the new entrant, Mexico, had chosen to opt out of most of these provisions. This decision by Mexican authorities is consistent with the fact that energy markets in that country remain under tight government control, with state monopolies continuing to dominate the scene.

Efforts to deregulate or restructure electricity markets in North America started largely after NAFTA came into force. The short but turbulent history of electricity market restructuring is dominated by developments in the United States and Canada, with regulatory changes in Mexico being more limited in scope.

This chapter documents and assesses some of the key changes in the structure of regulation applicable to energy industries in North America, with a focus on developments in Canada and the United States. Developments in Mexico will be discussed as appropriate. In later sections, I will argue that changes in regulatory structures have brought about a closer integration of crude oil and of natural gas markets in North America. The degree of market integration is weaker in the case of Mexico, especially when it comes to natural gas. The situation in electricity markets does not point to continentwide integration. Rather, aspects of the production and transmission of electricity suggest that a pattern of regional integration is more likely to emerge if the stalled restructuring efforts ever regain some of their lost momentum.

The next section of this chapter presents a brief overview of the regulation of Canadian and American energy markets before deregulatory efforts began in the late 1970s. This is followed by three sections that outline the key changes in the regulatory structures applying to crude oil, natural gas, and electricity, respectively. Yet another section then considers these developments from the perspective of their sustainability as broad policy directions and of their contribution to sustainable development.

The Regulation of Energy Markets in North America, circa 1977

In some sense, 1977 marked the apogee of the U.S. government's intervention in the markets for crude oil and natural gas – significant policy initiatives aimed at increasing the role of market forces were introduced in 1978. In Canada, the process of tightening regulation continued until 1980, with the introduction of the federal government's National Energy Program (NEP). Within a few months, however, key aspects of the NEP had begun to unravel, and the march toward the deregulation of crude oil and natural gas transactions had begun in Canada.

Since the world oil price shock of 1973–4, the U.S. government had progressively moved away from a 'self-sufficiency' view of that country's crude oil market to a recognition that crude oil imports would be an integral part of the American energy picture for years to come and that not all foreign sources of crude were likely to be equally reliable. As a result, by the end of the 1970s, there were few regulatory impediments to the penetration of Canadian- and Mexican-produced crude oil on American markets.

In 1977, there were still widespread wellhead price controls: the Federal Energy Regulatory Commission (FERC) was responsible for regulating the price of American-produced crude oil. It seems that this price regulation was based not on concerns about the possible exercise of market power due to the presence of significant natural monopoly elements, but rather on the need to protect American consumers from the vagaries of OPEC-dominated international transactions.

At the time, crude oil in the United States was sold mainly on short-term contracts, and pipelines were in the business of providing transportation services. Fees and tolls were regulated (based mostly on natural monopoly arguments); however, access to the transportation infrastructure was not an important tool of discrimination, since pipeline companies did not own the crude oil that was shipped using their facilities. Finally, the prices of refined petroleum products were subject to sporadic controls at the state level, but were not an important part of the overall regulatory framework: market forces were the main drivers of the pricing decisions of retailers.

The situation in Canada was broadly similar in many respects: crude oil was sold on short-term contracts and was not owned by the pipeline companies that transported it; refined product prices were not subject to systematic regulation by the provinces. Canadian-produced crude oil involved in interprovincial and international trade was subject to price regulation by the federal government; output and other volume restrictions were also imposed on Canadian production and exports. By the mid-1970s, a declared (although never achieved) objective of Canadian energy policy was to limit crude oil exports to the United States to exchanges (or swaps): *net* exports to the United States (the destination of almost all Canadian crude sold abroad) were to be reduced to zero.

The basic set-up of the natural gas industry was quite similar in Canada and the United States: a large number of producers would sell their output to merchant pipelines, which would transport the gas they owned and sell it to regulated franchise monopolies (local distribution companies, LDCs), with all of these transactions occurring under contracts with terms as long as thirty years. An important element of these contracts was so-called take-or-pay clauses, whereby purchasers at both ends of the pipe (pipeline companies and LDCs) agreed to pay for specified volumes of natural gas even if they chose not to take delivery.

Prices of natural gas were typically regulated at two points in the value chain: some form of wellhead (or equivalent) price controls was imposed at the same time as prices to final users were regulated. In the United States, the FERC exercised its federal mandate to set wellhead prices and determine pipeline charges, while state (and sometimes local) public utilities boards determined end-use prices. In Canada, prices at specific delivery points of gas sold domestically (but outside Alberta) were set by the federal government, and pipeline charges were determined by the National Energy Board (NEB). Export prices were also determined by the federal government, whereas end-use prices were set by provincial utilities boards. Much of this natural gas price regulation in Canada and the United States was implemented in reference to oil prices, either crude or specific products (typically 'resid' or heavy fuel oil). The effects of crude oil price regulation were thus also felt on natural gas markets.

Much of the regulatory apparatus described above was justified by appeals to economies of scale and scope. Economies of scale dictated that few pipelines should be built and that only one LDC should serve any given area. Regulation was thus in order, since there would not likely be much competition in the provision of these services. Technical aspects of natural gas transportation, combined with the fact that it was relatively costly to store (in comparison to crude oil and to refined petroleum products, for example) and that there was much seasonal fluctuation in demand (since an important end use of natural gas is as space-heating fuel), were used to justify 'bundling' together many links in the value chain. For example, economies of scope encouraged vertical integration and were used to justify the existence of merchant pipelines.

Volume controls were also quite common. In Canada, 'removal' permits were necessary to ship natural gas from either of the main producing provinces (Alberta and British Columbia), and any exports from Canada had to be authorized by the NEB. All jurisdictions applied their own testing procedures to determine whether additional removals or exports were deemed to be in the public interest; they also ruled, following extensive public hearings, on whether to allow the proposed long-term sales.

The electricity industry in Canada and the United States has evolved very differently from the other energy-producing sectors. In some sense, electricity is much more of a 'local product' than either crude oil or natural gas: a much smaller proportion of electricity production crosses a provincial, state, or international border on its way to consumers. As a result, by 1977 the role of provinces and states in regulating electricity production, transmission, and sales was of greater importance in the overall regulatory framework. As with natural gas, however, it was felt that the industry was characterized by significant economies of scale and scope; thus, regulation encouraged electricity companies to become vertically integrated franchise monopolies, whether they were privately or publicly owned. Prices to final users were regulated in one form or another, either through standard regulatory means or simply by decree.

Federal oversight of electricity export and import transactions was less pronounced in Canada than in the United States, since the NEB focused on authorizing export quantities (but not prices) and on regulating the construction of cross-border transmission lines. In addition, since most provinces had opted for public ownership of electric utilities, international electricity transactions typically involved an agency of a provincial government as a direct participant.

Mexico chose a different model of government intervention in energy markets: wholesale nationalization. Indeed, the history of the Mexican nation is intimately tied to that of its oil industry.[1] Conflicts with British and especially with American oil companies led to the creation in 1938 of Petróleos Mexicanos (Pemex) – the Mexican national oil company – and to the expropriation of the assets of British and American companies in the oil sector. Eventually, the Mexican state reserved for itself a monopoly position in the oil (and gas) industry, and designated Pemex as the agent to exercise this role, which extended to all sectors of the industry, from exploration and production to refining and retail distribution. In electricity, the government established the Comisión Federal de Electricidad (CFE) to operate as the monopoly electricity provider throughout the country.[2]

By 1977, Mexican international energy trade was dominated by exports of crude oil, with the United States being a significant destination. But Pemex had imposed an additional constraint on exports of crude oil (and refined products): no more than 50 per cent of export volumes could be directed at the United States (Grayson, 2001). This acted to restrict crude oil exports to that country for many years.

The First to Go: Crude Oil

Deregulation initiatives relating to crude oil markets in both Canada and the United States mainly took the form of an end-to-wellhead (or equivalent) price regulation combined with a lifting (or at least a significant softening) of volume restrictions on cross-border – especially international – transactions. The role of the state as the entity responsible for determining these key aspects of transactions was supplanted in favour of market forces: buyers and sellers were now free to negotiate the terms of purchase/sales contracts within the context of world oil markets.

A recent issue of the *Journal of Regulatory Economics* (January 2002) contains papers dealing with the processes and consequences of 'deregulation' and 'restructuring' initiatives in the United States and a few other industrialized countries. This collection includes a contribution on natural gas, another on electricity, and ... nothing on oil markets. In some sense, this is not surprising. After all, deregulated oil markets have been the norm in Canada and the United States for about twenty years. The deregulation process in the United States began in the late 1970s and was effectively completed by early 1981, as Table 2.1 indicates.[3] In Canada, there was a transition period that began around 1982 and ended in the first half of 1985, with the deregulation of crude oil market transactions. Neither in Canada nor in the United States was the process of deregulation especially difficult to implement, so the transition away from 'regulated' markets was a fairly smooth one.

We can probably trace the roots of this smooth transition to three main sets of causes. First, the structure and technological characteristics of the industry encouraged a greater role for market forces. Among these characteristics, the following were key:

• There were (and still are) many producers of crude oil in both countries, so issues of market power on the supply side did not arise, especially since the North American crude oil market was (and remains) so closely linked to the world market.
• Crude oil and refined petroleum products are relatively easy to store, so inventory stocks can act as relatively low-cost buffers to meet unexpected fluctuations in demand and (flow) supply.

A second set of factors revolves around the nature of the regulatory system that was in place when deregulation efforts were initiated. In particular:

- The long-distance transmission systems provided only transportation services; they did not own the crude oil that went through the pipelines. Thus, issues of access to these 'natural monopoly' systems had been resolved earlier.
- End-use markets (those for refined petroleum products such as gasoline and heating oil) were largely deregulated before similar initiatives were launched in North American crude oil markets. As a result, the necessary readjustments in buyer/seller relationships were limited to those dealing with crude oil.
- Regulators in both countries had not insisted on long-term contracts to govern crude oil transactions. For example, even before deregulation, Canadian crude oil was typically sold on one-month contracts. Therefore, as deregulation proceeded, there were no 'stranded cost' issues associated with long-term contracts that needed to be addressed.

Finally, the political climate was favourable to deregulation. By the beginning of the 1980s, crude oil prices were relatively low (and falling) on world oil markets, which meant that linking North American crude oil prices more closely with those prevailing on world markets did not give rise to serious objections from consumers. In addition, within Canada, the federal government and the governments of the producing provinces all had a positive view of deregulation, following a decade of bitter disagreements. Finally, the energy policies of the United States and Canada were aligned in one crucial aspect for the first time in more than thirty years: increased crude oil exports from Canada were seen as desirable by the governments of both countries.

As far as Mexico is concerned, however, there have been no significant moves toward lessening the state's role in crude oil transactions: Pemex continues to be in a monopoly position in both domestic and international trade (see Table 2.1). Over time, however, Pemex has increasingly perceived the United States as a desirable destination for its crude oil production; by mid-2001 it had lifted its self-imposed volume restriction on exports to that country (Grayson, 2001). Nonetheless, Mexico's basic approach to the North American crude oil trade has not changed since 1977: Pemex determines export volumes, and prices are set at world-equivalent levels (after correction for differences in quality and transportation costs).

Another relevant aspect of Mexican energy policy concerns the cooperation between Mexico and OPEC. Over the past few years, Mexico has been a staunch supporter of OPEC's moves to reduce the supply

58   André Plourde

TABLE 2.1
Some Milestones in the Development of Crude Oil Markets in North America

Canada	Mexico	United States
February 1977: Based on concerns about the security of Canadian crude oil supplies, the National Energy Board (NEB) recommends sharp reductions in the volumes of light and medium crude oil exported to the United States. Net exports are to be effectively eliminated by 1980; however, this policy objective would not be attained.	*March 1938:* President Cárdenas nationalizes the assets of foreign (mostly UK and US) oil and gas companies operating in Mexico.	*April 1979:* President Carter announces the phased deregulation of crude oil prices; 'new' crude oil prices are deregulated as of June 1979; 'old' oil prices are to be deregulated by September 1981.
October 1980: In its National Energy Program, the federal government unilaterally departs from the established practice of negotiating wellhead crude oil prices with the governments of the producing provinces, and announces specific plans for crude oil price regulation in Canada.	*June 1938:* The Mexican government creates Petróleos Mexicanos (Pemex), and gives it the mandate of operating the assets nationalized a few months earlier.	*January 1981:* In one of the first acts of his administration, President Reagan announces the immediate price deregulation of all US-produced crude oil.
September 1981: After a period of bitter disagreements, the governments of Canada and Alberta sign an agreement dealing with crude oil pricing. (Similar agreements would soon be reached with the governments of the other producing provinces.) A 'vintage' approach is used to price crude oil: 'new' conventional and synthetic production receives the world-equivalent price,	*1958:* The Mexican government enacts the 'Regulatory Law of Constitutional Article 27 in the Field of Petroleum' (known as the 'Petroleum Law'). It extends Pemex's monopoly position to include downstream activities in the oil and gas industry.	*April 1983:* The New York Mercantile Exchange (NYMEX) introduces a futures contract for West Texas Intermediate (WTI) crude oil; options would be introduced in 1986.
	1960: Article 27 of the Mexican Constitution is amended to enshrine the state's monopoly position (as exercised by Pemex) in the oil and gas industry. It also prohibits concessions and risk contracts in that industry.	*January 1989:* The Canada-US Free Trade Agreement comes into effect. The energy-related provisions, as these apply to the oil industry, have almost entirely been anticipated by the deregulatory thrust of the two countries' policy approaches of the last decade or so.
	1992: The Mexican government undertakes a structural reform of Pemex: the state monopoly is broken up into four subsidiaries, one	

TABLE 2.1 *(continued)*
Some Milestones in the Development of Crude Oil Markets in North America

Canada	Mexico	United States
while 'old' conventional crude oil receives a lower, regulated price.	of which is focused on exploration and production of oil and gas, and the transportation, storage, and marketing of crude oil and oil products.	
June 1982: Additional 'vintages' of crude oil are created, and world-equivalent pricing is extended to more categories of crude oil.	*January 1994:* NAFTA comes into effect, but the Mexican government opts to exempt the country's oil and gas industry from almost all of the agreement's trade- and investment-liberating provisions.	
March 1985: The governments of Canada and of the oil-producing provinces agree to deregulate crude oil pricing in Canada, and to lift any remaining regulation on short-term crude oil exports.	*2001:* Changes in the internal direction of Pemex bring about a more positive attitude toward increased crude and oil products exports to the United States.	
October 1985: The government of Alberta begins the process of eliminating its 'prorationing' system for the regulation of crude oil production within the province. Prorationing will finally be abandoned by Alberta in June 1987.		

of crude oil on world markets, and has voluntarily reduced its production, in concert with OPEC members. Mexico has succeeded in endearing itself to both key importing and exporting countries, by collaborating with OPEC even while allowing higher export volumes to the United States. The long-term sustainability of this kind of policy is far from established.

Perhaps the most obvious consequence of the downfall of crude oil price regulation in Canada and the United States has been the closing of the gap that existed between prices in these countries and those prevailing on world markets. As Figure 2.1 shows, the wide price differentials that existed during most of the 1970s have virtually disappeared since the advent of deregulation.[4] Existing price differentials among crudes are now largely due to quality and transportation cost differences, with West Texas Intermediate (WTI) emerging as a marker crude.[5] Market forces have thus acted to eliminate arbitrage opportunities. Although there have been some local price events, these have typically been linked to shortages in pipeline capacity, and have been the source of their own demise: such local price events induced expansions of pipeline capacity, which in turn led to the elimination of the scarcity rent earned by transportation facilities.

Figure 2.1 also reminds us that crude prices in Canada and the United States have been more volatile since the advent of deregulation.[6] But it is difficult to trace the roots of this phenomenon back to deregulation itself, since world oil prices have also been more volatile since the beginning of the 1980s, as Verleger (1993) has shown. The deregulated environment has responded by establishing mechanisms for dealing with this volatility: spot and futures markets for crude oil emerged shortly after the deregulation process had been completed in the United States. The continuing popularity of the NYMEX (New York Mercantile Exchange) contract for WTI – first introduced in 1983 – indicates that market participants have come to rely on financial instruments to hedge some (or all) of their exposure to crude oil price changes. Buyers and sellers of crude oil in Canada and the United States now bear the consequences of this volatility, whereas when prices were regulated this role fell, at least in part, on the shoulders of taxpayers, as governments sought to protect consumers from price fluctuations.

Deregulation has also led to lower transaction costs on North American crude oil markets. The type of situation described in Helliwell and colleagues (1989, 46–7), whereby governments had to work hard to enforce quality-based price differentials within an administered pricing system, simply does not arise in an environment where buyers and sellers are allowed to determine prices and quantities. In addition, it became possible to structure export deals in such a way as to avoid lengthy (and costly) public hearings. Although this reduced transaction costs, it also meant that market forces would play a bigger role in determining crude oil trade patterns in North America. Crude oil has increasingly become a commodity like any other. Buyers and sellers

Figure 2.1. Selected crude oil prices, 1970–2001

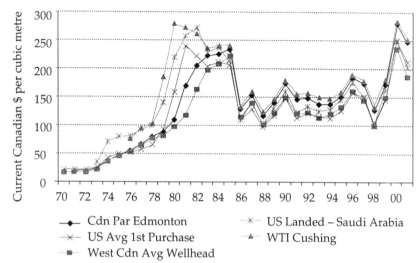

- ◆ Cdn Par Edmonton
- ✳ US Landed – Saudi Arabia
- ✕ US Avg 1st Purchase
- ▲ WTI Cushing
- ■ West Cdn Avg Wellhead

Sources: Statistics Canada; Energy Information Administration (EIA), U.S. Department of Energy; BP's *Statistical Review of World Energy*; conversions into Canadian dollars using exchange-rate data published by the Bank of Canada.

are free to negotiate the terms of contracts, but they also have to deal with the risks associated with these transactions.

Figure 2.2 shows the evolution of North American crude oil trade patterns since 1980, a period during which the United States has systematically been in a net importing position.[7] As Canada relaxed its export policy in the first half of the 1980s, export volumes grew sharply, as did the share of American net crude oil imports sourced in Canada. Since 1985 (when Canadian controls on short-term crude oil exports were effectively lifted), export volumes have continued to grow, roughly at the same pace as has the Americans' reliance on foreign sources of supply: Canadian crude oil has accounted for approximately 15 per cent of all American net imports since the mid-1980s. In volume terms, however, Canadian exports to the United States have almost tripled since 1985, rising to about 80 million cubic metres in 2001. Throughout this period of rapidly expanding exports, domestic production rose in concert: Canada remained a net exporter of crude oil (Figure 2.3).

At the beginning of the 1980s, Mexico provided the United States with almost 25 per cent of its net imports of crude oil. However,

62   André Plourde

Figure 2.2. U.S. net imports of crude oil from Canada and Mexico, 1980–2001

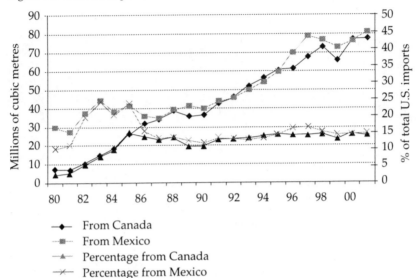

Source: Author's calculations based on data published by EIA, U.S. Department of Energy.

Figure 2.3. Net crude oil exports from Canada, 1980–2001

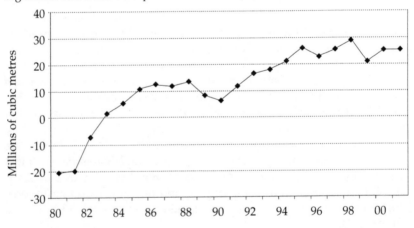

Source: Author's calculations based on data published by EIA, U.S. Department of Energy.

Figure 2.4. Share of U.S. crude oil consumption met by North American sources, 1980–2001

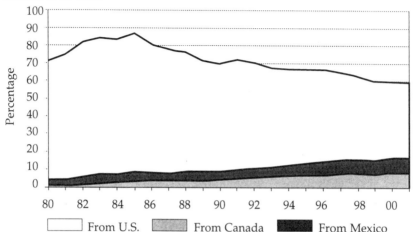

Source: Author's calculations based on data published by EIA, U.S. Department of Energy.

export growth from Mexico has only kept pace with that of Canada since the late 1980s – such that by the end of the sample period, both countries were providing the United States with approximately the same volumes of crude oil. Together, Canada and Mexico thus account for about 30 per cent of American net imports of crude oil, which corresponds to 16 per cent of total end use.

Over the years, these growing export volumes from Canada and Mexico have not been sufficient to counter the effects of the decline in American crude oil production. As Figure 2.4 shows, the share of American consumption met by North American sources has declined from a high of about 90 per cent in the mid-1980s, to about 60 per cent by 2001. Initiatives to reverse this situation are at the heart of the Cheney Committee report, tabled in May 2001 (National Energy Policy Development Group, 2001).

... And Then There Were Two: Natural Gas

As the 1970s progressed, the 'success' of deregulation initiatives in the American telecommunications industry – also previously thought to be a natural candidate for widespread regulatory intervention, with its natural monopoly elements and pervasive vertical integration – led to questions being raised about the inevitability of regulation for natural gas.[8] And then came the winter of 1977.

Shortages of natural gas were experienced in many parts of the United States, and these could not be traced back to the lack of pipeline capacity. The absence of price signals to producers was blamed, in that the regulated system failed to provide adequate supplies. Within a year, the Carter administration had set a course for natural gas deregulation within areas under federal jurisdiction – a process that would take fifteen years to complete, as Table 2.2 makes clear.

In Canada, federal controls on export prices and volumes were progressively relaxed throughout the first half of the 1980s. The intention to enhance the role of market forces in natural gas transactions was announced in 1985, and for all intents and purposes the deregulation process in Canada was completed by the end of 1988.

A number of factors played an important role in shaping the approach to the deregulation of natural gas markets in Canada and the United States. In particular:

- Transportation technology and costs are such that, for our purposes, the relevant market area for natural gas is North American in scope.
- Almost all aspects of natural gas transactions were regulated (including prices, volumes, pipeline tolls and tariffs, length of contracts, etc.); in both countries, retail sales and distribution of natural gas were regulated at the state or provincial level.
- Long-distance transmission pipelines owned the gas they carried.
- These merchant pipelines were linked to producers and LDCs by long-term contracts that included take-or-pay provisions.
- Demand for natural gas had a strong seasonal component, linked to its use as a space-heating fuel. Also, gas is more difficult (and hence more costly) to store than is crude oil. The combination of these two factors creates issues of load balancing for long-distance carriers that do not arise with crude oil.
- The deregulation of crude oil markets also had implications for natural gas transactions, especially in Canada: delivered prices of natural gas had been rigidly linked to the regulated price of crude oil. The end of crude oil price regulation meant that the stable anchor used to determine natural gas prices had effectively disappeared.

By the end of 1978, the government of the United States had enacted

TABLE 2.2
Some Milestones in the Development of Natural Gas Markets in North America

Canada	Mexico	United States
October 1980: As part of its National Energy Program, the federal government replaces the current negotiated approach to natural gas price regulation, with federal price regulation of natural gas in interprovincial trade. *September 1981:* The governments of Canada and Alberta agree on an approach to the regulation of natural gas prices in interprovincial trade: the price of natural gas delivered at Toronto is set at 65% BTU-parity with delivered crude oil prices. *July 1983:* The federal government acts to lessen price controls on natural gas exports. *April 1984:* The governments of Canada and Alberta agree to lower delivered prices for Eastern Canadian industrial gas users. *July 1984:* The federal government announces that it will allow gas exporters to negotiate prices directly with U.S. purchasers, subject to a floor price equal to that of natural gas delivered at Toronto.	*1958:* The Mexican government enacts the 'Regulatory Law of Constitutional Article 27 in the Field of Petroleum' (known as the 'Petroleum Law'). It extends Pemex's monopoly position to include downstream activities in the oil and gas industry. *1960:* Article 27 of the Mexican Constitution is amended to enshrine the state's monopoly position (as exercised by Pemex) in the oil and gas industry. It also prohibits concessions and risk contracts in that industry. *1980:* Natural gas export volumes to the United States grow significantly following the signing of a contract between Pemex and a California utility in 1979. *October 1984:* The Mexican government acts to suspend exports of natural gas to the United States. As the 1990s progressed, exports sales would be allowed again, but Mexico would remain a net importer of natural gas from the United States.	*April 1977:* President Carter proposes a series of measures aimed at changing the regulatory structure applicable to the U.S. natural gas industry; almost all of these measures are rejected by Congress. *September/October 1978:* Congress adopts the Natural Gas Policy Act. Among other things, the act renames the Federal Power Commission as the Federal Energy Regulatory Commission (FERC), and extends its regulatory authority to cover all U.S. natural gas production. The act also introduces a 'vintage' approach to the regulation of natural gas field prices and sets in motion a deregulation process, with the aim of having about 60% of U.S. gas production deregulated by 1985. *October 1985:* FERC Order 436 establishes rules allowing (but not requiring) pipelines to offer open access transportation service independent of natural gas sales service. *January 1987:* FERC Order 451 eliminates the 'vintage' approach to price

TABLE 2.2 *(continued)*
Some Milestones in the Development of Natural Gas Markets in North America

Canada	Mexico	United States
October 1985: The federal government and the governments of the gas-producing provinces reach agreement on the phased deregulation of natural gas prices and markets. Delivered prices are frozen until 1 November 1986, after which these will be deregulated. The NEB is given authority to approve, by order, exports contracts with terms of up to 24 months. Negotiated contracts are required to meet certain conditions, but terms are to be negotiated by buyers and sellers.	*1992:* The Mexican government undertakes a structural reform of Pemex: the state monopoly is broken up into four subsidiaries, one of which is focused on activities relating to natural gas transportation, distribution, and storage.	regulation, and sets a single price for all regulated natural gas production. *July 1989:* Congress adopts the Natural Gas Wellhead Decontrol Act, which brings an end to U.S. regulation of natural gas field prices.
July 1986: Following an assessment of the remaining regulatory structure, the federal government acts to require natural gas pipelines to unbundle their transportation sales from natural gas sales, and to provide access to their transportation facilities on a non-discriminatory basis to all shippers.	*January 1994:* NAFTA comes into effect, but the Mexican government opts to exempt the country's oil and gas industry from almost all of the agreement's trade- and investment-liberating provisions.	*April 1990:* The New York Mercantile Exchange (NYMEX) launches the world's first natural gas futures contract; options will first be traded on NYMEX in October 1992.
October 1986: The federal government replaces its border price test for natural gas exports with a price-monitoring process.	*May 1995:* The Petroleum Law is modified to allow for private (including foreign) participation in the transportation, distribution, and storage of natural gas.	*April 1992:* FERC Order 636 requires pipelines to unbundle sales of natural gas from sales of transportation services, and to provide comparable transportation services to all shippers; the order also introduces capacity release, thus creating markets for transmission capacity.
July 1987: The NEB adopts its 'Market-Based	*October/November 1995:* The Mexican government enacts the 'CRE Law' ('Comisión Reguladora de Energía'), and introduces the 'Natural Gas Regulations.' These specify that the transportation, distribution, and storage are regulated activities, and that local distribution companies are treated as franchise monopolies. 'First-hand sales' of	

TABLE 2.2 *(continued)*
Some Milestones in the Development of Natural Gas Markets in North America

Canada	Mexico	United States
Procedure' to assess whether long-term exports (contracts of more than 24 months) of natural gas are to be allowed.	natural gas must involve Pemex, but are subject to price regulation by the CRE.	
January 1989: The provisions of the Canada-US Free Trade Agreement come into effect. These largely reflect the deregulation efforts of the last decade in both Canada and the United States.	*March 1996:* The CRE adopts the Houston Ship Channel price as the benchmark for determining the (regulated) price of first-hand sales of natural gas in Mexico.	
	1996–7: The CRE gradually opens Pemex's natural gas transportation system to third-party access. The process is completed by 31 December 1997.	

sharp increases in the regulated wellhead prices of natural gas and set a timetable for eliminating price controls. American producers responded to these price signals by expanding their exploration and development activities, which led to greater gas supplies. But these new supplies were not reaching end users: merchant pipelines had long-term contracts with distributors. Gas-on-gas competition could not occur in this situation. In this way, the American gas bubble of the early 1980s emerged.

The FERC then began the long process of inducing pipelines to abrogate their long-term contracts, to strip themselves of their gas-marketing functions, and to grant access to their facilities on a non-discriminatory basis. These are the parts of the deregulation process that proved most controversial and that took the longest to realize. Eventually, the unbundling of the transportation and marketing functions led to increased investments in storage capacity to deal with the issue of load balancing.

Natural gas deregulation in the United States started rather inauspiciously for Canadian exporters. While the FERC was winding down the role of merchant pipelines, it made a series of rulings that effectively discriminated against Canadian-produced natural gas as far as access to transportation facilities in the United States was concerned. Canadian producers could not respond by shifting exports to another country, since there were no other export markets that could be tapped in a commercially viable manner. To make matters worse, there were regulation-imposed floors on natural gas export prices; those served to limit even more the scope of possible responses available to Canadian exporters. As a result, export volumes from Canada stagnated (Figure 2.6), and a large excess in production capability emerged in western Canada (Helliwell et al., 1989, 69–74).

The Canadian government and those of the gas-producing provinces responded to this situation first by lifting some of the remaining restrictions on export activities. This eventually culminated with the NEB-enforced position that the provisions of export contracts of twenty-four months or less in duration would no longer be subject to explicit regulation. As was the case with crude oil, buyers and sellers of natural gas would now be able to determine prices and volumes of exports from Canada.[9]

The governments of Canada and of the producing provinces also agreed to lift domestic price controls on delivered gas; in addition, they abrogated the long-term contracts linking producers and long-distance pipelines. These pipelines were also stripped of their marketing function and made to offer non-discriminatory access to their long-distance transportation facilities. But, in order for the effects of deregulation to be felt by end users in Canada, provincial regulatory agencies had to cooperate. The Ontario Energy Board, in particular, played a key role in ensuring that consumers would share in the benefits of deregulation.

At the beginning of the 1990s, the end-use market model that had emerged in most North American jurisdictions consisted of regulated LDCs operating within franchise areas, but subject to the competition of marketers and of direct sales by producers, who were granted non-discriminatory access to local distribution systems. End users could now choose between purchasing their supplies from regulated LDCs or from non-regulated alternative suppliers.

Figure 2.5 shows selected North American natural gas prices since 1970. As with crude oil, natural gas prices have progressively converged (once differences in transportation costs are taken into account) now that deregulation initiatives have been enacted on both sides of

Figure 2.5. Selected natural gas prices, 1970–2001

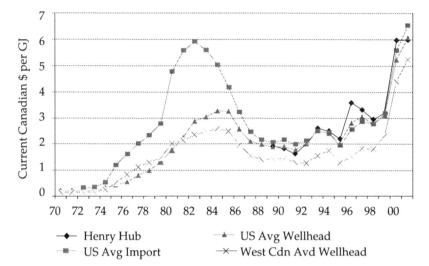

Sources: Statistics Canada; Energy Information Administration (EIA), U.S. Department of Energy; BP's *Statistical Review of World Energy*; conversions into Canadian dollars using exchange-rate data published by the Bank of Canada.

the border. Indeed, King and Cuc (1996) found that there was no north-south divergence in prices – if anything, different fundamentals seemed to be driving prices along an east-west split. Serletis (1997) has criticized these findings, arguing that natural gas prices were driven by the same factors all across Canada and the United States. Although these differences emphasize the fragility of the econometric techniques underlying the analysis, nowhere has it been argued that Canadian and American gas prices have diverged in the era of deregulation.

As with crude oil, natural gas prices have exhibited increased volatility since the advent of deregulation (Plourde and Watkins, 2000). Again, the consequences of this increased volatility have mainly been borne by buyers and sellers of natural gas, and financial instruments have emerged to help market participants manage this price risk. Henry Hub (Louisiana) is now the main pricing point in North America, and the natural gas contract introduced by NYMEX in 1990 has become a key instrument in risk management.

Leitzinger and Collette (2002) have argued that all benefits enjoyed by American gas consumers since deregulation can be traced back to the FERC actions that led to the abrogation of long-term contracts.

This allowed end-user prices to fall, at the cost of lower revenues for pipelines and producers. However, this argument fails to recognize that a number of developments (including falling prices for oil products – important end-use competitors for natural gas – and the rapidly emerging gas bubble) acted to place in doubt whether most of these long-term contracts would have been fulfilled in any case. Attempts to maintain the integrity of these contracts would likely have led to bankruptcies and lengthy legal disputes. It thus seems highly unlikely that much of the 'foregone' revenues would ever have accrued to pipelines and producers.

In any case, the transition from regulated prices to prices determined by the actions of buyers and sellers was relatively smooth in Canada and the United States. For example, the anticipated problems with load balancing did not materialize to any significant degree, because market participants acted to deal with these issues in the course of their day-to-day operations.

As access to American long-distance pipelines improved and as Canada lifted its export restrictions, volumes of natural gas exported to the United States increased sharply (Figure 2.6). Between 1986 and 2001, exports from Canada quadrupled until they exceeded 100 billion cubic metres (3 trillion cubic feet) and accounted for almost 16 per cent of total American consumption. During the same period, volumes shipped domestically increased steadily to meet the growing demand within Canada. Overall, Canadian natural gas producers aggressively capitalized on opportunities to expand both sales and market penetration in the aftermath of deregulation.

The story is quite different in Mexico, as Figure 2.6 and Table 2.2 remind us. Pemex has been unable to take advantage of the growing demand for natural gas in the United States, and remains a small net importer. This is the result of two things: decades of focus on oil-related activities, and a chronic shortage of investment funds (Nivola, 2002). Although there has been some relaxation of restrictions on private-sector participation in some aspects of the Mexican natural gas industry (Jiménez, 2000), exploration and development of Mexico's significant reserves of natural gas have remained the exclusive domain of liquidity-constrained Pemex. Mexico thus remains on the periphery of the North American marketplace. Opportunities, dating back to the early 1990s, to exploit the growing American demand for imported natural gas were simply not acted upon, and the prospects for this remain rather dim, at least in the short to medium term.[10]

Figure 2.6. U.S. net imports of natural gas from Canada and Mexico, 1980–2001

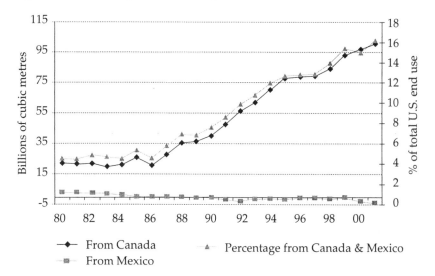

Source: Author's calculations based on data published by EIA, U.S. Department of Energy.

All Good Things Must Come to an End? Electricity

As the 1980s progressed, the electricity industry in the United States experienced severe problems. The fallout from 1979's Three Mile Island incident had placed the future of that country's nuclear power plants in doubt, and several power companies were facing financial crises. Changes were needed to address these problems. Furthermore, progress in electricity generation technology – especially the widespread commercialization of combined-cycle gas turbines – challenged the standard view that all aspects of the industry were subject to significant economies of scale, and thus that regulated monopolies were the desirable structure for electricity provision.

Buoyed by the success of its deregulation initiatives in crude oil and natural gas, as well as by early positive outcomes of electricity deregulation efforts in other countries (notably England and Wales, and New Zealand), the American government launched a similar process for electricity in 1992, with the enthusiastic support of authorities in many states (see Table 2.3).

TABLE 2.3
Some Milestones in the Development of Electricity Markets in North America

Canada	Mexico	United States
January 1996: The Power Pool of Alberta begins operations, as the province moves to implement a deregulated wholesale market and to foster competition in generation. Competition would be introduced by 1 January 2001 in all retail markets.	*1960:* The Mexican government nationalizes the country's electricity sector. Comisión Federal de Electricidad (CFE) is designated to exercise the state monopoly position in the production, transmission, and distribution of electricity as a public service.	*November 1978:* President Carter signs the Public Utilities Regulatory Policy Act. The key provisions of this act allow independent electricity producers to sell into wholesale markets. Although various conditions are attached to this initiative, the act signals the end of utility monopoly over generation.
1996–7: In response to FERC Orders 888 and 889, a number of Canadian provinces act to provide open access to the transmission systems within their boundaries (e.g., British Columbia, Manitoba, Ontario, Québec, and New Brunswick, in addition to Alberta).	*1992:* The Mexican government partially opens up the country's electricity sector to private participation; existing legislation is amended to provide an explicit definition of activities not considered as a public service in that sector.	*1992:* Congress passes the Energy Policy Act, which mandates the FERC to implement open access to electricity transmission systems. Over the next few years, a number of states will announce, and some will proceed with, broader deregulation initiatives (e.g., California, Pennsylvania, New Jersey, and Texas).
1999–2000: The government of Ontario announces plans for an in-depth restructuring of the province's electricity industry. At the centre of these plans is the termination of Ontario Hydro's monopoly position. In 2002, the government would curtail its announced plans to enhance the role of market forces in Ontario's electricity market, especially at the retail end.	*January 1994:* NAFTA comes into force, and the provisions relating to electricity are designed to reflect the post-1992 structure of the Mexican electricity sector. *October/November 1995:* The CRE is established and is given the mandate to regulate activities in the electricity sector, including the acquisition of electricity for public-service sales; supply and sales public service customers; private-sector generation; imports and exports; and transmission.	*March 1996:* NYMEX introduces electricity futures contracts for electricity delivered at two locations adjacent to the California border. Options would start trading by the end of April 1996. Additional contracts will be introduced by NYMEX and other exchanges over the next few years. None of these contracts will establish a sustained market presence.

TABLE 2.3 *(continued)*
Some Milestones in the Development of Electricity Markets in North America

Canada	Mexico	United States
		April 1996: FERC Orders 888 and 889 create a 'reciprocity' requirement for firms selling electricity into open-access systems in the United States: the 'selling' jurisdictions must also provide open access to their electricity transmission systems. In practice, these orders require exporting provinces to deregulate their wholesale electricity markets.
		April 1998: California is the first state to restructure its electricity market, which begins operation this month. The market would begin to collapse in the spring of 2000, and regulation would be reintroduced by the state government by mid-2001. A number of states subsequently curtail their planned restructuring efforts directed at electricity markets.
		December 1999: FERC Order 2000 requires transmission companies under FERC jurisdiction to form Regional Transmission Organizations (RTOs). This process is to be completed by December 2001. Given the interconnections between some U.S. and Canadian transmission grids, Canadian service providers are encouraged to participate in the RTOs.
		July 2002: The FERC issues a notice of proposed regulation on 'standard market design' aimed at standardizing the design and operations of wholesale electricity markets and of facilitating transmission across grids.

The desired industry structure that emerged from the early actions of the FERC and a number of state public utilities commissions was quite similar to the postderegulation structure of the natural gas industry: competition at the production/wholesale and retail ends, with transportation (in the electricity industry, the 'wires') remaining regulated, but characterized by non-discriminatory access to facilities. As more and more American states announced that they intended to put forward deregulation initiatives, some Canadian provinces (most notably Alberta) proceeded to outline similar plans.[11]

By the second half of the 1990s, however, it had become clear that any revamping of the electricity industry to allow market forces to play a more important role would be much more difficult to accomplish than had been the case for natural gas. Gradually, the literature in professional and industry circles as well as government documents began to refer to 'restructuring' efforts, as opposed to deregulation: a more limited agenda for reform was emerging. And then came the California disaster. For our purposes, it is sufficient to note that the 2000–2 crisis in California's electricity systems has significantly dampened the enthusiasm for electricity industry restructuring in most North American jurisdictions: plans previously announced by most states and provinces have been either curtailed or, in many cases, abandoned altogether.

A number of characteristics specific to electricity markets help explain the difficulties encountered in North American restructuring efforts. First, electricity is much more of a local 'commodity' than is crude oil or natural gas. All states and provinces have developed electricity supply industries – in many cases with significant public participation and ownership. As a result, regulatory frameworks differ – at least in details – across jurisdictions, and the role of federal authorities tends to be more limited than in crude oil and natural gas markets. Interconnections across systems are thus less important, and cross-boundary trade volumes account for a much smaller proportion of total sales. In the case of Canada, for example, in recent years more than 80 per cent of domestically produced crude oil and natural gas crosses at least one provincial or international border on the way to end users. For electricity, the comparable figure is about 15 per cent, and a single contract – the one between Newfoundland and Quebec – accounts for approximately one-third of these flows. By implication, it is difficult to see how market forces can operate to eliminate arbitrage opportunities on a national let alone a continental scale. It is also interesting to note that, contrary to the experience with crude oil and natural gas markets, there has been no successful introduction of formal financial instruments aimed at helping electricity market participants deal with the risks associated with price volatility.

Second, technological constraints are such that it is extremely costly to store electricity. This means that at all times the system must be maintained in a position of flow demand/supply balance. Third, as Hogan (2002, 110) emphasizes, there are 'complex externalities associated with the flow of power across constrained transmission systems' – in other words, changing power flows to meet demand conditions in one part of an interconnected system will affect the flow of power available in other parts of the system. Because of these two factors, there has to be a central coordinating function (sometimes called a 'system operator') in electricity that is absent from crude oil and natural gas markets.

As Figure 2.7 makes clear, it is very difficult to make the case that electricity price convergence has occurred at the national or continental level. There is not now, nor has there ever been, such a thing as a 'national' or 'continental' electricity market. The electricity industry in North America remains a collection of islands and of loosely (often very loosely) interconnected systems.

Figure 2.8 shows the main electricity trade flows among Canada, Mexico, and the United States. Despite a loosening of restrictions on electricity exports by Canada in the mid-1980s and by Mexico in the 1990s, there has been no significant growth in export flows to the United States. Canadian net exports still account for less than 1.5 per cent of total American end use, and Mexico remains a minor net importer of electricity from the United States.

On Two Aspects of Sustainability

Next, I assess the sustainability of the deregulation/restructuring efforts aimed at the Canadian and American energy markets. Two questions immediately arise: Are the market structures that have resulted from these initiatives likely to stand the test of time? And, are the new market structures likely to prove more or less susceptible than the structures they replaced when it comes to incorporating environmental considerations into decision making?

Figures 2.1 and 2.5 remind us that since the advent of deregulation, Canadian and American markets for crude oil and natural gas have functioned as expected. Buyers and sellers have been free to negotiate the terms of contracts, and the physical interconnections have been

Figure 2.7. Selected electricity prices, 1970–2001

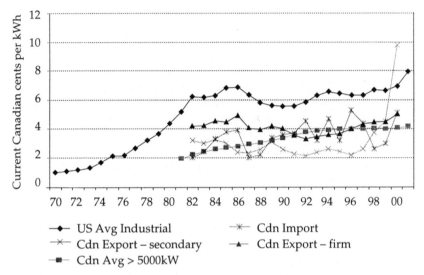

Sources: Statistics Canada; EIA, U.S. Department of Energy; conversions into Canadian dollars using exchange-rate data published by the Bank of Canada.

sufficient to allow market forces to eliminate arbitrage opportunities at a continental level. Crude oil and natural gas prices have fluctuated significantly, and financial instruments have emerged to help market participants manage this price risk. These developments indicate that well-functioning markets exist. In addition, although the sharp price fluctuations experienced over the past twenty-five years have greatly increased pressure on governments to intervene directly and reintroduce widespread price controls, with very few exceptions these pressures have been resisted. Market participants have been left to sort out the implications of these price changes among themselves.

Based on the above, it would seem that deregulated markets for crude oil and natural gas are to stay in place in Canada and the United States for the longer term. However, two clouds have recently appeared on the horizon. First, in mid-2002 both houses of the U.S. Congress passed energy-related legislation with an interventionist bent of a type not seen since the early 1970s. Proposed legislated restrictions on the choice of pipeline route for Alaska natural gas production, and the proposed subsidies for that output, are reminiscent of past policies of direct market intervention. The Bush administration has expressed its opposition to any extension of subsidies to Alaska gas production; however, it remains to be seen whether market forces will be allowed

Figure 2.8. U.S. net imports of electricity from Canada and Mexico, 1970–2001

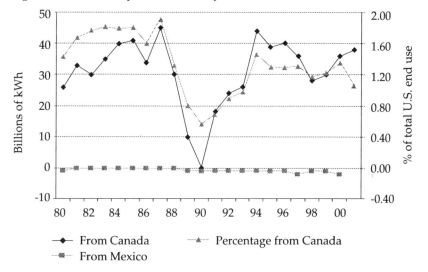

Source: Author's calculations based on data published by EIA, U.S. Department of Energy.

to determine whether (and, if necessary, how) Alaska natural gas will be produced and transported to end-use markets. The outcome of these policy deliberations will likely set the tone for American energy policy in general. A return to a more interventionist stance would clearly curtail the role played by the preferences of buyers and sellers in determining trade patterns on North American energy markets.

A second area of concern relates to the repercussions of the Enron debacle. Authorities in the United States are quite likely to tighten their regulatory oversight of energy industries to prevent the kinds of abuses (allegedly) perpetrated by Enron officials. The question here is whether it will be possible to tailor the added regulation, the intent of which is to discourage abuses, without affecting the legitimate transmission of market signals. Given the rather blunt nature of most regulatory instruments, it seems quite likely that such regulation will have unintended negative effects on market operations. But there is yet another dimension to the fallout from Enron. As a result of its questionable dealings, Enron has succeeded in casting doubt on the validity of risk management activities. Yet such activities are an integral part of well-functioning markets for energy commodities. Price fluctuations will not disappear, so for the sake of credibility, it is critical to return to risk management activities.

On the electricity front, efforts to date have not led to the creation of an integrated marketplace either in Canada or in the United States. It should also be clear, in the aftermath of the California disaster, that the current situation is not sustainable. The FERC seems to share this view and has recently produced documents dealing with proposed regional transmission organizations and electricity market design. Since there is no federal agency in Canada with the type of jurisdiction over electricity markets exercised by the FERC, developments in Canada will continue to be driven by provincial authorities. As a result, it seems inevitable that a number of distinct approaches will emerge in Canada, from the wholesale retention of regulated structures, to an aggressive restructuring along the lines of a modified natural gas model.

Technical characteristics and the recent FERC proposals combine to suggest that in both Canada and the United States, a pattern of regional integration might be more sustainable than the current situation. Such a market structure would offer more limited arbitrage opportunities, and electricity price differentials would thus reflect factors other than differences in transmission costs.

Given the changes in market design outlined above, what is the scope for environmental considerations to be reflected in energy-related decisions? As we know, market participants left to their own devices will not take environmental effects into consideration when making decisions on markets for energy – or any other product, for that matter. This is the nature of an externality. To overcome this, government intervention is required. But in generic terms, government intervention is exactly the kind of market manipulation that the deregulation initiatives were supposed to eliminate. This creates a communication problem for any government that is seeking to pursue both 'deregulation' and 'sustainable development' objectives: namely, not all market interventions are created alike, and some form of intervention is required (and economically warranted) if environmental externalities are to be addressed. Note, however, that this problem does not arise only in the newly deregulated markets for energy products – the same issues will be encountered in many other situations.

At a more general level, the experience of the years preceding the deregulation efforts in Canada and the United States suggests that environmental considerations were not of especially great concern to decision makers in energy markets, even in situations of public ownership. As a result, one might argue that deregulation initiatives are not likely to reduce the importance attached to environmental considerations in decisions relating to energy sales, purchases, and investments. But of even greater importance is the fact that the increased reliance on the forces of demand and supply to govern energy markets in North America means that economic instruments can now potentially play an even greater role in addressing environmental externalities. Indeed, these instruments can be made to work in conjunction with market forces to bring about more efficient (i.e., less costly) solutions to environmental problems.

But at the end of the day, the critical determinant for success in bringing environmental considerations to bear on energy market decisions is the political will of the relevant governments. The most learned discourses on environmental consequences and on ways of addressing them will not bring about any measurable progress on this front. Rather, what is needed are governments willing to take concrete steps toward bringing about more sustainable patterns of economic development. And again, there is nothing here specific to energy markets.

Conclusions

Markets for energy commodities in Canada and the United States have undergone a dramatic transformation since the end of the 1970s. From tightly regulated market designs have emerged frameworks wherein buyers and sellers of crude oil and natural gas can determine the terms of contracts, including prices and volumes transacted. This has allowed Canadian producers to seek new market opportunities in the United States. Their success has led to sharply increased export sales volumes; at the same time, these producers are shipping ever-increasing quantities to end-use markets in Canada.

These policy initiatives have led to the emergence of continental (i.e., Canada/United States) markets for crude oil and natural gas, in the sense that market forces have successfully eliminated arbitrage opportunities: prices for these energy commodities tend to be governed by the same fundamentals, and differences in prices tend to reflect differences in quality and transportation costs. Financial instruments have emerged to allow market participants to manage the risks associated with the greater price volatility observed since the advent of deregulation.

The new market designs for crude oil and natural gas have been in place for at least the past decade – even longer in the case of crude oil – and have provided for orderly transactions between buyers and sellers. Their future looks bright.

The experience with electricity market restructuring has been much more problematic. Initial plans to pursue deregulation along lines similar to those followed in the case of natural gas soon proved inappropriate. The more local nature of markets (and the related lack of system interconnections), and characteristics of the production and delivery of electricity, combined to impede the functioning of the new market designs. The meltdown experienced in California has slowed the pace of electricity restructuring across Canada and the United States. Furthermore, the situation currently prevailing on electricity markets is not sustainable: additional changes are to be expected. Recent proposals by the FERC suggest that a patchwork of regional markets could well emerge as restructuring progresses. One outcome that will not emerge, however, is an integration of Canadian and American electricity markets of the type found for crude oil and natural gas.

Mexico has mostly opted not to follow the example of its two North American partners. It continues to allow state monopolies to operate on the supply side of energy markets. Pemex has pursued opportunities to expand exports of crude oil to the United States, but its chronic shortage of investment funds has left it incapable of increasing natural gas production sufficiently for it to become a significant exporter. The Mexican electricity industry continues to be dominated by CFE, and minor reforms dating back to the early 1990s have not brought about any significant increase in private-sector participation. As with natural gas, exports to the United States remain negligible. Mexico thus remains on the periphery of North American energy markets.

It is difficult to make a case that the new energy market designs are likely to provide a less favourable framework for allowing environmental considerations to affect energy market decisions. This is partly due to the less-than-stellar treatment afforded these considerations under the earlier, regulation-intensive designs, and partly due to the fact that economic instruments can now be allied with market forces to provide solutions to environmental problems. However, whatever the market design, a critical element in bringing environmental considerations to bear on energy-related decisions is the political will of governments to deal with these issues.

NOTES

I wish to thank Danielle Moffat for her able research assistance. The comments and suggestions of Bruce Doern, Joseph Doucet, and two anonymous reviewers were very helpful in revision. All remaining errors and omissions are mine.

1 Krauze (1998) provides a fascinating overview of the emergence of the modern Mexican state.
2 There is a minor exception to this statement: another state-owned company about one-thirtieth the size of CFE operated (and continues to do so) in and around Mexico City.
3 The three 'milestones' tables included in this paper are designed to provide a quick overview of some of the key factors that have influenced the evolution of energy markets in North America. The tables are not meant to convey a complete description of North American energy market development.
4 The price data used in this paper are drawn from three sources: the U.S. Department of Energy's Energy Information Administration, Statistics Canada, and BP's *Statistical Review of World Energy*.
5 On this, see Horsnell and Mabro (1993, Part IV).
6 For an analysis of the volatility of Canadian crude oil and natural gas prices before and after deregulation, see Plourde and Watkins (2000).
7 In an effort to ensure consistency across concepts and units of measurement, all quantity data used in this paper were drawn from publications (and websites) of the U.S. Department of Energy's Energy Information Administration.
8 On this, see Kahn (2002), among others.
9 The NEB (2002, 19) reports that in 2001 almost 80 per cent of Canadian gas exports were traded under short-term contracts.
10 Recently, the Mexican government has taken steps to increase the responsiveness of natural gas markets in Mexico to developments in the rest of North America. Domestic prices of natural gas are now linked by regulation to the Houston Ship Channel price. On this, see Brito and Rosellón (2002).
11 For an overview and analysis of the Alberta experience, see Daniel, Doucet, and Ploude. 2002.

REFERENCES

Brito, Dagobert L., and Juan Rosellón. 2002. 'Pricing Natural Gas in Mexico: An Application of the Little-Mirrlees Rule.' *Energy Journal* 23, no. 3: 81–93.
Daniel, Terry, Joseph Doucet, and André Plourde. 2002. 'Electricity Industry Restructuring: The Alberta Experience.' In Andrew N. Kleit, ed., *The Challenge of Electricity Restructuring*. Forthcoming.

Grayson, George W. 2001. 'Pemex, the President and His Dream Team.' *Petroleum Economist* 68, no. 10: 32–4.

Helliwell, John F., Mary E. MacGregor, Robert N. McRae, and André Plourde. 1989. *Oil and Gas in Canada: The Effects of Domestic Policies and World Events.* Toronto: Canadian Tax Foundation.

Hogan, William W. 2002. 'Electricity Market Restructuring: Reforms of Reforms.' *Journal of Regulatory Economics* 21, no. 1: 103–32.

Horsnell, Paul, and Robert Mabro. 1993. *Oil Markets and Prices: The Brent Market and the Formation of World Oil Prices.* Oxford: Oxford University Press for Oxford Institute for Energy Studies.

Jiménez, Jorge. 2000. 'The Great Impact of NAFTA in the Energy Sector: A Mexican Perspective.' *Journal of Energy and Natural Resources Law* 18, no. 2: 159–94.

Journal of Regulatory Economics. 2002. Special issue, vol. 21, no. 1.

Kahn, Alfred E. 2002. 'The Deregulatory Tar Baby: The Precarious Balance between Regulation and Deregulation, 1970–2000 and Henceforward.' *Journal of Regulatory Economics* 21, no. 1: 35–56.

King, Martin, and Milan Cuc. 1996. 'Price Convergence in North American Natural Gas Markets.' *Energy Journal* 17, no. 2: 17–42.

Krauze, Enrique. 1998. *Biography of Power: A History of Modern Mexico, 1810– 1996.* Transl. Hank Heifetz. New York: HarperPerennial.

Leitzinger, Jeffrey, and Martin Collette. 2002. 'A Retrospective Look at Wholesale Gas: Industry Restructuring.' *Journal of Regulatory Economics* 21, no. 1: 71–101.

National Energy Board. 2002. *Annual Report to Parliament 2001.* Calgary: National Energy Board.

National Energy Policy Development Group. 2001. *National Energy Policy – Reliable, Affordable, and Environmentally Sound Energy for America's Future.* Washington, DC: U.S. Government Printing Office.

Nivola, Pietro S. 2002. 'Energy Independence or Interdependence? Integrating the North American Energy Market.' *Brookings Review* 20, no. 2: 24–7.

Plourde, André, and G.C. Watkins. 2000. 'Relationships Between Upstream Prices of Crude Oil and Natural Gas – Evidence from Canada.' Discussion Paper 2000–3, Department of Economics, University of Aberdeen, UK.

Serletis, Apostolos. 1997. 'Is There an East-West Split in North American Natural Gas Markets?' *Energy Journal* 18, no. 1: 57–62.

Verleger, Philip K., jr. 1993. *Adjusting to Volatile Energy Prices.* Washington: Institute for International Economics.

Chapter 3

Energy Policy and Sustainable Development

ROBERT W. MORRISON

Energy is essential for sustainable development. This fact poses two challenges for policy, one at the front end of energy fuel cycles and one at the back:

1 *Meeting demand:* Are there adequate, affordable, and accessible energy supplies to sustain anticipated growth in global economic activity?
2 *Impact:* How can energy be used to achieve global economic goals without undermining the environmental support systems that sustain human civilization?

Demand for energy services, driven by population and economic growth, is increasing steadily. In developing countries, energy is required to provide basic needs. Two billion people lack access to modern forms of energy, including electricity (Worldwatch, 2002). In industrial countries, energy is required to maintain living standards and to accommodate new technologies. Scenarios for the world's energy future differ widely regarding the total amount of energy that will be consumed and the impact of this consumption (Nakicenovic, Grublen, and McDonald, 1998; Laponche, 2001). The differences among these scenarios are largely policy-driven. As was established at the 2002 Earth Summit (Economist, 2002), energy concerns are closely related to other key concerns on the global policy agenda such as health, food, air and water quality, biodiversity, poverty, and personal and international security. Energy policy faces great uncertainties as well as great opportunities.

A useful definition of sustainable development is that of Brundtland:

Sustainable development is development that meets the needs of the present without compromising the ability of future generations to meet their own needs. It contains within it two concepts:

- The concept of needs, in particular the essential needs of the world's poor, to which overriding priority should be given; and
- The idea of limitations imposed by the state of technology and social organization on the environment's ability to meet present and future needs. (Brundtland, 1987, 43)

Sustainable development, as a concept, seeks to build a future world by balancing three sets of factors over time: economic, environmental, and social. It sees these dimensions as complementary rather than competitive. This chapter outlines the relationship between energy and sustainable development, and the implications of this relationship for policy in Canada and the world. It will focus on the economic and environmental dimensions of energy, while emphasizing that the human (i.e., social) dimensions are the most important.

Rhetoric aside, environmental policy in the short term in most countries is subject to overall economic development policy. Few politicians have campaigned successfully on platforms of declining wealth and fewer jobs. Issues of wealth distribution are easier to address when growth will make people better off. Energy policy has long meant ensuring adequate and affordable energy supplies to meet development needs.

In the long term, the economy is subject to the environment. We need clean air and water, arable land, diverse ecosystems, and, generally, the carrying capacity of the environment in order to sustain life on this planet. In energy and other policies, most governments are increasingly taking longer-term environmental considerations into account.

Brundtland's definition takes us straight into two very broad political issues: equity today, and equity for future generations. Ethically, one can make a strong case for both these goals, and the world's poor are justified in their demands for access to more energy. Any energy policy agenda for sustainable development will have to address both equity and growth.

At the heart of this concept lies a rational and universal human interest. We want to preserve the environment, not for its own sake but because of our needs. The issues involve everyone and pervade every aspect of human behaviour. So it is fundamental to put people first. Governments and industry must play leadership roles, but success in these broad ventures will require a high level of public understanding and participation. People must believe in the importance of sustainable development and in the legitimacy of the solutions being proposed.

We look first at the front end of energy fuel cycles to see how sustainable they are from the perspective of resource availability – a traditional concern of energy policy. After this, we consider fuel cycle sustainability from the back end, that is, from the perspective of health, environmental, and social impacts. If we value the environment and the future, we will have to find ways to assign a value to these impacts, and incorporate those values in our decisions.

Limiting Factors for Sustainable Development: The Availability of Energy Resources

Population and Economic Growth, and Energy

The global population and economic growth that is expected over the next half-century will require vastly more energy services. The challenge will be to decouple the necessary growth in energy services from the growth in energy use and its impacts, and to benefit from those services without undermining the natural environment. This is easier said than done, because population and economic growth tend to overwhelm gains in efficiency.

At present, the world's population is 6.1 billion, and it is growing at an annual rate of 1.3 per cent (UN, 2001). The world's annual population growth rate peaked around 1970 at 2 per cent, and it is expected to continue to decline at a rate faster than was anticipated a few years ago. World population is now expected to reach 9.3 billion by 2050. In business-as-usual scenarios, the world's economy is projected to continue growing at 3 per cent annually until 2020. If current annual rates of decline in energy intensity continue at 1 per cent, primary energy consumption will grow at 2 per cent – that is, it will double about every thirty-five years (IEA, 2001a). Only dramatic changes in prices or policies are likely to change these trends.

There are plenty of reasons why energy use is increasing, and why this increase is a good thing. Global population growth adds about 80 million people to the planet every year. The use of dung or firewood for household energy depletes local biomass resources and causes severe indoor air pollution, which is responsible for several million deaths each year (World Bank, 1999). Modern energy services such as electricity could greatly improve this situation.

The more developed countries, with 20 per cent of the world's population, currently use 55 per cent of the energy – about five times as much on a per capita basis as the 80 per cent who live in less developed countries (Nakicenovic, Grublen, and McDonald, 1998). In the near future, all of the growth in population and most of the growth in energy use will be in the less developed countries. This means that by 2020, those countries will surpass today's world average per capita level of energy consumption, roughly that of Portugal. By that time, those countries will be producing 55 per cent of the world's energy, reversing the current situation. Sustainable options for meeting the growth in their energy demand should be a focus of policy.

Energy Sources

Fossil fuels provide about 90 per cent of the world's commercial energy, and that proportion is expected to remain steady over the next two decades. Oil constitutes 40 per cent of the world energy market. In mid-range projections, it will retain its market share until 2020, largely because of its importance in transportation. Coal and gas will change places, with gas increasing from 22 to 25 per cent and coal falling from 25 to 22 per cent. The rest of the world's commercial energy is mainly hydro and nuclear. However, other renewables are growing rapidly at 2.8 per cent a year and increasing their share of the market from 2 to 3 per cent (IEA, 2001a).

Known conventional oil reserves are good for about forty more years of production at current rates. Conventional oil production should peak in the next decade or so and then gradually decline. Some observers predict an earlier peak and a more rapid decline (ASPO, 2002). Unconventional sources will expand to meet increasing demand, and this may allow another forty years of world oil supply at these rates (IEA, 1998). The price is expected to rise somewhat, because unconventional oil is more expensive to produce. In the past, the price of oil has followed political decisions rather than the market laws of supply and demand (Walsh, 2002).

Currently, about one-third of global oil production is traded across international borders. Most of the OECD countries, including the United States, are major importers of oil, and their dependence on imports is likely to increase. About 65 per cent of the world's conventional oil reserves are in the Middle East (BP, 2002), and these are generally the lowest-cost reserves. This suggests that political pressures on the price of oil are likely to continue, and that the security and diversity of energy supplies will continue to be a major issue in energy policy (IEA, 2002).

Gas is at an earlier stage of exploitation than oil, and world gas reserves seem to be adequate for the increased use foreseen over the next half-century, although they, like oil reserves, are also concentrated in specific areas. The former Soviet Union and the Middle East hold 72 per cent of the world's proven gas reserves (BP, 2002). Many of the leading industrial countries will become increasingly dependent on imported gas. Global coal resources will last for centuries and are widely dispersed.

Of the non-fossil sources, nuclear energy can certainly increase significantly from a resource perspective, but it is also expensive, and there are deep public concerns about accidents, waste, its use in weaponry, and, more recently, its vulnerability to terrorist attacks. Theoretically, renewable energies could grow tremendously. The constraints on renewables will be cost, land use, material intensity, and the need in some cases for backup because of their intermittent nature. Biomass will require careful management to ensure that it is indeed used in a renewable way.

Energy Uses

The IEA divides energy use into three categories: electricity, transportation, and stationary sources. Each combines industrial with commercial and residential uses. Globally, electricity and stationary uses each take about 40 per cent of primary energy, whereas transportation takes 20 per cent (IEA, 1998, 412 [table]). Electricity and transportation are the fastest-growing sectors. They will grow at 3 per cent a year, whereas stationary uses will grow at about 1.5 per cent.

It is important to incorporate efficient, low-impact technologies into facilities and equipment when they are first built, in order to decouple growth in energy services from the impacts of energy use. This clear need to limit the impacts of growth in energy use strongly suggests that the less developed countries (where growth will be strongest) and the transportation and electricity sectors are key policy areas (Morrison et al., 2001). Much of the growth in electricity in less developed countries will be based on coal.

Canada's Energy Resources and Uses

Canada is abundantly endowed with energy in most forms – coal, oil (including the tar sands), natural gas, hydroelectricity, and uranium, as well as biomass, wind, and solar. Canada's energy exports amount to $36 billion annually – roughly 10 per cent of our total exports (National Resources Canada, 2000). All of our gas, oil, and electricity exports go to the United States. Access to markets will be important if Canada is to realize the full potential of its energy industries.

By market share, Canada's sources of energy production are as follows: oil 37%; gas 29%; coal 11%; hydro 10%; nuclear 8%; other 5% (National Climate Change Process, 2000). Canada has a relatively low-carbon energy supply; it relies little on coal and much more heavily on natural gas, hydro, and nuclear power. Despite this advantage, our per capita carbon emissions are about double those of European countries, because of our high per capita energy use.

NRCan's most recent projection (1999) is that between 2000 and 2020, Canada's economy will grow at 2.3 per cent a year; its primary energy growth will be about 1 per cent. This suggests a rate of decrease in energy intensity of about 1.3 per cent. At current rates of production, Canada has about ten years of proven oil and gas reserves. Future discoveries should extend the resource base considerably, and the tar sands, with about 300 billion barrels believed to be recoverable, should ensure this country's oil supply for several centuries. Canada's coal resources should last for a similar period. There are significant hydro resources in northern Canada, and this country's base for uranium and renewables is large.

In general, the fossil-based economies of Canada and the world seem to be sustainable for the next half-century from the perspective of oil and gas supply, even with increasing demand. The physical availability of oil and gas resources will not be the limiting factor over this period. However, there are obvious problems globally, relating to the geographical concentration of oil and natural gas. OECD countries will become more dependent on oil and gas imports, although Canada seems well placed to continue as a major exporter of energy. Diversification of energy sources will be more important. Timely investments will be necessary in all energy sectors to ensure continuity of supply. Prices are likely to increase, but not so as to threaten continuing development. For the longer term, it would be prudent to start building the foundations for a post-fossil or at least lower-emission economy. But we have yet to deal with the environmental impacts of energy use.

Limiting Factors: Impacts of Using Energy Resources

Let us begin with an intuitive judgment: the most important impact of energy use is climate change. Thus, climate change can serve as a proxy for sustainable development issues as they relate to energy (IEA, 2001b). Most of the man-made greenhouse gases (GHGs) come from the use of fossil fuels. Climate change has the power to change the course of human civilization, at least in some regions, by threatening some of the environmental foundations that support life. Northern regions will be especially affected. Significant changes are already happening with the world climate as a result of the increase in atmospheric GHG concentrations. Climate change could be a show-stopper.

There are other important impacts of energy use. Probably next to climate change in importance is regional air quality, especially in big cities. Because of its immediate local impact, air quality may be a stronger driver of action than climate change, which is more diffuse and long term in its causes and effects. Working on both together would bring useful synergies. Other energy system problems such as waste management, land use, and industrial accidents could have serious regional consequences but are not likely to threaten the basis of human civilization.

However, the point of analysing the impacts of energy use is precisely to quantify and compare them from a risk management and policy perspective. Several approaches to valuing the impacts are touched on briefly below.

Present and Future: The Discount Rate

Let us consider how we value the needs of future generations – a basic concern of sustainable development. This is not a simple task (Arrow et al., 1995). We cannot be sure how many people will be around at any given future point, or what they will want. Clearly, we have to use our own best judgment on their behalf. We want to leave them a range of options. How should we balance their anticipated priorities against our own?

One approach is to ask ourselves what discount rate we should apply to the future. A market rate, roughly equivalent to a required rate of return on investments, might be 10 per cent or higher. At 10 per cent, the present value of income received seven years from now is halved, and the future beyond twenty years or so has effectively zero value. Decisions made on this basis attribute little value to the future. The counterweight is that they generate wealth faster, and so offer more options for both present and future generations.

Along these lines, some argue that we should invest more in immediate development and poverty elimination than in sustainability (Lomborg, 2002). Wealthy countries are the cleanest and most environmentally sensitive, whereas poor ones place stress on the environment. So we should make the poor countries richer faster by using a high discount rate and investing directly in projects with rapid paybacks. The environmental impacts will then take care of themselves, because wealthier societies will have more capacity to address those impacts. From this angle, any drag on economic growth is depriving future generations of their heritage.

But that is precisely the issue – racking up financial wealth while ignoring the environment could lead us to overshoot the earth's carrying capacity and degrade our basic life support systems: clean air and water, food supply, protection against disease. This being the case, financial wealth would not be a good indicator of overall human health and welfare, and would not be sustainable in any case.

In more specific energy terms, a high discount rate favours those with low start-up costs, short lead times, and less need for R&D. Natural gas power plants are currently preferred over hydro, nuclear, or renewable plants. Too much short-term emphasis on natural gas will deplete that resource more quickly and lead to underinvestment in the technologies necessary to replace it.

A lower effective discount rate, or an anticipated rise in the value of scarce natural resources, would make longer-term investments more attractive. Some economists talk of public and private discount rates, and there is a lively discussion about what the public rate should be (Arrow et al., 1995). Without going into this debate in detail, the case can be made that there is a role for governments to undertake investments that have a lower rate of return but important consequences in the longer term. This would apply to R&D and to education. It would also apply to policies and programs that preserve and enhance the value of resources and the environment (e.g., by mitigating the impacts of climate change), as well as to more capital-intensive projects of the sort that will bring significant longer-term benefits. So one of the challenges for policy is how to balance short-term growth with longer-term sustainability and with adaptation to changes already built into the system. Sustainable development implies that we should invest more in the future and find ways of incorporating longer-term health and environmental impacts into our policy decisions. Given the uncertainties, we should act incrementally and flexibly, keeping long-term goals in view.

The Structure of Energy Supply

A useful approach to looking at energy-related activities from a sustainable development perspective is to reflect on the contribution of different factors to a particular impact – say, impact A – as follows (Schipper, Unander, and Marie, 1999, Coombs 1992):

Change in impact A = Population change
x Change in activity per capita (broken down into different modes)
x Change in energy per unit activity
x Change in impact A per unit energy

One could also add a factor for the degree to which the impact is mitigated – for instance, for the capture and sequestration of carbon dioxide, or the neutralization of the impact of a chemical effluent.

The activity in question could be a specific measure such as passenger-kilometers or square metres of floor space to be heated or cooled. The impact could be, say, carbon dioxide emissions or land degradation. Analyses that provide these sorts of breakdowns point to areas where policy can be most effective in reducing the impact (National Resources Canada, 2002). For instance, population change is not likely to be affected by energy policy. Nor is the level of economic activity. Indeed, these factors tend to *drive* growth in energy demand. Economic growth is generally seen as desirable, and the energy to fuel that growth is expected to be available. Governments do not want to be seen as restricting activity levels. Passenger kilometres, floor space, and the like are for individual actors to decide. There are often several ways to carry out a given activity. For example, one can travel or move freight by car, bus, train, or plane, and one can live in a detached home or in an apartment. Each activity will have a range of values for energy per unit of activity, or energy intensity. Switching to less energy-intensive modes could allow the same levels of activity with lower energy consumption. However, this would involve lifestyle choices, which to date have tended to favour the higher-energy modes.

Supplying a level of activity in a preferred mode with less energy or less impact sounds like a good thing, and policies tend to focus on these two areas. The public is happy to have the activity, the reduced energy intensity or impact is seen as a benefit, the change may save money, and the savings may be shared between different players. One model for how Canada could meet its Kyoto targets for reducing GHGs through domestic actions alone, using tradable permits, suggests that 42 per cent of the cuts would come from efficiency gains and 31 per cent from fuel switching (Jaccard, 2001). Efficiency is clearly a useful area for policy development, since it can ensure the same services or levels of activity with less energy, and reduce the impact proportionally. Ideally, the gains should pay for themselves. Any net economic cost could be traded off against the imputed value of the improvement to public health or the environment; this underlines the need to account for externalities. The public's willingness to pay must be tested in specific cases.

Gains in efficiency are often offset by increased levels of activity, leading to a net increase in energy use. Gains in fuel efficiency have encouraged people to buy larger and more powerful vehicles and to drive more. Houses have become more efficient but also bigger. Nonetheless, efficiency gains remain an important policy goal. Reducing the health or environmental impact per unit of energy is another useful field for policy. Changes in this regard are achieved essentially by switching fuels, since different fuels have different impacts. Looking at carbon impacts, natural gas emits half as much carbon dioxide as coal per unit of energy. Thus, replacing coal with gas, even at the same efficiency, will cut emissions in half for a given activity. However, if natural gas displaces a non-carbon source such as nuclear, hydro, or other renewables, it will add significant emissions. Also, non-carbon sources have other impacts, such as radioactive waste, land degradation, and the need to flood reservoirs. These can be compared using life-cycle analysis, as outlined below.

Another approach to reducing the impact of coal is to capture and sequester carbon from large point sources. In some cases, the carbon dioxide can even be used to generate revenue; for example, it can be injected into oil reservoirs to enhance recovery. Coal bed methane projects, which sequester carbon dioxide and convert coal resources to natural gas, would also be helpful (Reeve, 2000; Gunter et al., 1998).

Biomass can absorb carbon directly from the atmosphere. The amount of carbon in the global biomass reservoir is roughly equal to that in the atmosphere, and about ten times less than in fossil fuels (McBean, Weaver, and Roulet, 2001), so biomass will not store all the carbon from the burning of fossil fuels. Nonetheless, biomass and land for fuel, food, fibres, and so on must be managed effectively, so as to be part of the solution and not part of the problem (Biocap, 2001).

Governments are reluctant to touch activity levels; even so, it may become necessary at some point to revisit the issue of whether increased activity is inherently good, or whether there is a risk that we may exceed the earth's carrying capacity or the norms of social cohesion. Prime Minister Chrétien once mused about this (Travers, 2002).

We could also ask whether we could achieve the same quality of life with less energy by changing the nature of activities or the overall design of energy-using systems. To what extent could people substitute conferencing by phone, video, or the Internet for physical meetings? How willing would they be to live in a denser urban environment with good public transit instead of commuting from a suburb? Experiments could test which factors are important in these decisions and what it would take to bring about significant change.

Forms of Capital

We depend on a number of different forms of capital. This capital generates income of various kinds. When we preserve that capital, we can live steadily off the flow of income. When we deplete that capital, our income flows diminish.

Economic accounts of wealth and growth have long been based on financial and man-made capital. This includes buildings, ships, and infrastructure such as highways, mines, and pipelines. For sustainability purposes, a full accounting requires us to look at natural, human, and social capital as well. These are essential components of our overall wealth, yet until recently they have not been included in national accounts (Pearce, 1993). Natural capital includes the natural resources we depend on and the ecosystems that supply those resources. These resources include air, water, soil, metals and minerals, biomass for food and energy, medicine, wood, and fibre. Thus, ecosystems have an intrinsic value because of the resources and stream of services they supply: renewal of air and water, recreation, information, future use of various kinds, or simply beauty. The loss or degradation of natural ecosystems or of biodiversity will reduce those services. By enhancing the integrity of natural systems, we add to their value. By measuring and monitoring the value of natural capital, we gain a clearer picture of sustainability.

Of course, placing a value on natural entities is not easy. They may not be measurable in strictly economic terms, or people may disagree on their value. Some possible measures are our willingness to pay to preserve them, to avoid damaging them, to accept compensation for their loss, or to control impacts on them. Or we can assign real estate or tourism values to natural environments such as coastlines and rain forests. Various physical measures may be necessary to take full account of their significance for us.

Efforts are underway to include the value of natural capital in national accounts. This sort of 'green accounting' leads to a green GDP or to an index of 'genuine savings' that factors in resource depletion and pollution costs (Hamilton, 1999). There are many sets of broad indicators that reflect progress toward sustainable development across the range of human activity (NRTEE, 2002; Pembina, 2000). Air quality and other energy impacts are often among the key indicators.

Human and social capital encompasses knowledge, skills, and capability, including science and technology, but also cultural skills. It includes institutions such as governments, legal and financial systems, and companies, schools, and hospitals. It also includes values, customs, and public policies. Indeed, in this era of mobile capital and knowledge, policies and institutions are among the main features that distinguish one country from another.

There is a view that as people become more numerous and the natural environment comes under increasing pressure, natural capital will become relatively more important (Hawken, Lovins, and Lovins, 1999). However, recent efforts to value different forms of capital tend to underline the overriding importance of human capital in its individual and collective forms. Clearly, it is human capital that establishes the value of other forms of capital. Resources are not a fixed stock; rather, they are a changing function of human ingenuity in funding and making use of natural materials. Our impact on the environment is a function of our behaviour and technology, which can both be traced back to institutions and values. And in the Information Age, man-made capital clearly depends increasingly on human capital – for example, the assets of high-tech companies are the imaginations of its employees.

Initial studies of national wealth, in which natural, human, and man-made capital are assessed together, suggest that human capital is by a wide margin the most important for almost every country (Hamilton, 1999). This points again to the need to place people first. Attempts to value natural and human capital are worthwhile in that they force people to think about what truly contributes to sustaining the value of human civilization. We implicitly place a value on natural and human capital in our decisions, so it would be helpful to make this value explicit.

When one form of capital can be substituted or traded off for another, we are in a condition known as *weak sustainability*. This allows for considerable flexibility. We do not have to guarantee a given level of a given resource in order to ensure that future generations will be able to maintain the same standard we enjoy. If it were otherwise, we would be unable in good conscience to use any non-renewable material (Voss, 2001).

There is nothing wrong in principle with using non-renewable resources such as fossil fuels, as long as we can use some of the wealth generated from them to produce an equivalent or greater amount of man-made and human capital that will ensure access to energy services for future generations (Canada, 2001). In the energy sector, we will need to enhance these other forms of capital in many ways: by finding alternative sources of energy and ways of using them, by including nuclear and renewables with hydrogen as potential carriers, by building up new infrastructures, and by carrying out R&D and social experiments (Jaccard, 2001) on different systems of more efficient, lower-impact energy production and use.

In other cases, we will find that there are environmental assets that have no substitutes and cannot be traded off. This is a condition of *strong sustainability*. There are things in nature that we can neither produce nor reproduce (Hawken, Lovins, and Lovins, 1999). We cannot do without clean air and water, or arable land, and there may be ecosystems or parts thereof that are fundamental to our survival, and variations in climate that would be unacceptably extreme. For these, we will have to set strict physical limits that will protect essential elements of natural capital for the indefinite future, effectively assigning them a high value and a zero discount rate. Much of the debate about the environment, including climate change, will centre on how far we can go before we cause significant, irreversible damage.

Life Cycle Assessment (LCA) and Externalities

A useful approach to looking at products and processes involves assessing their health and environmental impacts over their entire life cycle, from extraction of resources (at the front end), through processing, manufacture, and use, to disposal or recycling (the back end) (UNEPIE, 1995; EPA, 2001). LCAs try to capture, in a systematic and transparent way, the full range of material and energy flows associated with a given product or service.

Generally, most health and environmental impacts have not been factored into consumer prices. These are 'external' costs, and they are borne by the general public, the environment, or future generations. They tend to be less visible in cost/benefit calculations and in comparisons between alternatives. But external costs *should* be paid by consumers; this would send them the right signals about the effects of their decisions.

As with natural and human capital, it is difficult to place a value on health and environmental impacts. These impacts are diverse, and they affect a range of targets or groups over space and time. Fossil fuels affect regional air quality and the global climate. Hydro dams flood huge tracks of land and change stream flows. Other renewables use land and materials intensively. Nuclear energy produces radioactive wastes.

In order to use real data, LCA studies focus on specific facilities, sites, and times. They are static snapshots of particular projects. The results are specific to the technology used, the environmental mitigation factors applied, and local weather patterns, watercourses, and population distributions. Thus, they may not be generalizable to other situations and must be updated to include developments in technology, population distributions, and the like. Nonetheless, they provide valuable insights, and they focus attention on the key impacts.

Some analysts favour trying to reduce all impacts to a single indicator, usually money. This allows them to apply traditional economic techniques, to compare the impacts directly, and to add them together.

Others prefer to describe the impacts in physical form and to carry out qualitative comparisons.

Some indicators specific to the energy sector have been suggested (IEA, 2001b, 64):

Economic	Subsidy per unit energy
	Per capita consumption of final energy
Energy supply	Reliability – percentage of time a source is available
	Import dependency
	Diversification
Environmental	Greenhouse gases
	Local emissions
Social	Affordability – percentage of household income devoted to energy
	Education – hours of lighting available to schoolchildren
	Health – impact of energy-related health problems, e.g., respiratory

This list is a useful one that spans the dimensions of sustainable development. It also illustrates the breadth of the impacts of energy use and the challenge of trying to compare them.

The most comprehensive study of energy externalities using a life-cycle approach is the ExternE study sponsored by the European Union (European Commission, 1995). It looks at impacts from a range of complete fuel cycles in specific European situations and then expresses those impacts in monetary terms. This study is highly informative; however, it leaves behind considerable uncertainties, and its results should be applied with caution (Pearce, 2001).

Its main conclusions are that the principal impacts arise from mortality and health problems, caused largely by emissions from fossil fuels, especially particulates from coal and lignite, and especially from older plants. Nuclear energy and renewables – especially wind, hydro, and natural gas – have generally lower impacts.

Areas of controversy in the analysis revolve around how the impacts are assigned values – in particular, the impacts on health and climate change. The health impacts bring out the problems inherent in assigning value to human life (value of years of life lost as a function of age, value of a life in wealthy countries versus poor ones, etc.). The impacts of climate change, which arise largely from the burning of fossil fuels, are estimated to be at least as large as the short-term health impacts, and probably larger; but they are also highly uncertain owing to their global scale and long lead times. In the summary tables of the original ExternE study, the impacts of climate change were not included. The choice of discount rate has an important bearing on the results for present value.

For fossil fuel facilities, both the health and the climate change impacts are mainly the result of routine operations. For nuclear energy, the main impact is through accidental releases of radioactivity, and, in some cases, through routine releases integrated over the entire globe and over very long time frames. Both sets of impacts are subjects of controversy.

Nuclear energy proponents make the case that nuclear energy internalizes a larger proportion of its costs, through tighter health and safety regulations, liability insurance schemes, and charges to current customers for future waste management and decommissioning expenses (NEA, 2000), whereas the external costs from fossil fuels are only beginning to be internalized.

Using an approach similar to that of ExternE, Voss (2001) studied a range of energy sources in Germany, using up-to-date technologies. He then compared external and internal costs. Climate change impacts, valued at 19 euros per tonne of CO_2, were comparable to the health impacts. He found that coal and lignite were again the sources with the greatest external costs, comparable to the existing commercial price, whereas the external costs of natural gas were about 30 per cent of the existing price. Internalizing those costs would double the cost of electricity from coal and add 30 per cent to the cost from gas. Wind, hydro, and nuclear had very low external costs. Interestingly, photovoltaics (i.e., solar panels) had external costs comparable to those of gas because of the material intensity, and because processing the materials in Germany would rely heavily on coal-fired power. However, given that photovoltaics were already expensive, the external costs did not add much in percentage terms to the cost of electricity from that source. Even though the external costs were relatively large, internalizing them did not greatly change the relative ranking among energy sources. The main effect was to make nuclear energy more competitive vis-à-vis fossil fuels. Internalizing costs clearly sends the right signals to consumers. Values for climate change impacts are likely to increase, and costs for renewables are likely to decrease, further narrowing the gap between renewables and fossil fuels.

There is a reasonable consensus on external costs, which can be internalized through a range of policy instruments. Regulation can get rid of the worst-performing facilities and equipment through minimum standards; it can also set appropriate standards for existing and new equipment. Economic instruments such as taxes and 'cap-and-trade' permit schemes can internalize these costs directly. Taxes directly influence prices and enable emissions to find their own levels. Tax levels can be adjusted to suit. Cap-and-trade schemes fix the level of emissions and then let prices find their own levels. Caps can be adjusted to suit. The policy challenge is to design taxes and/or trading schemes that can achieve emission reduction goals and that are also politically acceptable.

Awareness of external costs as generated by LCA studies can help consumers make effective choices. Education campaigns, and labelling and certification schemes, can teach people to use present equipment and choose new products more effectively. A small but growing share of the market can be allocated to high-performance equipment (Jaccard, 2002). That way we can begin moving toward large-scale changes, but without risking damage in the near term. R&D can develop new technologies with higher efficiencies and lower impacts, and targets can measure progress toward the goals of sustainable development. Specific experiments and pilot projects can test the acceptability and utility of new technologies, programs, and behaviour patterns.

Conclusions and Implications for Policy

Growth in energy use is essential to meet the needs of the world's people, especially its poor, whose needs are a priority under the definition of sustainable development. Almost all the near-future growth in energy use will be in the less developed countries. Energy supply will not be a major limiting factor for growth over the next fifty years. Constraints on energy use will arise mainly from the environmental and health impacts of using fossil fuels – more specifically, from climate change and air quality. The challenge thrown down by sustainable development is to decouple the necessary growth in energy services and energy use from the impacts. Policy changes will be required to achieve this goal.

Most industrialized countries will become increasingly dependent on oil and gas imports. This should mean increased policy emphasis on efficiency and on the security and diversity of supply. Canada is an exception, as it should have enough energy resources to continue as a major exporter. But precisely because we are a major producer and user of energy, with a large northern landmass that is sensitive to climate change, we should be leading the world in reducing the impacts of energy use and in adapting to large-scale changes that are already inevitable.

We need energy policies that explicitly value the future and that encourage longer-term investments which will reduce impacts without impeding current growth or placing an undue burden on any particular regions or sectors of society. A tall order! From the perspective of supply, and also from that of impacts, it would be prudent to begin laying the foundations for an economy based on non-fossil or low-impact fossil sources, including renewables and nuclear energy. We should carry out the necessary R&D and pilot projects to ensure acceptable safety costs, and impacts of new sources and technologies. This will require us to develop innovation and regulatory policies.

At present, efficiency and fuel switching are the main policy focuses. Both offer many possibilities. Cost will be key, and internalizing the external costs will be critical to sending the right signals. Reducing economic welfare will never be popular, so it may be fruitful to look at ways to provide the same the level of welfare or amenities by using less activity, or by using different activities with less impact – for example, by moving toward denser urban structures and more efficient supply chains, and by moving information rather than people.

From a natural capital perspective, we should move towards ensuring maximum value from fossil fuels as they become scarcer. This will have to involve increased resource recoveries, greater efficiencies of production and use, and lower emissions. It will also involve pursuing the capture and sequestering of carbon, mainly from coal, so as to ensure the full use of this important resource. As well, we should maximize the value of biomass: agriculture, forests, wetlands, and soil. Biomass can contribute both to energy supply and to carbon capture. Government policy and funding support, and partnerships with industry, will be necessary if we are to move toward these longer-term goals.

Kyoto does not reduce emissions greatly and will have even less impact on atmospheric concentrations of GHGs. To stabilize concentrations at acceptable levels, we may ultimately have to reduce emissions to one-third of where they are today. But Kyoto is a start, and it can be extended. Avoiding commitments now because they are too small to do any good, but too large to be politically acceptable, does not make sense. The Canadian government's commitment to ratify Kyoto has at least launched a vigourous public discussion.

Meeting the Kyoto target by 2010 will be a stretch, for Canada and for many other industrial countries. Canada represents only about 2 per cent of global emissions and will have to act in concert with the international community. We cannot get out too far ahead of the United States, which is by far our main trading partner and competitor for investment. But given the lead times required for major changes, we can at least begin the work, even though it may not bear fruit until the period beyond Kyoto. Clearly, further policy development will be necessary in this area, as well as high levels of public participation.

Regarding externalities, it would be useful to look at ways to internalize costs on a consistent basis in the Canadian context. Studies to date suggest that burning coal using current technologies is not a sustainable practice. This underlines the need for positive policy incentives to develop low-cost capture and sequestration, and for disincentives for emissions. Renewables have low external costs. The key is to get their internal costs down and to get more experience with their operation in different practical situations. Wind is a good place to start. Nuclear energy also has low external costs. We should continue to ensure that our nuclear program is safe, secure, and reliable as our reactors age, and we should take steps to resolve the waste management issue. For new reactors, and for life extensions of existing reactors, lower capital costs will be essential.

Replacing oil as the main fuel for transport, and coal and natural gas as the main fuels for electricity, will require alternative fuels. We should move toward eventual hydrogen-based electricity and transport systems; ideally, these will be based on hydrogen from non-fossil sources. Government support is justified here.

Although there are many uncertainties, the outlines of the challenges Canadians face in energy policy are clear. In the near term, the biggest challenge will be to find effective, fair, affordable, and adequate energy supplies that have less impact on health and the environment. In the long term, it will be to move toward a more sustainable system. So far, we seem to have good programs in a wide range of areas, and there have been some encouraging developments (National Resources Canada 2001; Canada 2000). Overall, however, activity levels continue to outweigh the progress we are making on impacts through efficiency gains or fuel switching. We still have a long way to go in terms of policy development, plans, and public consultation before we can claim to have blazed a clear trail forward in terms of sustainable development and climate change. Governments have a legitimate role to play in policy development and funding for the longer-term public goods aspects of sustainable development. Industry and individual citizens have responsibilities as well.

If we take the challenges seriously, we face significant changes in how we produce and use energy. Making those changes will require difficult decisions and intense negotiations based on the best available information and public understanding we can develop. Many other issues are competing for the public's attention, but this is clearly a fundamental one for the longer term. The sooner we begin addressing it in earnest, the better.

REFERENCES

Arrow, K., et al. 1995. 'Intertemporal Equity, Discounting and Economic Efficiency.' In *Climate Change 1995*. Contribution of Working Group III to the Second Assessment Report of the Intergovernmental Panel on Climate Change. Cambridge, MA.

ASPO. 2002. Press Release. Founding Conference of the Association for the Study of Peak Oil, Uppsala, Sweden. May. www.oilcrisis.com/aspo/iwood/ASPO_Press.doc[.]

Biocap. 2001. *Canada's Green Advantage for a Bio-based Future*. Kingston, ON: Biocap Canada Foundation, February.

BP. 2002. *BP Statistical Review of World Energy 2002*. www.bp.com/centres/energy2002[.]

Brundtland, Gro-Harlem, Chair. 1987. *Our Common Future*. World Commission on Environment and Development. Oxford: Oxford University Press.

Canada. 2000. *Canada's National Implementation Strategy on Climate Change: National Climate Change Process*. Ottawa. October.

– 2001. *Energy and Sustainable Development: A Canadian Perspective*, Ottawa: Public Works and Government Services Canada.

Coombs, Al. 1992. *International Comparison of CO2 Decomposition*. Working Paper. Ottawa: Energy Mines and Resources Canada.

Economist. 2002. *A Few Green Shoots*, 29 August.

EPA (Environmental Protection Agency) and Science Applications International Corporation. 2001. *LCA 101: Introduction to LCA.* www.epa.gov/ORD/NRMRL/lcaccess/lca101.htm[.]

European Commission, Directorate-General XII. 1995. *ExternE: Externalities of Energy.* Vol. 1. Summary. Brussels: European Commission. externe.jrc.es[.]

Gunter, W.D., et al. 1998. 'Large C02 Sinks: Their Role in the Mitigation of Greenhouse Gases from an International, National (Canadian) and Provincial (Alberta) Perspective.' *Applied Energy,* 61.

Hamilton, Kirk. 1999. *Genuine Savings as a Sustainability Indicator.* Second OECD Workshop on Frameworks to Measure Sustainable Development. Paris: OECD. September.

Hawken, Paul, A. Lovins, and H. Lovins. 1999. *Natural Capitalism.* New York: Little Brown.

IEA (International Energy Agency). 1998. *World Energy Outlook 1998.* Paris: IEA.

– 2001a. *World Energy Outlook 2000.* Paris: IEA.

– 2001b. *Highlights: Toward a Sustainable Energy Future.* Paris: IEA, May.

– 2002. *Toward Solutions: Sustainable Development in the Energy Sector.* Paris: IEA, May.

Jaccard, Mark. 2001. 'Costing Greenhouse Abatement: Canada's Technological and Behavioural Potential.' *Isuma* 2, no. 4: 45–52.

– 2002. 'Since We're Stuck with Kyoto, Stalling Will Only Cost Us More.' *Globe and Mail.* 3 September, 7.

Laponche, Bernard. 2000. *Energie et developpment durable: l'avenir est ouvert.* Paris: International Conseil Energie.

Lomborg, Bjorn. 2002. 'Earth's a Tough Mother.' *Globe and Mail.* 23 August, B1.

McBean, Gordon, Andrew Weaver, and Nigel Roulet. 2001. 'The Science of Climate Change, What Do We Know?' *Isuma,* 2, no. 4: 16–25.

Morrison, R.W., D. Layzell, and G. McLean. 2001. 'Technology and Climate Change.' Climate Change 2, Canadian Technology Development Conference, Toronto. October.

Nakicenovic, N., A. Grubler, and A. McDonald, eds. 1998. *Global Energy Perspectives.* Cambridge: International Institute for Applied Systems Analysis, and World Energy Council.

Natural Resources Canada. 1999. *Canada's Emissions Outlook: An Update.* Ottawa: Natural Resources Canada. December.

– 2000. *Energy in Canada 2000.* Ottawa: Natural Resources Canada.

– 2001. *Sustainable Development Strategy, Now and for the Future.* Ottawa: Natural Resources Canada.

- 2002. *Energy Efficiency Trends in Canada, 1990 to 2000*. Ottawa: Natural Resources Canada. June.

NCCP (National Climate Change Process). 2000. *Canada's National Implementation Strategy on Climate Change, Annex 3*. Ottawa: Public Works and Government Services Canada. October.

NEA (Nuclear Energy Agency). 2000. *Nuclear Energy in a Sustainable Development Perspective*. Paris: OECD. December.

NRTEE (National Roundtable on the Environment and the Economy. 2002. *Summary of the Draft Environment and Sustainable Development Indicators*. National Roundtable on the Environment and the Economy. Ottawa. June.

Pearce, David. 1993. Blueprint 3, *Measuring Sustainable Development*. London: Earthscan.

- 2001. *Energy Policy and Externalities: An Overview*. Paris: Joint IEA/NEA Workshop on Externalities. December.

Pembina Institute. 2000. *Alberta Sustainability Trends 2000*. Calgary: Pembina Institute.

Reeve, David. 2000. *The Capture and Storage of Carbon Dioxide Emissions: A Significant Opportunity to Help Canada Meet Its Kyoto Targets*. Ottawa: Natural Resources Canada. October.

Schipper, Lee, F. Unander, and C. Marie. 1999. *The IEA Indicators Effort: Extension to Carbon Emissions as a Tool of the Conference of Parties*. Paris: IEA. Spring.

Travers, James. 2002. 'Chretien Ties 9/11 to Western "Greed."' *Toronto Star*. 12 September, 2.

United Nations. 2001. *World Population Prospects: The 2000 Revision*. New York: UN Population Division.

UNEPIE (United Nations Environment Program Industry and Environment Centre). 1995. CP 16, *Life Cycle Assessment and How to do it*. New York: UNEPIE.

Voss, Alfred. 2002. *LCA and External Costs in Comparative Assessment of Electricity Chains: Decision Support for Sustainable Electricity Provision?* Paris: Joint IEA/NEA Workshop on Externalities. December.

Walsh, John. 2002. *The World Energy Situation after the Peak in Conventional Oil Production Has Passed*. Proceedings of the Canadian Association for the Club of Rome, Series 3, no. 3. March.

World Bank 1999. *Fuel for Thought: Environmental Strategy for the Energy Sector*, World Bank Group Sector Strategy Paper. Washington: World Bank. July.

- 2002. *World Development Report*. Washington: World Bank.

Worldwatch. 2002. *World Summit Policy Brief #1*. Washington: Worldwatch Institute. February.

Chapter 4

Accounting for the Uncountable: Valuing the Environment in Energy Policy

BILL JARVIS

This chapter has three purposes. The first is to make the case that environmental issues will be the driving force behind energy policy for a sustainable development world. To this end, I will look at the characteristics of past energy policy and analyse the links between energy and the environment. The second is to provide a framework for such a policy that is meaningful in environmental management terms but also grounded in a utilitarian context that is consistent with our democratic institutions.[1] The third is to point out the vital necessity of implementing such a policy and of developing and launching explicit accounting processes, at both the corporate and national levels, to report on the environmental impacts of energy use and production.

The case is often made that it is immoral, impossible, or impractical to develop explicit prices for environmental assets and integrate those prices into rational (economic) decision making in fields such as energy investment, supply, and use. It is widely perceived that environmental assets resist reductionist processes such as cost benefit analyses, which require explicit prices. Briefly put, that environmental assets are uncountable (see, for example, Daly and Cobb, 1989, 55). Even where explicit pricing is possible, operational barriers, including aggregation problems, quality adjustments, multiple use issues, and the notion of non-use values for environmental assets create enormous difficulties.

Yet regardless of such limitations, decisions respecting protection of or damage to the environment are taken every day. These decisions are based on the information available (we manage what we measure); they are also based on the tools that can fit that information into a 'decision-making framework.' These decisions are all about choices – choices made by individuals, by corporations, and by society. Our ability to make such choices explicit is what enables us to evaluate, make, and understand important decisions. Without explicit valuation,[2] the choices with respect to the environmental consequences of many decisions can only be unclear, or misunderstood, or ignored. The solution to this is for us to take explicit, monetized account of how we use our natural environment and of the damage done to it by human activities. When we fail to do this, we risk impoverishing our community by allowing some of our most valuable assets to steadily deteriorate. More importantly, we must change the way we think about the environmental consequences of our activities. In this chapter I argue that instead of viewing the environment as peripheral or external to our activities, we must recognize the environment and its health as integral to what we do and how we do it – just like labour, capital, and material supplies. Early and widespread application, however imperfect, will create both the capacity and the incentive to improve valuation in many areas. Waiting for completeness in theory, or avoiding the issue altogether, is no answer.

Regarding the energy industry, given its association with environmental issues, the absence of formal mechanisms for including environment constraints in decisions will mean significant and growing uncertainty as the pressure on our environmental assets increases and as awareness of environmental issues rises. Two paths are open. First, we can relegate environmental decision making to politicians and, it follows, to the interest groups that vie for access to policy instruments. Second, by explicitly accounting for environmental assets, we can bring these decisions into the more predictable domain of the markets.

The consequences of the latter approach could well be an energy market that serves the broadest interests of all Canadians, that operates within the parameters of integrated and coherent sustainable development, and that has the potential to overcome those barriers to progress which are reflected in the concern that environmental values are being sacrificed for narrow economic gains.

Energy Policy Drivers and Objectives

Energy policy has been central to public policy in Canada for at least the past fifty years. This is not surprising, because energy accounts for 6.5 per cent of GNP, 8 per cent of consumer spending, almost 20 per cent of private investment, and 10 per cent of the value of Canada's export earnings. Just as important, energy is vital to transportation, to housing, and to industry. In a large and often frigidly cold country whose economy is still quite dependent on resource extraction and processing, Canadians rely on energy for life, for health, for transportation, and for their high living standards.

Energy policies have a number of goals that are sometimes congruent and sometimes competing: to secure supplies of energy for all Canadians at low prices, with minimal environmental impact; to build Canada's social infrastructure; to create wealth and employment; and to husband this country's natural resources to benefit both current and future generations. Although each of these objectives is constantly in play, the historical record indicates that at any particular point in time, energy policies tend to be dominated by a single element or major driver.

- In the 1950s and 1960s, regional and national *industrial development* drove energy policies. Energy prices were both low and stable. Industry players received support from governments to begin developing their capacity. Governments established a reserved market for Canadian oil, financed delivery systems, such as pipelines, to link Eastern markets with Western resources (pipelines), set favourable rates for electricity so as to encourage that sector's expansion, and backed large energy projects.
- After the oil embargo in 1973, and especially after the 1979 revolution in Iran, *security of supply* became the driving force in energy policy. The concerns raised by the Club of Rome's report, *Limits to Growth*, were also a factor in this (Meadows et al., 1972). Efforts were made to reduce oil dependency. Frontier exploration, massive 'off-oil' programs, major hydro and nuclear development, dedicated R&D programs, and export caps were other outcomes of energy policies, which focused on anticipated price rises and supply shortages for hydrocarbons.
- After 1985, a process of deregulation began. This involved *the establishment of a market-driven energy economy* as a response to energy surpluses in Canada and throughout the world. This cleared the way for an era of policies based on *competitiveness in the energy sector*, which would be market driven and export led, but which would also receive significant support for large capital projects that would make the most of the previous decade's invest-

ments. The performance of Canada's energy sector with respect to the amount and value of exports has been nothing less than spectacular. This success has increased pressure on the environment.

- In the early 1990s, environmental issues began to rise in prominence. This influenced how energy supply projects were developed. Concerns over nuclear waste management, the impacts of energy mega-projects, and combustion-based air pollution slowed development. Policies now focused on *efficient energy use* as both an economic and environmental necessity. Governments and also the electricity industry introduced programs to pursue economically attractive demand reductions.
- By the end of the 1990s, *climate change* arising from emissions of greenhouse gases (GHGs) had become the dominant issue in energy policy (Government of Canada, 2002). It was now perceived that there had to be a coordinated global response to changes in the atmosphere. A reduction in the use of carbon-based fuels has, for new reasons, once again become the main policy priority.

As we look to the future, is it possible to discern what the next major driver for Canadian energy policy will be? In this chapter I argue that environmental issues are the most likely candidate for this, and I outline how we can make progress in defining and implementing that policy.

The first argument for an environmental focus is that energy production and energy use both make extensive use of our environmental resources. Most of the costs of this impact on the environment are not borne by the energy industry, nor are they borne directly by energy users – a clear case of market failure. Rather, they are borne by the 'owners' of the natural environment – the citizens of Canada. Second, it is likely that continuing population and economic growth – including growth in both energy production and energy use – will place growing demands on our environmental assets. This growth will be required for domestic needs, but it may be greatly accelerated by opportunities in export markets, especially the American market. Third, because much of the environment is not included in marketable transactions, the normal mechanisms for adjusting to the pressures (scarcities) caused by continuing increases in demand will not be sufficiently responsive to protect the interests of Canadians. Most of the time, the need to address environmental issues will outweigh other energy policy considerations, precisely because this is where markets are unable to deliver desired solutions. Policies will not target what the markets can accomplish – that is, they will not allocate resources to production and apply commercial energy for profit and individual welfare maximization. Rather, they will target the area where markets cannot function. It is in these areas that governments must act.

This is not to say that commercial issues, security issues, and development issues will not continue to be important. Indeed, energy supply crises are depressingly regular, and governments would be short-sighted not to be ready for them over the next decade or two. Also, regional, jurisdictional, and constitutional issues remain. But given a continuing expansion of global and Canadian populations and economies, the increase in environmental stress is likely for the foreseeable future to drive energy policies not only in Canada but through most of the industrialized world.

It would be useful to start by reviewing why energy is so close to the centre of environmental concerns and policies. The following sections consider this from two perspectives: energy use and energy production.

Energy Use and the Environment

Assessments of national environmental performance typically include indicators that describe the state of the environment (e.g., the quality of the water in our rivers and lakes), as well as indicators that describe the pressures humans are placing on the environment (e.g., toxic releases into the air or water). There is sometimes a third type of indicator – one that does not have any direct relationship to the natural environment, but rather describes the size of the economy overall as an indicator (perhaps) of limits to the carrying capacity of the earth (Wackernagle and Reese, 1996).

Perhaps surprisingly, energy use is a common indicator in environment/sustainable development assessments (OECD, 2001; Estey and Cornelius, 2002). It is useful to ask why the use of energy, as opposed to the use of health services or food, is so often identified as an environmental 'bad.' There are several possibilities, which perhaps work together. Some public (and policy) views are rooted in ideas that have been discredited by academic research or that are not relevant to the Canadian situation. Others reflect philosophical positions regarding the fundamental nature of our society. The first step in designing a robust policy framework in this area is to understand what problems are being addressed and what objectives our society might want to establish. We can start by examining the various ideas that underlie the perception that energy use is, in and of itself, a 'bad' thing. The candidates:

- *Finite energy resource.* If energy is ultimately absolutely limited, then 'overuse' now is diminishing the potential of future generations to use energy. This basic idea has a long history; it is identified with Thomas Malthus (1798) and is reflected in the reports by the Club of Rome (Meadows et al., 1972). It remains powerful in the public mind, even though history has repeatedly confounded its predictions.
- *Energy as a proxy for industrial development.* The assumption here is that the source of environmental degradation is modern industrial development, given the close links between energy use and industrial activity. Whether or not this idea has merit, the existence and promotion of the modern industrial state is not very likely something that can or should be dealt with through the relatively narrow lens of energy policy.
- *Overconsumption.* Here, high levels of energy use are directly associated with an immoral or unsustainable lifestyle. Sometimes this is couched as an equity issue (i.e., relative to most people in developing countries) and sometimes as a sustainability issue (i.e., our children will run out). Again, this points to societal issues, which are much more profound than energy issues.
- *Waste.* Here, high levels of use are associated with waste, the implication being that the elimination of waste could lead to clear and sharp gains in welfare. However, waste in this context is being closely equated with inefficiency. As Lee Schipper (Schipper et al., 2001) of the IEA points out, and as others point out as well, intensive use of energy is not always or even usually the same as *inefficient* use of energy. Higher levels of energy use do not necessarily imply inefficiency. (When nations are being compared, this poses difficulties for energy-intensive countries like Canada).
- *The mercantilist argument.* For most of Europe and for the United States, energy – especially carbon-based energy – is a major net import. This has strong implications for trade accounts and competitiveness. In this context, reducing energy use is 'good' for the nation in that it preserves foreign currency. Environmental arguments are sometimes resorted to in order to 'protect' nations from

excessive import requirements. (This is a discredited nineteenth-century argument, yet it still holds some power.)

- *Externalities* (from production, transmission and use). There are significant external costs attached to the use of environmental assets associated with virtually every form of usable energy (more on this later). This argument has some merit, but it is constructed in a way that could lead to quite perverse policy conclusions. The environmental problem is, in fact, the externality (e.g., the emissions of sulfates), not energy use per se.

In spite of the limitations of these explanations, the public tends to strongly identify high levels of energy use with deleterious environmental consequences. This is why the environmental aspects of energy policy must be made painstakingly clear as to their objectives. If the real issues (most of which relate to the unaccounted use of public goods) are not identified and dealt with, misrepresentations of energy use issues will drive policies toward solutions that can't achieve useful goals.

Energy Production and Environmental Stresses

Almost no one denies any more that energy production, transmission, transformation, and use result in waste streams that can degrade our air, water, and land and damage human and non-human health. GHGs, oil spills, nuclear waste, noxious emissions from internal-combustion engines, volatile organic compounds leaking from filling stations, noise pollution from windmills, disposal of used solar panels – almost every energy supply form is associated with some undesirable waste. Land use issues are of concern for hydroelectric plants, pipelines, and refinery complexes, as well as for oil and gas exploration. And so on.

Why is this deemed more important in the energy sector than in many other sectors? It is unlikely that environmental issues will dominate industrial, health, agricultural, or even transportation policies in the coming decades, although environmental issues will be addressed in each of these sectors. There are certain characteristics of the energy sector that raise all of these pointed concerns:

- *Scale.* Economies of scale and resource distribution lead to highly concentrated energy production facilities (e.g., nuclear plants, dams, refineries, tar sands production facilities). This concentrates

the environmental impact, so that the stresses on local environments can be large. (Thus, very small hydroelectric projects are
often perceived as relatively benign, whereas large projects, which
may have less impact per unit of energy produced, are seen as
environmental concerns.)

- *Visibility.* The air quality problems faced (mostly) by large urban
  centres are highly visible, directly linked to citizens' health, and
  almost entirely associated with the burning of fuel to produce
  energy. Smoke-belching vehicles and stacks are glaring sources and
  symbols of environmentally damaging waste. Large oil spills from
  tankers create sudden, dramatic, and often massive environmental
  damage. Transmission pipelines and wires cut through often
  pristine countryside. Urban centres, where most Canadians live
  and where most energy is consumed, are most affected by problems of this kind.
- *Scope.* It is in the nature of air-born pollutants to migrate, often over
  long distances. Thus, smog and acid rain can be created in one
  community, and end up as environmental problems in another;
  both easily cross regional, provincial, and national boundaries. It is
  especially galling to have one's air quality or cottage lake damaged
  by the waste of people far away. With ozone depletion (not an
  energy issue) and atmospheric change, local actions are now seen
  as having a global impact. The distance between the cause and the
  consequences of combustion emissions raises particular concerns
  about fairness and redress.
- *The energy industry.* An outgrowth of economies of scale is a high
  concentration of corporate wealth and power in the energy sector.
  The energy giants, be they private and publicly owned, become
  targets for disempowered groups in society. These concerns are
  often expressed as environmental concerns. Powerful economic
  entities are perceived as difficult to hold to account for environmental damage and as indifferent to how they affect populations.[4]
- *Political opportunism.* To 'sell' policy reform, politicians often find it
  convenient or necessary to identify 'villains' – that is, those who
  can be blamed for the problem that needs fixing. But such villains
  must be carefully chosen. In transportation, the villain is the vast
  majority of citizens – the car-driving. In agriculture, the belea-
  guered farmer makes a poor villain. It is much easier to get a
  political consensus and call for action when the villain is a large,

often multinational corporation extracting rents from Canada's resource endowment.

As populations grow and economies impinge ever more on our environmental resources, creating scarcities that our society will want to address, energy (both its production and its use) is likely to be the first area of focus for environmental policies. An effective energy policy will need to understand this, and be designed to address it.

Let us conclude, then, that concerns over the environment should be the most important driver of energy policy over the coming decades. This provides guidance on broad objectives. But the task of creating the tools to enable implementation presents us with another set of problems. These problems are basically three: First, how do we construct the specific objectives of the policy? Second, how do we measure environmental use and assets so that we can make informed decisions? Third, how do we influence the behaviour of citizens to achieve those objectives? These three questions can be addressed by applying basic tools that have been developed within economics and by finding innovative ways to apply them.

Utilitarian versus Romantic Approaches

It would be useful to address a key philosophical issue that sometimes makes clarity difficult to achieve when it comes to setting policy objectives in the area of the environment. Competing ideologies as they relate to environmental goals result in sharply differing views on whether it is appropriate to apply economic models to environmental matters. Yet the policy debates that influence environment policies are usually framed in economic terms.

Ronald Brooks, in an article challenging some of the premises of sustainable development, usefully condenses views on environmental conservation into two myths: the utilitarian (unlimited consumerism) and the romantic (green) (see table 4.1). In his view, the utilitarian view (which he reasonably claims 'the majority of society holds most of the time') has two fundamental flaws. First, its objectives (measured activity) do not correspond to societies' actual interests: 'The point is that a lot of the things we're interested in, in terms of conservation, don't produce measurable amounts of money compared to other things' (2000, 68). Second, the utilitarian view rests on the notion

Table 4.1
Two world views

Romantic	Utilitarian
Biocentric	Anthropocentric
Strong sustainability	Weak sustainability
No trade-offs	Trade-offs
Limits to growth	No logical limits
Harmony	Competition
New society	Selfish behaviour
Skinner–nurture	Darwin–nature
Philosopher prince	Democracy

that more is always better and that 'resources – especially human and renewable resources – are limitless.' He illustrates the difficulties inherent in such a view through some examples of the geometric expansion of growth (population and invested wealth).

Brooks is no more comfortable with the romantic view. He attacks the assumption that preindustrial civilizations were in harmony with nature by referring to the actual behaviours of societies throughout history, many of which were damaging to the environment and to other creatures. He argues that 'the destruction of the environment is not merely a cultural trait, nor even a species trait, but a characteristic of any organism that has evolved by Darwinian selection' (ibid., 72). He continues: 'Short term gain always triumphs over long term stability. Long-term stability is *merely a consequence of balanced strategies and counterstrategies selected at the level of purely greedy individuals*' (my emphasis).

Not surprisingly, Brooks is gloomy about the possibility of resolving these dilemmas. I have used his characterizations because of their admirable clarity and because, notwithstanding his concerns about the utilitarian view, I believe he has pointed out an approach to resolving the dilemmas. The stability he seeks, I argue, is inherent in our societies to a much greater extent than he admits.

The philosophical debate that requires resolution is precisely the debate between Brooks's utilitarians and his romantics. The romantic approach is entirely incompatible with a set of policies based on an economic framework, because such policies must inevitably include certain trade-offs between the natural environment and human wants and needs. For the romantics, the very idea of putting a price on our environmental assets is anathema, precisely because it would permit such trade-offs. Such a non-anthropocentric perspective may be a perfectly legitimate approach to our environment by an individual, and may even be implementable in some limited contexts. But it cannot, I argue, form the basis for a broad policy construct for Canada. The reality of everyday decisions, at all levels of society, is that they require choices between all of those things we value.

Simply put, the romantic vision cannot be accommodated to democratically-based policies. Brooks points out: 'People can hold a green view on occasion, but revert to a utilitarian view for most of their day-to-day decisions' (ibid., 67). The implication is that self-interested behaviour is simply the consequence of millions of years of evolution. In other words, a democratic government – which must serve the interests of its citizens if it is to be re-elected – is confined to a utilitarian approach by the fundamentals of human nature; fundamentals that, as Steven Pinker shows in *How the Mind Works* (2001), have evolved over the millennia. But what, then, are we to make of Brooks's demonstrations of the fundamental flaws of the utilitarian approach?

Brooks's take on the utilitarian approach is too limited. A broader and more accurate interpretation of utilitarian models can resolve in principle, and perhaps in practice, the concerns identified. And in fact it is precisely the interpretation of sustainable development adopted by the Canadian government (among others) – one that balances economic, social, and environmental objectives – that can lead to such a resolution.

Resolving Limitations in a Finite World

We must first distinguish between the *conceptual space* of economics and the *practical use* of economics as limited by information constraints. First-year economic textbooks generally identify the economic problem as consisting of people wanting more than they can have, of unbounded needs colliding with limitations, of available resources at a given point in time being unable to satisfy everyone's needs and wants. The mechanism for resolving this tension is the effects of scarcity on behaviour. When a resource, which can be any resource (human, natural, or man-made), becomes more scarce relative to other resources, its value increases. The increase in value encourages investment in increasing its supply; it also discourages its use. In a market economy, the signal that sets all of this in motion is a price. In practice, we often use only priced transactions to measure changes in welfare (GDP). In theory, all things of value are included.

Environmental scarcities, just like scarcities of marketable commodities, place pressures for resolution on societies and their governing instruments. But many environmental assets are different; unlike marketable commodities, their scarcity does not generate a price signal that encourages reductions in demand (use) and increases in supply. Other mechanisms emerge to cause the required response, and the more urgent the scarcity, the higher the pressure for response. When it was shown in 1969 that the citizens of the Grassy Narrows Reserve near Kenora, Ontario, were affected by mercury poisoning, the source was identified and new rules (regulations) were established for the pulp and paper industry in Canada. Under the 1986 Settlement Act, compensation was provided to those affected. This example shows that responses *do* emerge, and that for non-market problems, those responses can be very slow – sometimes too slow to avoid tragic and non-reversible consequences. As Thomas Homer-Dixon (1999) points outs, unresolved environmental problems (scarcities of environmental 'assets') can, if not resolved by other means, lead to civil unrest as an ultimate adjustment mechanism.

But what is meant in this context by a scarcity of environmental assets? The emerging literature on natural capital offers a perspective on the value of our environmental assets that fits nicely with our understanding of economic forces. We 'use' natural capital (including 'renewable resources,' ecosystem services such as clean air and clean water, and so on) just like we do human-produced capital in the course of satisfying our needs and wants. The natural environment 'invests' in these capital assets: forests grows; species reproduce; organic materials decompose; water replenishes lakes and rivers in the form of rain and snow melt. When the use of environmental assets, at any particular time and place, exceeds the reinvestment being done by natural events, natural capital is diminished. If these excesses of use over investment (renewal) occur on a continuing basis, ultimately society will be faced with a shortage (scarcity) of the natural capital affected.

Environmental problems are quite often assessed not as changes in the value of the stock of the asset, but as flows of by-products from our human activities that have deleterious effects on the environment. Emissions from combustion, residuals from forest product production, and chemical effluents from manufacturing processes or from mining operations are examples of such by-products. These by-products can correctly be seen either as having negative value or as being a cost of the activities they are associated with (i.e., the cost of use of the environment to dispose of the by-product). What makes them the subject of concern and policy intervention is that they are not always (or even normally) accounted for as part of the price of the good or service being produced.

These two concepts – of changes to natural capital stock and of the negative value of waste flows – are compatible, and can actually be seen as mirror images of each other. From an accounting perspective, there is a one-to-one mapping between environmental resource (capital) consumption and the production of environmental by-products (Gollop and Swinand, 2001).

Implementation

From the rather abstract arguments above, I propose that we can start to answer the questions posed earlier relating to the implementation of an energy policy that is driven by environmental concerns (scarcity).

The first question was one of objectives. The utilitarian school of thought seeks to maximize the delivery of goods and services on which humans place value. It is completely anthropocentric; it sees value in nature only as this is deemed to be of value to human beings (i.e., there is no 'existence value'). Welfare, according to this school of thought, is typically assessed by proxies within the national accounting system (GDP, GDP per capita, income per capita, and sometimes government and trade balances).

However, the failure to explicitly consider the non-market value of environmental goods and natural resource depletion in existing accounts misrepresents the current state of well-being, distorts the representation of the economy's production and substitution possibilities, and fails to inform policy makers on the important link between economic growth and the environment (Hrubovcak, Leblanc, and Eakin, 2000). A complete (and therefore useful) assessment of the objective of the utilitarian approach must logically include all things of value to citizens, not just those which are measured in the economic accounts. However, increasingly severe obstacles are likely to arise as the National Accounts move further from the boundaries of the marketplace (Nordhaus and Kokkelenberg, 1999). It is relatively easy to construct, through a thought experiment, the case for such inclusion. One need only consider the fate of a corporation whose operating profits are always less than the value (depreciation) of its use of its capital assets. Bankruptcy is inevitable, since the corporation's net worth will decline eventually to zero. The case is the same for a society whose GDP has risen by less than the value of the natural capital (or other non-marketable capital assets such as the legal system) that has been diminished in the process. Nonetheless, the truism that we manage what we measure remains a constraint for both the public sector and the private one.

Unless and until we can provide appropriate and useable accounting for those things which we value but which are not subject to market transactions, the expression of our objectives in the context of a utilitarian view of the world will be dangerously incomplete.

Inclusive Accounting

Our accounting frameworks (including both business accounting and national accounting) are criticized more for what they omit than for flaws in what they actually measure. For the energy sector, the most prominent failure relates to the absence of the value society attributes to the use of environmental assets (or, as pointed out earlier, the negative value of disposal of substances into the environment). Simply put, those who produce and use energy are regularly making use of resources that belong to all of society, yet they are not accountable for that use. It is like a neighbour using your backyard to dispose of his garbage, without any permission from or compensation to you. Our objective, from the arguments made earlier, should be to ensure that producers and users of energy act as if the value of those environmental assets are fully reflected in their decisions, and to ensure as well that they compensate society as a whole for the value of their use. The principle is clear – the application is difficult.

Corporate Accounting

We must start from this question: Why might it be in the interest of corporations to account for their use of those public goods which they receive without any cost? A large amount of literature is emerging which suggests that corporations ought to look beyond the interests of their shareholders and act more in the interests of society as a whole –

that is, they should practice corporate social responsibility (CSR). In an ideal world, we might look to the public-spirited behaviour of corporations to address the problem. But can that be sufficient?

In a study produced for the California Global Accountability Project, *Beyond Good Deeds* (Leighton et al., 2000), environmental and human rights issues for multinational companies are examined with reference to CSR and how to foster better corporate performance in those areas. The business case for corporations to engage in CSR is based on the idea that 'good environmental and social performance generates tangible financial benefits, which can be captured by companies and investors.' According to the report, these benefits arise from the preferences of consumers, investors, and workers for doing business with 'responsible' companies, or from reducing costs and improving quality.

The results of the case studies investigated by the Leighton report are mixed, according to the authors; there has been a relatively low rate of uptake of CSR among firms. 'One reason,' the study suggests, is that 'markets cannot discriminate very well between good and bad performers,' largely because of serious information gaps. The study points out that environmental and social information gaps stem from:

- Minimal statutory requirements for company disclosure;
- Company fear and refusal to voluntarily disclose internal information, including fear of liability or other reprisal, or of being disadvantaged relative to a competitor, or divulgence of trade secrets;
- Greenwashing, by providing information as a public relations gimmick;
- Lack of a reporting template, which hampers comparability and generates confusion among the public and within companies; and
- Lack of clarity in private sector responsibility for human rights norms.

These concerns, which are reflected widely in the literature, are not so much arguments against CSR as evidence of CSR's limitations. Two remedies can be drawn from these concerns. First, better and standardized information is vital if CSR is to be of much value to corporations. As pointed out in the report from the Canadian Democracy and Corporate Accountability Commission, *The New Balance Sheet* (Bennett and Broadbent, 2002, 22), 'corporate law requires disclosure of information to shareholders on financial matters, in order to remain accountable to investors, but other information is disclosed only if it has a significant "material" effect on the bottom line – a serious environmental or social impact without financial costs may not be "material."'

Second, only governments can provide a level playing field to ensure that all corporations will report in a consistent manner so that free riders cannot take unfair advantage of voluntary reporting systems. Legal requirements of disclosure are the first necessary condition for an effective corporate accounting system that recognizes the value of environmental use. The key to understanding the power of accounting is to understand that consistency and comparability are sometimes more important than being absolutely right (Rubenstein, 1994). Consistency and comparability are unlikely to emerge without specific governmental reporting frameworks and requirements.

Another approach to addressing the use of the environment within corporations – one that is distinct but not necessarily separate from CSR – is a risk management approach. The arguments in the first parts of this chapter suggested that at some level of scarcity (depletion or damage), society will act to recognize explicitly the value of our natural assets. The most important decisions a corporation makes are decisions respecting new investments. Especially (although not uniquely) in the energy sector, those investment decisions set the course for corporate activities for many years or even decades. If they are made assuming that the value of the natural environment as a means of waste disposal or material input is zero, or significantly below its value to the community as a whole, the investment could be at real risk. Including the potential costs so that they reflect the real value of the resources used would enable corporations to discriminate between projects with significant risks of additional future costs on the one hand, and those involving less use of environmental assets on the other. To make such calculations, one must be explicit about the expected use of the environment (or the anticipated waste streams), and at least estimate costs of prevention or remediation. Ideally, shadow prices of the (negative) value of emissions would be explicitly included in rate-of-return calculations for investment purposes.

As concern for the environment grows, the value to corporations of the capacity to make such calculations will increase. The argument can be made that valuing environmental assets such as 'air sheds' and water quality is beyond the means of corporations. Yet in decision frameworks, corporations *do* value many non-market assets (corporate reputation, brand, and various types of economic and physical risk, and so on). A number of approaches can be taken, depending on the perceived corporate issues (risks) and the nature of the environmental asset and damage. A list of options is provided by Rubenstein (1994):

- *Social cost value* – subjective evaluation of worth to society;
- *Non-utilization value* – amount paid to prevent use (ie payment to Newfoundland fisherman not to catch cod);
- *Remediation cost* – cost to repair known damage;
- *Rehabilitation cost* – cost to restore ecosystem to prior state;
- *Value of alternative use* – what else could be done with the resource such as tourism;
- *Compensation value* – the cost of compensating directly affected people as in the Grassy Narrows Settlement;
- *Future scarcity value* – estimated value in 100 years of intact environmental asset;
- *Infinite value* – from 'romantic view' discussed above – not a useful construct in this context.

A final concern of corporations with respect to calculating and reporting the value of their use of environmental assets is that governments might use this information to ensure that market signals reflect those values and protect society's interest by making them explicit (i.e., by charging for the use of public assets). This is a realistic concern, and indicates where the public interest diverges from private interests. But avoiding the issue will not make it disappear. The policy implication, which should be one of the pillars of a new energy policy, is that governments should create a standardized reporting framework. Furthermore, over time, as the usability and acceptability of the framework is established, governments should require mandatory reporting on the use of publicly owned environmental assets by energy producers and users. This does not require that the entire issue be resolved before implementation. What *is* necessary is that the implied values be widely accepted within society, as a precondition for incremental implementation.

National Accountability

In 1915, Canada's Commission on Conservation wrote about the need to live within natural cycles saying: 'Each generation is entitled to the interest on the natural capital, but the principle should be handed on unimpaired.' Work by the World Bank (Hamilton, 2000) and others has provided a capital framework that conceptually represents all built, human, environmental (natural), financial, and social capital – a national balance sheet. This provides a coherent and logical framework that countries can apply when making decisions that will advance the welfare of their citizens – provided that we can identify and value all of these assets. We are far from that state.

In a study commissioned by the U.S. National Research Council regarding the integration of environmental and economic accounting (Nordhaus and Kokkelenberg, 1999), a distinction is made between the development of accounts for the purposes of 'scorekeeping' and for the purposes of management. In the first case, aggregate information on the physical state of environmental assets is sufficient to guide policymakers with regard to whether we are living off our environmental capital. The current work by the National Round Table on the Economy and the Environment (NRTEE) focuses explicitly on targets such a 'scorekeeping' perspective.

However, in their role as stewards of the environment on behalf of citizens, governments are obliged to go beyond mere reporting and to undertake an explicit management role. An added dimension of information is important for management decisions: 'This perspective focuses on the sources, transportation, and ultimate disposal of residual pollutants, particularly their contribution to outcomes of economic and ecological consequence. Knowing to what extent particular emissions of residuals come from utilities, automobiles, or volcanic eruptions is critical to developing strategies for control' (Nordhaus and Kokkelenberg, 1999, 36).

This suggests that two separate but related sets of information are needed. The first is a continuation of the work done by Statistics Canada on natural capital accounts. These clearly need to go beyond physical flows and consider value terms that can be integrated with the existing national accounting system.

R.D. Cairns, in an unpublished report prepared for Environment Canada, puts it this way with respect to water. 'Some may argue that the best way to determine how well society is using its water is to use aggregates of physical quantities as the fundamental statistics. That argument is an intellectual dead end, however. Adding up physical quantities that are not commensurable in terms of social objectives has no logical basis. It gives no means of assessing the roles of water in society. Rather, the way forward is to improve methods of valuing goods that are not sold in markets.'

This work can and should proceed incrementally, using shadow prices based on concepts such as hedonic pricing (which values assets in terms of the value of the multiple functions that they have) which can be expanded over time as better information becomes available. As noted in the report from the CISE (Canadian Information System for the Environment) Task Force, we will require greatly improved environmental information if we are to track the physical changes in environmental assets on a consistent and coherent basis. And this endeavour should be driven by and linked directly to the work on environmental sustainability indicators being conducted by NRTEE.

The second bundle of information – that is, the information required for program definition – can and should be assembled from the data required from corporations regarding their use of the environment. This would then be combined with the data gathered through the monitoring of emissions from combustion in widespread applications (like transportation).

Influencing Behaviour

As our knowledge about the value of publicly owned resources increases, these values will need to be reflected in signals that affect decisions by both energy producers and energy users. Making the information widely available will have some effect on its own. Programs such as the National Pollution Release Inventory (NPRI) can make damaging emissions transparent and thereby influence companies to reduce them. However, by far the most efficient way of accomplishing this is to make use of the market economy, and place explicit charges[5] (taxes and so on) on the use of the environment. This type of charge is most often associated with the work of A.C. Pigou (1912). Notwithstanding the issues raised by R. Coase (that under certain extreme conditions, free markets could lead to optimal solutions), and public choice theorists (who argue that government policies suffer from systemic failures), 'most economists still advocate Pigovian taxes on pollution as a much more efficient way of dealing with pollution than government-imposed standards' (Henderson, 2002, 44). The revenues from these charges, being derived from the use of publicly owned resources, should go into general government revenues, to be used according to the decisions of our democratically elected governments.

Conclusions

A successful policy framework must have a number of critical characteristics. It must deal with the most prominent and important issues from the perspective of constituents. It must be clear in its intent. It must address the problems with tools that are congruent in time and depth with the problem. The results must be observable. And, finally, it must be do-able.

This chapter has proposed a new energy policy for the coming years that focuses on accounting for the environmental consequences of energy production and use. It has made the case that scarcity of environmental resources is now evident, and that that scarcity will continue to increase, with Canadians demanding that ever more attention be paid to the protection of their environmental heritage. The objective of this policy should be to protect the welfare of Canadian citizens by developing mechanisms to protect the environment, in an economic in which market failure precludes appropriate valuation and management of public goods.

The problems are not temporary, nor are they amenable to 'one time' solutions. The tools for addressing them must include mechanisms for monitoring the use and the state of our environment, to gather information that can be used for making explicit the choices our society faces. And we need to know whether we are making progress. Corporate financial accounting systems and the national economic accounts systems provide models for this, and we need a similar system for environmental management. Once the information has been gathered, policies – in particular, explicit environmental charges that take full account of our environmental interests – can be implemented.

The final criterion – that of do-ability – is the most difficult. Some constituencies strongly resist the 'commodification' of the environment. Their concerns are both ideological and practical. Ideological concerns leave no room for using formal tools (implicit prices) to address the choices that are inevitably the stuff of daily decisions at all levels of society. Calculating implicit prices is seen (correctly, I think) as the first step toward condoning and enabling trade-offs at the margin between environmental assets and economic or social assets. I contend that governments, in their role as stewards of the environment, can and must do more than leave these issues to resolution by rhetorical and political tests of wills.

The practical concerns are well articulated by Daly and Cobb (1989) in *For the Common Good*: 'What the discipline requires' necessitates a simplification so drastic as to be erroneous and likely misleading to policy-makers. This is an important caution. The problem with this view is that the failure to attempt explicit valuation will most likely result in significant undervaluing of the environment in decision making simply because useful data are lacking. Although significant problems of calculation will remain, it would be unfortunate if progress in this area were to be forestalled by an insistence that only complete and unchallengeable information be considered. Better to include environmental costs at some level than to ignore them altogether.

For certain, there are more issues to be resolved than those of accounting for our environmental assets as described earlier. Issues of jurisdiction, arguments over valuation, concerns over government intervention, arguments about competitiveness, and worries about the commodification of assets of spiritual value will need to be addressed. But the alternative is surely worse. Without mechanisms for making realistic allocations, overuse of environmental assets will continue until pressure builds to take drastic action. Overnight, the cost of certain activities will soar from zero to infinite, as regulatory fixes are used to address scarcity, often at great economic cost. Adjustments will be so slow that permanent environmental damage will be highly likely and legitimate grievances will grow within society.

We need an energy policy framework that starts with the recognization that we must be explicit about the environmental consequences of energy production and use. The first step toward this is to be clear in our understanding of the utilitarian values that drive modern societies. The second is to gather the knowledge we need to understand what should be done. The third is to translate that knowledge into action through instruments that can affect market prices and create the conditions for behaviour that accounts for all of our valuable assets. These steps are not panaceas, but they can and should provide instruments that will significantly improve the performance of public policy in the energy sector. 'It is when the hidden decisions are made explicit that the arguments begin' (Hardin, 1968).

NOTES

All views in this paper are those of the author and do not necessarily reflect the views of Environment Canada or the Government of Canada.

1 Essentially anthropocentric, responding to the wants and values of a voting citizens.
2 Explicit valuation as used here refers to the quantitative expression of the equivalent of a market clearing price. While acknowledging the existence of 'consumer rents' that reflect different values for different people, the point here is to provide a common basis for decision-making. The point is not whether this quantification of value produces the 'right' price, but rather whether we can derive a common and consistent basis for decisions about public choice.
3 'The petroleum industry is probably scrutinized more closely than any other sector of the economy. Activists and non-governmental organizations of every stripe – be they environmentalists, labour organizers, proponents of sustainable development, or advocates of human rights and democracy – have at one time or another found reasons to inveigh against Big Oil' (Leighton, Roht-Arriaza, and Zarsky, 2002).
4 Charge here is used as a general concept of which a tax is a specific type.

REFERENCES

Bennett, Avie, and Edward Broadbent. 2002. *The New Balance Sheet*. Report from Canadian Democracy and Corporate Accountability Commission. Toronto: McClelland and Stewart.

Brooks, R. 2000. 'Earthworms and the Formation of Environmental Ethics and Other Mythologies: A Darwinian Perspective.' Pp. 151–71 in Ward Chesworth, M. Moss, and V. Thomas, eds., *Malthus and the Third Millennium*. Guelph: University of Guelph.

Coase, Ronald. 1960. 'The Problem of Social Cost.' *Journal of Law and Economics* 3: 1–44.

Daly, R., and J. Cobb. 1989. *For the Common Good*. Boston: Beacon Press.

Dennett, D. 1995. *Darwin's Dangerous Idea*. New York: Simon and Schuster.

Estey, D. and P. Cornelius. 2002. *Environmental Sustainability Index*. New York: World Economic Forum.

Gollop, Frank, and G. Swinand. 2001. 'Total Resource Productivity.' Pp. xx–xx in *New Developments in Productivity Analysis*. Chicago: University of Chicago Press.

Government of Canada. 2002. Speech from the Throne. Ottawa: Government of Canada.

Hamilton, Kirk. 2000. *Genuine Savings as a Sustainability Indicator*. Washington: World Bank.

Hardin, Garrett. 1968. 'The Tragedy of the Commons.' *Science* 162: 222–30.

Henderson, D.R. 2002. *The Concise Encyclopedia of Economics.* www.econlib.org[.]

Homer-Dixon, T. 1999. *Environment, Scarcity and Violence.* Princeton: Princeton University Press.

Hrubovcak, James, M. Leblanc and K. Eakin. 2000. 'Agriculture, Natural Resources and Environmental Accounting.' *Environmental and Resource Economics* 17: 148–160.

Leighton, Michelle, Naomi Roht-Arriaza, and L. Zarsky. 2002. *Beyond Good Deeds.* Berkeley, CA: Nautilus Institute for Security and Sustainable Development.

Malthus, T. 1798. *An Essay on the Principle of Population.* London: Johnson.

Meadows, Donella, Dennis Meadows, Jorgen Randers, and William Behrens. 1972. *Limits to Growth.* New York: Potomac Associates.

Nordhaus, W., and K. Kokkelenberg, eds. 1999. *Nature's Numbers.* Washington, D.C.: National Academy Press.

OECD (Organization for Economic Co-operation and Development). 2001. *OECD Environmental Indicators.* Paris: OECD.

Pigou, A.C. 1912. *Wealth and Welfare.* London: Macmillan.

Pinker, S. 1997. *How the Mind Works.* New York: Norton.

Rubenstein, D.B. (1994) *Environmental Accounting for the Sustainable Corporation.* Westport, CT: Quorum Books.

Schipper, Lee, F. Unander, S. Murtishaw, and M. Ting. 2001. *Indicators of Energy Use and Carbon Emissions.* Paris: IEA.

Wackernagle, Mathis, and Bill Reese (1996) *Our Ecological Footprint: Reducing Human Impact on the Earth.* London: New Society Publishing.

Chapter 5

Electricity Restructuring in Canada

DONALD N. DEWEES

Although in principle electricity restructuring can mean any change in the structure of the electricity sector, the most significant changes in recent years have been those that have introduced competition to supplement or displace prices that were previously set by regulations. This chapter focuses on the introduction of competitive generation markets for determining wholesale electricity prices and for providing incentives for investment in new generation. In a competitive market, wholesale prices are set by the interaction of supply and demand, not by the interaction of monopolists and regulators. If supply is down and demand is up, the price will be high; if supply is up and demand is down, the price will be low. Investment in new capacity is determined by private investors risking their own equity, not by monopolists seeking a regulated return on investment. New capacity will be built when investors anticipate prices that will earn a satisfactory rate of return on their investment. Retail prices are set by competition between retailers or, for customers who do not choose a retailer, by regulators based on the wholesale price (Wilson, 2002). Because of the risk of market manipulation or of the exercise of market power, even the competitive wholesale market must be subject to some regulation, and transmission and distribution businesses usually remain as regulated monopolies. The introduction of competition may mean different regulation, but it does not mean the end of regulation.

Environmentalists have criticized the electricity generation sector for harming the environment through air pollution and massive hydro dams; they also worry that competitive markets will be even less environmentally responsible than regulated markets. I am about to suggest that competition is in fact *more* environmentally friendly.

This chapter explains what is involved in introducing competitive wholesale electricity markets; examines the effects of this restructuring on pricing, investment, and choice of fuel; and considers whether these effects move us toward or away from environmental sustainability. It also examines the problems that arose in California in 2000 and examines the systems in Alberta and Ontario. Finally, it considers the processes through which electricity markets are developed and the risks these processes pose for market design.

What Is Restructuring?

What happens when restructuring introduces competition in electricity generation? The traditional monopoly that a utility enjoys over electricity generation is replaced by a competitive market in which anyone who meets technical and prudential requirements is entitled to generate electricity and sell it to customers. In some cases, restructuring requires the existing monopolist to sell or lease some generation plants in order to create a competitive pricing structure; competitive behaviour then sets the wholesale price of electricity. In other cases, the big utilities remain the dominant generators, with regulated prices, but customers are free to purchase power from a competitive generator. In either case, separate wholesale prices are determined for every hour of every day, adjusting continuously as market conditions change (Wilson, 2002; Joskow, 1997).

Although electricity at the wholesale level becomes competitively priced, the long-distance transmission of that electricity, and its local distribution, remain natural monopolies subject to rate regulation. The transmission grid is required to transmit electricity from all generators to consumers. The local distribution companies are required not only to distribute electricity but also to accept 'default' retail customers who have not chosen competitive retailers and provide them with a standard rate package.

At this point, the various models diverge. In some, the local utilities remain intact, purchasing portfolios of power contracts in a competitive market and delivering power at regulated rates to captive customers; those utilities, however, remain subject to some regulatory oversight regarding the prudence of the purchase decisions. Other models adopt retail competition whereby retail customers can choose to secure supply from a competitive retailer rather than the local utility. Other design differences relate to whether an independent system operator dispatches the power from generating stations, using a bid process to determine the hourly price, and whether generators and consumers are required to enter into bilateral contracts for the supply of power every hour.

In the retail choice model, independent retailers should emerge who purchase power from generators and sell it to customers, competing with the regulated default supply price of the local distributor. These retailers may offer fixed prices in contrast to the default price, which often varies with the spot market price. The retailers may offer special services, such as load management, or special meters, including time-of-use metering and interval metering that records consumption separately for every hour of every day.

If generation plants are initially owned by a single public enterprise, some must be sold to create a competitive structure. In principle competition could arise among generators owned by different municipalities and other governments, as in Norway; in Canada, however, the most likely way to achieve a competitive structure would be to privatize some plants. If the transmission and distribution networks are initially owned by public enterprises, they may be privatized; however, privatization of these monopolies is not necessary for successful restructuring.

Why Restructure?

Over much of the twentieth century, the minimum size of efficient electricity generating stations increased, so that most cities were served by a small number of large stations. Coal was the least-cost fuel. In the 1980s, the combined cycle gas turbine (CCGT) emerged as an efficient power source that was economical at a much smaller scale than coal-fired plants, although with average total costs somewhat above those of coal. Although natural gas is much more expensive, per unit of energy, than coal, CCGT plants use less than two-thirds as much energy to produce a megawatt-hour of electricity as do coal-fired plants, and they produce less CO_2 and very little sulphur dioxide or particulate pollution. CCGT plants can be built in as little as two years, compared to five or more years for coal-fired plants, and they inspire few environmental objections of the sort that can add five years to the approval process for coal plants. As CCGT became the preferred new source of power, its smaller scale offered the promise of competitive generation using many plants rather than one single monopoly source of power (Joskow, 1997.)

In addition, many electric utilities in the 1980s were saddled with high costs from bad investments – usually expensive nuclear plants. Large industrial customers who chafed at paying high, regulated average total cost (ATC) prices to utilities learned that the ATC of new CCGT plants was less than the price they were currently paying. They pressed for competition so that they could get access to cheaper CCGT power (Joskow, 1997; Ando and Palmer, 1998).

Ideas and experience were two other important factors. Economists had been preaching the virtues of competition for decades, and there was a substantial literature about the capture of regulatory bodies by the regulated firms and the inefficient operations of regulated monopolies. Surely competition would improve efficiency, which many observers associated with lower prices. These arguments had led to the deregulation of railway and trucking rates, long-distance telephone charges, and airline prices, as well as American natural gas prices, and in most cases the result was significant cost and price reductions. Why not bring the same benefits to electricity?

In Ontario, there were two additional factors. Some executives at Ontario Hydro felt that the limitations of a regulated Crown monopoly offered insufficient challenges for the talents of the firm. With restructuring, Ontario Power Generation – the successor to the generation portion of Ontario Hydro – would be able to buy generation units across North America and become successful on a much larger scale; Hydro One, the successor to the transmission and distribution portions of Ontario Hydro, could extend its expertise in transmission to grids across the continent. According to other people, Crown ownership of Ontario Hydro had offered too many opportunities for government meddling in the utility's affairs; in other words, the government was using the utility to create jobs or to subsidize certain consumers. For example, in 1993, when prices began rising to pay for the expensive Darlington nuclear station, the government froze them. The consequence was financial losses at Ontario Hydro and an increase in its debt until the prices were unfrozen in 2001. Competition, and perhaps privatization, could limit the government's ability to intervene, and thereby improve efficiency.

Are Restructured Electricity Markets More or Less Sustainable?

Wholesale Pricing in Restructured Markets

Basic price theory says that when firms are price takers, they will adjust their output until price equals marginal cost, whereas price-taking consumers will adjust their consumption until the marginal value of another unit just equals the price. These two conditions ensure that consumer surplus and producer surplus are maximized, at least when there are no externalities and the commodity is homogeneous. In other words, in the absence of externalities and transactions costs, marginal cost pricing should achieve efficient electricity production and consumption (Joskow and Schmalensee, 1983, 81). However, if consumers face a price not equal to marginal cost, they will consume too much (low price) or too little (high price) electricity, and producers and consumers jointly will be worse off than if marginal cost pricing had been applied. Because electricity cannot be stored, and because supply and demand shift continuously, efficient pricing of electricity generally involves setting the price at least every hour of every day.

In the long run, new capacity should be installed only if it increases net surplus – that is, if it has net social benefits. In a competitive market, investors will build new capacity when they expect that they will cover all capital and operating costs from the expected market prices. If market prices will not cover the cost of the investment, that investment is socially excessive so long as the private discount rate of investors matches the social discount rate. Thus, if discount rates meet this criterion, then contrary to what Schott says in the next chapter, we should expect marginal cost pricing to induce socially optimal capital investment as well as socially optimal production and consumption.

How does pricing by a regulated monopoly match the model of efficient pricing? In a vertically integrated monopoly utility, the regulatory agency approves retail prices, while the wholesale price is usually not visible. We need to look instead at retail prices. Twenty years ago, Joskow and Schmalensee (1983, 88) stated bluntly that wholesale and retail power prices 'are currently not generally based on marginal cost pricing principles.' Today, little has changed for regulated utilities. Regulated rates for small commercial and residential consumers in the United States and Canada are usually fixed for a year or more at a time in the form of block declining rates. Reliance on a meter that measures only the cumulative kWh used between readings – which are taken at intervals ranging from one to three months – precludes changing the price to reflect short-run cost variations. Large and medium-sized industrial and commercial customers use a 'demand' meter that records the kWh used and also records the maximum rate of use, in kilowatts (kW), between readings. The customer pays both a kWh charge and a demand charge for peak use. This is intended to be a peak load–pricing system, although the customer's peak may not coincide with the system peak. The rates for kWh and kW are fixed in advance for periods of a year of more. The largest industrial customers are often connected directly to the high-voltage transmission grid, and they generally use an interval meter that records their electricity consumption every ten minutes or so. Some may pay a fixed price, and some pay a price that varies with time (Dewees, 2001b).

Some jurisdictions also offer time-of-use (TOU) prices. California began to require TOU pricing for large customers in the 1970s; Central Vermont Power introduced and expanded TOU pricing in the last quarter of the twentieth century (Spine, 2002). A TOU meter combines two or three kWh meters, with power run through one or another meter at different times of day according to a fixed schedule. In Los Angeles, for example, the summer (May through September) peak period is weekdays 11 a.m. to 6 p.m. and the semipeak is weekdays 6 a.m. to 11 a.m. and 6 p.m. to 10 p.m. All other times are off-peak. The TOU meter records cumulative kWh consumption for each period at the time of meter reading. The peak period price may be four times the off-peak price or even more. The combination of TOU metering and seasonal price changes allows considerable flexibility for tailoring prices to *expected* marginal costs – although not to actual costs as they unfold. However, in the prerestructuring North America, only a small fraction of all customers were on TOU metering (Dewees, 2001b).

One further step is possible with rate regulation: the adoption of some form of regulated real-time pricing. Georgia Power has introduced real-time pricing for its largest customers (O'Sheasy, 2002), and Faruqui and George (2002) describe a dynamic pricing system that could be applied by regulated utilities. The question is how rapidly such pricing systems will spread in jurisdictions that retain traditional rate regulation.

Regulated rates generally cover the expected average cost of all power generation for a year or more. Even predictable hourly, daily, and seasonal variations in marginal costs are lost with fixed annual rates. With TOU rates, they are partially lost. Equally important, the regulated rates may bear no relation to actual marginal costs during the year as unplanned outages influence supply and unusual weather influences demand. There is no reason for the expected average cost for the year to equal the load-weighted average of the actual marginal costs for the year or to equal the marginal costs of new generation capacity. In short, the variability of system marginal costs over time means that rate-of-return regulation based on fixed prices will fail to transmit to customers the true marginal cost of the power they consume at any time. This failure is sometimes spectacular. Joskow (1997, 126–7) reports that in the mid-1990s, the regulated price of electricity generation in the American Northeast and in California was in the range of 6 to 7 cents/kWh, while the short-run marginal cost of wholesale electricity was about 2.5 cents/kWh, and the long-run marginal cost was between 3 and 4 cents. In 2000, the marginal cost of wholesale electricity in California soared to many times the regulated price for days at a time.

A major advantage of electricity restructuring that involves an hourly spot market with competitive structure and behaviour is that the wholesale price of electricity approximates the marginal cost of generation. The largest industrial and commercial customers usually pay the wholesale price, and if they pay the spot price they face the marginal cost of generation on an hourly basis. They have an incentive to conserve electricity when the price is high and to increase their consumption when price is low. Instead of utility officials begging customers to curtail usage when demand threatens to outstrip supply, we have large customers shedding load to minimize their costs.

Even in restructured markets, medium-sized industrial and commercial customers and all small commercial and residential customers usually do not face such hourly prices. To pay an hourly price, a customer must have an 'interval meter' that records the kWh used in every hour of every day and transmits the data to the electricity supplier from time to time. Although the costs of such meters have fallen steadily, they are not yet economic for most small customers, so the majority of demand after restructuring is still served through demand or kWh meters (Dewees, 2001b).

Although competition does not achieve all of the efficiency gains that theory suggests could be available, its benefits can be substantial. Perhaps one-quarter of the total load may be on interval metering and thus be fully responsive to both predictable and unpredicted price variations. If most of the remaining customers pay the monthly average spot price – as in the initial Ontario and Alberta market designs – they will pay higher prices in summer and winter and lower prices in spring and fall. If supply and demand cause unusually high prices at any season, they will have an incentive to adjust their thermostats and their use of electric appliances. Thus, most of the total load will have some price responsiveness. If demand grows and investment languishes, the price may be high for a few years, leading all consumers to conserve electricity until the new investment comes on stream, prices fall, and profligacy can return. Because the initial Ontario and Alberta markets passed the spot price on to all consumers who had not chosen a retailer, they secured more of the benefit than jurisdictions employing fixed retail prices.

In the absence of market manipulation the competitive wholesale market provides information that simply is not available in a regulated market – a market-determined, readily available indicator of the marginal costs of electricity for every hour of every day. It provides a planning basis for the utility division of any large consumer that wants to reduce its energy costs. It provides a basis for energy service companies to develop and market energy conservation strategies that take advantage of this detailed information. Even residential consumers are induced to consider their electricity bills and how to conserve money by saving electricity.

What about the overall level of prices? Some advocates of competition promise higher efficiency and therefore lower prices. Environmentalists have objected to electricity restructuring in the expectation that it will reduce average electricity prices and thereby encourage more consumption and more pollution. However, although restructuring has reduced average prices in some cases, that result is not guaranteed by theory or experience. In Canada, where most utilities are Crown corporations, restructuring that involves privatization will increase the cost of capital and involve the payment of new taxes, and this will at least partly offset the cost savings from higher efficiency. Moreover, some restructuring designs increase the risks faced by market participants, and risk management is costly. Risk management costs must be passed on to consumers. I believe that in the long run, efficiency gains from restructuring in Canada will outweigh the increased costs, but the opposite result is possible. Furthermore, whatever the long-term average trend, there will be times when demand is high or generation capacity is short and prices may be higher for days, months, or even years until investors are attracted to install new capacity, just as there may be times when demand is low, capacity is high, and prices are low for months or even years. Finally, some jurisdictions may benefit from securing some portion of their power from inherently low-cost sources, such as the Adam Beck generating station in Ontario or many of the early low-cost hydroelectric sites in Quebec.

As these jurisdictions expand their capacity, the average cost of power will have to rise to cover the costs of new generation that is more expensive. But if pricing moves to a marginal cost basis, power will generally be priced at the cost of the newer high-cost units, and the legacy generators rather than the customers will reap the benefits of the low-cost generation. In short, it would be imprudent to promise any particular level of prices for any particular time in a restructured market.

Electricity Pricing and Sustainable Responses

What does this pricing have to do with sustainability? If customers pay marginal cost prices on an hourly basis, peak demands will be reduced as those customers find ways to reduce their usage when the price is high. Residential water heaters can be turned off for a few hours. Commercial buildings can turn off the air conditioning chillers for a few hours, especially if they have installed some 'cool storage' in the system. Electricity-intensive industries may decide to operate at night rather than in the daytime, or to shut down for a few days or weeks when the price soars. One meat packer in Australia noted that the electricity price was near zero at night, and virtually eliminated his electricity costs by running his freezers only at night, storing ice that kept the meat cold during the day. These economic responses to high prices will reduce peak demand. Reduced peak demand will in turn reduce the need for new generation capacity. This will reduce the environmental harms associated with the construction of that capacity. Since the facilities used for peak generation are usually energy-inefficient (low capital cost, high operating cost) and highly polluting, smoothing out the peaks and valleys in demand will reduce total air pollution even when there is no reduction in the total amount of electricity generated.

Moreover, customers with large heating or air conditioning demands will discover that the price is high just at the time these systems are used the most, and will be induced to invest in more efficient systems and better insulation. They will lower their thermostats in the winter and raise them in the summer. This will reduce total electricity consumption, thereby reducing total air pollution from the burning of fossil fuel.

It is sometimes argued that we are facing an electric utility crisis as a result of our inability to increase generating capacity. All the good hydroelectric sites have been exploited (except perhaps in Quebec), nuclear is too expensive, coal is too dirty, wind power is expensive, all fossil fuels discharge CO_2, and natural gas will be very expensive if it is used to supply all of the anticipated demand expansion over the next decade. I do not want to argue the factual basis for these worries, but let us assume for the moment that some of them are valid and that it will therefore be difficult to significantly expand our generation capacity. Under traditional rate regulation, when demand increases and capacity does not, prices remain steady at average total cost and brownouts and blackouts become more common. Under competition, the wholesale price rises steadily – as does the retail price, except for customers on fixed price contracts – as demand pushes up the steeply sloping supply curve. Prices may be high, but shortages are much less likely when enough of the load faces some form of real-time pricing. In short, the competitive system should be better able than traditional regulation to limit demand in the event of a supply shortage. If environmental concerns limit new investment in capacity, high prices will limit consumption. Energy conservation projects that have stood dormant because the payback periods are too long will be dusted off and implemented. In short, restructured markets can be the environmentalists' best friend. We should not be unguarded in our enthusiasm for this price mechanism, however, since the California, Alberta, and Ontario experiences remind us that angry consumers may ask governments to intervene just when the price mechanism is doing its most valuable work.

One fear expressed by environmentalists about electricity restructuring is that demand-side management (DSM) programs funded by small, regulator-approved price increases will be cut back or disappear, and this has in fact occurred in many jurisdictions. However, the link between rate regulation and DSM is not inevitable. A government could restructure the electricity market and levy a charge on all wholesale electricity, with the revenues dedicated to funding DSM programs. Alternatively, the government could fund a program out of tax revenues, as with other socially desirable programs. So it is possible, at least in theory, to decouple decisions about DSM programs from the decision to restructure the electricity market.

Does the Price Reflect Environmental and Resource Concerns?

How should electricity markets respond to concerns about pollution damage? Economic theory says that the efficient rate of pollution discharge and the efficient rate of product output will be achieved if the producer pays the cost of the marginal harm for every unit of pollution discharged (Baumol and Oates, 1988, ch. 4). Making this payment will cause the producer's perceived marginal production cost to include the marginal harm – that is, the externality. Thus, efficient pollution control and electricity output should result once the generator of electricity is required to pay for the marginal harm caused by that generation, be it in a regulated monopoly or a competitive market.

This is not, of course, how most pollution regulation works. Fossil-fuelled generating stations have long been subject to emission regulations that limit the discharge of pollution in proportion to the fuel burned. If the ministry represents the public interest, these regulations should strike the right balance between costs and pollution damage. The polluter will pay for the pollution control but not for the remaining harm, so the cost of electricity will not fully reflect the pollution damage being caused (Dewees, 2001c). Moreover, some pollutants such as greenhouse gases (GHGs) are not yet regulated, and others may be insufficiently regulated. Nuclear power does not discharge much air pollution, but few rate structures include in the price of electricity the eventual cost of decommissioning those plants and disposing of their radioactive waste. Although the marginal cost of operating an existing nuclear reactor is small, the price of electricity will have to rise substantially before private investors begin building new ones, especially if they have to shoulder full financial responsibility for accidents, decommissioning, and waste disposal (Dewees, 2001a). Whether regulated or competitive, the price of electricity does not fully encompass the environmental harm that generation may cause.

There are, however, one or two bright spots. With respect to air pollution, the Ontario government has instituted a system of emissions trading to control sulphur dioxide and nitrogen oxide emissions from the electricity generation sector.[1] Emissions trading automatically causes the emission of the regulated pollutant to appear as an opportunity cost to the emitter. Thus, any province that has instituted such a system has – to the extent that it has chosen the appropriate pollution limit – corrected the underpricing of that pollutant in the economics of generation.

Simple calculations suggest that a vigorous approach to global warming may significantly increase electricity prices. Suppose that Canada imposed policies to implement the Kyoto Protocol that cost $10 per tonne of CO_2 controlled – the lower value considered in recent studies for the federal government (Canada, 2002). With a domestic emissions-trading system for CO_2, every tonne discharged by an electric utility would cost $10. In a competitive market such as in Ontario and Alberta, coal would be the fuel in the marginal plant that set the price of electricity much of the time. Every MWh of electricity generated from coal burning would lead to the emission of about 0.9 tonnes of CO_2, which would increase the price of electricity by $9/MWh. If natural gas burned in CCGT plants were on the margin, the price increase would be closer to $4/MWh. Remember that in many competitive markets, all generators receive the price bid by the highest successful bid taken, so that hydroelectric and nuclear generators receive the price established by the marginal coal or gas plant. If Canadian wholesale electricity prices were $30 to 50/MWh, a $10/tonne price of CO_2 permits would cause price increases of 10 to 20 per cent for all electricity in the competitive market. In a competitive electricity market that relied on fossil fuels, strong GHG policies would result in serious electricity price increases. This is, however, good news for environmentalists, because the price increase would reduce demand and would bring renewable electricity sources closer to being economically competitive.

Suppose on the other hand that the same emissions trading program were instituted in a traditional (i.e., regulated) electricity sector. In Ontario, where coal supplies about 25 per cent electricity, and nuclear and hydroelectric power supplies most of the rest, the above cost increases would apply to only 25 per cent of the power. Since the regulated wholesale price equals the average cost of generation, the increase in wholesale prices would be one-fourth as great as it would be if the coal plants set the market price competitively. Thus, competitive markets are much better than regulated markets at reflecting environmental costs in the price of electricity.

For environmentalists, then, restructuring brings good news. Competition will bring an opportunity to introduce cap-and-trade emissions controls, which will prevent air pollution from growing with the economy. These two systems will ensure that the price of electricity fully reflects the environmental costs of the fuel that is setting the price. Higher prices will constrain demand. Apparently, competitive electricity markets are more sustainable than traditional rate regulation.

Green Power

Environmentalists would prefer that electricity be generated from renewable sources (i.e., 'green' sources) rather than from nuclear power or the burning of fossil fuels. Renewable power sources are generally more expensive than traditional power sources, especially coal. Advocates of renewable energy are promoting regulations or laws that would require utilities to purchase renewable energy at prices above the marginal cost of conventional power, or to purchase a fixed percentage of their total power from renewable resources. The latter approach is often referred to as a renewable portfolio standard (RPS). The RPS is essentially a subsidy to renewable power, paid through a higher price on all electricity. Restructuring has reopened the debate about RPS, yet there is no inherent inconsistency between a restructured market and an RPS requirement if that is how a jurisdiction wants to subsidize renewable power.

There have also been calls for rules that would allow retailers to label and sell 'green power,' subject to an audit to ensure that the source is indeed renewable. The Ontario Market Design Committee provided for the definition of 'green power' and established rules under which retailers could label and market qualifying electricity (Market Design Committee, 1998, 5–6). Any generator can invest in green power, certify the source, and then advertise this power to customers. Typically, green power comes at a premium price because it is more costly to generate. Experience shows that only a small fraction of customers are willing to pay more for green power, so sales are usually modest. The problem is the usual one with public goods – if I purchase green power, I share the benefits with all residents of southern Ontario, yet I pay the full price. Thus, green power marketing is best seen as a niche market and as a means of initiating the generation of renewable power. It is not a means of making substantial inroads into the supply of conventional power.

The debate over RPS and other subsidies to renewable power sources raises a question: Why do we want to encourage renewable power? Is it because there is too much pollution from conventional power? If so, the more direct solution would be to tighten our regulation of that pollution until we have achieved the desired level. If the optimal regulations are so costly that renewable energy becomes competitive with conventional power, renewable power will begin to succeed on its own. And if not, we should not worry because we will still get the environmental result that we wanted in any event. Raising the cost of conventional power will lead to overall power conservation, whereas subsidizing renewable power provides no incentives to conserve. Moreover, once we start down the road of subsidies, the program may be moulded by the industry to promote generation that is not necessarily as renewable as we might wish.

Will the California Crisis Be Repeated in Canada?

There is considerable worry that the debacle in California might be repeated in other markets, including those in Canada. California instituted a competitive market and within two years was suffering brownouts, blackouts, and skyrocketing prices. Utilities went bankrupt, and consumers grew furious. Government intervention virtually destroyed the market and is going to cost Californians tens of billions of dollars. Will it happen here?

The California Problem

The California power market opened in March 1998, after eight years of economic expansion during which no new generation capacity was built by the regulated public utilities, although non-utility generators installed smaller plants. After initial price drops, wholesale prices skyrocketed in 2000, propelled by drought, heat waves, market manipulation, inadequate generation capacity, and even air pollution emission limits. A retail price cap protected consumers from high prices and thus discouraged conservation. That price cap cost distributors, who were buying electricity at high wholesale prices, $10 billion in one year. Because of the distributors' financial distress, suppliers refused to sell to them without secure payment. Consumer prices were raised 30 per cent in 2001, distributors went bankrupt, the state guaranteed wholesale price payments, wholesale price caps were imposed, and environmental standards were suspended to unleash all available generation. San Diego completed its retirement of stranded debt during 2000, so its customers were not covered by the price cap after that time. This exposed them to spot prices, and they released their wrath upon the California government, which was accused by many of bungling restructuring. The state entered into long-term electricity purchase contracts when prices were high, then repudiated those contracts when prices fell. It is now questionable whether California still has a competitive market at all (see, for example, Joskow, 2001; Joskow and Kahn, 2001; Chandley, Harvey and Hogan, 2000; Duane, 2002).

Although California's problems were many, a few are central:

• The wholesale price was competitive, but retail prices were set at a price just below prerestructuring levels. When wholesale prices skyrocketed, losses for distributors were inevitable and ultimately ruinous. Worse, consumers had no financial incentive to conserve power even as blackouts rolled over them. The problem was not, as Schott suggests in the next chapter, that demand exceeded supply, but rather that the retail price, being fixed, could not function to match demand to supply.

- The distribution utilities were encouraged to sell their generation plants but were discouraged from entering into long-term supply contracts, because their customers could flee to competitive retailers at any time.
- The separation of the day-ahead PX market from the dispatch of the independent system operator, along with a system of scheduling coordinators, provided rich opportunities for generators to 'game' the system and raise prices.
- The price of electricity was uniform over substantial areas, instead of varying according to grid congestion, and this created further opportunities for generators to game the system.
- Other design aspects facilitated price manipulation by generators, especially when supply was tight and prices were already high.

The limited supply and surge in demand would have led to a power shortage in 2000 with or without restructuring. The flaws in market design turned this shortage into a crisis and a financial disaster.

The Alberta and Ontario Designs

The original Ontario and Alberta markets adopted a mandatory power pool and passed the spot prices directly to consumers, with distribution costs and other fees added on. There was no price cap, so distributors could not be caught between a fluctuating wholesale price and a fixed retail price. The wholesale price was determined by bids from generators, so the system operators could dispatch plants in merit order. Neither jurisdiction adopted locational marginal cost pricing (which would have allowed prices in different locations to vary with transmission line congestion), although in Ontario, locational pricing was supposed to be examined eighteen months after the market opened. Consumers in both jurisdictions who were worried about price fluctuations were encouraged to consider purchasing electricity from retailers offering fixed price contracts. These designs were fundamentally more sound than California's.

The Alberta market design, developed from the Electrical Utilities Act[2] of 1995, was robust; however, it did impose the risks of price fluctuations on consumers. They were encouraged to purchase fixed price contracts, or contracts for differences, from retailers, but few did. Despite steady economic growth, there was no new investment in generation capacity for five years or so pending the resolution of some market design issues. By 1999, prices had doubled from their 1996 values, and in 2000 they rose even higher. Consumers complained, and the government implemented a consumer protection plan, the regulated rate option (RRO). Residential consumers in 2001 paid a high regulated price, 11 cents/kWh, but received a rebate of $40 per month, yielding an average electricity cost of 6.5 cents/kWh for the average consumer. The RRO set a high marginal price for electricity, which preserved the incentive to conserve electricity; then the fixed monthly rebate relieved the financial burden of the high price. For medium and large commercial and industrial customers, the price was the same as in the RRO, but there was also a per-kWh rebate that reduced the net price to 7.6 cents/kWh. Beginning in 2002, utilities offered their own RRO rates, which in November 2002 ranged from 4.8 cents to 6.8 cents/kWh; at the same time, retailers offered fixed price contracts.[3] This RRO has apparently brought stability to the Alberta market while encouraging conservation. However, the generation market is highly concentrated, with two firms often setting the price, so a truly competitive result seems improbable.

The original design for the Ontario market included a feature intended to restrict the exercise of market power by the dominant generator, Ontario Power Generation, that also protected consumers from price increases until a competitive market structure was achieved. If the wholesale price received by OPG averaged over 3.8 cents/kWh for a full year, OPG would have to take its excess revenue, multiply it by a fraction representing roughly the proportion of Ontario demand served by OPG, and distribute this as a rebate to all Ontario consumers in proportion to their electricity consumption during the year in question. In the first year of market operation, the rebate would have been half or more of the excess of the annual average price over 3.8 cents. The purpose of this rebate, as specified in the Market Power Mitigation Framework, was to restrain OPG from exercising the market power it enjoyed as a result of its dominant position, until OPG sold or leased most of its generating stations to others and the market structure became competitive. It also gave OPG an incentive to decontrol or sell off price-setting generation plants to reduce the rebate. The stability that this rebate was to give consumers in the first few years of the market operation was an additional and valuable benefit.

By the time the Ontario market opened in May 2002, the California disaster and the Alberta gyrations had been well publicized. Almost one-quarter of Ontario consumers purchased fixed price contracts before the market opened, ensuring price security for themselves. Still, during 2002 the wholesale price was far above 3.8 cents, averaging over 5 cents for the first six months of market operation, the result of a drought, the failure to restart two nuclear units, and record high summer temperatures. Consumers seemed not to understand that they were to receive a rebate, or they were unable to wait until the following year to receive it. Even more disturbing is that many simply saw that their bills were 50 per cent higher than the previous summer and failed to recognize that their heavy use of air conditioning accounted for perhaps half this increase. They also seemed unaware that the price had been frozen between 1993 and 2001 and would have to increase significantly if generation costs were to be covered and the stranded debt repaid, quite apart from restructuring. They showed no interest in the fact that high prices would lead to conservation, which would mitigate the supply crunch. In any event, consumers complained and the government responded.

On 11 November 2002, Premier Ernie Eves announced that the retail price of electricity would be capped at 4.3 cents/kWh and that the cap would be made retroactive to 1 May 2002. Wholesale prices would be unaffected, but there would be a subsidy for the difference between that price and 4.3 cents. Consumers would receive a rebate cheque of $75 before Christmas and a further cheque the following spring. It seemed that the money for this would come from OPG, thus increasing the stranded debt. In a single stroke, the government had embraced the most serious defect in the California market: a retail price cap with a market-determined wholesale price. The government said that the price cap would be self-financing – this, even though wholesale prices were likely to stay above 5 cents at least until two nuclear units returned to service (which would not occur until the fall of 2003). This price cap scheme had several unintended effects. First, it discouraged electricity retailing, since nobody could make money competing with 4.3 cents. Second, it discouraged electricity conservation, since it eliminated price as a means of restraining demand. Third, potential investors in new generation now wonder how long it will take the government to tire of subsidizing the difference between the wholesale price and 4.3 cents and cap the wholesale price as well. Only a reckless investor would put equity into Ontario generation after 11

November 2002 without a long-term price guarantee by the government. OPG still has a 70 per cent market share and a duty to sell or lease the majority of its generating capacity to create a competitive structure, but no investor is likely to pay much for its plants, given the risk of further government intervention. Prospects for decontrol are now as moribund as the prospect of new investment, and consumer prices have been capped for several years, Ontario's competitive market has been destroyed by the government. It took them just half a year.

The election of a Liberal government in October 2003 was quickly followed by a statement that the price cap was too costly for the government to sustain and that it would be raised within a month. Increasing the price cap will reduce the government's fiscal problems and induce some electricity conservation; yet so long as any price cap remains, investors will worry about the government meddling in the market. And even if the price cap is replaced with a regulated price, we will still have a 'competitive' wholesale price set by a highly uncompetitive market structure. Most generating capacity will still be owned by the government, investment in generation by the public generator will continue to fail the market test, and retail prices for small consumers will still not vary with market conditions. This is nobody's idea of a well-restructured electricity market. The new government must come up with a renewed vision of restructuring and move forward with that model to restore coherence to electricity policy in Ontario.

The Experience Elsewhere

More than a dozen markets have restructured, and in many of the others it has worked well. In England and Wales, generation costs fell dramatically after restructuring began in 1988. This was partly the result of declining coal and gas prices and partly the result of increased labour productivity and improvements in the performance of nuclear plants. Consumer prices fell, contrary to Schott's assertion in chapter 7, but not as much as profits of generators rose. In Victoria, Australia, a monopoly generator was split into five one-plant firms; this was followed by similar divestment in four other states. By 2001, there were seventeen generators competing in a national market; the result was improved plant utilization, better reliability, lower costs, and reduced prices to consumers. In New Zealand, a monopoly gen-

erator was split into two principal firms and a market power mitigation agreement was imposed. Consumer prices for electricity fell about
20 per cent between 1992 and 2000 and new capacity has been built. In
1977, utilities in eastern Pennsylvania, New Jersey, Delaware, and eastern Maryland initiated a regional bid-based electricity market. The
incumbent utilities are still in place, but customers can now choose
their supplier, and generation is competitive. The market seems to be
working smoothly. These systems show that restructuring can be carried through without crisis.

Special Issues for Electricity Restructuring in Canada

Ontario has six thermal plants that will set the price much of the time.
If we are to achieve a competitive generation structure, the largest of
these plants will have to be owned and operated by separate firms.
Not only must one firm not own two of them, but the owners should
not compete in other markets, lest they compete less here for fear of
retaliation there. Because of the varying sizes of the six thermal plants,
a competitive structure is possible although it will not be easy to
achieve. Worse, government statements about retiring coal plants in
the near future have made them difficult to sell – a problem exacerbated by uncertainty regarding the vigour with which the federal government will pursue its Kyoto commitments. Without a competitive
structure, the risks of market power, market manipulation, and high
prices are considerable.

If a competitive structure will only be achieved with difficulty in
Ontario, how can smaller provinces with fewer generation plants
achieve competitive structures? Given the vast geography of most provinces and the limited capacity of transmission lines, to what extent can
generators actually compete with one another? Can competition among
provinces supplement competition within provinces? Is such competition feasible at times of peak demand, when it is most necessary but
the lines are most congested? There are substantial challenges to spread-
ing the model of competition in Canada.

Another Canadian problem is that most provinces have a long tra-
dition of public ownership of electric utilities. Public power is part of
the provincial culture, and the public holds the government responsible for price and reliability. It may be difficult for the public to
accept a competitive market and not blame the government when
prices rise. It may be difficult for the government to give up responsi-

bility for a large economic activity with its opportunities for satisfying the public demand for cheap power, for creating jobs, and for subsidizing favoured customers. It may be difficult for the government to sell generation assets that the public has regarded as 'theirs' for decades.

Governing the Restructuring Process

In the early stages of its market design, California was warned about the dangers of some features it was considering, yet it stayed the course to disaster. How could California have ignored principles that in retrospect seem self-evident? Some answers to this question are ominous for all jurisdictions. An electricity system is an intricate web that offers enormous opportunities for market participants to impose externalities on one another (Wilson, 2002). Extensive rules are necessary to minimize these opportunities and to ensure an economically efficient market design. In short, the electricity market is quite artificial and is basically a system of extensive, detailed rules. Yet every jurisdiction is different, so the market must be custom designed each time. The market is so complex that those who participate in it must be involved in the design to ensure that it meets all local needs and to ensure that everyone understands it well enough to participate intelligently when it opens. But when big generators, big transmission companies, big energy traders, and big energy-using industries gather around the table, who will stand up for economic efficiency? Who will look out for the public interest generally, and the interests of small consumers? Once the rules have been written, how are we to ensure that powerful interests will not change them to their own advantage? Some of California's design flaws were the result of demands by powerful interests, who were well served by them until the collapse.

The second problem is that the public will not easily understand the merits of fluctuating prices, nor of high prices at times of power shortage, nor even of prices high enough to cover costs, so long as increasing debt seems capable of keeping prices low. Evidence for this is the public demand for protection from high prices that arose in California, Alberta, and Ontario. Governments have difficulty resisting public demands for protection when prices rise, as evidenced by the reaction in those three jurisdictions. Yet private investment will occur only if investors can reap the high prices as well as the low prices. The business press has denounced Ontario's 11 November 2002 price caps as having crushed any hope of new private investment in generation. The greatest risk in competitive electricity markets may not be power shortages or heat waves but government intervention – sovereign risk. It is not clear what governments can do to block their own future intervention, nor to reassure investors once they have intervened.

These are public choice problems for which the solutions are not obvious. When we become disillusioned about economic regulation after real regulators are captured by industry or other powerful interests, how can we think that a democratic restructuring process will not succumb as well? In short, the market design process itself may not be sustainable. It is too early to tell how often this process will create competitive markets that achieve the efficiency gains for which they are admired.

Conclusions

The environmental effects of electricity sector restructuring seem to be mixed. On the one hand, restructuring may (although it need not) sweep aside demand-side management programs and subsidies to renewable generation that are not competitive economically, leading to increased pollution emissions. On the other hand, if competition means more real-time pricing for consumers, demand may be curtailed and resources saved that might have been devoted to new facilities. If environmental concerns seriously limit new construction, competition will direct new investment toward those power sources that can meet those environmental concerns at least cost. Competition may increase the financial pressure to use low-cost coal in place of cleaner natural gas, but it may also increase the attractiveness of building new plants fired by natural gas because of their short lead times. Competitive markets may better incorporate the shadow price of pollution discharge into the price of electricity. Competitive markets permit the selling of 'green' power, which provides a niche market for certain environmentally friendly technologies. The net environmental effects of these forces are uncertain, but competition combined with strict environmental standards could easily lead to environmental improvement.

Competition promises more efficient use of electricity because prices will then reflect marginal costs so long as the market is truly competitive. In many jurisdictions, however, restructuring has led to only modest changes in the price structures faced by most consumers, so that only some of the environmental gains that might come from restructuring have been achieved. Furthermore, some jurisdictions that passed the spot price on to consumers disabled that price mechanism after prices rose, raising questions as to whether efficient pricing is politically feasible. In addition, some real-time pricing is possible in regulated markets. Much work remains to be done on the design of retail price structures to ensure that competition will lead to more efficient pricing.

The California crisis of 2000 has raised concerns whether competitive electricity markets are sustainable. Electricity markets are extremely complex, and it is unlikely that any legislature will understand them well enough to choose efficient designs by itself. A public choice analysis of the restructuring process suggests that powerful industry stakeholders may try to control the process of writing the rules initially, and of revising them over time, to their advantage and perhaps against the public interest. In addition, when prices rise, as they will from time to time, the public will demand that the government protect them. The California and Ontario cases show that a government's response can devastate the market. At a minimum, this should lead us to pay more attention to design processes and to the processes by which rules are revised after the market opens. It remains to be seen whether governments can actually develop designs that achieve the efficiency gains for which competition is admired, and whether they can sustain those designs over time.

NOTES

I am grateful to Lisa Chapman for her able research assistance on this chapter.

1 *Emissions Trading*, O.Reg. 397/01.
2 R.S.A., 2001, c. E-5.5.
3 See www.customerchoice.gov.ab.ca/elect/images/summary_2002.pdf[.]

REFERENCES

Ando, Amy W., and Karen L. Palmer. 1998. *Getting on the Map: The Political Economy of State-Level Electricity Restructuring.* Discussion Paper 98/19 Washington DC: Resources for the Future.

Baumol, William J., and Wallace E. Oates. 1988. *The Theory of Environmental Policy*. Cambridge: Cambridge University Press.

Canada. 2002. 'A Discussion Paper on Canada's Contribution to Addressing Climate Change.' Ottawa: Public Works and Government Services Canada.

Chandley, John D., Scott M. Harvey, and William W. Hogan. 2000. 'Electricity Market Reform in California.' www.aei.org/past_event/conf010614b.pdf[.]

Dewees, Donald N. 2001a. 'The Future of Nuclear Power in a Restructured Electricity Market.' Pg. 147–73 in G. Bruce Doern, Arslan Dorman, and Robert W. Morrison, eds., *Canadian Nuclear Energy Policy*. Toronto: University of Toronto Press.

– 2001b. 'Price and Environment in Electricity Restructuring.' Paper presented to the Canadian Law and Economics Association, 26 September 2001, University of Toronto. www.chass.utoronto.ca/ecipa/archive/UT-ECIPA-DEWEES-01-01.pdf[.]

– 2001c. 'Emissions Trading: ERC's or Allowances?' *Land Economics* 77, no. 4: 513–26.

Duane, Timothy P. 2002. 'Regulation's Rationale: Learning from the California Energy Crisis.' *Yale Journal on Regulation* 19, no. 2: 471–540.

Faruqui, Ahmad, and Stephen S. George. 2002. 'The Value of Dynamic Pricing in Mass Markets.' *The Electricity Journal* 15, no. 6: 45–55.

Joskow, Paul L. 1997. 'Restructuring, Competition and Regulatory Reform in the U.S. Electricity Sector.' *Journal of Economic Perspectives* 11, no. 3: 119–38.

– 2001. Working Paper 8442, 'California's Electricity Crisis.' Cambridge, MA: National Bureau of Economic Research.

Joskow, Paul L., and Edward Kahn. 2001. 'A Quantitative Analysis of Pricing Behavior in California's Wholesale Electricity Market During Summer 2000.' Washington, DC: AEI-Brookings Joint Center. Working Paper 01-01.

Joskow, Paul L., and Richard Schmalensee. 1983. *Markets for Power: An Analysis of Electric Utility Deregulation*. Cambridge, MA: MIT Press.

Market Design Committee. 1998. *Second Interim Report of the Market Design Committee*. Toronto: Ontario Market Design Committee.

O'Sheasy, Michael T. 2002. 'Is Real-Time Pricing a Panacea? If So, Why Isn't It More Widespread?' *Electricity Journal* 15, no. 10: 24–34.

Spine, Havel Nos. 2002. 'Demand Response: The Future Ain't What It Used To Be – Or Is It?' *Electricity Journal* 15, no. 5: 78–86.

Wilson, Robert. 2002. 'Architecture of Power Markets.' *Econometrica* 70, no. 4: 1299–1340.

Chapter 6

Canada–U.S. Electricity Trade and the Climate Change Agenda

SCOTT VAUGHAN, C. LINE CARPENTIER,
ZACHARY PATTERSON, AND PAUL MILLER

One of the most contentious debates in Canada in recent memory has been over the ratification of the Kyoto Protocol. In early September 2002, following a highly divisive political debate, the prime minister announced at the Johannesburg, South Africa, World Summit that the Canadian Parliament would be asked to vote on ratification of the Kyoto Protocol (Chrétien, 2002). Since that announcement, the climate debate has intensified. The sharpest point of controversy involves economic costs. This chapter does not endeavour to answer the cost question directly; rather, it looks at the Canadian electricity sector in the context of the Americans' decision not to ratify Kyoto, the evolving nature of the North American electricity market, and the implications of these for greenhouse gas (GHG) emissions and Canada's GHG reduction commitments under the Kyoto Protocol. This chapter first reviews the Intergovernmental Panel on Climate Change (IPCC) and Kyoto Protocol commitments and their implications for Canada in terms of CO_2 emission reductions. Then it considers trends in and possible future scenarios for Canada's electricity sector in the context of CO_2 emissions. The chapter discusses the factors influencing Canada's electricity trade, focusing especially on political support for electricity trade expansion and integration, market restructuring, and NAFTA. Because the future of the electricity sector is so closely tied to market restructuring, important lessons on the future of the electricity sector and CO_2 emissions can be drawn from past work that considered the environmental implications of market restructuring. From this work, it seems that CO_2 emissions are likely to increase as a result of restructuring and that trade is also likely to increase. As a result of the relationship between electricity trade, market integration, and restructuring, the costs that Canada will face in satisfying its commitments under the Kyoto Protocol are likely to increase. That having been said, there is a fair bit of quiet convergence on a range of other policies, namely on energy efficiency, renewable energy and emissions trading. Although these policies are unlikely to entirely offset the costs of Kyoto, there is obvious potential for Canada to reduce the overall costs it faces to satisfy its commitments under the Kyoto Protocol.

The IPCC, the Kyoto Protocol, and CO_2

An extensive body of scientific literature has demonstrated the links between energy use, GHG emissions, and climate change. Since the late 1980s, scientific literature produced by the IPCC has shown that different energy sources emit different amounts of carbon. Thus, coal and petroleum emit relatively high amounts of GHGs, natural gas emits less of them, hydroelectric power less still, and nuclear, wind, and solar power very little or none. Although work in calibrating the precise impact of these fuel groups on climate change continues, the scientific consensus within the IPCC is that fossil fuels are a powerful source of GHGs and that reductions in GHGs will be necessary to stabilize the global climate (IPCC, 2001).

The Kyoto Protocol was agreed to in December 1997, at the Third Conference of the Parties to the UN Framework Convention on Climate Change. A key component of the protocol is that all Annex 1 (developed) countries have agreed to reduce their emissions of GHGs by at least 5 per cent below 1990 levels sometime between 2008 and 2112. On the initiative of the Canadian delegation, this country set its commitment at 1 per cent higher than the average required reductions (i.e., at 6 per cent).

An extensive body of literature exists on how countries will meet their commitments by 2112. Given the potentially high adjustment costs involved, the protocol identifies three so-called flexible mechanisms: Annex 1 Joint Implementation, the Clean Development Mechanism, and International Emissions Trading. (A fourth approach, involving a variation of the 'bubble' approach, is a regulatory concept in which two or more emission sources are treated as a single source.)

Planned Capacity and CO_2 Emissions in Canada

Flexible policies are intended to reduce the implementation costs of Kyoto. For example, price-formation effects stemming from Kyoto's flexible mechanisms are already creating new markets in areas such as emissions trading and the Clean Development Mechanism (CDM). (Some estimates suggest the global carbon offset market will exceed US$20 billion per year [UNCTAD, 1998]; however, more recent estimates are lower.) As a Kyoto participant, Canada can participate fully with other Kyoto parties in these activities. As a non-party, the United States either cannot do so or is limited to some market-based activities. Even though they reduce costs, these market-based measures will not offset costs. The situation in Canada will probably look something like this: the price of carbon-intensive fuels (in particular, coal and petroleum) will rise, and their demand will decline. Depending on our assumptions about cross-price elasticity, the demand for fuel substitutes will increase. However, an overall reduction in total energy demand will likely occur, leading to slower growth in productivity, reduced capital formation, the reallocation of some labour markets (from skilled to lower-wage jobs), and a decline in gross national product. This is the picture that emerges from one exercise that modelled a tax on carbon-intensive fuels in the United States to address climate change (Jorgenson and Wilcoxen, 1998).

How does this very general scenario fit with Canada's planned capacity expansion in one important energy subsector – the electricity sector? *Environmental Challenges and Opportunities of the Evolving North American Electricity Market* (CEC, 2002a), a report sponsored by the North American Commission for Environmental Cooperation, made estimates of the potential CO_2 emissions from new power generation in Canada (and the other NAFTA countries).

Unlike electricity forecasts, such as those produced on a regular basis by the National Energy Board (NEB) and Natural Resources Canada (NRCan), the CEC analysis used a publicly available database of announced new power plant projects (along with announced planned closures) to estimate CO_2 emissions associated with generation capacity changes through the year 2007 (RDI/Platts, 2001). This database provides excellent insight into actual planned capacity.

Because there are at present no mandatory programs for reducing CO_2 emissions in Canada, the analysis does not assume CO_2 controls in 2007. The analysis has a 'high boundary' scenario which assumes that all announced power plant projects will go forward, and estimates the CO_2 emissions associated with that scenario. However, since on average, less than 40 per cent of announced power plant projects are actually completed (NEPDG, 2001),[1] the CEC analysis also includes a 'low boundary' scenario that includes only power plants already in advanced stages of planning, construction, or startup. Potential future CO_2 emissions from new generation likely fall somewhere between the two scenarios.[2]

Table 6.1 displays the projected range of future CO_2 emissions in Canada associated with new power plant projects through 2007, as well as the sector's contribution to CO_2 emissions in 1990. The amount of potential CO_2 emissions reflects fuel choices that are presumably influenced by a variety of cost factors, including the cost of natural gas relative to coal. To place the CO_2 emissions in perspective, the table includes total CO_2 emissions from electricity generation during a recent year, 1998. This is not a projection of future growth in CO_2 emissions, since the new plants may displace some currently operating plants. If the displaced generation comes from older, relatively less efficient fossil fuel power plants, this will offset to some extent the growth in CO_2 emissions from new plants. The point of placing the new CO_2 emissions against the total amount from a recent year (1998) is to achieve a sense of the scale of CO_2 emissions Canada may face from new fossil fuel power plants still to come on line while it is seeking to reduce current CO_2 emissions to meet Kyoto targets.

By 1998, according to the CEC's estimate, the electricity sector's emissions had increased by 28 per cent over 1990 levels (Miller et al., 2002; Environment Canada, 2002a). For the 2007 low-boundary case, the increase in CO_2 emissions is relatively low relative to 1998 emissions – only about 3 per cent. This figure reflects the projection that most new fossil fuel capacity in Canada will be from natural gas (about 4,400 MW). The high-boundary scenario, however, places this same figure at about 15 per cent. This reflects not only more announced natural gas projects (about 8,600 MW), but also a much larger share of CO_2 from planned projects using more carbon-intensive coal (1,750 MW).

Canada is expected to ratify the Kyoto Protocol. The pressure of new CO_2 emissions from the fossil fuel choices made by the Canadian electricity sector raises the possibility of changes in the sites chosen for new plants. If Canada accepts the functional equivalent of a carbon cap in order to meet its Kyoto targets, while the United States continues without one, new generating plants may well try to locate in the United States while continuing to serve Canadian markets. Something similar has already happened in the context of smog along the California–Baja California border. Southern California has a serious smog problem, and fossil fuel power plants can emit large quantities of

Table 6.1
Summary of national emission totals in the reference inventory case and the high and low boundary scenarios.

Country scenario	Annual CO_2 (tonnes)
Canada 1990 CO_2 emissions from electricity sector	95,300,000
Canada 1998 CO_2 emissions from electricity sector	122,000,000
Canada high boundary, 2007	18,828,537
Canada low boundary, 2007	3,743,487

Source: Miller et al., 2002, 46; Environment Canada, 2002a, 5

nitrogen oxides, a pollutant that contributes to smog formation. In Southern California, there is a cap on the total amount of nitrogen oxides that can be emitted, and new sources are required to offset their emissions from existing sources in order to stay within the cap. This can be expensive for large sources, such as power plants, so there can be a financial advantage to locating outside the capped area.

Power plant developers have been building facilities fuelled by natural gas south of the California border, in Baja California. These will sell electricity back to California. Even if the new power plants meet the same stringent emission limits as California's (some power developers say they will), these plants will not offset the new pollution they produce by seeking equivalent or greater reductions from existing sources within the same air basin. Regarding GHGs, the planet's atmosphere is essentially one 'air basin.' This means that siting plants in order to avoid emissions caps cannot but undermine those caps' integrity, no matter where sources locate outside the capped region. Of course, siting decisions are also influenced by access to transmission lines, transportation costs of fuel, and other factors, so decisions on where to place new power plants are not entirely unconstrained.

At least one factor could dilute this effect – the fact that although American utilities do not operate under any CO_2 constraints, they do face emission caps for other air pollutants – notably nitrogen oxides (NO_x) and sulfur dioxide (SO_2) – under the U.S. Clean Air Act regulations and potentially under the proposed 'Clear Skies' initiative. Since there is a strong relationship between CO_2 and these other controlled substances (see Figure 6.1), there may still be constraints (even if indirect) on the amount of CO_2 these plants can emit.

Figure 6.1. Average emission rates for U.S. power plants in 1998, by fuel type

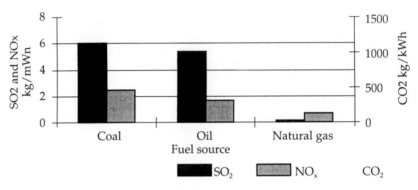

Source: EGRID 2000 Database (EPA, 2000)

Trends and Factors in Canada's Electricity Trade

GHG emissions from the electricity sector, and from Canada more generally, will be affected by how the trade in electricity develops. First, though, it is important for us to place electricity trade in perspective. The energy sector contributes approximately 6 per cent to Canada's gross domestic product, and it directly employs around 293,000 people (NEB, 2002). Energy exports to the United States represent 12 per cent of total Canadian export earnings. Between 1990 and 2001, the Canada–U.S. trade in energy tripled to $37.3 billion, the Canada–Mexico trade quintupled to $295 million, and the U.S.–Mexico trade doubled to $13.5 billion (all in USD). In 2001, energy exports generated $58 billion in earnings – a high point to date, and an increase from $54.5 billion in 2000 and from $30.4 billion in 1999 (ibid.).

Petroleum and natural gas account for almost 75 per cent of Canada's energy exports to the American market. In contrast, electricity exports comprise only six per cent of Canada's total energy export earnings. However, the relationship between the natural gas and electricity markets is strong; a significant proportion of Canadian natural gas exports go to fuel electricity generation in the United States. This trend is expected to continue: the majority of planned expansion in electricity generation in the United States as well as Canada is going to be based on natural gas.

At present, a number of factors are driving the convergence of the Canadian and American electricity markets. Four of these are discussed below: political support for a North American electricity market; the restructuring of some electricity markets in the United States and Canada; the evolution of very large regional transmission organizations; and NAFTA.

Political Support

The integration of the Canadian and American energy markets has been underway for some time. In contrast, the political interest in forging stronger policy and regulatory links is relatively recent. This political focus found expression in a common statement from the three leaders of the NAFTA countries that established the North American Energy Working Group (NAEWG), a technical-level forum intended to foster communication and coordination efforts in support of efficient North American energy markets.[3]

The objective of the NAEWG has its roots in the emphasis that the Bush Administration has placed on finding hemispheric approaches to managing energy interdependence. In March 2001, the United States described the relationship as follows:

> Mexico and Canada are two of the most important and secure suppliers of oil to the United States, and the U.S. is the biggest market for their oil. In addition, the United States is also a net importer of natural gas from Canada, and recently, at least, a net exporter to Mexico. As new fields of both oil and gas are developed in the Atlantic by Canada, both the Maritime Provinces and New England will have access to more affordable energy. (Abraham, 2001, 28)

Market Restructuring

Industry analysts continue to track the changes in electricity markets. Considerable research has been done regarding how electricity markets can be opened to competitive forces. The debate over this in Canada has its own internal dynamic but has tended to follow the initiatives that began in the United States and are continuing there. The exception is Alberta, which began restructuring before most American efforts.

The U.S. Federal Energy Regulatory Commission (FERC) formally launched a national restructuring of the wholesale electricity market in the United States with FERC Orders 888 and 889. These orders sought to open electricity generators' access to transmission lines outside their traditional service territories, for the purpose of promoting greater competition among producers of electricity at the wholesale level. Several American states pursued their own restructuring at the retail level. Common features of retail restructuring include the unbundling of monopolistic or oligopolistic vertically integrated utilities into distinct components within markets. This unbundling has generally involved creating stand-alone electric power generation companies, for-profit transmission entities, and financial intermediaries (including power brokers and traders), as well as various electric end-use service providers.

The restructuring of the American electricity sector is far from complete. Of interest here is how strongly regulatory reforms underway in that country have influenced changes in Canada. It is clear that Canada – with the possible exception of Alberta – has been a follower rather than a leader of market reforms, and that the reference point is, not surprisingly, the United States. For example, an analysis by the International Energy Agency of the OECD notes that the views of FERC 'have had a major impact on the development of policy in Canada. It is likely that competitive markets will continue to develop in some provinces to bring about domestic market structures to conform, in part, with US FERC policies' (IEA, 2000, 13).

In Canada, the pace of change toward open competition remains highly uneven. Alberta is still the front runner in introducing restructuring. Since 1 January 2001, consumers in Alberta have been entitled to choose among electricity producers. This greater choice on the retail side is the most visible sign of Alberta's restructuring initiative, which began in 1996. At one point, reforms in Ontario were well underway, most visibly with the breakup of Ontario Hydro into distinct corporate entities. However, as Dewees discusses in chapter 5, Ontario's restructuring was effectively halted by policy actions announced in November 2002. Several other provinces, notably New Brunswick, British Columbia, and Nova Scotia, have signalled their willingness to initiate market restructuring.

The Evolution of Regional Transmission Organizations (RTOs)

FERC Orders 888 and 889 initiated some of the most important reforms affecting competition policy in the American electricity sector.

However, some obstacles persisted, especially for smaller or independent power producers attempting to access transmission grids. In response, the FERC issued Order 2000, which ensured open access on a non-discriminatory basis to transmission grids by segregating power marketing and power transmission activities. The centrepiece of FERC Order 2000 is the establishment of huge regional transmission organizations (RTOs). In essence, the RTOs will set the ground rules for ensuring a seamless transmission grid; they will also coordinate the planning and integration of the transmission infrastructure and set rules for transmission-related investments.

RTOs will have profound implications for the Canadian electricity trade, both international and interprovincial. Improved integration of transmission planning and investments may mean that Canadian exporters will be able to improve their access to the American market. This assumes that better planning of transmission policies will, over time, alleviate transmission congestion. There is evidence that such congestion in transmission grids has led to a reduction in hydro exports from Quebec to New England (Vaughan et al., 2002, n147). So a crucial question is, how will Canada respond to the creation of RTOs? If these RTOs result in seamless transmission grids, should Canada remain a distinct entity with non-discriminatory access to that grid, or should it position its transmission policies within RTOs? Following the release of FERC Order 2000, the NEB noted: 'Canadian entities are not subject to FERC regulations, but due to the integrated nature of the North American transmission system, it appears that Canadian involvement in RTO formation could be potentially beneficial to all market participants, provided proper approaches for joint overseeing of cross-border RTOs are adopted' (8). Basically, the NEB was stating that it would benefit Canadian-based electric utilities to join the RTOs which are subject to the regulatory overview of an American federal regulatory body. But the NEB was unclear about what 'joint overseeing' might entail and how it might be received by the FERC.

NAFTA Chapter Six

Canada must decide whether to remain outside the RTOs. This reflects the concern that we might not be guaranteed equal access to American transmission grids. That said, the main purpose of FERC Order 2000 is to address discriminatory practices within the United States regarding access to the grid. In principle, NAFTA disciplines discriminatory practices that affect international market access; it also provides an additional impetus for integrating the Canadian and American electricity markets.

NAFTA came into force in January 1994. Its Chapter Six (Energy and Basic Petrochemicals) establishes commitments for the energy sector, including trade in electricity. Under NAFTA, electricity is categorized as a good and falls under the schedules in the Harmonized System (2716.00).[4] NAFTA's Chapter Six encompasses not only trade in electricity itself, but also trade in electricity-related services and trade-related investment in the sector. Moreover, NAFTA prohibits or constrains several kinds of trade restrictions, including import and export restrictions, the use of export taxes, and other export measures.

So far, NAFTA has had a marginal impact on the cross-border electricity trade. The export of bulk electricity began well before NAFTA, mainly in the late 1970s, after the oil price shocks. Most reallocation effects relating to Canada-U.S. trade preceded NAFTA, with the implementation of the Canada-U.S. Free Trade Agreement. Given the frequency with which the trading partners engage in trade disputes (softwood lumber, steel, agriculture, textiles), it is hard to imagine a market the size of the one for electricity not being subject to trade disputes, although up to this point there has been no NAFTA jurisprudence dealing with trade in electricity (Horlick and Schuchardt, 2002).[5]

Assessing the Environmental Effects of Trade in Electricity

A key question is whether this convergence of electricity markets and related competition policies will make the Kyoto targets easier or more difficult to reach. Put another way, does Canada's role as a net exporter of electricity to the United States make a commitment to Kyoto easier or harder?

One way of answering this question is to examine the environmental effects of cross-border electricity under the more general rubric of measuring the environmental impacts of free trade. Methods include those developed in 1994 by the OECD (OECD, 1994), by the United Nations Environment Programme (UNEP, 2001), and more recently by the North American Commission for Environmental Cooperation (CEC, 2002a and 2002c). At the sectoral level, analysis of air pollution effects from Canada–U.S. electricity trade underlines the importance of comparable air regulations (for NO_x and SO_2) between the trading partners (Plagiannakos, 2002).

Conceptually, most assessment methods assume that free trade may affect the environment through scale effects. For example, when Canada accesses an export market ten times its own size, a proportion of its total electricity generation and associated environmental impacts occur because of trade. Although the figure varies from year to year, roughly 9 to 10 per cent of the total electricity generated in Canada ends up in the United States. With American electricity demand expected to increase by as much as 20 per cent by 2009 (EIA, 2001), some Canadian utilities are building new power plants explicitly to access the American market. For example, by early 2002, at least two new electric power generating projects – one in Alberta, the other south of Montreal – had been announced whose primary market would be the United States.

Changes in where electric power is generated, coupled with growth in export markets, are altering the distribution and intensity of pollution. Back-of-envelope estimates of Canadian electricity exports to the United States, for which total electricity exports are broken down by province, fuel source, and emission factors per fuel source, have found that total Canadian electricity exports to the United States in 1999 were equivalent to 3.6 million tons of CO_2 emissions,[6] some 28,300 tons of SO_2, and almost 10,000 tons of NO_x (Vaughan et al., 2002).

This relatively crude analysis suggests that Canadian electricity exports to the United States have contributed to the overall carbon levels that Canada must now reduce under the Kyoto Protocol. In order to deepen this obviously simple observation, the authors refer to a more robust analysis underway by the Energy Modeling Forum (EMF, Stanford University), which is examining the general environmental effects of restructuring. This line of inquiry is useful, because restructuring exerts changes in relative prices *within* markets that are very similar to the changes that trade liberalization exerts *between* markets. That is, the assumed benefits of electricity restructuring include reduced end prices through efficiency gains associated with the removal of the market failures of monopolies. As well, restructuring can cause changes in relative prices that are not uniform between regions, thereby prompting an expansion of interregional trade.

From the perspective of environmental quality, changes in relative electricity prices between regions are crucial. The EMF estimates that under a 'Baseline' scenario for restructuring, average wholesale electricity prices in the near term will be between $24 to $34 per MWh

(1997 USD). Prices are then expected to fall marginally over time, to $20 to $30 per MWh (EMF, 2001). Relevant to this discussion, however, is the divergence in prices between North American Electric Reliability Council (NERC) regions as restructuring proceeds.

Under the 'alternative competition' scenario, the EMF study estimates that the largest price increase relative to the baseline assumption will involve a 27 per cent price hike in the Midwestern MAIN region of NERC. The largest reduction, 22 per cent, will take place in the New York region. Many assumptions and caveats guide these regional price changes. That said, the EMF analysis reaches this important conclusion: 'In general, the lowest prices are experienced in regions which have existing low cost coal and nuclear generation sources. Regions more reliant on oil and gas-fired generation and those with higher delivered fuel costs have higher prices' (viii).

Put simply, by favouring least-cost electricity producers, restructuring will shift demand toward at least one least-cost generator – coal. This is the very worst outcome from a GHG emissions perspective. A long-standing fear of environmentalists relates to the fate of the coal-fired electric power stations in the American Midwest. These stations are presently producing under capacity. Moreover, they are benefitting from the single largest distortion in the American electricity market – 'grandfathering,' whereby air pollution limits are weaker for existing plants than Clean Air Act requirements for new plants.

Restructuring and some limited privatization in the electricity sector will increase the pressure on power plants to seek competitive positions, reduce costs, and expand markets. This could well create an incentive to run low-cost and largely depreciated units more heavily than in the past. These trends would tend to increase emissions of SO_2, NO_x, and CO_2.

To be sure, there are caveats to this. Conceivably, the shift to lower-cost production could result in more generation from hydropower and nuclear electricity; this would result in lower CO_2 emissions and thereby make it easier for Canada to satisfy its Kyoto Protocol commitments. Similarly, if more generation occurred in the United States to serve the Canadian market, GHG production would take place in the United States and thus would not have to be reduced in Canada. The point is simply that in most models, electricity market restructuring is often associated with increases in CO_2 emissions. Clearly, this is an area ripe for further research.

Forecasts Remembered

The above discussion of models was presented to give a sense of the types of results that are produced when models consider the environmental effects of electricity market restructuring. In this context, it is important to recognize that models produce results that are only as good as the assumptions that go into them. One way of testing models is to compare their predictions with actual outcomes. As part of the CEC's work on electricity and the environment (Woolf, Keith, and White, 2002), actual electricity sector emissions were compared with estimated emissions of the electricity sector found in the 1996 Final Environmental Impact Statement (FEIS) for FERC Order 888.

One assumption the FEIS made was that changes in air pollution emissions are almost entirely determined by changes in the relative prices of gas and coal (technological changes played almost no part in the analysis). The FEIS assumed that over time, coal prices would rise and natural gas prices would fall, thereby contributing to a change in the fuel mix and a relative decline in CO_2 emissions.

Compared to the actual 2000 data, analysis shows that the 'competition favours coal' scenario – the worst-case scenario from the climate and more general environmental perspectives – comes closest to the FEIS projections. Under this worst-case scenario, however, projections of CO_2 emissions from the utilities sector underestimated actual CO_2 emissions by 8 per cent. Among the conclusions of the analysis were the following:

- From 1996 to 2000, natural gas prices remained relatively high, while coal prices remained relatively low. Since projections were based almost entirely on relative fuel prices, FERC's 'competition favors coal' scenario comes closest to capturing industry trends in the United States. A key finding of the analysis is that the move to open competition under prevailing price differences is more likely to lead to increased air emissions as opposed to decreased air emissions. It is important to underline that this conclusion assumes a status quo in environmental regulations, including air pollution emission caps. In the case of Canada, accession to the Kyoto Protocol is equivalent to a cap on CO_2 emissions.
- FERC's projection of American electricity demand from 1996 to 2000 was lower than the actual growth of 4.6 per cent. This is the

main reason why CO_2 emission projections were lower than actual experience. FERC's underestimate of CO_2 emissions, however, was greater than its underestimate of electricity demand, indicating a more carbon-intensive generation mix than originally predicted.

Cooperative Efforts

It seems that the path Canada is on (ratifying Kyoto while increasing market integration and restructuring, resulting in increased trade in electricity) could make it more difficult for Canada in general – and for the electricity sector in particular – to implement the Kyoto Protocol. That having been said, there is also convergence on a range of policy fronts, such as those on energy efficiency, renewable energy, and emissions trading. While unlikely to completely offset the costs of Kyoto, these developments have at least the potential to lower those costs. Examples of such efforts follow, for the areas of energy efficiency, renewable energy, and emissions trading.

Energy Efficiency

Increasing energy efficiency is often touted as one way to reduce energy use and its associated emissions without compromising either competitiveness or quality of life. The first example of political convergence on this front was the establishment of the North American Energy Working Group, referred to earlier. One task that the NAEWG set itself at its May 2002 meeting was to examine energy efficiency standards in each of the countries and to 'continue efforts in information sharing [on] electricity, energy efficiency standards-related issues' (NAEWG, 2002).

Second, in both Canada and the United States, there are at present two major product and service energy labelling programs, one mandatory and the other voluntary. Energy Guide in the United States and EnerGuide in Canada are mandatory labelling programs that provide information on the energy efficiency of products. The labels are placed on many different products, from appliances to automobiles. Similarly, both Canada and the United States have voluntary labelling programs for energy efficiency. The American federal government promotes energy efficiency levels above minimum performance standards through its Energy Star program, which extends to approximately forty product categories and to more than 500 environmental management companies. Once a company or manufacturer meets the criteria, it can use the Energy Star seal of approval on products, in its product promotions and advertising campaigns, and for other activities. The main categories of products covered are office equipment (including fax machines, printers, copiers, computers, and monitors), residential light fixtures, exit signs, transformers, residential heating and cooling equipment, insulation, and major household appliances such as consumer electronics, television sets, and VCRs. The program estimates that in 2000, Energy Star products 'avoided' more than 864,000 pounds of CO_2 emissions, and that the cumulative cost savings from the program will have exceeded $60 billion (USD) in saved energy bills by 2010.

In Canada, the main environmental labelling program in place is the Environmental Choice program. Created in 1998, this program has awarded the Ecologo to approximately 20,000 products and services in roughly a hundred categories. Like many labelling schemes, the program uses life-cycle analysis to some degree, in that it examines the environmental characteristics of the products during their manufacture, as well as their end-use energy profiles. Examples of products covered under Environmental Choice include dishwashers, rechargeable batteries, and office products such as fax machines, photocopiers, and printers.

With respect to energy efficiency, an important cooperative move took place in July 2001, when the EPA announced a joint program with the Canadian government (through Natural Resources Canada) that would make Energy Star labels available to Canadian consumers.

Renewable Electricity

Another area in which there has been some policy convergence and political support for collective action is renewable energy. Alternative fuels are of interest to the NAEWG, and many different levels of government in North America are pursuing various renewable energy policies. For example, the Canadian government is now subsidizing wind-generated power: this program will run until at least 2007. The government expects to spend $260 million (CDN) on this incentive. Another example is the production tax credit from the American government of 1.5¢ per kWh for the first ten years of wind-generated electricity. In 1998, this program was estimated to have been worth $20 million (USD) (Moomaw, 2002). Another example of incentives to increase the supply of renewable energy is the Canadian Renewable

Energy Deployment Initiative (REDI), which offers a 25 per cent rebate for businesses and institutions installing solar and biomass systems (Environment Canada, 2002b).

There are also many initiatives at the provincial, state, and municipal levels, including the following:

• Renewable portfolio standards (RPSs) set a minimum proportion of electricity required to be from 'renewable' or cleaner sources in a given jurisdiction. Generally, these establish a proportion of electricity generation or consumption that is required to be renewable, as well as which sources of electricity qualify as 'renewable.' So far, eleven American states have adopted RPSs. RPSs are being considered in several Canadian provinces.[7]
• More than ten American states and cities have renewable energy policies, and this number is expected to increase. For instance, in June 1999, Santa Monica became the first American municipality to purchase 100 per cent renewable electricity for its facilities. It buys approximately 5 MW of electricity from geothermal plants. Based on its 1998 energy consumption, the city expects the switch to reduce GHGs by 13,672 tons, NO_x emissions by 16.2 tons, and SO_2 emissions by 14.6 tons annually. In March 2000, Santa Barbara began buying 100 per cent certified renewable power for city facilities.
• The state of New York has an executive order mandating that state buildings obtain 20 per cent of their energy from renewable sources by 2010. The same order appointed a task force to reduce emissions in New York and combat global warming.

Emissions Trading

Emissions trading is a market-based mechanism whereby firms or countries can only emit regulated substances up to the levels allowed by their emissions allocations. The right to emit usually takes the form of permits, which emitters can trade among one another. Permit prices are determined by demand and supply in the permit market. For most trading programs implemented so far, governments have initially allocated permits to companies, prorated to the existing contribution of the given pollutant by the company at the time the program was launched.[8]

In theory, firms (or countries) with low abatement costs will lower their emissions and sell excess credits as long as the value of the credits is higher than the firm's (or country's) costs of emission reduction, and vice versa for the buyers of permits. The use of tradable permits should result in a given level of emissions at least cost and create an incentive to achieve more abatement than under a uniform performance standard.

There is a growing amount of experience with emissions trading systems in North America, including trading systems aimed at reducing SO_2, NO_x, and lead in gasoline. These programs have generally been considered successful at attaining their environmental goals cost effectively (Russell, 2002). Although emissions trading seems to be a potentially effective and important tool in environmental management, its implementation is complex and requires careful planning. In particular, before any such system can work, emissions of all participating sources, be they firms, regions, or countries, must be known. This requires comparable and transparent methods for quantifying emissions among all participants.

Common methodologies are also necessary to calculate 'additionality' – that is, to ensure that future reductions in the given environmental medium will actually be over and above what any given participant would have done in the absence of the trading system. A third important issue is the need for common approaches to ensure that any emission reductions or removals will be verifiable (i.e., certifiable). A fourth important issue is 'fungibility,' in the sense that credits earned in such a system must be recognized by others in the system if they are to have any value. Finally, it is important to make it clear which pollutants are being traded; the success of trading programs depends heavily on the nature of the pollutants, for it is their nature that determines the breadth of such schemes. If the pollutant contributes to a global problem (e.g. CO_2), the greater the reach of the trading system, the better.

Tradable 'green' certificates are another example of how emissions trading could help reduce GHG (and other) emissions. Green certificates (also known as green tags, renewable energy certificates, or tradable renewable certificates) represent the environmental attributes of a specific quantity (commonly one MWh) of renewable energy. They can help develop renewables by broadening the potential market for the environmental services of a particular renewable generation source beyond its grid. Green certificates 'decompose' the energy commodity and the renewable attributes that can be sold on different markets. This allows renewable electricity to be generated in one location. The environmental benefits of this generation can then be sold to a customer in another, possibly distant location. Thus, a renewable electricity generator could conceivably have clients all across the continent, even where the local utility company or utility regulatory commission does not offer electricity generated from renewable sources.

The use of green certificates is in its infancy in the United States. Some power generators, such as the Los Angeles Department of Water and Power, are beginning to sell green certificates. Other companies are beginning to offer green certificates to retail consumers in states that do not have renewable energy facilities. The Center for Resource Solutions is continuing to work at bringing the trading of green certificates into the mainstream. The situation in Europe is quite different. Four European countries have green certificate systems in place, and trading has actually begun in Austria. There has also been considerable buy-in to two different extragovernmental international renewable certificate trading regimes (RECS and RECerT).

Trade in green certificates is complicated and still faces a number of hurdles. Definitions and information associated with green certificates are not yet standardized, and the processes and rules of the various programs are not yet compatible. Other hurdles include uncertainties regarding property rights, other legal issues associated with the various renewable attributes, the difficulty in explaining such programs to the public, the potential for the double-counting (and double-selling) of renewable attributes, and the lack of market structures (i.e., structures that would give value to green certificates) that would help encourage capital investment in renewables.

Clean Development Mechanism (CDM) and Joint Implementation (JI)

The official formulation of joint implementation (JI) is based on the 1992 UNFCC Convention, Article 4.2a, wherein countries included in Annex I (developed countries) may 'implement such policies and measures jointly with other parties and may assist other Parties in contributing to the achievement of the objective of the Convention.' Based on this, the joint implementation concept has evolved based on discrete emission reduction units that can be credited to the investor country for reduction projects realized in the host country. Reduction credits would be based on the actual, project-related avoidance, reduction, or sequestration of GHGs. In this way, the reduction of global GHGs could be reduced in a cost-effective manner. The clean development mechanism is a similar instrument, but based on agreements between Annex I and non-Annex I (or developing) countries. Both JI and CDM offer possibilities for project-based emission reduction 'credits,' referred to as 'emission reduction units' for JI and as 'certified emission reductions' for transfer of credits from non-Annex I countries envisioned in CDM. Since the United States will not be ratifying the Kyoto Protocol, JI is unlikely to be relevant to the North American context; however, CDM will still be available to Canadian investors interested in making carbon-saving investments in Mexico.

The one thing these different initiatives have in common is that all have the potential to lower Canada's adjustment costs resulting from its Kyoto commitment. The amount of this potential is unclear and is the subject of debate and much serious analysis. The fact remains, however, that such initiatives could prove very important in helping Canada keep its Kyoto commitments, and at the same time reduce the costs of satisfying those commitments.

Conclusion

The North American electricity market is becoming more interconnected. Estimates of the costs to Canada of ratifying the Kyoto Protocol are fuzzy. However, earlier work on the relationship between CO_2 emissions and electricity market restructuring is potentially informative.

This analysis suggests several things. It seems that CO_2 emissions will increase with increased restructuring as production is shifted toward lower-cost/higher-emission sources of electricity generation. A corollary of this shift will be an increase in trade between higher- and lower-cost electricity-producing regions. As a result, it would appear that market integration, market restructuring, and the concomitant increase of trade in electricity is likely to make it more difficult for Canada to satisfy its commitments under Kyoto Protocol because of higher CO_2 emissions associated with electricity generation.

Of course, there are caveats to these conclusions. It is conceivable that the shift to lower-cost production could result in more generation from hydropower or nuclear sources, resulting in lower CO_2 emissions and facilitating Canada's reduction commitments. Similarly, if more electricity were to be produced in the United States to serve the Canadian market, then GHG production would take place there and would not have to be reduced in Canada. What has been argued in this chapter is simply that in most models as well as in hindsight, electricity market restructuring is often associated with increases in CO_2 emissions. Clearly, this area is ripe for further research, especially with respect to how restructuring and trade integration will influence overall emissions from this sector, in the Canadian context, in particular.

That having been said, there is a fair bit of quiet convergence on a range of other policies, namely on energy efficiency, renewable energy, and emissions trading. Although unlikely to entirely offset the costs of Kyoto, this definitely indicates potential for reducing Canada's overall costs of satisfying its commitments. There remains room, however, for greater cooperation on policies to help in the reduction in the emission of GHGs.

Appendix

The following describes the calculation for estimating emissions associated with Canadian electricity exports. Emissions per unit of electricity by province were derived from emissions data by province from Miller et al. (2002) and generation data for Canadian provinces from the Canadian Electricity Association (CEA, 2000). Total emissions attributable to electricity exports were then calculated by determining total exports by province based on provincial contribution to electricity exports CEA (ibid.), and then multiplied by the emissions per unit numbers (described above). This resulted in the following estimates of national totals of pollutants emitted from electricity generated for export to the United States: CO_2 (tonnes): 3,629,725; SO_2 (tonnes): 28,278; NO_x (tonnes): 9,669.

NOTES

1 The average refers to power plants built in the United States in the 1990s, over a five-year period.
2 For a more detailed description of the approach, see Miller et al., 2002.
3 Statement available in full at usinfo.state.gov/regional/ar/summit/ north22.htm.

4 The staging category of HS 2716.00 for Canada and the US is 'D' (duty free treatment), with a zero tariff rate. Mexico's schedules for 2716, under category B, allowed for a 10 per cent duty, which was reduced to zero by 1998. Mexico has a number of important exceptions to Chapter Six commitments, including investment and other barriers intended to protect the state-owned nature of its electricity company, CFE.

5 See also NAFTA Secretariat web pages 'Decisions and Reports' and 'Status Reports' at http://www.nafta-sec-alena.org/english/index.htm.

6 For the purposes of this discussion, these CO_2 numbers say little about net environmental impacts, which for climate change is the issue. For example, it is difficult to say whether net GHG emissions would have been higher or lower in a situation of autarky, since it is difficult to identify which sources of electricity – and which fuel types – are being displaced at any given time by electricity from foreign sources, with different fuel mixes. However, Hydro Quebec proposes that it can. Estimates prepared by Hydro Quebec and submitted to the CEC suggest that net total exports of electricity generated from Canadian hydropower displaced 14.4 million tons of CO_2 that otherwise would have been produced in the US had it relied on electricity generated from fossil fuels.

7 The CEC Electricity and Environment Database contains information on RPS standards introduced or adopted in jurisdictions in North America. Available from www.cec.org/electricity.

8 The U.S. Acid Rain Program also auctions off a small portion of allowances each year.

REFERENCES

Abraham, Spencer. 2001. Speech given at 5th Hemispheric Energy Initiative Ministerial Conference, Mexico City, 8 March. www.energy.gov/HQDocs/speeches/2001/marss/mexico.html (accessed September, 2002).

CEA (Canadian Electricity Association). 2000. *Electric Power in Canada, 1998–1999*. Ottawa: Minister of Public Works and Government Services.

CEC (Commission for Environmental Cooperation). 2002a. *Assessing Environmental Effects of the North American Free Trade Agreement (NAFTA): An Analytic Framework (Phase II) and Issue Studies*. Montreal: CEC.

– 2002b. *The Environmental Effects of Trade: Papers Presented at the North American Symposium on Assessing the Linkages between Trade and Environment*, ed. Scott Vaughan. Montreal: CEC. October.

– 2002c. *Environmental Challenges and Opportunities of the Evolving North American Electricity Market*. Montreal: CEC.

Chrétien, Jean. 2002. Address by Prime Minister at the World Summit on Sustainable Development, 2 September, Johannesburg, South Africa.

EIA (Energy Information Administration). 2001. *Annual Energy Outlook 2001.* www.eia.doe.gov/oiaf/aeo/aeotab_2.htm (accessed July 2001).

EMF (Energy Modeling Forum). 2001. EMF Report 17, *Prices and Emissions in a Restructured Electricity Market.* Stanford University.

Environment Canada. 2002a. *Canada's Greenhouse Gas Inventory: 1990–2000.* Ottawa: Government of Canada. www.ec.gc.ca/pdb/GHG (accessed October 4).

– 2002b. *Assessing Barriers and Opportunities for Emerging Renewable Energy in North America.* Presentation by Environment Canada at CEC meeting. 18 February.

EPA (Environmental Protection Agency). 2001. *The Emissions and Generation Resource Integrated Database (EGRID 2000).* www.epa.gov/airmarkets/egrid[.]

Horlick, Gary, and Christiane Schuchardt. 2002. 'NAFTA Provisions and the Electricity Sector.' Background Paper #4 produced for the CEC's Electricity and the Environment Article 13 Initiative. Montreal: CEC.

IEA (International Energy Agency). 2000. *Energy Policies of IEA Countries: Canada 2000 Review.* Paris: OECD.

IPCC (Intergovernmental Panel on Climate Change). 2001. 'Summary for Policymakers: A Report of Working Group I of the IPCC: Third Assessment Report.' www.ipcc.ch/pub/spm22-01.pdf (accessed September 2002).

Jorgenson, Dale W., and Peter J. Wilcoxen. 1998. 'Reducing U.S. Carbon Dioxide Emissions: An Econometric General Equilibrium Assessment.' In Dale W. Jorgenson, ed., *Growth: Energy, the Environment and Economic Growth.* Cambridge: MIT Press.

Miller, Paul J., Zachary Patterson, and Scott Vaughan. 2002. 'Estimating Future Air Pollution from New Electric Power Generation.' Background Paper #2 produced for the CEC's Article 13 on Electricity and the Environment. Montreal: CEC.

Moomaw, William R. 2002. 'Assessing Barriers and Opportunities for Renewable Energy in North America.' Background paper produced for the CEC's Article 13 Initiative on Electricity. Montreal: CEC.

NAEWG (North American Energy Working Group). 2002. 'North America: The Energy Picture.' www.eia.doe.gov/emeu/northamerica/engintro.htm (accessed 15 October 2002).

National Energy Policy Development Group. 2001. *National Energy Policy: Reliable, Affordable, and Environmentally Sound Energy for America's Future.* Washington, DC: NEPDG. May.

NEB (National Energy Board). 2002. 'Annual Report: 2001.' Calgary: Government of Canada. See www.neb-one.gc.ca/pubs/ar/2001/ar2001_e.pdf (accessed September 2002).

OECD (Organization for Economic Cooperation and Development). 1994. *Methodologies for Environmental and Trade Reviews*. Paris: OECD.

Patterson, Zachary. 2002. 'Modeling Techniques and Estimating Environmental Outcomes.' Background Paper #5 produced for the CEC's Article 13 on Electricity and the Environment. Montreal: CEC.

Plagiannakos, Takis. 2002. 'Will Free Trade in Electricity Between Ontario/Canada and the United States Improve Air Quality?' Montreal: CEC.

RDI/Platts. 2001. *NEWGEN Database*. Boulder, CO. August.

Russell, Douglas. 2002. 'Policy Considerations for North American Emissions Trading.' Paper produced for the CEC. Montreal: CEC.

UNCTAD. 1998. 'International Emissions Trading Update.' Geneva: UNCTAD.

UNEP (United Nations Environment Program). 2001. 'Economic Reforms, Trade Liberalization and the Environment: A Synthesis of UNEP Country Projects.' Geneva: UNEP.

Vaughan, Scott, Zachary Patterson, Paul Miller, and Greg Block. 2002. 'Environmental Challenges and Opportunities of the Evolving North American Electricity Market.' Background Paper #1 produced for the CEC's Article 13 on Electricity and the Environment. Montreal: CEC.

Woolf, Tim, Geoff Keith, and David White. 2002. 'A Retrospective Review of FERC's Environmental Impact Statement on Open Transmission Access.' Background Paper #3 produced for the CEC's Article 13 on Electricity and the Environment. Montreal: CEC.

Chapter 7

Sustainable and Socially Efficient Electricity Production: How Will Ontario Satisfy the Criteria?

STEPHAN SCHOTT

The deregulation, restructuring, and privatization of electricity markets has become a popular agenda for many countries, provinces, and states. The notion that electricity generation, transmission, and distribution is a natural monopoly and, therefore, should be either state-owned or heavily regulated is increasingly being challenged. Supposedly, once electricity markets are opened to new suppliers, incumbents will be pressured to achieve more efficient production, and new and innovative technologies will enter the market. However, the supply, transmission, and distribution of electricity is a more complex and integrated process than the ones for providing ordinary private goods, and the secure supply of electricity at stable prices is crucial to a well-functioning economy.

Experiences with electricity deregulation and privatization have not provided convincing evidence that these are preferable to public ownership. The recent Californian experience in electricity deregulation has sent a warning signal and provided some insights about the general drawbacks of opening electricity markets. The British experience pointed to some of the inherent flaws of a decentralized system with a few suppliers that have substantial market power. Social cost–benefit studies and other examinations of the market structure have found that a regulated domestic franchise might be preferable to a fully liberalized supply market (Newbery, 2002; Green and McDaniel, 1998; Newbery and Pollitt, 1997). It is clear now that all of the restructured and privatized markets have required regulation of either prices or investments as well as rules about transmission and distribution. Thus, we can only wonder how much deregulation is actually possible and how much consumers and taxpayers can expect to save. It is debatable whether a competitive electricity market will ever emerge and whether there will be sufficient and proper capacity investments.

The key ingredients for sustainable and socially efficient electricity supply are long-term investment planning for capacity, the consideration of all social and external costs (pollution and nuclear waste being the major ones), and the optimal pricing of electricity in various demand periods. An open electricity market, in which prices are determined by demand and supply, is a step in the direction of more efficient pricing, but it does not lead to a socially efficient and sustainable electricity supply, even when suppliers behave competitively. Private owners have different investment incentives than a social planner with a long-term horizon; they also face different investment costs, and they often behave strategically in their supply and pricing decisions. Furthermore, a deregulated market increases price and supply uncertainty and introduces additional costs to consumers and taxpayers. Leaving supply decisions up to the discretion of private investors and deregulated owners seems risky and unnecessary. This is not to suggest that the current government-controlled pricing model is ideal. Regulatory design and pricing decisions need to be revised, especially in Ontario. Pricing should be based on demand fluctuations throughout the day and between seasons.

This chapter establishes criteria for sustainable and socially efficient electricity production, and discusses which ownership structure is likely to meet those criteria, as well as which institutional setup. First, it reviews the lessons from electricity privatization and restructuring in the United States and United Kingdom. Then it suggests some key criteria for sustainable and socially efficient electricity production, and discusses which barriers to the implementation of these criteria are encountered under regulated and deregulated electricity markets. The efficiency and sustainability of Ontario's electricity market is evaluated, and an alternative model for Ontario is suggested that could be an improvement over the Ontario Hydro era as well as the recent attempts at privatization and deregulation.

Lessons from the United States and United Kingdom

The California power crisis began in the summer of 2000, with significant increases in consumer prices in San Diego, followed by a rise in wholesale rates. This crisis led to severe deficits, bankruptcies of private suppliers, rolling blackouts, and substantial government intervention. This was the world's first close look at the severe economic and social consequences of mishandled electricity restructuring. Some defenders of electricity privatization contended that the problems were specific to California – that it had made certain terrible mistakes such as introducing price caps, failing to provide real-time metering, starting deregulation too late, and so on. California's experience, however, also pointed to certain basic challenges inherent in the opening of electricity markets. Electricity is a complex market that involves generation, transmission, and distribution. The California debate was a reminder that generators exercise market power and withhold electricity when supplies are tight (Brennan, 2001). Electricity markets are also highly vulnerable to temporary load imbalances: the system can break down if supply exceeds demand, and blackouts occur when demand exceeds supply (ibid.). Therefore, a reliable and stable supply requires substantial coordination by a regulator, and this is more complicated and costly under a privatized scheme.

Retail competition in electricity markets started in the United States in 1996 with Rhode Island, followed by California, Pennsylvania, and Massachusetts (Trebing, 2000). A controversial econometric study by the U.S. Department of Energy DOE) predicted that competition would reduce national electric prices in all regions of the country by 2010 (Trebing, 2000; U.S. DOE, 1999). The study was soon challenged by the U.S. Department of Agriculture (USDA), which applied the same model and showed that there would be significant savings in five high-cost states, moderate savings in twenty-one states, and net economic losses in nineteen states (Trebing, 2000; USDA, 1999). A DOE staff study in March 2000 found evidence of prices in excess of competitive levels in the United Kingdom, California, the middle Atlantic States, and Colorado (Trebing, 2000; Newbery and Pollitt, 1997). Horizontal and vertical mergers, cross-industry mergers, and alliances in the United States provide evidence of growing market concentration since the start of privatization (Trebing, 2000). Market trading had also increased price volatility in the United States. Consumers are generally risk-averse and seek to hedge risks by entering long-term contracts with high markups over average prices.

The British government under Margaret Thatcher began privatizing and restructuring electricity markets in 1990. Before restructuring, most electricity in that country was produced from coal or nuclear. The mandate of the Central Electricity Generating Board (CEGB) was to use British coal at a premium rate over world prices in order to protect domestic coal production. With privatization, this protection for coal was abandoned, which led to a reduction in electricity production costs. Yet this decline in unit costs of electricity production did not result in falling output prices; instead, it increased the producers' profits, as indicated by electricity share prices rising significantly higher than the rest of the stock market (Newbery and Pollitt, 1997). Almost half of the new capacity in combined cycle gas turbines was built by the incumbents, and this helped them secure their market power (Newbery, 1998). In the first five years of privatization, two companies – National Power and PowerGen – set the price of electricity in the pool almost 90 per cent of the time (Newbery, 1998). The move away from coal as a fuel for electricity generation had a positive impact on environmental quality, by reducing Britain's contribution to global warming as well as the negative effects of SO_2, NO_X, mercury, lead, and so on. The reduction in SO_2 alone led to significant drops in mortality rates, and depending on how one values life (in statistical terms), could offset all other costs of deregulation. If the value of a statistical life is indeed that high, pollution could be further reduced by the continued entry of clean energy sources such as small-scale hydro, biomass, wind, and solar. The increased reliance on gas imports, however, is a source of concern for some British policymakers, because gas prices fluctuate sharply and future supplies are likely to be drawn from politically unstable countries.

Before privatizing and restructuring an electricity market, it seems crucial to determine a desirable energy source portfolio for electricity generation – that is sustainable over a long period, that considers the harm to public health and to the environment, that can guarantee a stable and secure supply of electricity, and that is efficient. Once long-term objectives have been established, it can then be decided which institutions, ownership structures, and regulatory designs will meet the desired objectives most efficiently. Letting the market determine energy source portfolios without adequate institutional frameworks and appropriate policies could lead to a lack of public support, inadequate long-term investments, and extraordinary social costs of the sort experienced in some American states as well as in Ontario and Alberta (see Dewees, this volume) and in Great Britain.

Criteria for Sustainable and Socially Efficient Production

Sustainable and socially efficient electricity depends on a number of factors. Generally, the following must be considered: efficiency of production, proper investment in the most appropriate technologies, external costs of electricity production, uncertainty in supply, energy source prices, and external effects (such as pollution and nuclear waste). All of the factors contributing to sustainable and socially efficient electricity production are captured and explained below, under three categories:

- efficiency and price stability
- internalization of social costs
- security of supply and environmental uncertainty.

Efficiency and Price Stability

Efficiency requires the best use of inputs such as capital and labour, optimal pricing of electricity consumption, and optimal investments in capacity. Since transmission and distribution are natural monopolies, it is possible to economize by integrating these two sectors with generation. However, one large organization does not always use inputs efficiently. Only when the gains from efficiency in generation outweigh the losses from integration and cover the additional costs of running wholesale, retail, and transmission separately should a private system even be considered on economic terms.

Generation involves operating costs as well as capacity or capital costs. Prices always have to cover marginal operating costs and also have to recover marginal capital costs. Capital costs can be recovered exclusively during peak times, or they can be added to peak and off-peak marginal costs. Optimal capacity investments and pricing decisions depend on demand elasticities, the duration of peak demands, the cost structures of different technologies, and the fluctuation of demand between peak and off-peak periods. Crew and Kleindorfer (1986) found that efficient pricing can involve the full use of capacity during peak and off-peak periods (the 'shifting peak' case) or some unused capacity during off-peak (the 'firm peak' case). The latter is especially likely when capacity costs are not too high. When technologies differ with respect to capacity costs and operating costs, it is optimal to use the technology with the higher operating costs (but lower capacity costs) during peak demand only, in addition to other technologies. This only holds, though, if it is optimal to have unused capacity in off-peak. With shifting peak demand, it is optimal not to use the technology with the higher operating costs at all. Some large operating facilities such as nuclear reactors, large hydropower plants, and coal plants experience increasing returns to scale (economies of scale). In the latter case, marginal cost pricing will not necessarily cover capacity or fixed costs, and it might be optimal to produce at a loss to the producer (a loss that is outweighed by an increase in consumer surplus). The loss can then be recovered through taxes or other pricing schemes.

Price fluctuations are caused by changes in demand and supply. During the year, week, and day there are peak and off-peak periods. It is efficient to price according to demand fluctuations so that consumers can then determine when it is most beneficial for them to use electricity. This helps conserve energy and/or reduce capacity investments (see Dewees, this volume). Prices, however, also vary with changes in supply, which can be caused by capacity retirement, maintenance, or changes in capacity. Consumers do not like strongly fluctuating prices and are willing to pay a risk premium (or insurance premium) in order to secure stable prices. The premium that consumers are willing to pay to reduce the risk from fluctuating electricity prices should be considered a cost of deregulation (Schott, 2002). An efficient system also provides incentives for proper investment in R&D and new technologies. The best investments will only be made when the true costs of technologies are known and expressed in the market. This means there must be a mechanism for charging or internalizing the social or external costs of the production process.

Internalization of Social Costs

The social costs of electricity production include those arising from local and global pollution, market distortions, regulation, and transaction and transition costs. In most instances, the real social cost of electricity production is not reflected in the choices of markets, nor is it considered by central managers. The generation of electricity often contributes significantly to smog, global warming, and air pollution. Pollutants have direct regional health impacts in that they cause cancer, heart disease, and respiratory disease; they are directly responsible for a significant number of deaths.[1] Some have suggested that green labelling be used to signal the environmental friendliness of energy sources (see, for example, Grant, 2002). Consumers can then choose to buy electricity from clean resources at a premium. There are two fundamental problems with this approach. First, individual consumers have an incentive to free ride on others who are willing to pay premiums for cleaner sources; as a consequence, not too many people will voluntarily purchase electricity from green sources. Second, this approach assumes that people do not have a right to clean air and should have to purchase that privilege. Effective pricing of external effects requires us to measure the marginal damages arising from electricity emissions, as well as the cost of reducing emissions (marginal abatement costs) and the transaction costs involved in monitoring and enforcing emission reductions. Marginal damages from electricity generation often reach beyond the boundaries of regional electricity markets. In these circumstances, several states, provinces, or countries must establish target levels. Jurisdictions that are upwind may well face fewer social costs than downwind jurisdictions. This is why cross-border pollution problems often lead to one-sided benefits from pollution reduction, and require common emission reduction programs or markets.

In a deterministic world, the optimal energy source portfolio is achieved when the social marginal cost of each technology is the name. (This cost includes marginal damages due to pollution, as well as capacity and operating costs.) If one energy source could produce all of the electricity demanded at the lowest marginal social cost, and if there were no input price uncertainties, we would use only that source to produce electricity. This would, however, be risky, if the price of the energy source tended to fluctuate heavily or if energy supplies were insecure. For these reasons, many jurisdictions have invested in a diversity of technologies.

Security of Supply and Environmental Uncertainty

A sustainable system should also be judged with respect to supply security and environmental uncertainty. A system that, for example, consists of 100 per cent wind energy will have supply problems and will not be as secure as a system that consists of 100 per cent nuclear energy. The latter, however, will impose environmental uncertainty because of the difficulty of managing nuclear waste and the burden that management will impose on future generations.

The use of coal to produce electricity has a tremendous impact on the environment, mortality rates, global warming, and so on. This is why the use of gas in combined cycle gas turbines (CCGTs) has gained popularity. Natural gas as an energy source generates considerable emissions, but it is still much cleaner than coal. However, the marginal operating costs of natural gas plants are higher than those for coal plants, especially with recent developments in energy markets. Natural gas prices fluctuate tremendously; as a result, a market that relies too much on gas as an energy input would risk strong volatility in electricity prices.

Nuclear power adds almost nothing to water and air pollution; however, a great deal of uncertainty surrounds nuclear waste removal and its effects. Environmental taxation or pollution permit markets would make the use of nuclear power more lucrative, because of its comparative advantage over coal and gas. The uncertainties of waste removal and fears about the long-term effects of nuclear accidents have limited the attractiveness of this energy source. Since the terrorist attacks of 11 September 2001, there is also fear that nuclear power stations could be targeted by terrorists. The chief concern here is that private owners do not spend as much on security, because they do not bear the full consequences of a terrorist attack or a nuclear accident.

Renewable resources offer clean alternatives that do not depend on energy markets and that do not create pollution or uncertainty about environmental impacts (with the possible exception of large-scale hydropower). Most renewable energy sources are not competitive yet, partly owing to the lack of R&D investment and poorly thought out environmental targets. The health impacts of air pollution, for example, are not fully considered when environmental targets are set or when the external social costs of electricity generation are determined. Large-scale hydropower has proven itself to be efficient and able to supply entire domestic and export markets (as, for example, in Quebec). It enjoys large economies of scale and can be cost-efficient, but it also imposes social costs, in that it causes flooding and forces the relocation of settlements. Furthermore, it has uncertain ecological effects. In contrast, small-scale hydropower, can be relatively cost-efficient without too many detrimental effects. Wind energy has recently become more popular (e.g., in Denmark and Germany). It is a clean energy source; however, it depends on wind conditions and for that reason could result in fluctuating electricity supplies. Solar energy is still relatively expensive as an initial investment, but it is capable of providing a relatively reliable source of energy on a small scale for households or small companies. A number of other alternative resources, such as biomass and geothermal, have not received much attention yet, but they will become increasingly popular in the future as environmental pressures continue to increase (domestically and internationally).

This brief description of the various energy sources available indicates that it would be dangerous, risky, or too expensive to rely on a single energy source. An exception is large-scale hydropower, in which heavy investments have already been made. With hydropower, most of the damage has already been done, so it is better to keep using it than to invest in polluting or less efficient technologies. Where large-scale hydropower is unavailable, other renewable energy sources should probably receive larger market shares, but they must not yet be relied on as exclusive energy sources. The optimal energy source mix, therefore, depends on the investments already made, the social costs of electricity production (which vary from region to region), the availability and supply stability of energy sources, the environmental risks of electricity generation, the operating and capital costs of various technologies, and the differences and cross-elasticities between peak and off-peak demand. The electricity market is extremely complex (see Dewees, this volume). Extensive rules are necessary to control all of the factors that together ensure the efficient and sustainable functioning of electricity generation, transmission, and generation. We cannot rely on an unregulated market to guide us; that being said, government monopolies are open to political abuse and require careful oversight. The next section discusses public versus private ownership of generation plants.

Ownership, Regulation, and Institutions

Theoretically, state ownership of the electricity sector could satisfy all of the criteria for sustainable and socially efficient electricity production. A public owner could carefully plan capacity investments, changes in technology, and energy source mixes; it could fully internalize social costs; and it could price according to demand fluctuations even while keeping supply stable. Yet it cannot be said that state ownership automatically leads to sustainable and efficient electricity production. Direct government ownership has the disadvantage of following political objectives; governments fear making policies that could make consumption more expensive or that would require citizens to adjust their consumption habits (e.g., special night-time rates or price increases to reflect demand increases). Dewees in chapter 5 proposed competition between electricity generators as a solution to government lethargy. In his view, reliance ought to be placed on demand and supply in wholesale markets rather than on regulation of rates and careful investments in capacity. He adds, however, that an electricity market is rather artificial and must work within certain guidelines, rules, and regulations. Privatization and deregulation models often require much *more* regulation than a government ownership model. Demand and supply in hourly wholesale markets introduce great uncertainty, and this does not help either investors or consumers. Also, there are coordination issues among transmission, distribution, and generation that must somehow be addressed. Markets do not support cooperation; instead, they make the process of supplying electricity at different times more strategic. In short, the wholesale market introduces a new game for its participants. Is it worth risking all of the costs of fundamental institutional change simply to force regulators to price differently? Or are there other, more promising reforms besides the regulated monopoly model?

The generation of electricity was perceived to be a natural monopoly until it was challenged by contestable market theory (Schiller, 2001; Demsetz, 1968; Baumol, Panzet, and Willig, 1982; Bailey, 1981). It was long thought that electric power was most cheaply produced by a single supplier because of its large fixed costs and economies of scale. Contestable market theory suggests that the threat of entry could force even monopolies to price competitively. The contestability of markets, however, is threatened by the strategic behaviour of incumbents and new entrants that have too large a market share. This was the experience in the United Kingdom and in many American markets (Trebing, 2000; Newbery, 1998). The interaction between spot markets and contract markets is complex, and there are often multiple market equilibria, which together cause uncertainty over output, price, and capacity. Especially when incumbents have spare capacity, they tend to maximize their baseload contract cover; this in turn increases volatility in the spot market and deters entry (Newbery, 1998). Public ownership of large-scale power generation is perhaps inefficient with respect to operating and administration costs, but it also has this advantage: it discourages strategic behaviour by firms that have market power. Private producers that enjoy any kind of market power will not price at marginal cost and will invest in a socially inefficient capacity. Private monopolies or monopolistic competitors will attempt to maximize their profits and to price discriminate. This will significantly reduce consumer surplus. Also, when running at lower capacity, the industry is less flexible when it comes to accommodating demand fluctuations, and this increases the likelihood of blackouts. A competitive market can only emerge when there are a large number of firms that cannot significantly influence prices by adjusting or shutting down supply individually. That is why there will probably never be a truly competitive electricity market. The exception might be areas that are supplied exclusively by electricity generated from diesel or natural gas.

The key to a successful privatization program, then, is to discourage market concentration or the allocation of too much capacity to one producer. Most electricity markets have a few large producers, (e.g., nuclear reactors and large coal-fired power stations), which can service large proportions of the market. In order to restrict market power, either large producers must be regulated, or capacity must be split up, or production must stay in public ownership. But reductions in capacity, plant size, or firm size in order to prevent market power will be inefficient, when there are economies of scale in the production of electricity. This is because larger output levels (and therefore larger market shares) result in lower average costs and more efficient production. Trebing (2000) has found that at present, larger rather than smaller generating units seem more cost effective. Kleit and Terrell (2001) have shown that a private market could increase efficiency for some natural gas plants, but have also found that natural gas plants typically operate at increasing returns to scale. This creates a dilemma: it is desirable to have larger firms producing at lower average costs, yet at the same time, large firms could abuse their market power to their own advantage.

One of the goals of deregulation and privatization is to reduce excess capacity requirements by charging higher prices during times of peak demand and lower prices during off-peak times. Large price variations could cause consumers to switch consumption from peak to off-peak periods; this would smooth out spikes and result in a more efficient use of capacity. It could also place less strain on increasingly scarce sustainable energy sources. Some technologies, such as nuclear and hydro, have high capacity costs but relatively low operating costs; in contrast, natural gas plants have much lower capacity costs but relatively high operating costs. Competition could lead to industries with high capacity costs being underbid by those with low capacity costs during peak periods. Industries with high capacity costs would then have to raise their off-peak prices to recover their investment costs. The result would be large unused capacity in off-peak times and excessive demand during peak periods as a result of lower peak prices and higher off-peak prices. This could even have the effect of equalizing prices between peak and off-peak. This in turn would reduce incentives to shift consumption to off-peak, and which in turn would result in a very inefficient use of capacity, which in turn would require that large new energy sources be acquired. Marginal cost pricing therefore does not miraculously lead to the most efficient prices and long-term capacity investments. In some cases, therefore, it is better to regulate the entry of technologies and to coordinate pricing instead of leaving it up to competition.

Planning horizons for public electricity providers are usually twelve to fifteen years (interview with R. Franklin, *Electrical Equipment News*, 1988); private suppliers have different planning horizons. Private firms also face higher financing costs than government-based suppliers, and, therefore, work with different discount rates. This is another reason why the private sector makes suboptimal (from the perspective of society) capacity investment decisions.

Price distortions, and instability in the supply and price of electricity, affect residential and small business consumers the most. The latter are willing to pay a premium to reduce price fluctuations and ensure a stable price for electricity. For consumers, higher average electricity prices that are also stable are a preferred alternative to lower average prices that fluctuate.

Even after generating facilities are privatized, governments will be required to continuously assess whether firms are trying to fix prices, or collude, or withhold capacity. Firms must be regulated, and as necessary, market concentrations must be broken up. This requires substantial information about suppliers' production costs, in order to justify regulation measures and to set proper taxes or subsidies. When incumbents have market power and create barriers to entry, regulators may need to subsidize potential entrants in order to secure sufficient electricity production. The cost of monitoring, regulation, enforcement, and subsidies should be accounted for when the costs of public versus private ownership are compared.

Most electricity industries rely strongly on fossil fuels, which create significant emissions, or they operate nuclear reactors that create waste. An efficient system will impose taxes or establish pollution permits to price the social cost of emissions or waste removal. This will add additional monitoring, regulation, and enforcement costs. The regulator must measure individual firms' emissions at different output levels in order to monitor compliance with environmental policy instruments. When a firm's emissions decrease with an increase in output, and that firm has relatively large capacity, environmental instruments could cause additional increases or use of capacity and therefore could create even larger barriers to entry. In the opposite case (when emissions or outputs increase with total output), environmental policy instruments could reduce barriers to entry.

The Canadian government is currently trying to find ways to implement the Kyoto Protocol, and it is going to have to drastically reduce GHG emissions over the next ten years. This could soon translate into very low carbon emissions from electricity production – perhaps even none. This means that firms that invested exclusively in fossil-fuelled production may have to declare bankruptcy, which will lead to government bailouts, and that there may be no further investment in coal or natural gas plants. The ratification of Kyoto could also lead to legal disputes between firms and provinces, and between provinces and the federal government. Provincial ownership of coal-fired, oil-fired, and larger gas-fired plants could facilitate the implementation of Kyoto in Canada, since implementation is not going to depend on the compliance of firms but rather on that of Crown corporations or government ministries. However, the actual implementation of emission reduction instruments and the considerations of social cost in pricing and investment decisions may end up depending on the political will and determination of ruling governments and opposition forces.

A deregulated market requires fair and equal access for producers to transmission and distribution networks. So the ownership and organization of the transmission grid and of the distribution must be separated from the ownership of production facilities. This can have undesirable effects. California's experience has shown us that an electricity market's equilibrium price and supply can be very volatile. A reliable and well-functioning market requires either coordination of supplies or central management of the grid (Brennan, 2001). An independent system would limit coordination possibilities. In a study of several American electric utilities, Kwoka (2002) showed that cost savings from vertical integration are significant for all but the smallest utilities. Furthermore, deregulation reduces consumer surplus, as each vertical market segment charges markups on output prices. An independent system or market operator might have to run a profit in order to secure extra capacity for periods of power shortages. Retailers will provide medium-range and long-range contracts for consumers at considerable premiums. However, consumers will also incur transaction costs because they need to inform themselves about all of the markets, possible contract options, and prices, and they will have to deal with non-requested solicitations. When the non-integrated system fails to supply enough electricity at certain times, blackouts may occur and the system may break down. At that point, the government will probably step in at a considerable cost in order to restabilize the electricity supply. The recent North American blackout of 14 August 2003 is a good example of the magnitude of costs resulting from an interruption in electricity (for twenty-four hours, in most jurisdictions). Ontario took longer than any other jurisdiction affected by the blackout to return to normal operations, as a result of the tightness of supplies and insufficient monetary incentives to reduce consumption due to the price cap. The government had to appeal to Ontarians to voluntarily conserve electricity for almost a week. Federal and provincial government employees were missing work days in order to curb demand and to avoid further blackouts. Private firms could exploit situations like this. Recently, for example, British Energy received a bailout loan of £650 million from the government (*Economist*, 17 October 2002) as a bridge across its financial troubles in operating nuclear reactors.

Privatization can provide a competitive yardstick for incumbent utilities, but it also introduces other costs and increases market volatility and can lead to suboptimal capacity levels and energy mixes. Consumers likely will face similar or higher prices than without privatization. It is the shareholders of electricity providers that are the beneficiaries of privatization. Taxpayers are not likely to gain, since a well-functioning private market requires substantial restructuring costs, ongoing regulation, market assessment, and environmental regulation costs. A separation of electricity generation, transmission, and distribution will introduce inefficiencies in the coordination of the market and will increase volatility in the supply and price of electricity. Because of the additional costs, the introduction of price and output uncertainty, the potential loss of consumer surplus, and inefficiencies of vertical disintegration, a private market is likely to be preferred only for industries that have several small producers and that are relatively clean. Several small companies are more likely to behave competitively, and regulation is less costly and complex when companies do not pollute or create waste. It is questionable, though, whether several small, non-polluting companies will be able to accommodate the entire demand at all times.

Before the industry is restructured, it should be evaluated, using a comprehensive cost–benefit analysis, regarding whether there is at least

investment in new capacity, and some old plants were (and still are) being serviced. Political pressure arising from drastic price increases and from the financial strain these imposed on residential and small business consumers led the Conservative government to cap electricity prices for consumers at 4.3 cents per kilowatt hour. Suppliers still received the spot market price, but the difference between the spot market and the consumer price was financed by taxpayers in both the short run (through taxes or cuts elsewhere) and the long run (in the form of further debt accumulation). Since its implementation, the average hourly spot market price has consistently been well above 4.3 cents/kWh; the result has been enormous additional costs or debt for taxpayers. Consumer price caps are very inefficient because consumers are not charged the true price of electricity; instead, they pay the spot market price indirectly, through taxes or debt retirement, and thus are not encouraged to reduce their consumption. This artificial market sets improper signals for new investors as well. New investors cannot determine the true demand at uncapped prices, and their only incentive is to invest in low-capital-cost plants such as gas power plants for relatively short time horizons. Ontario Hydro had planning horizons of twelve to fifteen years for new capacity investments and had the advantage of receiving the same credit ratings for bonds as the provincial government. This enabled long-term planning and financing at much better rates than private firms can ever receive. So far we have not seen any major investments in new capacity.

Electricity production from nuclear and coal is relatively large-scale at the moment, as it is generated by a small number of relatively large plants. On average, individual nuclear plants contribute 9.12 per cent of total market capacity, and coal plants contribute 5.1 per cent of total market capacity (derived from IMO, April 2002). It is not clear whether the larger plants are experiencing economies of sale. With economies of scale, higher production at fewer plants would be efficient. Interruption of services in individual plants (as currently experienced with Pickering A) can seriously disturb the market, and individual plants are large enough that they can have a noticeable impact on supply and on prices. A perfectly competitive market is not very likely to emerge, but perhaps monopolistic competition with some degree of price-setting behaviour is possible. This would result in prices above marginal cost and inefficient consumption and capacity levels.

Restructuring has introduced fluctuating prices, and this is a step toward more efficient pricing. Supply, however, has proven to be tight and volatile, resulting in sharp price fluctuations and a visible increase in prices. Price capping for consumers has introduced more inefficiencies and significantly increased the debt. This in turn has discouraged energy conservation and caused supply to remain tight and spot market prices to remain high. A new institution, the IMO, has had to be established, at considerable expense to taxpayers and consumers. The IMO charges consumers a wholesale market service charge, a transmission charge, and a debt retirement charge, all of this on top of the market price of electricity. Retailers also demand a markup, and consumers face transaction costs, because they need to inform themselves, 'shop around,' and study contract options, contract length, 'fine print' provisions, and the spot market. Privatization and restructuring overall have, therefore, probably reduced efficiency and led to more price volatility relative to the earlier Ontario Hydro model (Schott, 2002).

While this book was going to press, Dwight Duncan, the new Liberal government's energy minister, announced five guiding principles for an electricity reform plan (Ontario Ministry of Energy, 3 November 2003). The Liberals are going to lift the current price cap of 4.3 cents per kilowatt hour so that prices will better reflect the true cost of electricity. However, the price will not be determined in the spot market; instead, it will be regulated again in a stable and predictable manner. An arm's-length body will regulate prices based on the public interest.

This Liberal's plan is clearly a step in the right direction. Duncan realizes that a volatile spot market hurts consumers, businesses, and investors. In order to reduce capacity requirements in the long run, consumers should, however, be slowly introduced to the idea of fluctuating prices during the year and during the day. It is possible that in the short run they will receive assistance in the form of electricity vouchers or fixed rebate amounts on their electricity bills. The latter approach succeeded in Alberta (see Dewees, this volume). Fixed rebate amounts have these advantages: prices need not be capped, and consumers have a much greater incentive to reduce their electricity consumption. Early in the process, the rebate will help households deal with increased energy prices. As households cut back, demand will dwindle; this in turn will allow the government to reduce its rebate cheques. The rebate/voucher system will allow a gradual phasing out of financial assistance; in contrast, price caps would not have changed demand and would have imposed a long-lasting drain on provincial finances. When adjusting to price fluctuations, households will have to receive more frequent meter readings or will have to be equipped with real-time meters – something that still is a bit too costly.

It will be interesting to see which regulatory design the Liberals choose when making pricing and capacity decisions. We can hope that the new body will implement more efficient pricing that sets proper incentives and that enables the shifting of consumption from peak periods to off-peak periods during the day. Pricing should be directly linked to capacity requirements and to investments in the optimum energy mixes. The current government also has some work to do regarding the internalization of social costs for coal, natural gas, and nuclear facilities. Emissions from natural gas and coal plants will have to be taxed so as to reflect the true social cost of electricity production. There also must be a fee for nuclear waste production to better reflect the true marginal cost of electricity from nuclear.

Internalization of Social Costs

Air pollution from electricity production has increased tremendously in Ontario since the mid-1990s due to increased reliance on fossil fuels (OPG, October 2001). Total emissions of CO_2 totalled 38.6 million tonnes in 2000 – an increase of 160 per cent over 1994 levels (see Figure 7.1 and OPG, October 2001a). Air pollution from electricity generation is caused almost exclusively by fossil fuels (which account for 99.74 per cent of total CO_2 emissions). The Nanticoke Power Plant alone created over half (55.84 per cent) of the electricity industry's total CO_2 emissions and was also responsible for significant proportions of SO_2 and NO_X emissions. OPG's coal plants were responsible for 34 per cent of Ontario's airborne mercury emissions, 23 per cent of Ontario's SO_2 emissions, 14 per cent of Ontario's NO_X emissions, and 20 per cent of Ontario's GHG emissions (OPG, 2002; the Ontario Clean Air Alliance, 2002). In a comparison with twenty-five American states, OPG ranked twelfth in terms of total NO_X emissions and thirteenth in terms of total SO_2 emissions (OPG, 2001b). But the biggest sources of smog and many other pollutants in Ontario are the upwind American states. Thus, an effective solution for controlling $SO_2$and NO_X, will have to involve all of the polluters in the airshed. Ideally, all of the states and provinces should agree on a target level that corresponds to acceptable total emissions levels (which are related to marginal abatement costs and to the marginal damages of emissions), and negotiate an

Figure 7.1. Ontario Hydro/OPG greenhouse gas emissions (millions tones CO_2)

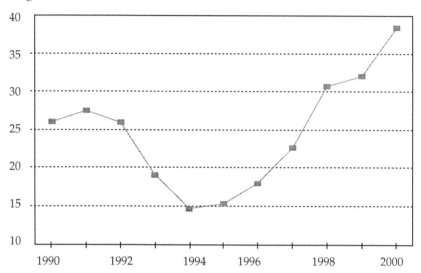

Source: OPG, October 2001.

emission reduction program. A consensus on target levels has not yet been developed, but the Ontario government has made progress in the trading of emission reduction credits with polluters in several American states. Emission reduction credits are based on historic emission rates, and allow firms to trade emission reduction credits with other firms that have not met their targets or have not reduced their emissions. This program is a start in the right direction, but it lacks a binding cap as well as trade aggregate pollution limits based on environmental damage and emission reduction costs.

Regarding further privatization of OPG's plants, controlling and regulating private firms' emissions will result in significant monitoring and enforcement costs for Ontario regulators. Ontario will need to invest heavily in agencies dealing with market concentration assessments, emissions monitoring, the enforcement of regulation rules, and adherence to environmental standards and pollution allowances. This could only be avoided by replacing some of the coal power plants with cleaner technologies in the grid (hydro, wind, biomass, nuclear, and solar). The IMO allows green energy sources (solar, wind, small-scale hydro and so on) to contract directly with customers (Grant, 2002). Customers are expected to buy electricity from clean sources at a premium. This will lead to inefficient outcomes because people normally do not voluntarily contribute enough to the reduction of global warming and to improvements in air quality. It follows that the optimal level of air pollution will not be reached in this way; to achieve this goal will require regulation of dirty generating plants and the implementation of efficient policy instruments.

As the Kyoto commitments take effect, carbon emission levels considerably lower than even in the early 1990s will have to be achieved. Ontario's Liberals have promised a complete phase-out of coal by 2007 (Ontario Clean Air Alliance newsletter, September 2002). They will need to demonstrate that this is the most efficient way to deal with emissions. For meeting Kyoto targets and reducing other emissions, Ontario has a number of options. It could invest more in greener technologies or emission reduction technologies for coal-burning plants, and/or it could curb demand increases through demand-side management or more effective pricing.

Ontario Hydro was more concerned about providing a stable supply of electricity than about reducing emissions or dealing with nuclear waste. It chose not to reduce its investments in coal power or reactivate some of its small-scale hydropower plants. And it did not seriously consider renewable energy. With sufficient political will, the government and the public could have imposed stricter environmental standards and cleaner technologies and placed pressure on Ontario Hydro. The government had auditing options, and it could have appointed a new board. Private firms are more difficult to regulate because governments lack information about authority over their practices. When firms gain market power and emission reduction programs are imposed on them, they reduce supply and increase prices even further.

Security of Supply and Environmental Uncertainty

Ontario has a relatively large nuclear sector, and this raises concerns about waste management, the safety of facilities, and nuclear power's uncertain effects on the environment. Ontario Hydro has had a very good safety record with respect to nuclear power management. It is unlikely that private firms would be as careful and spend as much money on maintenance and safety – after all, they would not be bearing the same public responsibility and consequences.

There is also political uncertainty regarding federal policies toward implementing the Kyoto Protocol. Ottawa has the authority to impose sanctions on provinces or firms that are not meeting environmental standards or targets. Provinces such as Alberta that do not support federally negotiated agreements can oppose implementation at the provincial level. Here it might be easier for a federal government to impose regulation on individual firms instead of relying on the individual provinces to follow the Kyoto guidelines and emission targets through their provincial energy policies. Private firms, however, are generally reluctant to invest in technologies that will be placed under tight regulation in the near future. Coal plants, therefore, are likely to remain in provincial hands.

It is also unclear how much private firms will invest in capacity and what technologies they will choose. Any further investments in Ontario are likely to be in natural gas plants and perhaps small-scale hydropower or wind energy. Ontario Hydro had an impressive international reputation for consistently providing a secure supply of electricity, but it was criticized domestically for investing too much in capacity. Ontario is, however, currently experiencing supply shortages, as Ontarians noticed during the blackout of 14 August 2003. Owing to a lack of new investment, the Conservative government was at one point in 2003 planning to avoid blackouts by temporarily providing extra capacity in the form of highly inefficient and polluting diesel generators. This highlights the drawbacks of not having one responsible entity such as Ontario Hydro to carefully plan capacity investments by applying a long-term vision.

Market restructuring has made us think more about the marginal costs of generation, about off-peak versus baseload demand, and about political barriers to more efficient pricing policies. This lesson has come at a significant cost for Ontarians. Now is the time to learn from the mistakes in Ontario and other jurisdictions and to return to an improved version of the government ownership model.

Conclusions

Electricity is unlike any other consumption good. Capacity can be used at various times and at different prices. Careful planning of long-term capacities and their integration into the grid is one of the key objectives of electricity provision. Pricing, however, should not be determined by the profit-maximizing approaches of private monopolists or oligopolists; instead, it should discriminate efficiently between consumer groups (e.g., residential or commercial) and time of use, and it should be linked to socially efficient and sustainable capacity investment decisions.

Many governments are trying to increase generation efficiency by opening markets to the private sector, without considering the full range of costs and benefits to society. Empirical evidence confirms that consumers lose when markets privatize, and that taxpayers often lose as well. The argument that government-owned production is not efficient overlooks the benefits of an integrated system, ignores the need for regulation, coordination, and transaction costs, and underestimates the benefits of secure supply and relatively stable electricity prices. The efficiency of electricity generation cannot be judged in isolation from all other functions a government owner carries out. The government has a role as a coordination agency, insurance agency, and planning body for new investments. Privatization introduces more volatility in prices and capacities, and more uncertainty about environmental consequences and the type of investments. Any disadvantages of government ownership are unlikely to be worse than the disadvantages of privatization and deregulation.

Instead of breaking up a complex, stable system of electricity production, transmission, and distribution, new mechanisms could be applied to make government management more accountable and transparent. First, the mandate of the corporation in charge of capacity and generation should be changed from producing power 'at cost' to optimal pricing and socially efficient capacity investment. This change in mandate should be manifested in a new Power Corporation Act. This act would have to define and interpret the terms 'optimal pricing' and 'socially efficient capacity investment.' The provincial auditor could regularly verify progress in adopting and implementing sustainable electricity production objectives.

Time-invariant prices should be abolished, because they discourage conservation and do not provide any incentives for consumers to shift electricity use to off-peak periods. Everyone would benefit from lower consumption; this in turn would cause prices to fall. Instead of a capped energy charge, a distribution charge, a transmission charge, a wholesale market charge, a debt retirement charge, and a customer charge, Ontario should have one price that depends on the actual demand at the time of use and that covers socially optimal capacity and operating costs.

The next step would be to treat the social cost of emissions and nuclear waste management as input costs for electricity production. This could be achieved by forcing OPG (or the public corporation in charge) to fully internalize all external social costs of electricity generation. This would cause OPG to weigh various options for technology investments and/or phase out dates for dirty technologies in order to meet capacity requirements in the most sustainable manner.

Since substantial investments have already been made, it will probably be a good idea to work with the current institutions. Ontario Power Generation could make long-term investment plans based on demand projections and differences between peak and off-peak demand. The IMO could make recommendations about optimal pricing strategies to OPG and could continue to analyse market demand. This coud be reviewed by the Ontario Energy Board. Additional research with respect to cross-price elasticities between peak and off-peak demand must be conducted. In order to make more efficient capacity investments, Ontario needs to find out how responsive consumers are to price changes and to what extent they will shift consumption to off-peak periods. This in turn will determine whether it is economical to provide more frequent readings or real-time meters to households and small businesses. The IMO should also continue to inform and perhaps educate consumers about prices through regular television, newspaper, and website announcements.

A public corporation could plan a sustainable path to technology adoption and retirement; this could guarantee relatively stable prices, secure generation capacity, and socially acceptable pollution levels. Private suppliers and innovators should be considered for integration into the grid if they are not likely to gain significant market power. Consumers, OPG, and private suppliers would all benefit from careful long-term planning in a secure and stable market. Price volatility and uncertainty are favoured by neither producers nor consumers.

NOTES

1 The Ontario Clean Air Alliance and the Ontario Medical Association estimate that 1,800 people die every year in Ontario due to air pollution (Ontario Clean Air Alliance, 2002).

REFERENCES

Alesina, A., and Summers, L. 1993. 'Central Bank Independence and Macro-economic Performance.' *Journal of Money, Credit and Banking.* May. 151–62.

Bailey, E.E. 1981. 'Contestability and the Design of Regulatory and Antitrust Policy.' *American Economic Review* 71 (May): 178–83.

Baumol, W.J., J.C. Panzet, and R.D. Willig. 1982. *Contestable Markets and Theory of Industry Structure.* New York: Harcourt Brace Jovanovich.

Brennan, T. 2001. 'Drawing Lessons from the California Crisis.' *Resources* 144 (Summer): 8–12.

Crew, M.A., and P.R. Kleindorfer. 1986. *The Economics of Public Utility Regulation.* Cambridge, MA: MIT Press.

Demsetz, H. 1968. 'Why Regulate Utilities?' *Journal of Law and Economics* 11 (April): 55–65.

Economist. 2002. 'High Tension.' 17 October.

Friedman, Lee S. 2002. *The Microeconomics of Public Policy Analysis.* Princeton: Princeton University Press.

Grant, J. 2002. 'Ontario's New Electricity Market.' *Policy Options* 23, no. 4: 56–62.

Green, R., and T. McDaniel. 1998. 'Competition in Electricity Supply: Will "1998" Be Worth it?' *Fiscal Studies* 19, no. 3: 273–93.

Independent Electricity Market Operator of Ontario. 2002. '10-Year Outlook: An Assessment of the Adequacy of Generation and Transmission Facilities to Meet Future Electricity Needs in Ontario.' 3 April. www.theimo.com/imoweb/months/Years/monthsAhead.asp[.]

Kleit, A.N., and D. Terrell. 2001. 'Measuring Potential Efficiency Gains from Deregulation of Electricity Generation: A Bayesian Approach.' *Review of Economics and Statistics* 83, no. 3: August. 523–30.

Kwoka, J.E. 2002. 'Vertical Economies in Electric Power: Evidence on Integration and Its Alternatives.' *International Journal of Industrial Organization* 20, no. 5, 653–71.

Newbery, D.M. 1998. 'Competition, Contracts, and Entry in the Electricity Spot Market.' *Rand Journal of Economics* 29, no. 4: 726–49.

– 2002. 'Problems of Liberalising the Electricity Industry.' *European Economic Review* 46: 919–27.

Newbery, D.M., and G. Pollitt. 1997. 'The Restructuring and Privatisation of Britain's CEGB: Was It Worth It?' *Journal of Industrial Economics* 14, no. 3: 269–303.

Ontario Clean Air Alliance. 2002. www.cleanair.web.ca and www.electricitychoices.ca

Ontario Ministry of Energy. 2003. 'News Release: A Responsible Approach to Electricity Pricing, for a Change.' www.energy.gov.on.ca (accessed 3 November 2003).

OPG (Ontario Power Generation). 2001a. *Greenhouse Gas Action Plan – 2000.* Submitted to Canada's Climate Change Voluntary Challenge and Registry Inc., www.opg.com/envComm?E_emissions_air.asp (accessed October 2001).

– 2001b. *Towards Sustainable Development – 2001 Progress Report.* www.opg.com/envComm?E_emissions_air.asp

– 2002. 'Environment and Community-Emissions.' www.opg.com/envComm?E_emissions_air.asp

Schiller, T. 2001. 'Rewiring the System: The Changing Structure of the Electric Power Industry.' *Business Review* 1: 26–33.

Schott, S. 2002. 'Are There Any Convincing Economic Reasons for Electricity Privatization and Deregulation in Ontario?' *Policy Options* 23, no. 7: 44–6.

Trebing, H.M. 2000. 'Electricity: Changes and Issues.' *Review of Industrial Organization* 17: 61–74.

USDA Office of the Chief Economist. 1999. *Electric Utility Deregulation: Rural Effects.* Briefing to Senior USDA Policy Officials. January.

U.S. DOE (Department of Energy). 1999. *Supporting Analysis for the Administration's Comprehensive Electricity Competition Act.* Washington: USDOE. May.

Chapter 8

Alberta's Oil and Gas Industry in the Era of the Kyoto Protocol

KEITH BROWNSEY

On 2 September 2002, the world turned upside down for the Alberta oil patch. At the Johannesburg Summit on a Sustainable Environment, Prime Minister Jean Chrétien announced that Canada would both ratify and implement the Kyoto Protocol on Climate Change. Canada's formal commitment to reduce its greenhouse gas emissions (GHGs) to 6 per cent below 1990 levels was widely perceived by various oil patch representatives and also by the provincial government as having a negative impact on the industry. The Alberta oil patch had been living in the shadow of the Kyoto Protocol since its very inception in December 1997 and had adapted to the reality of a federal government committed to a policy of sustainable development (Sharpe, 2002); even so, the September announcement came as a surprise. Both the oil and gas industry and the Alberta government had expected further consultations and a commitment that Kyoto would not place the oil patch at a disadvantage with its major competitors. For example, Lorne Taylor, Alberta's environment minister, 'immediately denounced the move as a betrayal of his province akin to the imposition of the hated National Energy Program of the early 1980s' (*Calgary Herald*, A1).

This was a surprising turn of events. With the dismantling of the National Energy Program (NEP) in 1985 and the implementation of the Canada–U.S. Free Trade Agreement in 1989, the federal government had abandoned its efforts to manage the oil and gas industry. Although Ottawa had kept for itself a role in competition and environmental regulation through its strategy of sustainable development, it was continuing to rely on the free market as the best means of ensuring inexpensive and secure supplies of energy for Canada (Natural Resources Canada, 2000, 7). Moreover, in 2001 it had loudly announced its approval of the Bush administration's National Energy Plan and promised to do everything it could to sell Alberta's oil and gas to the voracious American market.

The renewed federal interest was, however, very different from past attempts by Ottawa to intervene in Alberta's oil patch. The NEP of the 1980s had had a nationalist thrust; this time, the Chrétien government had a very different reason for intervening. The new federal initiatives have a multilateral emphasis that is the antithesis of the continentalist focus of the Alberta oil and gas industry, the provincial government, and the Bush administration. Ottawa's goal was not to secure supply or to share in the wealth of the oil and gas sector. Through its sustainable development framework and its ratification of Kyoto, the Liberal government was seeking to counter the new-sovereignist tendencies of the Bush Administration (Hirsh, 2002, 18–43; Ikenberry, 2002, 44–60) and to regain a place in the oil and gas sector through an environmental policy designed to promote a multilateral approach to climate change. Federal efforts to resist the north–south pull of the United States and to regain at least some influence in the oil patch are attempts to reduce the harmful effects of global warming by reducing GHG emissions. But they are also attempts to maintain Canada's position in global affairs as a supporter of multilateralism in the international community, and to counter the unilateralism of the United States.

As an international agreement to reduce GHGs, the Kyoto Protocol is central to the federal government's sustainable development and environmental strategies, but it is also a step toward integrating the oil patch with the international community. Throughout the 1980s and 1990s, the Alberta oil and gas industry sought to end the NEP and defended both the 1988 Canada–U.S. Free Trade Agreement and the 1993 North American Free Trade Agreement (NAFTA). Although the industry had fought for continental integration of the oil and gas industry – its version of globalization – it had not foreseen Canada's extension of global commitments beyond the opening and securing of markets. The oil patch had adopted much of the rhetoric and program of the federal government's strategy of sustainable development. The industry had even praised the federal government's continuing support of oil sands and heavy oil development as well as its continuing efforts to sell Alberta natural gas and oil in the American and international markets. But the idea that globalization could mean anything but the ability to explore, produce, and sell oil and gas was unthinkable. The debate over the Kyoto Protocol does not reflect the traditional continentalist–nationalist tension in Canadian politics; rather, it suggests a possible new paradigm that would pit the continentalist tendencies of George W. Bush's new-sovereignist foreign policy against the expanding multilateralism of the Canadian government and its environmental policies, as embodied in a program of sustainable development and the Kyoto Protocol.

The Alberta Oil Patch

Alberta is by far Canada's leading producer of crude oil and natural gas, accounting for 70 per cent of Canada's total petroleum production. At the end of 2001, Canada had 6.6 billion barrels (bb) of conventional crude oil reserves – 6.6 per cent of the world's reserves (BP Amoco, 2002, 4, 20). Regarding natural gas, Canada has an estimated 733 trillion cubic feet (tcf) of ultimate resource potential reserves – 13.3 per cent of the world's total (National Energy Board, 1999, 43). Alberta has 19.7 bb of crude oil and 200 tcf of natural gas in the form of potential recoverable reserves (AEUB, 2002a, 2).

Alberta has the largest oil sands (crude bitumen) deposits in the world. Alberta oil production from raw bitumen – the tar sands and heavy oil – exceeded conventional oil production for the first time in 2001. Under anticipated technology and economic conditions, it may be possible to recover 315 bb of conventional oil from this resource. This compares very favourably with Saudi Arabian reserves, which are estimated to be 261.1 bb. The total in situ and accessible remaining established reserves are 174 bb. These figures are not considered in totals of world reserves by the International Energy Agency (IEA), the U.S. Department of Energy (DOE), or the BP Amoco annual survey of world supplies. By the end of 2001, only 2 per cent of Alberta's established crude bitumen reserves had been produced.

Alberta's remaining reserves of conventional crude oil are estimated at 1.75 bb, and its ultimate potential recoverable reserves at 19.7 bb. These estimates are based on the hope that 'improvements in technology could improve the current recovery efficiency of 27 per cent.' Alberta's 2001 production from conventional oil, oil sands, and pentanes was 1.53 million barrels per day (mbd).

Since the mid-1970s, Alberta's conventional reserves of crude oil have been steadily declining. Reserves are estimated at 19.7 bb, and annual production in 2000 was 893,000 bpd. Thus, at current rates of production, Alberta's supplies of conventional crude will run out around 2060. Demand for oil is expected to rise over the next decade, so Alberta's conventional reserves are likely to deplete long before this date. Although conventional oil production will continue to decline, the AEUB estimates that production of bitumen will triple by 2011. This figure will account for as much as 75 per cent of Alberta's total oil supply. In 2000, production reached 605,000 bpd. Around C$85 billion of investment has been announced for the tar sands since 1996. This investment is expected to double current oil production in Alberta. The future of Alberta's oil and gas industry rests with the production of oil from bitumen reserves.

Natural gas reserves in Alberta are estimated at 200 tcf. At the end of 2001, Alberta had 42 tcf remaining in its established reserves. New drilling has not replaced natural gas production since 1982; production in 2001 replaced only 67 per cent of production from the previous year. This compared to 90 per cent replacement in 2000. Natural gas reserve estimates do not include coalbed methane, which the AEUB believes has the potential to add significantly to Alberta's reserves. If this projection is correct, gas supply could be revised upward by a considerable amount.

The oil and gas industry is essential to Alberta's prosperity. In fiscal year 2000–1, an exceptional year for oil and gas prices, non-renewable resources accounted for $10.58 billion of the province's revenues (41.3 per cent). This figure declined sharply in fiscal years 2001–2: the total revenue from non-renewable resources was $3.7 billion on provincial revenues of $19.2 billion. This was a decline of $6.8 billion, or 65.03 per cent. Non-renewable resources accounted for just 19.3 per cent of total provincial revenues in fiscal year 2001–2 (Finance Alberta 2001, 2002).

Canada is the second-largest foreign supplier of oil to the United States as well as that country's largest supplier of natural gas. Since the release in May 2001 of the Bush Administration's National Energy Policy, American attention has focused on Canadian reserves of oil and gas as a secure and accessible source of energy. In 2000, Canada provided 12 per cent of American natural gas supplies and approximately 11 per cent of its oil imports (Alberta, n.d.). As conventional supplies of oil decrease, the oil sands will become more important to energy supply in both Canada and the United States. The Bush Administration describes the continued development of this non-conventional source of oil as a 'pillar of sustained North American energy and economic security' (National Energy Policy Development Group 2001, x-x). The Bush National Energy Policy has stimulated American interest in Alberta's tar sands as a safe and secure source for oil and other petroleum products. The continuing integration of the North American energy markets – especially in the oil and gas sector – is going to be vital to Alberta's tar sands and heavy oil development. Simply put, Alberta's oil patch is going to depend on increasing production of non-conventional sources of oil and natural gas and on access to American markets. It has been the policy of the provincial government to support both the development of non-conventional oil production and the integration of the provincial industry with the American market.

Alberta's Oil and Gas Industry, 1905–92

The Alberta government's oil and gas policies have largely been a response to federal intrusions into what the province sees as a purely provincial jurisdiction. Under section 109 of the Constitution Act, 1867, Canada's provinces were given control over natural resources. But that Constitution also assigned the federal government authority over interprovincial and international trade, as well as other powers. The jurisdictional disputes that have arisen between Ottawa and Alberta have strongly influenced the evolution of the province's oil and gas industry.

The history of the Alberta oil patch can be divided in four phases: the semicolonial period, 1905–30; the era of multinational domination, 1930–69; the years when the multinationals withdrew and the industry was Canadianized, 1969–85; and, since 1985, the switch to non-conventional oil recovery, the rise of natural gas as the industry's dominant segment, and the increasing reliance on market mechanisms to provide low-cost and plentiful supplies of oil and natural gas. Ottawa's re-entry into the provincial oil and gas industry through the Kyoto Protocol may signal the end of the free-market continentalism that has dominated the oil patch since the mid-1980s and the beginning of a new phase driven by environmental regulation of the industry.

The Colonial Period

The early days of Alberta's petroleum industry were characterized by federal control and neglect. Under sections 92 and 109 of the Constitution Act, 1867, the provincial governments controlled natural resources; however, between 1869, when Canada assumed control of the Hudson's Bay Company lands, and 1930, twenty-five years after the creation of Alberta and Saskatchewan and the formalization of Manitoba's provincial boundaries, Ottawa retained control over natural resources in the prairie provinces. The Dominion Lands Act of 1872 provided the legal framework for federal control of natural resources in the Northwest Territories and in the provinces of Alberta, Saskatchewan, and Manitoba after 1905 (Breen, 1993). After years of protest over this semicolonial status, the prairie provinces were finally given control over their natural resources in 1930.

Although there are many stories of native and early European encounters with gas leaks and tar, the first producing well in Alberta was drilled at Waterton in 1902. This well, which produced 300 bpd, started a boom in oil and gas exploration in southwestern Alberta. A small settlement, Oil City, was established near that original site. In 1912, a pipeline was built from Bow Island to supply natural gas to Calgary. In 1914, a well was drilled in Turner Valley, southwest of Calgary, and provided fuel for that city. Financed by A.W. Dingman, Bill Herron, Senator James Lougheed, and R.B. Bennett, Dingman No. 1 ignited an oil boom in Calgary. As many as five hundred companies were formed, but only about fifty wells were drilled. The First World War brought an end to the Turner Valley boom; interest was renewed in the field in 1924, when Royalite No. 4 began producing large quantities of natural gas. Almost all of the natural gas, however, was burned off. There are reports that residents of southwest Calgary were able to read by the light generated by this flaring more than fifty kilometers away (Pratt and Richards, 1979, 46–7). Yet Ottawa's interest in the distant oil fields of Alberta was minimal. There was no regulation of the industry, and the oil was depleted in less than four years. The only rule for the dozens of small local producers was to recover as much oil as quickly as possible.

The Era of Multinational Domination

The rapid depletion of oil and gas reserves continued after 1930, when jurisdiction over natural resources was transferred to the prairie provinces. In an attempt to curb the rapacious depletion of known reserves, the United Farmers of Alberta government established the Turner Valley Conservation Board in 1932. After fierce opposition from local producers, this board was disbanded within months. When the

Turner Valley Royalites No. 1 struck oil in 1936, it became the largest oilfield in the British Commonwealth. Finally, in 1938, at the instigation of Imperial Oil and other major producers, the Social Credit government of William Aberhart created the Oil and Gas Conservation Board. Modelled after conservation commissions in Oklahoma and Texas and in keeping with the ideology of the early Social Credit government, this board was an attempt to end the competition between Imperial Oil and the small local producers. Each side recognized that there had to be some form of regulation if the field was to be sustained and expanded and if recovery rates and profits were to be maximized (Breen, 1993, 55–8).

Aberhart died in 1943. His successor, Ernest Manning, encouraged multinational companies to develop Alberta's petroleum reserves as quickly as possible. In the postwar era, however, Turner Valley was in decline, and the future of Alberta's petroleum sector looked bleak. Imperial Oil, the Canadian subsidiary of Standard Oil of New Jersey, had decided to end its exploration program in the Western Sedimentary Basin. Then on 13 February 1947, the legendary Imperial drill foreman, Vernon 'Dry Hole' Hunter, brought in Leduc No. 1. This strike, and the establishment of the Oil and Gas Conservation Board, created the conditions for the entry into Alberta of multinational petroleum companies, most but not all of them American. For the next twenty years, the Social Credit government actively encouraged the development of Alberta's oil and gas reserves through the multinationals, at the expense of smaller Canadian firms.

The production side of Alberta's oil and gas industry in the 1950s and 1960s was dominated by the four Canadian representatives of the 'Seven Sisters.' The Seven Sisters were the large, vertically integrated, multinational oil and gas companies: Royal Dutch/Shell, British Petroleum, Imperial/Exxon, Texaco, Gulf, Standard Oil of California, and Mobil. Four of these firms operated in Canada: Shell, Imperial/Exxon, Gulf, and Texaco. These 'Big Four' dominated the Canadian oil market and had significant interests in the natural gas sector.

As the 1950s began, Alberta oil and gas producers were lobbying the federal government to protect them from low-priced foreign imports. In response to these requests, the Diefenbaker government appointed Henry Borden to examine Canada's energy situation. The Borden Inquiry discovered a conflict between the multinational oil companies and local producers. The Canadian subsidiaries of the Big Four were the biggest producers of Alberta oil and gas, and they had little interest in shipping Alberta crude to central and eastern Canada. Through their multinational parents, the Big Four provided their refineries in the Montreal area with cheap imported oil. There was little incentive to sell expensive Alberta oil to consumers in Ontario and Quebec.

Alberta's producers wanted secure markets. Because various restrictions kept them out of the United States, their alternative was central and eastern Canada. The local companies wanted a more efficient pipeline than the existing Interprovincial line to Ontario, and they wanted a tariff on imported oil. What the Alberta producers got was a compromise. The federal government erected an artificial barrier, the Ottawa Valley line. Markets west of the line were reserved for Alberta oil, whereas those east of the Ottawa River, would continue to rely on inexpensive imported oil and gas. The National Oil Policy was established in 1960 at the same time as the Organization of Petroleum Exporting Countries (OPEC) in order to prevent the Seven Sisters from driving oil and gas prices any lower (Foster, 1979, 27–31).

In the 1950s and 1960s, other developments were taking place in Alberta's oil and gas industry. The major issue of the multinational era was how to transport Alberta oil and gas to market. Geology had blessed the province with petroleum resources; geography had cursed it. Alberta is far from the consumers of its oil and gas and must spend considerable sums shipping those products to market. This has been reflected both in debates over freight rates and in debates over petroleum pipelines.

By the mid-1950s it had been determined that Alberta's reserves of natural gas were sufficient to supply markets on the West Coast and in central Canada. Three major pipelines were constructed during this decade to ship these reserves to market. The largest is TransCanada Pipelines Ltd. (TCPL). Created by the federal government in the late 1950s, TCPL was designed to bring Alberta gas to markets in central Canada. Although subsidized and partially constructed by the federal government, TCPL was a privately held corporation. Its creation was a strong sign of Ottawa's interest in Alberta's reserves of natural gas and oil. This was the first major federal incursion into the oil patch since 1930, when Ottawa ceded control over natural resources to the prairie provinces.

The Alberta Gas Trunk Line (AGTL) was incorporated by the province in 1954 to serve as a common carrier for natural gas. Its purpose was to stabilize the price of natural gas and to ensure Albertans that they would have voting shares in the new provincial enterprise. To that end, these shares were distributed among Alberta's utilities, gas processors, and export interests, as well as the government. Non-voting shares were made available to Alberta residents. Although the AGTL was funded by the province, it was controlled by the natural gas processors and the utilities. This reflected Manning's aversion to Crown corporations and his faith in the private sector. Also, it provided the province with a window into the industry as well as an advantage over the federal government in light of Ottawa's renewed interest in Alberta's petroleum reserves (Breen, 1993, 403–7). The third major pipeline built in the 1950s was Frank McMahon's Westcoast Transmission. Designed to transport natural gas to the British Columbia coast and eventually to American markets, this met with federal, provincial, and American resistance.

By the late 1960s, conventional reserves were declining. The Big Four were looking outside the province for new reserves. As a consequence, wildcat drilling – exploration away from known reserves – dropped by 40 per cent between 1969 and 1971. Over the same period, Alberta's share of exploration dropped from three-quarters of the Canadian total to just over half. By the early 1970s, the Big Four had pulled out of Alberta, having concluded that there were no more large deposits of oil or gas – what the industry calls elephants – to be found in Alberta. Their focus was now on the Arctic and overseas.

The Nationalization of Oil and Gas

In the late 1960s and early 1970s, a number of factors combined to alter the structure of Alberta's oil and gas industry. After the Big Four abandoned the province for other locations, the exploration side of the business was left to the smaller multinationals and to a number of emerging Canadian-owned companies. There had always been Canadian companies in the Alberta oil patch, but they were small as well as few in number. As the 1960s ended, 98 per cent of the provincial oil and gas industry was under foreign (mainly American) control.

The withdrawal of the multinational oil and gas companies from Alberta in the late 1960s paved the way for political change in Alberta. In August 1971, the Progressive Conservatives led by Peter Lougheed defeated the thirty-six-year-old Social Credit government. One of the reasons for the Social Credit defeat was concern that Alberta was not receiving its fair share of oil and gas revenues. The Social Credit government had placed few controls on the multinationals. Royalty rates were reviewed only once every ten years, the multinationals were consulted on any changes to government policy, and Canadian investment was actively discouraged. Manning saw his role as providing a stable political environment for the foreign-based industry. Lougheed, in contrast, did not trust the big oil companies. He understood that the interests of the multinationals did not necessarily coincide with those of the province. He was willing to offer incentives to smaller Canadian companies, but he did not advocate a policy of rapid depletion of conventional reserves by the large, foreign-based oil and gas companies. His campaign focused on the problem of what do when the oil and gas ran out (Foster, 1979, 38–41).

The debate between the Alberta and federal governments over energy pricing shifted suddenly in October 1973, after the OPEC oil embargo. In response to Western, especially American, support for Israel during the Yom Kippur War, OPEC cut off shipments of crude oil to the West. The price of a barrel of crude oil shot up from approximately US$3 per barrel to over $12 per barrel WTI. The OPEC oil shock of 1973 sent the multinationals scrambling to find secure supplies of crude and natural gas. One obvious place to look was Alberta. The price jump in oil was an incentive for the multinationals to return to the Alberta oil patch.

Ottawa was embarrassed by statements made by the natural resources minister, Joe Greene, in the House of Commons in June 1971, to the effect that Canada had a 923-year supply of oil and a 392-year supply of gas (ibid., 51). Also, it had been caught by surprise by the OPEC embargo in October 1973. So the federal government thought it necessary to create a national oil and gas company with various national goals. Among these goals were to increase domestic ownership of the industry; to develop reserves not located in the West; to gather better information about the petroleum industry; to ensure security of supply; to lessen Canada's dependence on the large multinational oil corporations, especially the Big Four; and to increase revenues flowing to the federal treasury from the oil and gas sector (Fossum, 1997). These goals were very similar to those of state-owned corporations in other countries, yet they were controversial in Canada (Olav Fjell, president of the Norwegian State Oil Company, Statoil, news conference, World Petroleum Conference, Calgary, 14 June 2000). In 1974, the federal government established a state-owned oil company, Petro-Canada. Petro-Can was resented by both oil patch veterans and the provincial government. The oil patch players had a self-image of rugged individualism, and they resented any state incursion as an unnecessary impediment to their God-given right to drill, produce, and market oil and natural gas (House, 1980). In this context, Petro-Canada was a means for the federal government to enter into the petroleum industry.

Lougheed had committed his government to economic diversification through increased oil and gas revenues. Any attempt by Ottawa to reduce these revenues or to interfere in any way with Alberta's efforts to create a viable oil and gas economy was strongly resented. As a result, Canadian and Albertan energy policy lack a coherence found in other jurisdictions. Instead of working together to maximize revenues and recovery, the two levels of government were in constant conflict over the direction and control of the oil and gas industry (Fossum, 1997).

A second oil shock came on the heels of the 1979 revolution in Iran. Although the Shah's overthrow was welcomed by most Iranians, their country soon fell into the hands of Islamist fundamentalists, whose hatred of the West was profound. The revolutionaries simply stopped exporting oil to the West. After the 1979 seizure of the U.S. Embassy in Tehran and the taking of American hostages by state-sponsored protestors, the Americans imposed economic sanctions, froze Iranian assets in the United States, and prohibited imports of Iranian oil. Oil prices rose dramatically, from just under US$20 a barrel to $40, and were expected to go much higher.

Ottawa's response to all of this was to increase its involvement in the energy sector. As part of its National Energy Program (NEP), the federal government offered incentives for drilling in the Canada lands, increased export taxes on oil and gas, and established a variety of 'off oil' policies in an effort to conserve domestic oil and gas reserves while decreasing dependence on foreign energy supplies. The goals of the NEP were much the same as those which led to the creation of Petro-Canada. The federal government wanted to alleviate the shock of recent dramatic hikes in the price of oil and natural gas by keeping prices below world levels, by increasing its share of revenues from the petroleum industry, by continuing to promote the Canadianization of the industry, and by ensuring that Ottawa would play a national role in energy affairs. Although a number of domestic companies benefited from the federal initiatives, the NEP was strongly resented in the oil patch, as well as by the Alberta government and most of that province's people.

After a series of negotiations between Alberta and Ottawa, an agreement was reached concerning pricing and taxation. As well, Alberta and the other producing provinces were able to secure an amendment to the existing constitutional division of powers – one that would strengthen provincial control over natural resources. However, the constitutional amendments and the agreement that had been negotiated would both maintain the basic structure of the NEP.

The Era of Benign Neglect

The election of the Progressive Conservatives under Brian Mulroney in September 1984 changed federal oil and gas policy dramatically. The West was strongly represented in the government caucus and the Cabinet, so it was no surprise that both were open to demands from the Western oil and gas producing provinces that the NEP be dismantled. One of the Mulroney government's first acts was to negotiate an end to the NEP. In April 1985, the Western Accord was signed, which effectively dismantled the NEP.

World energy prices collapsed in 1986. Oil was suddenly selling for around US$12 per barrel, and natural gas for US$1 per thousand cubic feet. In the oil patch, thousands of workers were laid off. The federal government's response to the drop in oil and gas prices was one of benign neglect. During the negotiations to end the NEP, the Lougheed government had contemplated an arrangement whereby the federal government would guarantee a minimum price for both oil and gas. This proposal was taken off the table by Alberta in favour of establishing a market price for oil and gas. After Lougheed's retirement in the fall of 1985, the new Progressive Conservative premier, Donald Getty – a former provincial minister of energy and intergovernmental relations in the Lougheed governments of 1971–9, as well as an executive in the oil patch – faced a crisis. Getty had to manage a dramatic and sudden downturn in the price of oil and gas. Investment in Alberta's oil and gas industry had come to a halt, and with shrinking provincial revenues, Alberta faced a series of budget deficits.

The Getty government's response was to cut spending on various public programs, from health to education, and to increase subsidies to business in an effort to stabilize the energy sector. In April, June, October, and December 1986, new subsidies were announced and existing programs were expanded. The Royalty Tax Credit Program, the Alberta Petroleum Incentives Program, and the Exploratory Drilling Assistance Program were created. Combined with other energy subsidies, subsidies to the oil and gas industry amounted to $16 billion in 1987 (Taft, 1997, 46).

Questions about Canadian ownership and security of supply were no longer a concern of federal energy policy. Instead, Ottawa would rely on low prices and unfettered markets to supply Canadians with inexpensive oil and gas. With the signing of the Canada–U.S. Free Trade Agreement (FTA) in 1988, state intervention in the oil and gas sector was restricted. Simply put, under the terms of the FTA, Canada could no longer give preference to Canadians. American markets and businesses were to be given proportional access to Canadian oil and gas.

The Alberta oil patch was undergoing another type of change. In the mid-1980s, the multinational oil and gas corporations that had returned to Alberta in the early 1970s after the oil shock of 1973–4 began to shift their focus away from conventional petroleum reserves, toward the tar sands and heavy oil deposits in northern and central Alberta. Royal Dutch/Shell, Mobil, and several other multinationals announced huge investments in non-conventional reserves.

Ralph Klein and the Triumph of the Market

In the fall of 1992, Alberta underwent a political transformation. Faced with a series of budget deficits and an economic slowdown arising mainly from low oil and gas prices, the Getty government had become increasingly unpopular. One poll in the fall of 1992 placed Progressive Conservative support at 18 per cent of decided voters. On a trip through New England in September 1992, Getty decided to leave political life. In the bitter leadership race that followed, the Lougheed/Getty era came to an end with the selection of Ralph Klein, former Calgary mayor and provincial environment minister, as Progressive Conservative leader and premier. It was a historic shift.

Klein's focus as premier was on eliminating the provincial budget deficit and debt. In a series of spending decreases through the mid-1990s, Klein reduced provincial spending by an average of 20 per cent across all departments. Despite the massive reductions in provincial spending, the provincial government gave the oil and gas industry a royalty holiday of $250 million in late 1992. The new federal Liberal government's ratification of the North American Free Trade Agreement (NAFTA) in November 1993 further reduced the power of the federal and provincial governments to determine pricing and to secure the supply of oil and gas for domestic markets. The oil and gas industry was now integrated with the American market. The provincial and federal governments had removed any impediments to the full integration of Alberta's oil and gas industry with the North American and world markets.

The election of the Chrétien Liberals in October 1993 added another dimension to the federal–provincial energy mix. In their Election Redbook, the Liberals proposed an environmental–economic model of sustainable development for all its economic policies, including its energy policy. The first department to define sustainable development in its legislation and place it within its mandate was Natural Resources Canada (NRCan). Its *Sustainable Development Strategy* was tabled in Parliament in the fall of 1997. The department defined sustainable development as development that meets the needs of the present without compromising the ability of future generations to meet their own needs (NRCan, 1997, 6). This policy did not preclude tax breaks and other incentives for the development of the oil sands and heavy oil, nor did it preclude continuing efforts by Ottawa to sell Canadian energy in American and other markets. Ottawa's sustainable development strategy has seen the industry reduce emissions of various GHGs and other substances. At the same time, though, the Alberta oil and gas industry has successfully lobbied the federal and provincial governments for help in producing and marketing its products (Fairley, 2003, 40–3).

In February 1995, as part of the general restructuring and fiscal restraint initiatives of the Alberta government, the Energy Resources Conservation Board (ERCB) was merged with the Public Utilities Commission (PUC) to form the Alberta Energy and Utilities Board (AEUB), and its provincial grant was slashed by more than 20 per cent. The funding formula for the new AEUB was different from that of its predecessor. With an expanded mandate that now included both the petroleum and electricity sectors, the AEUB was to be funded 70 per cent by industry and 30 per cent by the province. The reorganized board faced a variety of problems. The most immediate was how to blend the two previously separate units – the ERCB and the PUB. The two organizations had different administrative styles that were difficult to reconcile. In April 1996, the Alberta Geological Survey joined the AEUB. During the transition, the old ERCB came to dominate the new organization. The AEUB has regulatory authority over all aspects of energy resource development in the province.

In the mid and late 1990s, there were more than 166 different acts of vandalism in the oil and gas fields around Beaver Lodge and Hythe near Grande Prairie, northeast of Edmonton. The individual at the centre of this controversy was Weibo Ludwig. Ludwig was certain that gas flaring near his religious commune had caused the stillbirth of several children and animals. It has been alleged that Ludwig, frustrated with the failure of the provincial environment ministry and the AEUB to act on his complaints, resorted to a series of sometimes violent acts to end the intrusion of oil and gas companies on his land and the land adjacent to his property. Although he was convicted on several counts of vandalism and public mischief, he was not charged with any of the numerous bombings of natural gas installations in the Hythe region. In fact, the RCMP and the Alberta Energy Company later admitted that they had used explosives to destroy a gas well shed as part of an elaborate scheme to implicate Ludwig in other similar incidents. Although the bombings and other acts of violence should not be minimized – especially the shooting death of a local teenager, Carmen Wylis, on Ludwig's farm – the incidents at Hythe demonstrated that the AEUB and the environment ministry were unable to address concerns over gas flaring and other issues associated with the exploration and production of natural gas (Nikiforuk, 2001).

The New NEP and Kyoto

On 11 December 1997, the Government of Canada and 159 other states signed the Kyoto Protocol to the UN Framework Convention on Climate Change. In doing so, Canada committed itself to reducing its GHGs to 6 per cent below 1990 levels by no later than 2012. The Kyoto Protocol – the final piece in the federal government's environmental policy – fit with the federal framework of innovation and sustainable development. Kyoto seeks to reduce GHGs – mainly CO_2, nitrous oxide, and methane emissions. These gases are generally agreed to be major contributors to global warming. GHGs arise from the burning of carbon-based fuels such as oil, natural gas, and coal. The protocol 'stipulates that progress in achieving this reduction commitment will be measured through the use of a set of internationally agreed-to emissions and removals inventory methodologies and reporting guidelines' (Olsen et al., 2002, iii). Kyoto will enter into force as soon as fifty-five signatories to the convention accounting for a total of 55 per cent of GHGs have agreed to ratification.

In 2000, Canada emitted into the atmosphere approximately 726 megatonnes (Mt) of CO_2 equivalent. This was a 19.6 per cent increase over 1990 levels. That same year, the electricity and petroleum industries accounted for 264 Mt, or 36 per cent, of total national emissions. Petroleum-related emissions accounted for 52 per cent of energy-generated GHGs in 2000. Since 1990, emissions have grown by almost 38 per cent in the electricity and petroleum sectors. The petroleum industry's emissions increased 40 per cent over this period. This rise was due largely to increased production of oil and gas for export. Alberta's energy sector contributed 223,000 kilotonnes of GHG emissions in 2000. This was 30.7 per cent of the national total. Ontario, in contrast, with three times the population of Alberta, contributed 207 (Mt) or 29 per cent of Canadian GHGs. Clearly, any effort to reduce GHGs is going to have a strong impact on Alberta, specifically, on the province's oil and gas industry and on the urban cowboys of Calgary who insist on driving oversized, urban assault vehicles commonly known as SUVs.

Through the provincial government and several industry organizations, the Alberta oil and gas industry has expressed its dislike of the Kyoto Protocol. In September 2002, the province launched a $1.5 million advertising campaign designed to weaken public support for Kyoto. On 17 October 2002, the Alberta government announced its own made-in-Alberta climate change plan. This initiative was designed as a partnership between the province, the federal government, and the private sector. Instead of the absolute reductions as defined in the Kyoto Protocol, the made-in-Alberta plan calls for cuts to GHG emissions intensity (emissions divided by gross domestic product) by 50 per cent below 1990 levels by the year 2020 (Alberta Environment, 'Finalized Made-in-Alberta Climate Change Plan Released,' 17 October 2002). Polling data indicate that the apocalyptic provincial advertising, with its warning that thousands of jobs may be lost and that living standards may be lowered, has succeeded. A majority of Albertans now oppose the ratification and implementation of Kyoto (Chase and Mahoney, 2002, A1).

The ratification and implementation of the Kyoto Protocol was not a total surprise to the oil and gas industry. However, the industry had expected to be informed of the ratification and implementation plans. From the perspective of the petroleum industry, Ottawa has no oil and gas policy, nor has it a clear strategy for implementing the requirement for GHG reductions mandated by Kyoto. Admittedly, consultations between representatives of the oil patch and the federal government gave the industry some input into the implementation process. After George W. Bush was elected in November 2000 and his administration rejected Kyoto, the Alberta government, various industry groups, and the federal government all agreed that Kyoto could not be implemented in its present form. Opponents of the agreement argued that any effort to require Canadian industry to reduce GHG emissions without the active participation of the United States would place Canada at a comparative economic disadvantage in relation to its largest trading partner. The Alberta oil patch, moreover, believed that it would carry a disproportionate burden in meeting the Kyoto targets. The province's conventional oil and natural gas would be affected by the implementation of Kyoto, but the non-conventional oil reserves (i.e., the tar sands and heavy oil deposits) would suffer the greatest blow. The costs associated with reducing GHGs would fall disproportionately on the non-conventional oil and raise recovery costs by as much as US$6 per barrel – based on the industry standard of West Texas Intermediate (WTI) oil – from the current US$18. With Middle Eastern oil averaging a recovery cost of $6 or less per barrel WTI, the costs of Kyoto would price Alberta non-conventional reserves out of the North American and world markets. Billions of dollars in planned investment could be lost, and Alberta's future economic prosperity could be threatened. In Alberta's oil patch, comparisons with the widely unpopular 1980 NEP abounded.

Six months earlier, the situation in Alberta's oil and gas sector had been very different. In May 2001, the Bush Administration had released its National Energy Policy. The policy – written by the National Energy Policy Advisory Group and chaired by Vice-President Dick Cheney, the former CEO of Haliburton Corporation, one of the largest oil and gas field service firms in the world – called for secure supplies of oil and gas for the United States through such mechanisms as enhanced recovery, increases in domestic supplies, and global alliances (National Energy Policy Development Group, 2001). Canada's deregulated energy sector has become the Americans' largest energy-trading partner as well as their leading supplier of natural gas, oil, and electricity. In 2000, Canada supplied 14 per cent of American energy needs through an integrated network of pipelines and electricity lines. Canadian energy supplies – especially natural gas and oil – were not described as foreign sources of energy but rather as part of the American domestic supply. The Americans' recognition of Canada's importance as a source of energy was seen as part of the evolution of an integrated North American energy sector.

The federal Liberal government supported the Alberta oil and gas sector's efforts to sell its oil and gas to American consumers. After years of distrust and some recent controversy – it was widely noted in the Alberta media that the prime minister had not visited Calgary during the 2000 federal election – Ottawa was making an effort to reassure the Western producers that it welcomed the Bush National Energy Policy and that it would do all it could to sell Alberta oil and gas in the United States. With the average price for a barrel of oil at US\$23 WTI, and with gas hovering around US\$3 mcf, the prospects for further investment, increased sales, and expanded markets looked very good.

Although the U.S. invasion of Iraq and its aftermath has propelled the price of oil to record levels, and reported shortages have pushed the value of natural gas to US\$6 mcf, there is recognition within the Alberta petroleum industry that these prices may not be sustainable. The downturn in energy demand following the 11 September 2001 terrorist attacks on New York and Washington had depressed oil prices to below US\$20 per barrel and gas prices to well under US\$3 mcf. The prospect that taxation would be resorted to to reduce CO_2 emissions of as much as US\$50 a ton threatened to drive investment out of heavy oil and tar sands. This situation was exacerbated by the vague nature of the federal government's commitment to Kyoto. The oil and gas industry and the Alberta government lashed out at the federal government for its contradictory policies toward Kyoto. The prime minister was committing Canada to meeting the standards set by the protocol, but Ottawa was not offering any clear signals as to how it proposed to meet these goals, and it continued to insist that it fully supported Bush's National Energy Policy.

The Alberta government now proposed its own made-in-Canada alternative to Kyoto. In October 2002, the Klein government released *Albertans and Climate Change: Taking Action* (Alberta Environment, 2002). While tacitly acknowledging the relationship between GHGs and global warming, the province argued that emissions should be reduced not absolutely, as mandated by Kyoto, but rather in terms of their intensity. In this way, the equivalent of 60 million tonnes of GHG emissions would be removed from the atmosphere by 2020. The difference between the two plans is profound. Factoring in the projected growth in provincial oil and gas production, the province's plan would, in effect, increase GHGs by some 45 per cent in absolute terms over 2001 levels. Emphasizing the need for flexibility, *Albertans and Climate Change* focused on the need for new technologies, industry consultation in the formulation of rules and regulations, and conservation measures, all designed to reduce emission intensity.

The ratification of the Kyoto Protocol signals a reregulation of the oil and gas industry by the federal government, albeit in a very different way than under the 1980 NEP. This time the federal government is not seeking to Canadianize the industry, or to secure oil and gas for domestic consumption and industrial advantage, or even to share in the profits generated by the Alberta oil patch. Instead, Ottawa has begun a process of horizontal environmental regulation – regulatory stacking. Combined with American efforts to secure a safe and reliable source of oil and natural gas, this has left Alberta's, and Canada's, oil and gas industry in a very unclear position (Doern, 1999, 82–97). The Alberta oil and gas sector is caught between the contradictory impulses of the federal government's multilateralist policies and the continentalizing impulses of the United States under Bush's new-sovereignty unilateralism. It is within this uneasy balance between the two competing forces that the Alberta petroleum industry finds itself.

Conclusions

The Alberta oil and gas industry is in a period of change. But what *kind* of change has not been determined. The industry now finds itself pulled between two competing and contradictory priorities. On one side is the Bush Administration's effort to secure a safe and plentiful supply of inexpensive energy. The continentalist initiative is supported by the provincial government of Ralph Klein and the oil and gas industry. The federal government continues to support Alberta's efforts to sell its oil and natural gas in the American and international markets, but it also plans to implement the Kyoto Protocol on reducing GHGs. It seems that the federal Liberals believe they can implement the Kyoto Protocol and their overall sustainable development initiative while at the same time continuing a policy of continental energy integration. This contradictory policy will allow Alberta's oil and gas industry and provincial government to continue to develop the oil sands and heavy oil deposits as well as natural gas reserves and conventional oil reserves. The provincial government has acknowledged the impact of GHGs on global warming, but the industry has not. Through various organizations, the Alberta oil patch is continuing to lobby the federal government for exemptions and reductions to soften the possible impacts of the Kyoto Protocol. These efforts have resulted in a Kyoto implementation plan that is, if not optimal, is at least acceptable to the industry.

The Alberta oil and gas industry has evolved in four distinct historical phases, each identified by the relationship between the provincial and federal governments. The first, from 1869 to 1930, was the colonial phase. During this time, the federal government had jurisdiction over Alberta's natural resources. When the province obtained control over natural resources in 1930, a second phase began. This era saw the provincial government focus on attracting and placating the large (mainly American) oil companies. The Social Credit government of Ernest Manning fostered a deliberate policy of discouraging domestic investment and encouraging multinational oil companies – the Big Four, as they came to be known – to exploit Alberta's oil and gas reserves as quickly as possible. The Manning government refused to impose any restrictions on the multinationals. There were no requirements to use Canadian labour, management, services, or goods.

The third phase in the history of Alberta's oil and gas sector began with the election of Peter Lougheed's Progressive Conservative government in 1971. Lougheed demanded concessions – however minimal – from the foreign-based energy companies. With the oil shocks of the 1970s, the provincial government was distracted from its goals of maximizing returns from a non-renewable resource because it had to focus on thwarting the efforts of the federal government to nationalize and manage the oil and gas industry. The nationalist era in the oil patch ended officially in 1985 with the signing of the Western Accord. The Western Accord effectively ended the federal Liberal's NEP and replaced it with a system of supply and distribution based on free-market principles. The official end of the NEP did not mean that it had not achieved several of its goals. For example, the Canadian oil and gas industry – within a few percentage points up or down – is now more that 50 per cent domestically owned and controlled.

The Alberta oil patch was surprised by the lack of consultation leading up to the announcement that Canada would ratify and implement the Kyoto Protocol on Climate Change. The oil patch had not embraced the environmental implications of the 1993 federal sustainable development strategy; even so, it had made efforts to reduce emissions from flaring and other environmental concerns, and it has certainly benefited from the various incentives and efforts of the federal government to exploit the heavy oil and oil sands reserves in Alberta. If sustainable development means that future generations will have access to the same energy reserves available today, the contradictory policies of the federal government seem to make sense. Sustainable development has been interpreted as not only a plan to reduce the industry's effects on the environment but also as a policy for ensuring that coming generations will enjoy adequate reserves of oil and natural gas.

The Klein government launched an aggressive $1.5 million marketing campaign against the Kyoto Protocol, using the Trudeau-era NEP as a stalking horse. The province's anti-Kyoto crusade has been effective in swinging public opinion in Alberta against the agreement. However, the 1980 NEP is fundamentally different from the 1997 Kyoto Protocol. The NEP was a nationalist enterprise designed to counter the continentalist pull of American markets and multinational oil companies; in contrast, Canadian ratification and implementation of Kyoto is a multilateral approach to the problem of climate change, and it is global rather than regional in scope. Moreover, the federal government is continuing to support oil sands and heavy oil development with tax breaks totaling $1.2 billion. Also, Prime Minister Chrétien personally lobbied American president George W. Bush on behalf of the oil sands and other industry projects. The result was a new dynamic between the continental strategy of the Bush administration and the international agenda of the Chrétien government as well as confusion over the direction of Ottawa's environment and energy policies (Fairley, 2003, 43).

The Alberta oil and gas industry is in a state of flux. The prime minister's announcement that Kyoto would be ratified and implemented created a climate of uncertainty that had not been seen for a generation. With the provincial government promoting a continentalist agenda, the federal government has juxtaposed an international agreement with its market-oriented energy policy of the post-NEP era. The final outcome of this tension between Alberta's continentalist polices and the federal government's multilateralist approach is uncertain. That said, the example of earlier nationalist-continentalist battles – especially the one over the NEP – indicates that the province's efforts to blunt Canada's Kyoto commitments and its efforts to evolve into a non-conventional source of American energy will triumph. The Alberta

oil patch may be the place where the regionalism of provincial politicians and the Bush administration triumphs over the internationalism
of the federal government and the international community.

REFERENCES

AEUB (Alberta Energy and Utilities Board). 2002a. *Alberta's Reserves 2001 and
Supply/Demand Outlook, 2002–2011.* Calgary: AEUB.
– 2002b. *2001 North American Oil Reserves.* Calgary: AEUB.
Alberta. n.d. *Alberta Oil and Gas.* Edmonton: Government of Alberta.
Alberta Environment. 2002. *Albertans and Climate Change: Taking Action.*
Edmonton: Alberta Environment.
BP Amoco. 2002. *BP Statistical Review of World Energy.* London: BP Amoco.
June.
Breen, D.H. 1993. *Alberta's Petroleum Industry and the Conservation Board.*
Edmonton: University of Alberta Press and the Energy Resources Conser-
vation Board.
Calgary Herald. 2002. 'Chretien Pledges Canada to Kyoto. Parliament Will Be
Asked to Ratify Pact.' 3 September, A1.
Chase, S., and J. Mahoney. 2002. 'Albertans Turn Against Kyoto in Poll.' *Globe
and Mail.* 8 October: A1.
Doern, G. Bruce. 1999. 'Moved Out and Moving On: The National Energy
Board as a Reinvented Regulatory Agency.' Pp. 82–97 in G. Bruce Doern,
Margaret M. Hill, Michael J. Prince, and Richard J. Shultz, *Changing the
Rule: Canadian Regulatory Regimes and Institutions.* Toronto: University of
Toronto Press.
Fairley, Peter. 2003. 'Digging a Carbon Hole for Canada.' *Alberta Views* 6,
no. 2: 40–3.
Finance Alberta. 2001. 2000–2001 Annual Report. Edmonton: Finance Alberta.
– 2002. 2001–2002 Annual Report. Edmonton: Finance Alberta.
Fjell, O. 2000. News conference by president of Statoil (the Norwegian state
oil company). Calgary: World Petroleum Congress, Calgary. 14 June.
Fossum, J.E. 1997. *Oil, the State, and Federalism: The Rise and Demise of Petro-
Canada as a Statist Impulse.* Toronto: University of Toronto Press.
Foster, P. 1979. *The Blue-Eyed Sheiks: The Canadian Oil Establishment.* Don
Mills, ON: Collins.
Hirsh, M. 2002. 'Bush and the World.' *Foreign Affairs* 81, no. 5: 18–43.
House, J.D. 1980. *The Last of the Free Enterprisers: The Oilmen of Calgary.*
Toronto: Macmillan of Canada.

Ikenberry, G.J. 2002. 'America's Imperial Ambition.' *Foreign Affairs* 81, no. 5: 44–60.

National Energy Board. 1991. *Canadian Energy Supply and Demand to 2025*. Ottawa: Queen's Printer.

National Energy Policy Development Group. 2001. *National Energy Policy: Reliable, Affordable, and Environmentally Sound Energy for America's Future.* Washington, DC: U.S. Government Printing Office.

Natural Resources Canada. 1997. *Sustainable Development Strategy: Now and for the Future.* Ottawa: Natural Resources Canada.

– 2000. *Energy in Canada, 2000*. Ottawa: Natural Resources Canada.

Nikiforuk, A. 2001. *Saboteurs: Wiebo Ludwig's War against Big Oil*. Toronto: Macfarlane Walter and Ross.

Olsen, K., P. Collas, P. Boileau, D. Blain, C. Ha, L. Henderson, C. Liang, S. McKibbon, and L. Morel-a-l'Huissier. 2002. *Canada's Greenhouse Gas Inventory, 1990–2000*. Ottawa: Environment Canada.

Pratt, L., and J. Richards. 1979. *Prairie Capitalism: Power and Influence in the New West*. Toronto: McClelland and Stewart.

Sharpe, Sydney. 2002. *A Patch of Green: Canada's Oilpatch Makes Peace with the Environment.* Toronto: Key Porter.

Taft, K. 1997. *Shredding the Public Interest: Ralph Klein and 25 Years of One-Party Government.* Edmonton: University of Alberta Press.

Chapter 9

The Smartest Steward?
Indigenous People and Petroleum-Based
Economic Development in Canada's
North

FRANCES ABELE

The winter 2002 edition of *The Far North Oil and Gas Review* put a photograph of Northwest Territories Premier Steve Kakfwi on its cover, with this rather triumphant headline: 'Full Circle: Kakfwi comes around.' Inside, the explanation: 'As a young man in the 1970s, Stephen Kakfwi vociferously opposed a Mackenzie Valley pipeline. As president of the Dene Nation in the 1980s, he fought to secure Dene rights to self-determination and a fair land claims process. Now, with the latter two issues largely behind him, Northwest Territories Premier Kakfwi has become the North's most vocal pipeline supporter' (Sarkadi, 2002, 23). This interpretation of the apparent reversal of many northern Indigenous people's views about non-renewable resource development in general, and oil and gas development in particular, is widely shared but not quite accurate. Here is what Premier Kakfwi actually said about the reasons for his current support of the Mackenzie Valley pipeline project:

> I don't think my ideology has shifted at all ... Political development is important. Once you have [an idea of the type of political institutions that you need] it also becomes apparent that you don't want to live on a handout and that free housing and free education and free government does not exist anywhere in the world. It does not lead to independent, self-reliant individuals and families and communities. So I mean a government by itself, an agreement [for self-government] by itself doesn't do anything ... Governments need to be financed, they have to be economical and affordable and they have to be workable. And the people that want to govern themselves have to accept that responsibility. (Ibid., 25)

Kakfwi's view – and that of many other people in the North (Legislative Assembly, 2000) – is that non-renewable resource development presents at least an opportunity to *complete* the process of decolonization that began in earnest about forty years ago. The negotiation of modern treaties and self-government is not 'behind him'; rather, these are developmental processes that have yet to be completed. The hope is that non-renewable resource development may help this process in two ways: first, by improving the fiscal independence of the territorial government, it will strengthen that government's ability to serve the interests of territorial residents; and second, by strengthening the territory's economic base, development will create jobs and business opportunities so that northerners themselves will be able to achieve personal economic independence.

Premier Kakfwi does not distinguish among the various forms of Indigenous and public self-government now being developed in the Northwest Territories, and indeed across the territorial North. Since he speaks as premier of the Northwest Territories, it is likely that territorial government is the particular political decision maker he has in mind. Whatever governing institutions are eventually developed in the NWT (and these are certain to entail firmly linked aspects of both public and ethnically exclusive governing authorities), these institutions will face similar difficulties as they try to find a stable economic base on which to build democratic government in the North. There would seem to be at least three important considerations in this regard: the need to find adequate means and measures to monitor and control the activities of huge international corporations; the minimization and mitigation of the environmental impact of resource development activity; and the devising of means to achieve these goals in ways that support and strengthen rather than erode community development.

In this chapter I consider some of the choices facing the people of the Northwest Territories, and the linked processes of economic and political change. First, I cast some light on an apparent change in northern opinion regarding non-renewable resource development by reviewing the major achievements of the 'Generation of '68,' of which Steve Kakfwi is a member. The experience in the Mackenzie Valley is instructive, for it marks one reasonably successful response to circumstances that prevail in much of Canada. In the second part of the chapter I examine some important institutions and processes through which the people of the Northwest Territories will choose their common future. All contemporary governments try to balance economic development with environmental protection. I argue here that despite some significant handicaps and complexities, there is a possibility that in the Northwest Territories, responsible governments and public authorities will achieve something closer to an appropriate balance than has been typical in other parts of Canada.

In the context of all other forms of development underway in or proposed for the Northwest Territories, petroleum development has the potential to either advance or disrupt the process of decolonization – or to use the jargon of the 1990s, the democratization of northern governments and societies. In fact, it seems likely to both disrupt and advance. In the course of recent northern history (say the last hundred years) pressure for non-renewable resource development has been a spur to political change, and the possibility for Indigenous people to disrupt development has given them some political leverage. At the same time, energy development itself has been a major force for direct and indirect social change. Also, it may cause major environmental damage, some of which is now evident. Besides being intrinsically undesirable, environmental damage in the form of pollution, disturbance of wildlife, and contribution to global warming threatens to undermine the land-based aspects of the northern economy and the viability of northern community life.

The Democratic Achievement in the North

Most Canadians live within a few hundred kilometers of the Canada–U.S. border, and in this region Aboriginal people comprise only about 3 per cent of the population (RCAP, 1996, v. 1 c. 2). In contrast, in the territorial North, and in the northern two-thirds of every province except those in the Maritimes, Aboriginal people form a majority or a large plurality of the population. The northern two-thirds of Canada is also where most of Canada's energy and other natural resources are produced. Thus, Aboriginal and non-Aboriginal people share these northern lands and the benefits and costs of their development in rough demographic equality; furthermore, they inhabit a resource hinterland where few major development decisions are actually taken.

Initially and for decades, Indigenous people in the northern two-thirds of Canada were ignored, marginalized, and colonized; today, the picture is strikingly different. Through activism and political organization, they have negotiated modern treaties (land claims agreements) and in many cases new political arrangements that have given them a measure of control over their circumstances. Over the past thirty years, many new institutions for collective representation and Indigenous self-government have been created. The configuration of public institutions in northern Canada has also been transformed, and along with it, the conditions in which future economic development will take place. In the following few pages, I present an egregiously abridged overview of the major events that have shaped present circumstances. For reasons of space, only the Northwest Territories is treated in any detail.

Mines, Oil, War, and Social Engineering

In the Northwest Territories as in the rest of the North, political development has always followed externally generated pressures for resource development. This was the case with Treaty 8 (1898) and Treaty 11 (1921), the first formal agreements in northwestern Canada between Indigenous peoples and emissaries of the Canadian government. Treaty 8, which was prompted by Indigenous people's concerns over the disruptions attending the Klondike Gold Rush, encompasses a large part of northern Alberta, some of northeastern British Columbia, and some lands in the southern Northwest Territories. Treaty 11, which covers most of the rest of the western Northwest Territories, was negotiated after private developers sought the rights to develop oil at Norman Wells. Both parties to the treaties sought stability and a regularization of relations; the Dominion government also sought control over Indigenous lands (Fumoleau 1973; Mair 1999; Asch 1997; Aasen, 2002).

After the treaties were negotiated, the once pressing matter of sovereignty over northern Canadian lands faded from the attention of the Dominion government. In most of the North, the only representatives of the federal government were Mounties and occasional touring scientists. Except for traders and missionaries, and some gold miners and oil workers in Yellowknife and Norman Wells, these were the only non-Aboriginal people most northern residents were likely to see.

The situation changed profoundly during the Second World War, which brought thousands of (mainly American) military personnel to the North. The relative isolation of even the Inuit was ended by this presence and by the construction of highways, airstrips, and – in the immediate postwar period – the Distant Early Warning line. During and immediately after the war, the Dominion's concern over northern sovereignty revived. There were concerns about the large American presence and Canada's relatively weak capacity even to monitor – never mind control – these personnel. From the perspective of northern Indigenous people, the question of sovereignty was raised in this period as well, although few would have used the term. The relatively sudden influx of large numbers of outsiders, and the events that followed their arrival, generated local interest in the opportunities their presence afforded even while they raised local concerns about how the negative impacts of their activities could be mitigated.

In southern Canada, another important consequence of the American and Canadian military presence in the North during and immediately after the Second World War was a growing awareness of very poor northern health conditions due to new diseases, and of economic hardships, including some deaths by starvation. These concerns found a ready reception in a federal state that was still geared up from the war effort and beginning to develop what we now recognize as the modern welfare state. There was a multifaceted federal response that led to a sharp increase in state intervention in northerners' lives (Rea, 1968; Grant, 1988). For example, strong efforts were made to enforce school attendance. This led many families to settle in communities near schools, so as not to be separated from their children. Health care was introduced to the Arctic in the form of medical visits by ship, and during this period many people suffering from tuberculosis and other diseases were sent to southern facilities for care. Social housing was introduced, and people began to leave their own accommodations to live in the settlements. Some programs were introduced to teach English and to teach women housekeeping skills appropriate to life in towns. This social engineering phase of northern administration probably reached its zenith with a program to relocate Inuit from communities on the Arctic Quebec coast and Pond Inlet on Baffin Island to the far northern settlements of Resolute and Grise Fjord.

During this period, federal policy was not entirely consistent. Although the relocation of Inuit to the High Arctic appears to have been motivated in part by the desire to protect them from the wage economy and social welfare dependency, there were other roughly concurrent initiatives designed to open the North to non-renewable resource development and to encourage other northern Indigenous people to enter wage employment. Prime Minister John Diefenbaker's 'Roads to

Resources' theme expressed in popular language a widely shared view that the North should be developed in the national interest as a resource hinterland to supply the burgeoning postwar American economy with Canadian power and raw materials. In the twenty years after the war, mines and hydroelectric dams were opened across the provincial North, and many unprecedented measures were taken. For example, a railway was built to serve the mine at Pine Point and – in line with the new approach to northern development – programs were introduced to subsidize the training of Inuit to work on the railway.

The Aboriginal people who lived through this period of massive social change are still alive, and they have been able to explain what the changes meant to them (RCAP, 1996, v. 4 c. 6; HAR, 1994; Snowshoe, 1977). There were as many different reactions, positive and negative, as there were people living in the North, but almost everyone there agreed that the lack of democracy in introducing all of these changes was intolerable. In the 1970s, these views coalesced in widespread opposition to two major pipeline projects, in the Mackenzie Valley and along the Alaska Highway. In the democratic response to these proposals was forged the new balance of political power in northern Canada.

The Rise of Aboriginal Peoples' Organizations

Across Canada and in the territorial North, there was a flowering of Aboriginal peoples' political organizations within a very few years. The Council for Yukon Indians, the Committee for Original Peoples Entitlement (in the Mackenzie Delta–Beaufort Sea area), the Indian Brotherhood of the Northwest Territories, the Metis Association of the Northwest Territories, and the Inuit Tapirisat of Canada were all formed between 1969 and 1973.[1] Despite many regional differences, these 'first generation' Aboriginal organizations shared a very similar goal: the negotiation of new political and economic arrangements in the North that would ensure that northern Aboriginal people had the means to protect their way of life and to shape their collective future, in cooperation with their non-Aboriginal co-residents. They began this work in the context of major changes in Canadian policy on Aboriginal land rights.

When northern Aboriginal people first began forming their political organizations, Canadian jurisprudence on Aboriginal rights recognized little and denied much. A series of important legal victories, together with political activism across the country literally transformed federal policy. In 1969, Jean Chrétien, the young Minister of Indian Affairs in the new government of Pierre Trudeau, issued what has come to be known as the infamous *White Paper on Indian Policy*. This document declared the treaties to be artifacts of a colonial past, best forgotten so that the conditions for status Indians to take their places as full citizens of modern Canada could be put in place. This perspective collided with the understanding and purposes of status Indians across Canada, who were seeking to negotiate treaties where none existed (as in British Columbia), as well as to rehabilitate respect for existing treaties where these had been ignored – the situation in many places. Indigenous people's political mobilization and a series of important court cases led to a federal policy that recognized Aboriginal rights and established a procedure for negotiating agreement on what this entailed (Weaver, 1975; Graham, Dittburner, and Abele, 1996, v. 1, chs 4 and 5).

Relations between Canada and its Aboriginal peoples were now being transformed at all levels in many parts of the country. In what was then western Northwest Territories, much political energy focused on a proposal to develop and transport northern energy reserves. In the early 1970s, a federally supported proposal to build a large-diameter natural gas pipeline in the Mackenzie Valley alarmed northern Indigenous people, as well as others in southern Canada who were concerned about the impact this project could have on the environment and on Canadian economic sovereignty (Dosman, 1976). As chapter 10 by Bankes and Wenig indicates, all of these groups found a forum and a focus in the hearings of the Inquiry into the Construction of a Mackenzie Valley Pipeline, chaired by Thomas Berger. In the recorded verbatim testimony to the inquiry, one finds an excellent compendium of community opinion and analysis. Many participants recounted the impact of past outside disruptions and noted that the pipeline and attendant development activities were likely to continue a destructive trend. Others noted that there was uncertainty about the technical feasibility of avoiding or mitigating environmental damage, which would destroy the basis of life as they knew it.

Participation in the Mackenzie Valley Pipeline Inquiry was one aspect of a general movement among the Indigenous peoples of the Northwest Territories toward negotiating increased control over impending economic development. Another was their engagement with comprehensive claims negotiations. These negotiations in the NWT have too complex a history to summarize here. Let it suffice to say that initial efforts by the Dene and Metis in the southern four-fifths of the NWT, and by the Inuvialuit and their co-residents in the Delta, did not lead to agreements. Instead, a series of regional claims agreements have been reached. The first was signed in 1984 by the Inuvialuit of the Mackenzie Delta–Beaufort Sea area, under the authority of the Committee for Original Peoples Entitlement (COPE). There followed agreements signed by the Gwich'in (1992) and by the Sahtu Dene and Metis (1993). The claims agreements provided certainty about land ownership, with identified collective holdings in fee simple, with other use rights to larger areas of the traditional territory, with specific participation in a variety of land and resource management boards, and with substantial cash payments for rights surrendered, which the various groups have since invested for collective purposes.

There are still some important outstanding land and governance issues in the Northwest Territories: for the Deh Cho Dene (whose homeland is southwest of Great Slave Lake); for the Dogrib (Tli Cho Dene in the Yellowknife area); for the Akaitcho Dene (southeast of Great Slave Lake); and for the Metis living in these same areas (for current information on each situation, see www.ainc-inac.gc.ca). These issues are being addressed within a framework of principles that recognizes Aboriginal entitlement and includes the possibility of diverse specific arrangements.

While negotiating their claims, residents of the Northwest Territories have also been engaging in several very thorough public discussion and research processes concerning their constitutional future. In 1981, territorial legislators formed the Constitutional Alliance, and through this body agreed to divide the Northwest Territories into two new territories: Nunavut in the east, and the Northwest Territories in the west. They then debated the appropriate constitutions for each new territory. In the NWT, a special public commission chaired by Jim Bourque recommended a highly decentralized or regionalized form of territorial government (Cameron and White, 1995).

In the meantime, the territorial government has been changed dramatically, as a result of two major processes: the large-scale participation of northern Indigenous people in electoral politics and increasingly in the administrative branch; and the concurrent increase in territorial government powers and scope as responsibilities devolve from the federal level. Since 1975, when the Northwest Territories Legislative Assembly[2] became an entirely elected body, the majority of representatives have been Aboriginal and only two government leaders (premiers) have been non-Aboriginal. Cabinet membership reflects the proportion of the various ethnic and national groups in the general population. The public service is changing more slowly, but gradually senior as well as middle-level positions are coming to reflect the demographic pattern of the population.

The existing territorial government was planted in the Northwest Territories after 1967, when the seat of government was transferred from Ottawa to Yellowknife. At that stage the legislature was composed entirely of appointed members, who still formally advised the Commissioner of the Northwest Territories, who was the supreme authority. The public service, both its functions and (often) its personnel, was transferred to Yellowknife in stages between 1967 and 1975, until by 1975 a functioning bureaucracy was lodged in the territory. In 1985, another wave of devolution commenced, this one involving the transfer of responsibility for a few more government services (such as fire control and health care) to the territorial level (Dacks, 1990). A third stage has been opened by the current Minister of Indian Affairs and Northern Development; this time, the intent is to devolve powers concerning land and natural resources to the territory. In this round, which deals with powers at the heart of economic development, all of the Aboriginal entities, along with the territorial government, will participate in negotiating devolution.

It should be evident by now that the northern constitutional and political landscape is extremely complicated and, as I recently heard a participant remark in quiet understatement, 'pretty process-oriented.' There has been a remarkable period of rich experimentation and mass public discussion of governance, of an extent and nature rarely seen Canadian history. Many of the deliberative processes have ended inconclusively; however, when one takes the longer view, some important changes can be marked. These have occurred in the span of about one generation.

Modern treaties have been negotiated for most of the current Northwest Territories, although the spirit of the earlier treaties has been retained. Northern Aboriginal people now participate fully in territorial electoral politics and territorial government, as well as in federal politics.[3] Certain practices with respect to non-renewable resource development have been developed and entrenched: consultation, benefits packages, and environmental mitigation and monitoring are now unquestioned features of any large development project. Finally,

232 Frances Abele

northerners – both Aboriginal and non-Aboriginal – have built up a
body of practices, expertise, and expectations concerning appropriate
levels of public participation. Twenty years of public political discussion, layered over concurrent comprehensive claims negotiations, have
created a sophisticated northern public with high standards of public
consultation and some practice in achieving consensus on difficult
issues. Many differences of opinion have yet to be resolved, but the
general consensus on the terms of public debate is clear enough:

- The discussion should be public.
- It should include all interested parties and all discernable
  perspectives.
- It should be based on community-based research, made public.
- It should culminate in a public, written report.

All four of these conditions are shaping the circumstances in which
northerners are confronting the major economic and environmental
issues now upon them. They also indicate that the mechanisms for
public discussion of such fundamental issues are more open and democratic – in short, more advanced – than in most other parts of Canada.
In the next section, we will see what these processes have enabled
residents of the Northwest Territories to accomplish.

Economy, Environment, and State Capacity

There are still some outstanding issues of Aboriginal self-government
and sovereignty to be resolved in northern Canada, and it will be
many years before all parties have ironed the kinks out of what are
essentially brand-new experiments in Canadian governance. No one
can know, in advance, how to create democratic governing institutions that will on the one hand respect Aboriginal rights and provide
practical settings for collective self-government, and on the other hand
deliver efficient and responsive government to all northern residents.
What we *can* see now is that a variety of different arrangements are in
place, to be revised and developed by the people who must live within
them.

The current interest in large-scale natural gas development raises
some new issues and resurrects some old ones. As important as the
Berger Inquiry was for northern political development, and as influential as its processes and analyses were for future northern decision

making, the inquiry did not, as many people think, halt the construction of a pipeline in the Mackenzie Valley. To be sure, the inquiry delayed the commencement of construction of the natural gas line past its 'best-before' date, and as a result, the project was abandoned for what has turned out to be nearly a generation. In 1981, however, just four years after Berger reported, and in advance of any land claims agreements being concluded, approval was given for the construction of a smaller-diameter oil pipeline about one-half the length of the proposed gas line, from Norman Wells to Zama in northern Alberta.[4] Furthermore, the delay of the Mackenzie Valley natural gas pipeline did not halt seismic exploration in the Northwest Territories, nor did it prevent the drilling of exploratory wells in several regions, including the Arctic offshore. This sort of energy development activity has continued throughout the gas pipeline hiatus. In addition, after a trough in the 1990s, there has recently been intense exploration and development activity in certain regions, especially around Fort Liard in the southwestern Northwest Territories, and in the Mackenzie Delta area, where Inuvialuit-owned companies have been prominent. In addition to this energy activity, the lands north of Yellowknife have been opened to diamond mining, of which there is surely more to follow. In short, the Northwest Territories is not poised on the brink of a massive economic change; it has already started the transformation.

The externally generated projects in petroleum and diamonds have taken place on terms somewhat different from what they might have been had there been no mobilization of Indigenous people over the past generation. Normal practice now involves the following: full public disclosure of plans in advance; community consultations or information sessions; and public hearings through several separate and joint federal, territorial, and Aboriginal authorities (including various levels of review under the Canadian Environmental Assessment Act as well as hearings by the Mackenzie Valley Environmental Impact Review Board and by regional environmental review boards, among others). For a project to be approved, it must provide a package of local benefits, which must always include employment, training, and small business opportunities. Is this enough? There are strong indications that northerners do not think so, especially as they have become concerned about the cumulative effects of various development projects. To illustrate, I will describe four very recent efforts in the Northwest Territories to come to public terms with the changes that are upon them.

Two linked initiatives of the Minister of Resources, Wildlife and Economic Development address the Northwest Territories' economic future.[5] In June 1999, the minister established the Economic Strategy Panel, a seventeen-member citizens' panel, with responsibility for proposing a new economic strategy for the Northwest Territories. After a year's research and deliberation, the panel published *Common Ground: NWT Economic Strategy 2000*, which contains fifty-nine recommendations covering Land, People, Community and Regional Development, Transportation and Communications, Diversification, Non-Renewable Resource Development, Political Structure, and Research and Development. The panel describes its approach this way:

> The term *'Common Ground'* has two meanings in this strategy. One literal and the other a more symbolic one. Literally, *'Common Ground'* refers to the land that we all inhabit, the trees, plants, rivers and lakes, the animals and the minerals and fossil fuels that are found under it.
>
> The Panel's vision states, *'For thousands of years people have lived on this land. Every generation has had its own economy and every generation has recognized that their economy was based on the land.'*
>
> Aboriginal residents have said the land is a gift from the Creator. But, it is a fragile gift. If we misuse it, we destroy the foundations of our economy and the economies of future generations of northerners.
>
> The symbolic meaning of *'Common Ground'* is that people with differing viewpoints can come to a consensus on important matters. Panel members see an urgent need for residents of the Northwest Territories to achieve a consensus towards the development of our economy.
>
> Common ground, based on respect for the land, can emerge from dialogue and discussion and a commitment to action. Each of us, and each group, must be willing to share our unique perspectives, interests, values and assumptions. Through this sharing, we will find a common ground and desire to work together. (Northwest Territories, 2000a, 11)

The panel endorses devolution, speedy completion of and respect for land claims agreements, and a diversified northern economy in which fossil fuel and other non-renewable resource development will provide an engine of growth while at the same time respecting the environment and the traditional economy. The specific recommendations that close the report amount to a list of good things to do, but there is no assignment of specific responsibilities, nor is there any apparent concern that the goals embodied in the report might be incompatible. Certainly the northern commitment to discussion and consensus building is well represented in this report. That said, a consequence of this approach is also evident: the common ground is reported, and concerns that do not fit with this approach are ignored.

Following the report of the Economic Strategy Panel, the Minister of Resources, Wildlife and Economic Development published *Towards a Better Tomorrow: A Non-Renewable Resource Development Strategy for the Northwest Territories*. This document focuses clearly on making the best use of fossil fuel and diamond exploitation to develop the territorial economy along the same path as other, similarly endowed jurisdictions. There is detailed empirical analysis of the various dimensions of such a path, in which diversification and growth in employment and business opportunities are the goals. Major concerns are the complexity of the regulatory system (which discourages private-sector development) and the continued control of key economic levers in Ottawa rather than the territory. Here, in a nutshell, is the Minister's message: 'The Northwest Territories is at an exciting crossroads. Non-renewable resource development, including oil and gas production, development of a Mackenzie Valley gas pipeline, and the continued expansion of the NWT diamond mining sector, can mean the difference between our ongoing dependence on federal transfer payments, and our becoming Canada's first "have" territory' (Northwest Territories, 2000b, n.p.).

Although *Towards a Better Tomorrow* expresses few qualms about an economic development strategy based on enthusiastic non-renewable resource development, there have been indications of concern in other documents. For example, the West Kitikmeot/Slave Study (WKSS) Report communicates a good deal of discomfort with some of the apparently contradictory features of northern economic development as well as concern over a lack of real information on which to base planning. Stimulated by the diamond boom of the 1990s, but with concerns not confined to diamond mining, the WKSS was funded and directed by 'a partnership of aboriginal and environmental organizations, government and industry that wish to make sure the effects of development on the environment, wildlife and people of the [West Kitikmeot/Slave Study] area are minimal and that northern people get the maximum benefits' (WKSSS, 2001). Nearly $10 million was raised from forty-nine 'partners' to support the five-year research initiative, which concluded on 31 March 2001.[6] The general purposes of the study were (1) to provide an information base necessary for the study partners to make sound resource management decisions; (2) to provide a basis for identifying and assessing cumulative effects for planning and development purposes; (3) to provide a forum in which to share information on issues, while respecting the diversity of interests: aboriginal, industry, environmental, governmental, and public; (4) to provide information necessary to enhance the understanding of potential impacts of exploration and development on ecological processes and communities; (5) to support a central role for both traditional knowledge and scientific knowledge, and to facilitate the linkage of research carried out in these systems; and (6) to ensure the accessibility of study research results and information to all partners and the public, while respecting the confidentiality of certain information.

Not surprisingly, not all of the goals of the WKSS were met in the first five years, and the organization is seeking funding for further work. The first five years' work identified serious gaps in the area of documenting traditional knowledge, community well-being, and the natural environment. There are too many such gaps to list here (at least seventeen are mentioned), but here is a sample (WKSSS, 2001, 54–61):

Traditional Knowledge: All areas of traditional knowledge are poorly documented throughout the Study area; the only Inuit traditional knowledge documented in the region is that done for WKSS. This applies to both the socioeconomic and natural environment.

Socioeconomic: [There is a need for] a number of areas of socioeconomic research and monitoring:

- the effect of increasing industrialization on community, family and individual lifestyles, including the effects of rotational work.
- A major element of this would be the effects on, and changes in, participation in renewable resource harvesting and changes in harvesting patterns.
- Troubling social behaviours have been emerging in WKSS communities – gambling, prostitution, organized drug activity – in addition to existing risky behaviours such as alcohol and drug abuse and smoking. These are not well studied, particularly at the community level.

Natural Environment:

- The influence of existing developments on water quality has been poorly documented, particularly in relation to hydroelectric developments.
- A great deal more research is required in relation to terrestrial, freshwater and marine ecosystems, and the interactions between them, e.g. nutrient cycling.
- Habitat limitations on wildlife populations, interconnectedness of prey and predator species and relationships between wildlife and the vegetation they eat, as well as the effects of fire and recovery of vegetation afterward, are all poorly documented.

Given that so much has changed in twenty-five years, it is striking how similar these concerns are to those raised in the early 1970s in the context of the Mackenzie Valley natural gas pipeline and again during the construction of the Norman Wells pipeline (Indian Affairs, 1974; Berger, 1977). Looking only at the behaviour of governments, it is as if there has been an implicit assumption in government that concerns about environmental impact and disruption of community life, and about the need to find policies that balance various forms of productive activity (including traditional land-based income generation), will disappear as northern Indigenous people gain more experience with wage employment. The expectation that such concerns will be resolved by wage economy experience has never been based on reality, given that Dene, Metis, and Inuvialuit have been working for wages and trading for cash for nearly a century without giving up land-based activities. If more confirmation is required, it is clear that more intensive experience with wage employment over the last generation has not led to abandonment of these concerns, which are reflected in other institutions such as the wildlife and resources management boards established under the modern treaties.

The West Kitikmeot/Slave study was an attempt at a comprehensive, empirically based assessment of the cumulative effects of various non-renewable resource development projects. Another cumulative effects study, in roughly the same area, is being planned by an independent environmental organization, the Canadian Arctic Resources Committee. Now in progress is the federally run NWT Cumulative Effects Assessment and Management [CEAM] Strategy and Framework, sponsored jointly by the Department of Indian Affairs and Northern Development and the Department of the Environment. Relying on a steering committee with members from Aboriginal organizations, environmental non-governmental organizations, the mining and oil and gas industries, the Government of the Northwest Territories, the two responsible federal departments, and the Mackenzie Valley Environmental Impact Review Board – with observers from the Government of Nunavut – this project aims to produce a strategy and regional plans of action.

The CEAM process suffers inevitably from the awkwardness of being an Ottawa-generated territorial initiative and from the general fatigue in northern communities with processes and consultations. Even so, it represents an effort by federal departments to develop a comprehensive and coordinated framework to shape federal policy and programs and to match these with those of other governments. After the work on the Strategy and Framework is complete, the major challenge will be to achieve in Ottawa a sufficient level of interdepartmental cooperation and coordination to ensure that some action will follow the planning.

Conclusions, Portents and Potentials: The Lady or the Tiger?

What passes for normal in this world is something incredible: billions spent on exploration, prolific tax credits for oil production, and growing household income spent on energy – all to sustain a fossil fuel status quo that, according to world scientific consensus, might ultimately end in catastrophe.

Gordon Laird, *Power: Journeys Across an Energy Nation*

As we enter the new millennium, Canada must become and remain the world's 'smartest' natural resources steward, developer, user, and exporter – the most high-tech, the most environmentally friendly, the most socially responsible, the most productive and competitive – leading the world as a living model of sustainable development.

Hon. Ralph Goodale, *The Minister of Natural Resources Sector*

Ultimately, market forces will prevail.

Tim Hearn, Imperial Oil Limited, commenting on fast-tracking approval of the proposed Mackenzie Valley Natural Gas Pipeline, quoted in the *Financial Post*, 12 September 2002

When one tries to imagine the likely path of development for the Northwest Territories, the example of Alberta, immediately to the south, is hard to avoid. Alberta is an oil and gas rich 'have' province with healthy public sector revenues and a burgeoning economy – as well as a seriously damaged boreal forest, depleted and polluted groundwater, air pollution threats from natural gas production, too-rapid population growth, and the attendant changes to quality of life (Pembina Institute, 2000).

In deciding how to make use of the opportunities presented by multinational interest in northern resources, the people of the Canadian territories face some difficult choices. Given the much smaller size of the territorial government and its relative jurisdictional weakness, can the people of the North expect to reap the benefits of the much-vaunted 'Alberta advantage' without paying Alberta prices?

I do not plan to answer this question fully, but I would like to suggest some relevant considerations. Some of these point to dangers that will have to be confronted and mitigated; others to potential sources of strength and development.

Territorial Fiscal Vulnerability

All of the northern territories depend heavily on Ottawa for their expenditure budgets. Sparsely populated, with widely dispersed populations in a high-cost regions, they face costs unknown in the provinces. By far the least dependent territory is the Northwest Territories, but even in this territory, even it its best years, more than half the expenditure budget comes in direct transfers from Ottawa. A major source of territorial wealth is not taxable. This is the income-in-kind (or 'domestic' sector), highly valued for practical and symbolic reasons. Hunting, gathering, fishing, and trapping, and the associated artistic and handicraft production, together generate substantial income in the form of food and well-being, but very little cash. Thus, the income-in-kind sector is never going to be a major source of tax revenue, and territorial and other governments seeking somewhat less dependence on federal transfers will inevitably rely more and more heavily on the economic activities financed by mainly huge, mainly international corporations interested in the North's mineral and other resources. The colonial political status of Canada's territories may come to be replaced by dependence on (and vulnerability to control by) multinational corporations.

A Young and Burgeoning Population

The territorial North has a greater proportion of young adults entering the labour force than any other region of Canada. These young people will need meaningful and suitable work. For reasons of geography and infrastructure, these opportunities will lie in the public sector and increasingly in the area of mineral development – oil and gas production, and mining of many sorts. There are also likely to be a steady but smaller number of new jobs in tourism, including ecotourism and the commercial exploitation of renewable resources such as fish and mammals. For the reasons just mentioned, it is most likely that the great engine of new jobs will be, directly or indirectly, the non-renewable resource development sector. Territorial youth constitute a source of pressure for economic development; at the same time, they are the territories' greatest resource for dealing with it, if enough of them acquire sufficient education to monitor, manage, and develop the sector in a favourable direction.

Significant Progress on Indigenous Rights

Indigenous people in the Northwest Territories are in a much more secure constitutional position than they were a generation ago. The Constitution Act and a growing body of jurisprudence confirm their rights to the land and to self-determination. This reality is embodied in the modern treaties that have been negotiated, in the self-government arrangements that are now being developed through treaty negotiations, and in the multiple processes of treaty and other agreement implementation now underway. Indigenous people as collectivities have significant land rights or are presently negotiating these; also, they enjoy constitutionally protected institutions through which they can exercise some control over the pace and pattern of economic development on their lands.

A Complex and Still Developing Array of Governing Institutions, Coupled with High Northern Expectations about Public Information and Process

The route taken in the Northwest Territories toward resolving outstanding treaty issues is extraordinarily complex – from the agreements reached already in the northern part of the territory (with attendant management boards and proposals for regional public government) to the still-evolving negotiations for self-government and treaties by the peoples of the southern half of the territory. It seems clear that whatever the final institutional outcomes – and these are becoming clearer – the NWT is pioneering an unusually decentralized and heterogeneous form of governance. In the short term, this means that economic development is taking place in a setting of some regulatory fluidity, complexity, and even confusion. These problems will need to be addressed during the devolution process.

An Evolving but Still Substantial Federal Role

The federal government remains a powerful actor in northern energy decisions, and for fiscal and constitutional reasons it will still be powerful after some responsibility for natural resources is devolved to the territorial level. Yet federal policy on northern economic development in general, and northern energy resource development in particular, seems vulnerable to the same sorts of incoherence and unresolved contradictions that have characterized it since the earliest days. It is no easier to see how to balance environmental concerns with the need for jobs and business development from Ottawa than it is in Yellowknife, and given that several federal departments have responsibilities in the North, it is plain that a heavy burden for coordination and implementation rests with federal officials as well.

What is the federal responsibility? The federal level possesses the spending power, the control over territorial expenditures, and a good deal of the regulatory authority to determine northern energy outcomes. However much northerners may wish to control decision making, and however much moral authority may reside with them, the federal government still possesses the stronger hand – constitutionally, fiscally, and in terms of sheer person-years – to apply to various problems and opportunities. This is true even though the federal capacity to understand the North and the northern environment is probably considerably weaker than it was just before the last round of northern energy enthusiasm, the one that began in the late 1960s.

As the discussion earlier in this chapter has suggested, northerners have undertaken some important research and deliberative initiatives designed to support decision making about environmentally sustainable economic development. These studies have provided a great deal of previously unassembled insight and information and have highlighted how incomplete our knowledge is of northern ecosystems and their interactions with broad forces such as climate change and energy megaprojects. We are a long way from the level of knowledge required to meet the technocratic ideal of predicting and mitigating the long-term negative impacts of any particular project. At the same time, compounding the problem, the weaknesses of program review in Ottawa limit capacity there. Even if the federal government will no longer 'row,' 'steering' requires a driver's licence that few public servants now possess. Thus, even after the requisite knowledge base has been developed, it is far from clear that Canada will possess the public sector capacity to make use of it, artfully and under the pressure of development.[7]

At the beginning of this section are three quotations from people who are concerned about northern development. Gordon Laird draws our attention to our seeming inability – or at any rate, our failure to date – to plan for economic development in the context of environmental limits. The one-time Minister of Natural Resources, Ralph Goodale, expresses a wonderful vision for the future, with Canada as the 'smartest' steward of natural resources – environmentally friendly and socially responsible. Mr Hearn, who heads one of the most powerful and influential corporations in Canada – and one with a huge investment in northern Canada – reminds us flatly where the power lies. To quite a large extent, what happens in the Northwest Territories over the next few years will show us which one of these observers has the inside track.

NOTES

I would like to thank Stephanie Irlbacher Fox, Linda Freeman, David Miller, Kevin O'Reilly, Peter Usher, Graham White, and several federal officials for helping me, not always successfully, to get a grip on these issues, and George Kinloch, as always for challenging insights and sustaining support.

1 The Council for Yukon Indians is now the Council for Yukon First Nations; the Indian Brotherhood is now the Dene Nation; Inuit Tapirisat recently renamed itself Inuit Tapiriiksat Kanatai. The Metis Association of the Northwest Territories has been replaced by regional bodies. COPE, which originally represented all Indigenous people in the Delta, disappeared in 1984 when the Inuvialuit signed a modern treaty. Their interests are now represented through the Inuvialuit Regional Corporation.

2 For simplicity, I use, anachronistically, the current names of all institutions. For example, in 1975 the body of elected officials was known as the Council of the Northwest Territories, not the Legislative Assembly. There have been so many changes of nomenclature in each rapidly developing territory that it is not practical to track them all here.

3 Several members of the postwar generation of activists are also important in federal politics. For example, Ethel Blondin-Andrew, a Dene, is MP for the Western Arctic and Minister of State for Children and Youth; Mary Simon, an Inuk from Nunavik (northern Quebec), was Canada's first Circumpolar Ambassador; Georges Erasmus, former president of the Dene Nation, was co-chair of the Royal Commission on Aboriginal Peoples and now leads the Aboriginal Healing Foundation.

4 The Norman Wells pipeline construction was accompanied by an expansion of the oil production facility at Norman Wells. Although the pipeline of course did not traverse the sensitive North Slope on the Arctic coast, it did fail to respect a major recommendation of the Berger Inquiry – that no pipeline be constructed in the Mackenzie Valley until Aboriginal land rights were settled. A study of the impact of the Norman Wells project on Indigenous people's participation in the wage economy appears in Frances Abele, *Gathering Strength* (Calgary: Arctic Institute of North America, 1989).

5 It is important to recognize that although the two initiatives discussed here were major aspects of the Territorial government's approach to the economy and the environment, they are not the only activities worth mentioning. Other examples include the Northwest Territories Greenhouse Gas Strategy of March 2001 (www.ssmicro.com/~ghgs/index.html) and the Northern NGO [non-governmental organizations] Statement of Principles for Oil and Gas Development, endorsed by the Canadian Arctic Resources Committee, the Canadian Parks and Wilderness Society (NWT and Yukon chapters), Ecology North, the Pembina Institute for Appropriate Development, the World Wildlife Fund Canada, and the Yukon Conservation Society.

6 The executive vehicle for the study was a non-profit society registered in 1996. Four partners contributed over $1 million each: the Government of Canada, the Government of the Northwest Territories, and two diamond-mining companies, BHP and Diavik. Other major contributors include Canamera Mining, the Government of Nunavut, De Beers, and Nunavut Tunngavik Inc. (who spent over $100,000 each) as well as forty-one other companies, Aboriginal organizations, and environmental non-governmental organizations.

7 Here the contrast to the 1970s is especially sharp. Before the Berger Inquiry was more than a smart intuition in the prime minister's brain, the Pipeline Application Assessment Group, chaired by Dr John Fyles and staffed by well-trained government scientists who had substantial knowledge of the North, was preparing a thorough review. This research was available to the Berger Inquiry and added to the strength of its report.

REFERENCES

Aasen, Wendy. 2002. 'Nothing Will be Done to Interfere with [Your] Way of Life: The Sovereignty Issue and Treaty 8.' ms. available from author: aasens@unbc.ca.

Asch, Michael. 1997. *Treaty Rights in Canada: Essays on Law, Equality and Respect for Difference.* Vancouver: UBC Press.

Berger, Thomas R. 1977. *Northern Frontier, Northern Homeland: The Final Report of the Mackenzie Valley Pipeline Inquiry.* 2 vols. Ottawa: Supply and Services Canada.

Cameron, Kirk, and Graham White. 1995. *Northern Governments in Transition: Political and Constitutional Development in the Yukon, Nunavut and the Western Northwest Territories.* Montreal: Institute for Research on Public Policy.

Dacks, Gurston. 1990. *Devolution and Constitutional Development in the Canadian North.* Montreal and Kingston: McGill-Queen's University Press.

Dosman, E.J. 1976. *The National Interest.* Toronto: McClelland and Stewart.

Fumoleau, René. 1973. *As Long As This Land Shall Last: A History of Treaty 8 and 11, 1870–1939.* Toronto: McClelland and Stewart.

Graham, Katherine, Carolyn Dittburner, and Frances Abele. 1996. *Soliloquy and Dialogue: Overview of Major Trends in Public Policy Relating to Aboriginal Peoples.* Ottawa: Minister of Public Works and Government Services.

Grant, Shelagh. 1988. *Sovereignty or Security? Government Policy in the Canadian North, 1936–1950.* Vancouver: UBC Press.

Indian Affairs and Northern Development Canada. 1974. *Mackenzie Valley Pipeline Assessment: Environmental and Socio-Economic Effects of the Proposed Canadian Arctic Gas Pipeline on the Northwest Territories and Yukon.* Ottawa: Pipeline Application Assessment Group.

Legislative Assembly of the Northwest Territories. 2000. *Towards a Better Tomorrow.* Fourteenth Legislative Assembly of the Northwest Territories. 21 March 2000. www.assembly.gov.nt.ca/Members/Better/Tomorrow.html.

Mair, Charles. 1999. *Through the Mackenzie Basin: An Account of the Signing of Treaty No. 8 and the Scrip Commission, 1899.* Intro. David W. Leonard and Brian Calliou. Edmonton: University of Alberta Press.

Northwest Territories. 2000a. *Common Ground: NWT Economic Strategy 2000*. Report of the Economic Strategy Panel. Co-Chairs: Richard Nerysoo, Darrell Beaulieu. Yellowknife: Minister of Resources Wildlife and Economic Development.

– 2000b. *Towards a Better Tomorrow: A Non-Renewable Resource Development Strategy for the Northwest Territories*. Minister's message. Yellowknife: GNWT.

Pembina Institute for Appropriate Development. 2001. *Alberta Sustainability Trends 2000: The Genuine Progress Indicators Report 1961 to 1999*. www.pembina.org.

Rea, Kenneth. 1968. *The Political Economy of Canada's North*. Toronto: University of Toronto Press.

RCAP (Royal Commission on Aboriginal Peoples). 1994. *The High Arctic Relocation*. Ottawa: Ministry of Supply and Services.

– 1996. *Report of the Royal Commission on Aboriginal Peoples*. Ottawa: Ministry of Supply and Services.

Sarkadi, Lauri. 2000. 'What Goes Around ... Comes Around.' *Far North Oil and Gas Review* (winter): 23.

Snowshoe, Charlie. 1977. 'A Trapper's Life.' Pp. 28–31 in Mel Watkins, ed., *Dene Nation: The Colony Within*. Toronto: University of Toronto Press.

Weaver, Sally. 1975. *Making Canadian Indian Policy*. Toronto: University of Toronto Press.

WKSSS (West Kitikmeot Slave Study Society). 2001. Introduction to *West Kitikmeot Slave Study Final Report*. Yellowknife. All the information about the West Kitikmeot Slave Study is drawn from www.wkss.nt.ca[.]

Chapter 10

Northern Gas Pipeline Policy and Sustainable Development, Then. And Now?

NIGEL BANKES AND MICHAEL M. WENIG

In 1977, Canada and the United States agreed to build a natural gas pipeline from the Prudhoe Bay area of Alaska along the Alaska Highway through the Yukon and down into British Columbia and Alberta. This route was selected after extensive hearings. It triumphed over competing routes across the North Slope of the Yukon and down the Mackenzie Valley. This pipeline was never built. Now, twenty-seven years later, we are again considering building a pipeline, and perhaps more than one. The basic justification for a northern pipeline is that demand for natural gas in North America is increasing and that the northern regions of Canada and Alaska may help meet this demand. In 1999, the National Energy Board (NEB) estimated that there were 9 trillion cubic feet (tcf) of discovered gas resources and 55 tcf of undiscovered resources in the Mackenzie-Beaufort Region (NEB, 1999, 44). It is estimated that Alaska's North Slope holds roughly 35 tcf of proven reserves and 100 tcf of estimated reserves (NEPDG, 2001, 7–11).

Historically, gas was used primarily for space heating, and secondarily as a petrochemical feedstock and to produce steam for industrial uses. But gas has now become an increasingly important fuel for generating electricity. Canadian gas consumption increased 60 per cent in the fifteen years between 1985 and 2000; American gas consumption increased at the same time. The future growth in gas demand in both countries is expected to continue to be 'robust' (NEB, 2000, 1).

This chapter examines the northern pipeline debates of then and now through the lens of sustainable development. Did sustainability values inform the decision-making process in the 1970s? Do such values inform current decision-making processes? We argue that sustainability values played an important role in the rejection of the

North Slope option in 1977 and a less important role in approving the Alaska Highway route. We also show that although the language of sustainability claims to inform current federal policy, the failure to integrate pipeline policy with an overall energy (and climate change) policy, and with a protected areas strategy, calls into question the strength of this commitment in the current decision-making process. We begin the chapter with a description of sustainable development criteria. We then apply these criteria to the decision-making process of the 1970s and to the current process. We acknowledge that to apply the term 'sustainable development' to the debates of the mid-1970s is technically anachronistic; however, we contend that the values embodied in that term were very much in play during the first northern pipeline debate. We explore those values in this next section.

Sustainable Development Criteria

As chapter 3 showed, the Brundtland Report of 1987 popularized the term 'sustainable development,' which it defined as 'development that meets the needs of the present without compromising the ability of future generations to meet their own needs' (WCED, 1987). However, attempts to implement sustainable development have generated many questions as well as strong debate. Among the questions are these: Should the emphasis be on 'sustainability' or on 'development'? Are there other, more qualitative measures of 'development' than growth measures? How can *sustainable* development be applied to non-renewable resources? How do we square the economic, social, and environmental pillars of the concept? What roles should be played by government regulation and by the market?

Instead of trying to answer these complex questions, we have sought further guidance from the terms of the federal Auditor General Act. That legislation requires federal departments to prepare and periodically update strategies for promoting sustainable development; it also provides a mechanism for monitoring the progress of federal departments toward achieving their goals. Because the act essentially legislates sustainable development as federal policy, its conception of the term is an appropriate basis for assessing federal pipeline policy. The act adopts the Brundtland Report's definition of sustainable development, but it also explains (in section 21.1) that the concept is 'continually evolving' and is 'based on the integration of social, economic and environmental concerns.' Section 21.1 of the act lists eight strategies as among those which can be followed to achieve sustainable development:

(a) the integration of the environment and the economy;
(b) protecting the health of Canadians;
(c) protecting ecosystems;
(d) meeting international obligations;
(e) promoting equity;
(f) an integrated approach to planning and making decisions that takes into account the environmental and natural resource costs of different economic options and the economic costs of different environmental and natural resource options;
(g) preventing pollution; and
(h) respect for nature and the needs of future generations.

A few explanatory words are in order regarding these criteria. Perhaps the most notable feature of this list is the repeated reference to 'integration' of social, economic, and environmental concerns and of planning and decision making. According to the *Green Guide*, which federal departments use when preparing sustainability strategies, an 'integrated approach' includes a 'full-cost accounting' of costs and benefits and 'ecosystem management.' This latter element is also implicit in the legislative strategy of 'protecting ecosystems' (Canada, 1995a). The 'equity' component is commonly understood to refer to both intergenerational and intragenerational equity (ibid., 13, 14). In the northern context, 'equity' is probably most relevant to policies related to settling Aboriginal claims, promoting Aboriginal resource management, and allocating to Aboriginals the risks and benefits of resource development.

As for the act's reference to 'meeting international obligations,' the *Green Guide* emphasizes the 1992 Framework Convention on Climate Change (FCCC) and the Convention on Biological Diversity (CBD) (ibid.). Under the former, Canada has agreed to 'aim' to reduce its greenhouse gas (GHG) emissions to 1990 levels. Canada has now ratified the more important obligations contained in the 1997 Kyoto Protocol. Thus, GHG emission reduction strategies will remain a high priority for Canada's overall sustainable development strategy. Canada's northern pipeline policy must be considered in this context.

(NRCan, 2000, 12, 36, 136, 140; DIAND, 2001b, 11, 15, 23, 27; Canada, 1995b, 22, 49). However, the implications of this linkage are not clear. Northern pipelines could either promote or frustrate Canadian and global efforts to reduce GHGs. Natural gas may facilitate a transition to a low-carbon economy by substituting for coal, or it may encourage continued dependence on fossil fuels.

Canada's implementation strategy for the CBD is spelled out in a 1995 paper that commits this country to 'conserve' biodiversity by *maintaining* species, genetic, and ecosystem diversity. The strategy also stresses the importance of 'ecological management,' including the completion of 'networks' of 'protected areas' (Canada, 1995b, 7, 20, 22, 26).

DIAND's own sustainable development strategy, adopted under the act, is another relevant guide because of DIAND's prominent role in managing northern resource development. However, DIAND's 2001–3 sustainable development strategy speaks largely in generalities (DIAND, 2001a, iii, 3, 24, 34, 38, 39, 42, 44, 45) and does not resolve fundamental tensions between, for example, the Arctic environment's sensitivity to global warming and the promotion of northern economic growth through the extraction of fossil fuels and other non-renewable resources. Similarly, although DIAND is committed to 'support' the territorial governments in 'preparing' protected areas 'strategies' that reflect a 'balanced' approach to land-use decisions (ibid., 78), this commitment lacks timelines; moreover, it lacks vision regarding the scope and distribution of protected areas required to fulfil Canada's commitment to maintaining northern biodiversity. The commitment also fails to consider how far resource development can proceed before the protected areas strategies are established.

Other writings suggest that the resolution of the tensions inherent in the application of sustainability to non-renewable resources will require, at a minimum, energy efficiency as well as internalization of the costs of environmental protection (Canada, 1988, 60). It may also involve the use of fossil fuel revenues (e.g., heritage funds [Lysyk, 1977] and other measures to enhance the renewable resource economy [Berger, 1977]). In sum, although the act and the *Green Guide* both provide general strategies for pursuing sustainable development, they lack a clear vision of a sustainably developing society and how that differs from the present. DIAND's strategy provides little *value added* in terms of articulating these visions; in fact, in some instances (e.g., its commitment, 'where appropriate,' to the act's strategy of 'protecting ecosystems'), DIAND's strategy seems to backtrack from the act and the *Green Guide*.

Northern Pipeline Decision Making in the 1970s

Ever since the Prudhoe Bay discovery of 1968, a central question for northern energy planners has been *how* to get Arctic gas reserves to southern markets as cheaply as possible and *when* to try and do so. Should the Canadian government promote the use of Canadian territory as a secure land bridge to the markets of the lower forty-eight? Could an Alaskan pipeline be used to piggyback Canadian Delta gas to southern markets, thereby realizing economies of scale and therefore lower transportation costs and higher netbacks for Canadian producers?

In 1977, the NEB and the government of Canada answered these questions by authorizing the Alaska Highway Natural Gas Pipeline. The pipeline was to be constructed as soon as possible. In this section of the chapter, we outline the process that led to that decision by answering three main questions. First, why was the Alaska Highway route for the pipeline approved over other competing routes? Second, to what extent did sustainability values influence the 1977 decision? Third, why was the pipeline (other than the so-called 'prebuild' portion) never built?

Why the Alaska Highway Route?

In 1977, there were four alternatives for bringing Prudhoe Bay and Delta reserves to market: the Canadian Arctic Gas Pipeline (CAGPL) proposal, the Foothills Maple Leaf proposal, the Foothills Alaska Highway proposal, and the El Paso project (see map 10.1). A few words are in order on each. The CAGPL proposal envisaged the construction of a pipeline from Prudhoe Bay across the Alaska and Yukon North Slope to the Delta, where it would pick up Canadian gas before heading south down the valley as a single, forty-eight-inch, high-pressure trunk line to Caroline, Alberta. The Maple Leaf proposal, as the name suggests, was a Canadian proposal to carry Delta gas to Canadian markets. The Foothills (Yukon) or Alaska Highway proposal was a late and opportunistic response to the fact that there was simply not

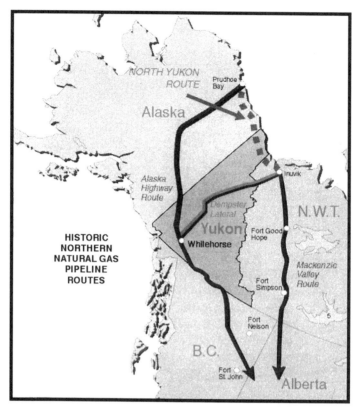

Map. 10.1 (Courtesy of Yukon Government, Energy, Mines and Resources)

enough discovered gas in the Delta to justify a stand-alone Mackenzie pipeline. Although the Alaska Highway Proposal was initially conceived as a means of getting American gas to American markets by following the Alaska pipeline right of way to Fairbanks and then tracking the Alaska highway, the NEB's review of the proposal incorporated the idea of a 'Dempster lateral' whereby the pipeline would serve Canadian interests in getting Delta gas to market (NEB, 1977). Finally, the El Paso project would have mirrored the Alaska oil pipeline; that is, it would have carried Prudhoe Bay gas to southwest Alaska, where it would have been liquefied and shipped by tanker to California. In theory, there was a fifth alternative: leave the gas in the ground and meet existing and projected demand through some combination of conservation and further exploration and development in the lower forty-eight and elsewhere in Canada. This option was raised by some of the intervenors in the regulatory proceedings.

Looking back at the events of the 1970s, it is possible to isolate several key features of the decision-making process that merit further discussion: (1) the legal and policy framework for the decision making, (2) the perceived urgency that attended the decision making, (3) the ad hoc nature of much of the decision making as the federal government responded to changes in project applications and configurations, and (4) the Dempster lateral.

The National Energy Board Act provides the main legal framework for making decisions about international and interprovincial pipelines. That act envisages that the NEB, as an independent quasi-judicial tribunal, should convene public hearings to determine whether a particular pipeline proposal is a 'public convenience and necessity.' Factors to be considered in that process are to include supply and demand, economic feasibility and financing, and the overall 'public interest.' The NEB has the legal authority to deny an application, and its decisions are final. A decision to approve an application takes the form of a recommendation to Cabinet, which retains the final say as to whether to issue a certificate authorizing pipeline construction.

The Government of Canada took care to provide additional policy guidance for the NEB and for industry in the form of its Guidelines for Northern Pipelines, introduced in 1970 and modified in 1972 (Canada, 1972). The key features of the 1970 guidelines included an emphasis on an energy corridor with only a single-trunk oil pipeline and a single-trunk gas pipeline. The 1972 revised version clarified the corridor concept and re-emphasized the environmental and socioeconomic concerns that would have to be satisfied. The emphasis on a single pipeline guaranteed competitive hearings and a single winner.

It was of great importance to make a decision on a northern pipeline, for two related reasons: the timetable prescribed by the U.S. Alaska Natural Gas Transportation Act (ANGTA), and projections that the United States would soon be facing an urgent need for natural gas. ANGTA required the president and Congress to decide on a route for Prudhoe Bay gas by September 1977, following recommendations from the Federal Power Commission (FPC). This unilaterally established deadline came to serve as a deadline for Canadian decision makers, who worried that if they failed to determine an acceptable route within this timetable, the balance would be tilted in favour of the all-American alternative, the El Paso project (Bregha, 1979). In its 1977 decision, the NEB frankly acknowledged that its haste to meet the Americans' schedule resulted in an inadequate decision-making record (NEB, 1977, 1–57).

ANGTA's artificial timetable was itself driven by the perceived shortage of gas. Although this now seems remarkable, we need to recall that by the mid-1970s, long periods of price regulation in the United States had brought about a deliverability crisis. This, coupled with the Arab oil embargo, led to demands for an early and timely decision.

Canadian policymaking was being driven by an American timetable, but it was also, to some extent, ad hoc. The NEBA and the Northern Pipeline Guidelines provided the basic framework for making a decision; however, the federal government thought it necessary to supplement this framework in a number of ways – most famously, by establishing the Berger Inquiry, which was to consider the CAGPL and Maple Leaf proposals. Berger's mandate was based on the Territorial Lands Act (TLA), pursuant to which the government would grant a pipeline right of way. The ad hoc responses spilled over to the Alaska Highway proposal with the appointment of the Lysyk Inquiry (to look at the socioeconomic issues), with the convening of an environmental panel, and ultimately with an international agreement with the United States and a special Act of Parliament (i.e., rather than an NEB approval) to green-light the project.

The primary purpose of the Alaska Highway Pipeline as originally conceived was to deliver Alaskan gas to American markets. The possible benefits to Canada of such a project included the opportunity to bring Canadian gas from the Delta to market more cheaply by applying the economies of scale associated with a pipeline sized to carry Prudhoe Bay gas; however, to realize this benefit, the NEB, in approving the Foothills proposal rather than the CAGPL, would have to address the problem of getting Delta gas to market. The NEB dealt with this by recommending that the southern Yukon portion of the route be modified by shifting it north to Dawson. Also, Foothills was required to make a formal application for the construction of the Dempster lateral.

The Role of Sustainability Values

In this section, we examine the role that sustainability values played in the NEB's decision, in the Lysyk Report, in the Berger Report, and in the government's subsequent decision as reflected in the Northern Pipeline Act and the Canada–U.S. Northern Pipeline Agreement. Justice Berger, who wrote his report a full decade before Brundtland wrote her own, did not use the terms 'sustainability' and 'sustainable development'; even so, sustainability reasoning underpinned much of his report. Critical ideas embraced by Berger included the following: the importance of cumulative impacts in weighing particular proposals; the importance of strengthening the renewable resource economy as well as the non-renewable economy; the need to capture the benefits for northerners; and the importance of protected areas, both to preserve critical habitat and to preserve wilderness values. These ideas informed concrete recommendations in Berger's report. For example, the importance of critical habitat led Berger to rule out the Northern Yukon route and to propose wilderness national park status for those lands, a whale sanctuary for the Delta, and endorsement of a number of International Biological Program sites for further protected status. Similarly, Berger believed that Aboriginal northerners should be able to reap the benefits associated with pipeline construction, and this led him to recommend that there be no pipeline down the valley for ten years.

The broad scope of Berger's recommendations reveals the extent to which he was attuned to the social and economic legs of sustainability as well as to the environmental leg. Their scope also reveals the extent to which he was able to offer truly integrated recommendations, unconstrained as he was by statutory mandate. Most of Berger's recommendations were accepted by the federal government and have since been implemented in whole or in part. One recommendation yet to be implemented is the Delta whale sanctuary.

Four elements of the NEB's decision merit attention here: (1) the need for the project and the conservation option, (2) the internalization of project costs, (3) subsidies, and (4) the environmental issues associated with the various routes. We also discuss the Lysyk Report here insofar as it deals with the socioeconomic impacts of the Foothills proposal.

Several intervenors opposed the pipeline applications as unnecessary. These intervenors had a vision of a conserver society in which energy use would grow no more than 2 per cent a year. They contended that this much growth could be met by non-frontier non-renewables and through greater emphasis on conservation and renewables. The NEB's reaction to this was mixed. On the one hand, it endorsed conservation as the lowest-cost option for balancing the energy budget; on the other hand, it did not believe it could close the gap in the near term. The NEB also noted that although federal and provincial policies and world events (the Arab oil embargo of 1973) were important influences on energy demand, they were not the whole picture; equally important 'were the choices freely made by the public at large on life styles and on social goals.' The NEB did not address the extent to which consumers' choices were in fact influenced by existing government polices – including price regulation – that favoured hydrocarbon sources.

The NEB had even more difficulty with the argument that it was premature to connect Delta gas before the potential of the Western Sedimentary Basin was exhausted; it responded, somewhat lamely, that although this argument 'might have some purely economic support,' a wiser strategy would 'draw on alternative sources of supply' (NEB, 1977, 1–84). We have already emphasized the importance of internalizing costs as a means of achieving a sustainable energy future. The NEB was unusually sensitive to this issue in its 1977 decision because of its characterization of the Foothills project as a project to get Alaskan gas to American markets. For the NEB, the problem was that although a large portion of the project's costs would fall on Canadians, and especially on northern Aboriginal residents, that project would largely benefit American consumers. The NEB thus took the unprecedented step of recommending that Cabinet approval of any certificate for the Foothills project require a number of undertakings from the proponent, including the following: (1) it would construct the Dempster lateral, (2) it would pay as much as $200 million to meet the indirect socioeconomic costs of the project, and (3) it would fulfil the various undertakings made during the hearings to mitigate socioeconomic impacts.

The Lysyk Report built on the NEB's recommendations and proposed that a Yukon Heritage Fund be established with an initial capitalization of $200 million, to be provided by Foothills. Further contributions over the life of the pipeline would come from 50 per cent of the property taxes attributable to the pipeline. This fund would be used to provide 'long term, tangible benefits' and to 'support positive steps that Yukoners ... will want to take to restore, maintain, and enhance the quality of life in the Yukon' (Lysyk, 1977, 150, 151). Lysyk also devoted considerable attention to the possibility of applying a property tax to the pipeline to enhance the territory's revenues.

The CAGPL frankly disclosed in its application that it would require government guarantees ('backstopping') in order to finance its pipeline. The NEB, echoing the FPC, adamantly rejected this idea – not, however, on the basis of getting the pricing messages right for consumers, but rather on the basis of perceptions of respective national interest and national benefits (NEB, 1977, 105). Foothills (Yukon) claimed that private finance could fund its project. The NEB was sceptical of this. In its view, a project of this magnitude would have to involve Foothills and AGTL mortgaging their Canadian assets to build a project for the United States. This would surely increase the cost of debt for these two regulated companies, and thereby force toll increases on the balance of their domestic systems.

The NEB was already in possession of the Berger Report, and its decision followed Berger on the routing question. It considered the North Slope impacts of the CAGPL unacceptable and not mitigable. In contrast, the environmental impacts of the Foothills Yukon and Maple Leaf projects *were* acceptable and mitigable. There was some uncertainty regarding the Dempster lateral (since there was no formal application to cover this proposal), but the NEB seemed willing to assume that any impact associated with this project would also be acceptable. The NEB did not address the need to set aside protected areas.

Cabinet and Parliament made several adjustments to the NEB's recommendations under the terms of the Northern Pipeline Act and the Northern Pipeline Agreement (the treaty). The overall tenor of these changes was to render less onerous the steps the NEB had proposed for internalizing the environmental and social costs of the project. The main points can be summarized as follows. (1) The route was amended to conform to Foothills's proposal; thus, the Dawson realignment was rejected. In return, American shippers were to pay for the tariff associated with the Dawson–Whitehorse leg of a Dempster lateral, provided there were no cost overruns. As costs rose, the obligation of American shippers to pay the full tariff would be reduced. (2) The government confirmed that the pipeline was to be privately financed without government backstopping. (3) Both abandoned were the NEB requirement of a $200 million fund for socioeconomic impacts, and Lysyk's recommendation for a Yukon Heritage Fund to be financed by Foothills. Instead, the treaty recognized that Yukon might impose a property tax, to be limited in value to $30 million per year, subject to a possible further increase if Alaskan property taxes on pipelines also increased. Special funds were expressly prohibited. Foothills's socio-economic undertakings were expressly endorsed by the act. Completely missing from the federal government's decision making (indeed, from the NEB's recommendations) was any consideration of the need for a network of protected areas.

What does all of this tell us about the extent to which what we now call sustainability values informed the decision-making processes in 1977? The key players showed differing levels of commitment to sustainability values. This commitment was most pronounced in Berger's report, which integrated environmental concerns with economic, social, and equity aspects of decision making. Berger's report acknowledged the importance of ecosystem approaches, and his respect for the value of wilderness was informed by his understanding of the needs of future generations. Berger translated sustainability thinking into concrete recommendations.

The NEB's decision showed less integration and less willingness to value equally environmental and economic values. We can see this in its dismissal of the conservation option and in its willingness to be stampeded into making a decision notwithstanding an incomplete record and considerable uncertainties surrounding the Dempster lateral and technical problems associated with discontinuous permafrost. The NEB made important recommendations on socioeconomic impacts, but judging from its reasoning, its concerns about internalizing costs were informed more by its perceptions of the national interest than by a commitment to internalization for the sake of fostering sustainability. The same perception of national interest informed its position on subsidies.

The Lysyk report was less integrated than those of Berger and the NEB, confined as it was to inquiring into socioeconomic conditions. That said, Lysyk's reasoning in relation to the Heritage Fund seems to have been informed by considerations of equity and the need to develop a balanced economy that would create options for future generations.

The Government of Canada's decisions are the most difficult to assess. On the one hand, it seems possible to say that the NPA and the treaty showed the least commitment to the values of sustainable development. The efforts of the NEB and Lysyk to internalize at least some of the socioeconomic costs of the project were rejected by the government. Its approval of the project now strikes us as cavalier in light of the uncertainties identified by the NEB. There were no contemporaneous commitments to create a network of protected areas.

Yet at the same time, the NPA and the treaty did not represent the sum total of Canada's policy commitments. The government did enter into negotiations with Yukon First Nations and with the Inuvialuit. One of the results of land claim settlements has been the creation of important protected areas in the Yukon and elsewhere, including the Ivvavik and Vuntut Gwich'in national parks in the northern Yukon.

Prebuild

The project that Foothills contemplated, that the NEB aproved, and that Parliament ratified has never been built. Foothills was a project to deliver Alaskan gas to American markets, with an opportunity to carry Delta gas to those markets as well as to Canadian markets. Instead, Foothills obtained the right, by Order in Council varying the terms of the NPA, to construct the 'prebuild' version of the project. First mooted by the NEB in its 1977 decision as a means of dealing with the so-called bubble of Alberta gas, the prebuild involved constructing pipelines in Alberta to ship Alberta gas to American markets. Two legs of pipeline have been constructed south of Caroline. The western leg takes Alberta gas to Kingsgate, British Columbia, where it connects with the Pacific Gas and Electric system for delivery to California and the Pacific Northwest. The eastern leg moves Alberta gas southeast from Caroline, through Alberta and Saskatchewan, to connect with the Northern Border system at Monchy for delivery to the American Midwest (Foothills, 2002). The basic facilities were completed in 1982. Efforts to challenge the prebuild approval as unconstitutional failed (*Waddell*, 1984).

Why was the project as originally conceptualized never built? The reason is simple. The dire predictions of gas shortages never came true. Fuelled by the perceptions of shortages and by price increases for natural gas, exploration efforts increased, and these added substantially to reserves within the lower forty-eight and in Canada's Western Sedimentary Basin (Office of the Federal Inspector, 1992, 3–5). These resources could be tied in to the existing pipeline system far more cheaply than could frontier resources. The same market conditions also led to the abandonment of other possible projects, including the Arctic Pilot Project and Polar Gas, both proposals to move high Arctic gas to international markets. In more recent years, the Canadian oil and gas industry has enjoyed considerable success exploring the Liard Basin in the southern Northwest Territories (Brackman, 2000). This points sharply to the wisdom of extending the existing pipeline system incrementally instead of taking a leapfrog approach by constructing a large-capacity northern pipeline.

Between Then and Now

Much has changed since the Alaska Highway Pipeline was approved in the late 1970s, but a few things have remained constant. Other essays in this volume discuss some of the changes. Abele draws attention in chapter 10 to northern developments, including the settlement of land claims and the maturing of territorial governments. We emphasize the following. Although progress has been made in settling Aboriginal claims, some claims – especially in southern Yukon and the southern NWT – remain unsettled. Also, claims settlements introduce vastly increased regulatory complexity when it comes to dealing with linear developments such as pipelines (Cowling, 2001). Federal petroleum leasing policies have evolved from the aggressive policies of the National Energy Program (NEP) to the current provisions of the Canada Petroleum Resources Act, which are avowedly designed to attract industry investment (DIAND, 1994). Protected areas strategies have been initiated in both the Yukon (Yukon, 1998, 2001) and the NWT (GNWT, 1999). Much of the actual responsibility for these strategies has devolved to the territorial governments, but the key controlling factor is the settlement of land claims, which remains a federal responsibility. Environmental NGOs have expressed concern that a northern pipeline may be authorized before a network of protected areas is in place, yet they also seemed encouraged by more recent DIAND announcements (WWF and CPAWS, 2000; CPAWS, 2002).

Doern and Gattinger (2003) note the general adoption of market-based approaches to regulation, which are evident in such measures as the abandonment of regulated pricing; the dominance of spot-market pricing; the abandonment of formal gas surplus determinations as a prerequisite for gas export approvals; the provisions of the Free Trade Agreement and NAFTA extending traditional non-discriminatory trade disciplines to energy commodities and services; the increased physical integration of North American pipeline systems through the construction of major new transmission pipelines such as the Alliance pipeline (NEB, 2000); and changing philosophies of regulation that emphasize the unbundling of integrated utilities, 'light-handed regulation,' and the fostering of pipe-on-pipe competition (Schultz, 1999).

Viewed collectively, these changes indicate that the values of the market have comprehensively replaced the interventionist approaches of the 1970s and 1980s.

Yet another contrasting trend is also identifiable. A number of global instruments, especially the FCCC and the CBD, now recognize that there are limits to market hegemony, and that these limits must be reflected in energy policies that are informed by concerns about climate change and appropriate development, as well as by ecosystem approaches that recognize the importance of landscape-level values. Domestically, these changes have been reflected in the legislatively based assessment process of the Canadian Environmental Assessment Act; in the stronger emphasis on cumulative impacts as part of project assessment; in the emergence of biodiversity values and landscape ecology as important components of project review; and in the importance attached to creating networks of protected areas as one of several critical means of maintaining ecosystem integrity.

There is a tension between the two broad trends identified above. The first set of trends reflects a hands-off approach with only limited and targeted government intervention the purpose of which is to create markets and make them work more efficiently. The second set of trends envisages more comprehensive regulation. Such regulation might be necessary in order to establish limits on the degree of landscape fragmentation in order to preserve ecosystem integrity, or it might be necessary in order to meet Kyoto-based GHG targets. Sustainable development requires us to reconcile this tension. One way is for government to implement new regulatory initiatives by setting overall standards (e.g., emission caps and landscape integrity standards) and then leaving the market to determine the most efficient means of attaining those standards.

With all of these changes, what, if anything, has remained the same? The National Energy Board Act is still the central permitting regime for a northern pipeline, although a proponent will also need to comply with the provisions of the Mackenzie Valley Resource Management Act (established pursuant to the Gwich'in and Sahtu claims) and with the screening and environmental impact assessment provisions of the Inuvialuit claim, as well as with other laws of general application such as the Canadian Environmental Assessment Act. In response to the obvious concerns this complexity raises for the possibilities of duplication and delay, the relevant regulators have been at pains to consult among themselves, and more broadly, to identify avenues for cooperation so as to avoid duplication. The results are embodied in a

Cooperation Plan and consolidated information requirements (Northern Pipeline Environmental Impact Assessment and Regulatory Chairs' Committee, 2002a, 2002b).

Now: Current Proposals and Interests

We now come to the status of the current proposals and identify the principal interests at stake. The two leading options are the Alaska Highway pipeline (AHP), for Alaskan North Slope gas, and the stand-alone Mackenzie Valley pipeline (MVP), for Delta gas. A third option, the 'over-the-top' pipeline, seeks to transport gas from both sources through a Mackenzie Valley pipeline that would extend from the Mackenzie Delta offshore to the Alaskan North Slope. Other options that are less likely include a proposal to pipe Alaskan North Slope gas to Valdez for liquefaction and ocean transport to Asian markets (YPC, 2002), and a process for converting the methane component of North Slope gas to liquid products that could be shipped down the existing oil pipeline to Valdez (Bradner, 2001).

The AHP appears to hold a regulatory advantage because its proponents – the Canadian and American companies that backed the original ANGTA proposal – still hold the certificate granted by the Northern Pipeline Act. But it is unclear whether that certificate covers the project as presently envisioned and how many additional regulatory steps will be necessary (Cowling, 2001). The proponents of the other two projects have announced that they intend to proceed with regulatory applications, but they have not yet filed complete applications with the NEB.

From another perspective, the MVP proposal holds the advantage because it is the only one of the three that is backed by a producer group. In fact, the Mackenzie Delta producers intend to own the MVP, in conjunction with an Aboriginal consortium. The Alaskan North Slope producers have concluded that the Alaska Highway and over-the-top pipelines remain uneconomic, under current market projections and absent any major new government incentives (*Houston Chronicle*, 2002; Earle, 2002). The political climate in the United States also favours the MVP insofar as Congressional proposals to offer subsidies to the AHP have lapsed and state legislation has tried to rule out the over-the-top option.

Each of the three main proponents has worked hard, with varying success, to gain the support of the Aboriginal peoples whose territories will be affected by the proposed routing options.

262 Nigel Bankes and Michael M. Wenig

Governments and Other Interests

The interests lining up behind and against each of the three main pipeline proposals are complex. On the American side, the chief players include the State of Alaska, which has vigorously promoted the AHP and adopted legislation effectively precluding state approval for the Alaskan portion of the over-the-top pipeline (Knowles, 2001). Alaska's pipeline preference has been supported by American labour unions, steel companies, consumers, and environmental groups. The latter apparently view an AHP as diverting attention from controversial proposals to drill for oil in the state's Arctic National Wildlife Refuge and as relatively environmentally benign because it would be constructed alongside existing transportation corridors (Morgan, 2002).

In their respective national energy bills, both houses of Congress have adopted provisions barring federal regulatory approval for the over-the-top route. The Senate's version also includes several subsidies, including a loan guarantee and a tax credit that would apply when gas prices were low, to be repaid when average prices were high (Morgan, 2002; Ruskin, 2002; Murkowski, 2002a, b). However, Alaska has thus far been unable to convince the White House, which, although eager to promote Alaskan gas production, has opposed the Congressional incentives and is insisting on staying neutral with respect to the choice of pipeline route (NEPDG, 2001, 7–11). The Federal Energy Regulatory Commission (FERC) has also expressed a preference for remaining neutral on this matter (FERC, 2001).

The interests in Canada are perhaps even more fractured than in the United States. The governments of the Northwest Territories and Yukon strongly support the AHP and MVP respectively, for their direct economic benefits, for the incentives they would provide for the development of each territory's own gas reserves, and as relatively cheap sources of power for mineral developments. Yukon has questioned the criticisms levelled by NWT and Ottawa against Congress's proposed financial incentives for the Alaska Highway pipeline, pointing to Canada's long history of subsidizing energy and other resource development projects in Canada as well as to the NWT government's own advocacy of federal loan guarantees for the Mackenzie Valley pipeline. (Varcoe, 2002; Weber, 2002).

British Columbia expects that it would experience direct and indirect benefits from the AHP similar to those for Yukon, yet it has been a far less vociferous advocate of the project. In fact, B.C. has been criticized for indirectly frustrating the project by conducting its recent referendum on 'principles' for negotiating future treaty settlements. This approach may frustrate the settlement of remaining treaties and other agreements necessary to clear the way for pipeline development (Dabbs, 2002b).

Alberta stands to benefit no matter which route is chosen, and it has backed both front runners. For either project, Alberta seeks to be able to extract liquids from the gas stream for its petrochemicals industry. There is also speculation that producers could use Delta gas to fuel their own Alberta oil sands production (*Calgary Herald*, 2002a; Lunan, 2002).

Canadian Aboriginal peoples may be in a position to withhold or provide support to particular pipeline developments. In general, the current mood is far more supportive of pipeline development than it was in the 1970s, but not all groups have signed on to the pipeline proposals in their respective regions. The dynamics are especially complex in the NWT. There, land claims are in various stages of settlement, and the various peoples are being wooed by the corporate proponents of two different pipeline proposals. In three of the four regional Aboriginal groups in the NWT, most leaders back the stand-alone MVP.

Canadian environmental NGOs may also be influential players. There has not yet been strong ENGO opposition to pipeline development per se, nor have ENGOs expressed a preference for any particular route. However, six prominent ENGOs have collectively endorsed a set of principles as a framework for northern oil and gas development, including pipeline construction. These principles call for the establishment, before significant developments are allowed, of an adequate network of northern protected areas; for land use planning and rigorous environmental assessment processes; and for frameworks for managing the cumulative effects of multiple developments (CARC, 2001, 3–5).

As for the federal government, there is no formal statement of federal northern pipeline policy, although we can identify three elements of such a policy. First, Canada is committed to an aggressive oil and gas disposition and exploration policy, and this implies support for some means to transport discovered reserves to southern markets. Second, Canada favours relying on the market to choose among gas pipeline routing options (Kergin, 2001). Third, Ottawa has vigorously opposed the U.S. Senate's proposed AHP subsidies, and also seems opposed to government subsidies – in the form of Aboriginal loan guarantees – for the MVP (Varcoe, 2002; Weber, 2002; *Natural Gas Week*, 2002).

Conclusions

How does current policy measure up against the sustainable development criteria we developed in the second section, which draw on the Auditor General Act, and against the emphasis those criteria place on the concept of *integration*? In the northern pipeline context, the integration strategy means that decisions on northern pipelines must be placed in a broader context. We discuss several aspects of that broader context below.

In 1977, Justice Berger recognized that decisions on a northern pipeline needed to be integrated with a wide range of environmental and social policies. For this to occur, decision makers must have the capacity to follow an integrated approach. Does this capacity exist, given the multiplicity of decision makers and the sector-specific focus of the NEB, which is Canada's chief pipeline regulator? Part of this capacity can be gained through cooperative arrangements among federal, territorial, and provincial decision makers. The 2002 Cooperation Agreement on NWT pipeline review is a considerable effort in this regard, but its primary purpose is to avoid duplication rather than to foster the integration of environmental, social, and economic values in decision making.

But do the decision makers themselves – especially the NEB – have a broad enough legal mandate to make decisions that reflect an integrated approach? On the one hand, the NEB's broad, 'public interest' decision-making authority suggests that it can and should consider a wide range of social factors in deciding whether to approve northern pipelines. On the other hand, the NEB's regulatory *power* is limited to pipelines, and this would make it impossible, for example, for it to directly require the creation of networks of protected areas that would maintain northern biodiversity, although the NEB should consider making its pipeline approval *conditional* on the completion of such networks.

We also question whether the NEB is well-positioned to give the same weight and respect to sustainable development policies as it accords to market policies. The NEB encounters little difficulty in giving concrete effect to the general move toward market values (NEB, 2002); it has considerably more difficulty in giving effect to environmental values (Athabasca Chipewyan First Nations, 2001).

In 1977, the Government of Canada stripped the NEB of its decision-making functions. Once again, legislative reform may be necessary in order to ensure that the NEB gives effect to international commitments on climate change and biodiversity, and to more specific federal policies, just as the NEBA was amended in 1993 in order to require the NEB to 'give effect' to NAFTA.

Pipeline policy must be consistent with a broader national energy policy. This has several implications. First, as other papers in this volume make clear, Canada's energy policy is going to be driven in part by national GHG reduction strategies, whether those strategies are established through ratification of the Kyoto Protocol or as part of a Canadian or North American approach. This means that Canada's GHG strategies will need to be factored into national supply and demand projections for natural gas, which currently fail to account for climate change commitments (NEB, 1999). Similarly, the boosterism of federal oil and gas disposition policies must be rationalized with future possible reductions in demand and dependence on fossil fuels.

Second, Canada's current energy policy does not resolve the tension between increased reliance on markets and the need for government regulation to achieve sustainable development. The government can resolve this tension, in part, by setting environmental and other limits within which emissions trading and other market mechanisms can flourish. This tension can be further resolved by government taking more responsibility for ensuring that market prices reflect the true social costs of renewable and non-renewable energy sources. Proposals to subsidize the construction and/or operations of a northern gas pipeline should be carefully scrutinized, as should price floors, because of their potential to distort the market choice between pipeline routes and, more fundamentally, between renewable and non-renewable energy sources.

Even without subsidies, the market does not accurately reflect the relative full costs of various energy sources. Thus, pipeline policy must fit within a broader energy policy that sets out to internalize the full environmental and social costs of pipeline construction and operation, and of the production and consumption of the gas shipped through those pipelines. The 1977 decision-making process made some effort to address this problem, but that effort must be more comprehensive, both in the specific context of setting conditions for pipeline approvals, and in the broader context of the overall energy market. Unfortunately, although we have turned increasingly to market solutions to environmental problems, and although other papers in this volume demonstrate that we know how to internalize costs, governments seem no more willing to grasp the nettle than they were twenty-seven years ago.

Much has changed since the 1977 Berger Inquiry, but the concerns for the just settlement of Aboriginal claims that motivated Berger, reinforced by the equity aspects of sustainable development, are still legitimate. The federal government has endeavoured to meet these concerns through the twin policies of devolution and settling Aboriginal land claims. There has been significant progress on both fronts, but there is still work to be done. The settlement of claims is a first step. This does not by itself guarantee that the Aboriginal peoples concerned will be able to take advantage of the opportunities presented by resource development within their territories. Much will depend on the educational and training attainments of community members. These are both long-term issues that require long-term governmental commitments and for which there is no quick fix. The enhanced level of Aboriginal support for the various pipeline proposals suggests a degree of confidence among Aboriginal leaders; however, that support is not unanimous and is most absent in those parts of the territories where claims have yet to be settled. A pipeline policy cannot require the settlement and implementation of land claims, but it can still pose the same types of questions that Berger posed in 1977. Will the Aboriginal residents of the area benefit if the pipeline is built? What can be done, besides settling claims, to maximize those opportunities? What level of risk, if any, should Aboriginal people bear in pipeline development? And, importantly, what role should the government play, relative to Aboriginal decision making, in answering these questions?

Berger urged a pipeline moratorium, in part because he felt that there was insufficient capacity to manage the environmental and socioeconomic effects of the boom in activity that would result from pipeline development. That capacity has improved greatly since the 1970s, but it remains an issue. In particular, the relatively young planning and assessment boards created by the land claim agreements are already under stress as a result of the ramping up of gas exploration and other northern resource development activities. Do these and other institutions have the capacity to handle the boom in pipeline activity, and if they don't, what steps are needed to remedy this problem?

In the mid-1970s, Canada decided it would make its decision on a northern pipeline within a timetable established unilaterally by the United States. In its decision, the NEB admitted that this schedule precluded it from properly assessing the competing proposals. Twenty-seven years later, there is a renewed urgency fostered by the Mackenzie producers, the NWT government, and the United States in the form of proposals to subsidize the Alaska Highway pipeline. In Canada, the position seems to be that the stand-alone pipeline must go first so as to allow Mackenzie producers to secure the speculatively higher prices that may be available before Alaska gas comes on stream. Although a 'fast track' timetable may serve private values, will it also serve sustainability values?

Governments approved a northern pipeline in 1977; the market decided that it would not be built at that time. The precious and limited resources of the applicants and intervenors were invested in that process, with some of the ENGO interveners making precisely the point that the market did not justify approving the pipeline. A similar fate befell the Arctic Pilot Project during the early 1980s, and again, the scarce resources of ENGOs, northern Aboriginal organizations, and governments were allocated to work on a proposal that ultimately lacked market support. Will the same thing happen now? Will producers conclude that it makes more sense to tie in the very large non-conventional gas reserves (i.e., coal bed methane; NEB, 1999, 42) before building a northern pipeline?

A pipeline approval system cannot avoid this sort of risk altogether, but the system should adopt tools to minimize the risk. These tools might include the following: (1) an early focus on the degree of market support and financial viability of the proposals; (2) continued clear articulation of government policy on energy policy generally, and specifically on subsidies so as to avoid considering proposals that depend on vain hopes of subsidies (the CAGPL position in 1977 until its dying moments); and (3) in recognition of the costs created for others, a meaningful program of intervenor funding. The absence of such a program within the NEB has long been contentious. Maybe its time has come.

REFERENCES

Aboriginal Pipeline Group. 2002. www.aboriginalpipeline.ca[.]

ArctiGas Resources Corporation. 2002. See www.arctigas.ca[.]

Athabasca Chipewyan First Nation, et al v. British Columbia Hydro and Power Authority and National Energy Board. 2001. 37 C.E.L.R. (N.S.) 147 (F.C.A.).

Berger, T. 1977. *Northern Frontier, Northern Homeland: The Report of the Mackenzie Valley Pipeline Inquiry.* Ottawa: Ministry of Supply and Services.

Black, Alexander J. 2002. 'Legal Principles Surrounding the New Canadian and American Arctic Energy Debate.' 23 *Energy Law Journal* 81.

Brackman, Calvin. 2000. 'The Northwest Territories Petroleum Industry.' Unpublished paper.

Bradner, Tim. 2001. 'Gasline Prospects Fade but Alternatives Await.' *Anchorage Daily News.* 30 December. www.adn.com/business/v-printer/story/747128p-799659c.html

Bregha, François. 1979. *Bob Blair's Pipeline.* Toronto: Lorimer.

Calgary Herald. 2002a. 'Premier Joins Push for Pipeline.' June 5: A2.

– 2002b. 'Bush Opposes Senate's Alaska Pipeline Subsidy.' June 29: D4.

Canada. 1972. *Expanded Guidelines for Northern Pipelines.* Ottawa: Ministry of Supply and Services.

– 1988. *Energy and Canadians into the 21st Century: A Report on the energy Options Process.* Ottawa: Minister of Supply and Services.

– 1995a. *A Guide to Green Government.* www.ec.gc.ca/grngvt/intro_e.html[.]

– 1995b. *Canadian Biodiversity Strategy – Canada's Response to the Convention on Biological Diversity.* www.bco.ec.gc.ca/documents/CBS_E.pdf[.]

CARC (Canadian Arctic Resources Committee). 2001. *Northern Perspectives.* (fall–winter).

Convention on Biological Diversity. 1992. www.biodiv.org/doc/legal/cbd-en.pdf[.]

Cowling, Robin. 2001. *Review and Regulatory Processes for Northern Pipeline Projects: Opportunities for Public Involvement.* Calgary: Canadian Institute of Resources Law.

CPAWS (Canadian Parks and Wilderness Society). 2002. *News Release: CPAWS Slams Federal Minister's Support For Fast-Tracking Mackenzie Valley Pipeline.* 16 September. www.cpaws.org/news/mackenzie-valley-2002-0916.html[.]

Dabbs, Frank. 2002a. 'Key Environmental Group Enters Pipeline Fray.' *Calgary Herald.* 14 June.

- 2002b. 'Campbell a Serious Danger to B.C. Resource Development.' *Calgary Herald*. 12 July: C2.
DIAND (Department of Indian Affairs and Northern Development). 1994. *Northern Oil and Gas Bulletin*. 1, no. 1. www.ainc-inac.gc.ca/oil/bul/Vol1_1_e.html
- 2001a. *Sustainable Development Strategy 2001–2003*. www.ainc-inac.gc.ca/pr/sus/index_e.html
- 2001b. *Sustainable Development – Action Plan North of 60° N*. www.ainc-inac.gc.ca/ps/nap/sust/docs_e.html
- 2002. *Oil and Gas in Canada's North*. www.ainc-inac.gc.ca/oil/bkgd/nor/index_e.html (26 April, 2002 update)
Doern, Bruce, and Monica Gattinger. 2003. *Power Switch: Energy Regulatory Governance in the 21st Century*. Toronto: University of Toronto Press.
Earle, Julie. 2002. 'BP Shelves Plans for Dollars 20bn Alaska Gas Pipeline Project.' *Financial Times* (London), 15 February: 19.
FERC (Federal Energy Regulatory Commission). 2001. *Testimony of Hon. Patrick Wood III, FERC Chairman, before the U.S. Senate Energy and Natural Resources Committee*. Washington: USGPO. 2 October.
Foothills Pipe Lines Ltd. 2002. www.foothillspipe.com (accessed 28 August 2002).
GNWT (Government of the Northwest Territories). 1999. *NWT Protected Areas Strategy: A Balanced Approach to Establishing Protected Areas in the Northwest Territories*. www.gov.nt.ca/RWED/pas/index.htm[.]
Houston Chronicle. 2002. 'BP: No Alaska Gas Pipeline Before Decade's End.' February 17, B7.
Kergin, Hon. Michael. 2001. *Letter to Hon. Spencer Abraham, U.S. Secretary of Energy*. Copy on file with authors.
Knowles, Gov. Tony. 2001. *Testimony of Alaska Governor Tony Knowles – United States Senate Committee on Energy and Natural Resource*. www.gov.state.ak.us/SPEECH/100201-Energy.html
Lunan, Dale. 2002. 'Opinion – Summer in the Patch.' *Oilweek Newsletter*. 24 June: 7.
Lysyk. 1977. *Alaska Highway Pipeline Inquiry*. Ottawa: Ministry of Supply and Services Canada.
Morgan, Dan. 2002. 'Senate Energy Bill Backs Alaska Gas Pipeline.' *Washington Post*. 25 April: A08.
Murkowski, Sen. Frank H. 2002a. *Press Release: Murkowski Wins Conference Committee Approval of Southern Route for Gas Pipeline*. 12 September. See energy.senate.gov/press

– 2002b. *Press Release: Energy Conference Resolves Host of Issues, Pushes Forward towards Final Bill.* 13 September. See energy.senate.gov/press
NEB (National Energy Board). 1977. *Reasons for Decision, Northern Pipelines.* Ottawa: NEB.
– 1999. *Canadian Energy Supply and Demand to 2025.* Calgary: NEB.
– 2000. *Canadian Natural Gas Market: Dynamics and Pricing: An Energy Market Assessment*
– 2002. *Reasons for Decision, Export Order Procedures.* MH-2-2002. Calgary: NEB.
NEPDG (National Energy Policy Development Group). 2001. *National Energy Policy.* May. www.whitehouse.gov/energy/National-Energy-Policy.pdf
Natural Gas Week. 2002. 'Government Anti-Subsidization For NWT Natural Gas Pipeline.' 15 November.
Northern Pipeline Environmental Impact Assessment and Regulatory Chairs' Committee. 2002a. *Cooperation Plan for the Environmental Impact Assessment and Regulatory Review of a Northern Gas Pipeline Project through the Northwest Territories.* Calgary: NEB.
– 2002b. *Consolidated Information Requirements for the Environmental Impact Assessment and Regulatory Review of a Northern Gas Pipeline Project through the Northwest Territories.* Calgary: NEB.
NRCan (Natural Resources Canada). 2000. *Energy in Canada 2000.* Ottawa: NRCan. www.nrcan.gc.ca/es/ener2000
Office of the Federal Inspector, Alaska Natural Gas Transportation System. 1992. *Report to the President on the Construction of the Alaska Natural Gas Transportation System.* Washington, DC:
Ruskin, Liz. 2002. 'Stevens Backs Off ANWR Plan.' *Anchorage Daily News.* 24 April. See www.adn.com/alaska/v-printer/story/989367p-1093230c.html
Schultz, N. 1999. 'Light-Handed Regulation.' 37 *Alberta Law Review* 387.
Varcoe, Chris. 2002. 'U.S. Pipeline Subsidy Will Die: Kakfwi.' *Calgary Herald.* 4 July: C2.
Waddell v. Governor in Council and Foothills Pipeline (Yukon) Ltd. et al. 1984. WWR 307 (B.C.S.C.).
WCED (World Commission on Environment and Development). 1987. *Our Common Future.* Oxford: Oxford University Press.
Weber, Bob. 2002. 'Subsidies for U.S. Pipeline Jolt Leaders.' *Calgary Herald* 17 April: D2.
WWF (World Wildlife Fund) and CPAWS (Canadian Parks and Wilderness Society). 2000. *News Release: DIAND Minister Nault Reneges on Federal Commitment to the NWT Protected Areas Strategy.* 29 June.
YPC (Yukon Pacific Corporation). 2002. *Project Description; Progress and Status.* www.csx.com/business/ypc/index_1.html

Yukon Department of Environment. 2001. *Yukon Protected Areas Strategy.* www.environmentyukon.gov.yk.ca/parks/ypas.shtml

Yukon Government. 1998. *Wild Spaces, Protected Places: A Protected Areas Strategy for the Yukon.* Whitehorse: Yukon Territory. Dept. of Renewable Resources.

Chapter 11

Alternative Dispute Resolution in Energy Regulation: Opportunities, Experiences, and Prospects

MONICA GATTINGER

When a conflict arises between two or more parties, there are two main approaches to resolving the dispute: adjudication by a third party, and joint decision making by the disputants themselves (Kheel, 1985). Canadian energy regulators, as quasi-judicial agencies, have traditionally employed the former means of resolving disputes in the energy sector.[1] A formal public hearing enables energy companies and parties affected by their applications to present their concerns to a third party, the energy regulatory board, which hears the various positions and renders a decision on the matter, approving, rejecting, or requiring modifications to an energy application. In recent times, many Canadian energy regulators are complementing this adjudicative regulatory model with practices that encourage joint decision-making between energy disputants. Alternative forms of dispute resolution such as negotiation, facilitation, and mediation can permit conflicting parties to settle disputes through direct interaction with one another, rather than through recourse to third-party adjudication.

This chapter considers the use of alternative dispute resolution (ADR) by energy regulators in Canada. My objectives are to identify the opportunities of ADR, examine energy regulators' experiences with this form of conflict resolution, and explore the prospects for ADR in Canadian energy regulatory decision making.[2]

This review reveals that a range of critical issues face energy regulators as they pursue and adopt ADR. At the program level, there are a number of challenges pertaining to ADR in areas such as enforcement, use in multiparty disputes, and the relationship between ADR and public involvement and consultation. This chapter argues that energy regulators will need to address these issues if they intend to further integrate ADR into their application processes. This includes the need to consider ADR's potential limitations in the energy regulatory context.

At a broader level, this chapter raises a number of fundamental concerns pertaining to the use of ADR in energy regulation. Specifically, does an ADR process, in contrast to a public hearing process, bear negatively on natural justice and procedural fairness, democratic considerations for openness and transparency in public decision-making, and the pursuit of the public interest? This chapter examines the potential implications of ADR as they relate to each of these three vital concerns, and argues that ADR may indeed hamper natural justice and procedural fairness, the openness and transparency of regulatory decision-making, and the pursuit of the public interest. As such, it is imperative that energy regulators reflect carefully and proceed cautiously when they design and adopt ADR programs.

The chapter proceeds in three parts corresponding to the three objectives noted above. The first section identifies the main opportunities of ADR. The second explores Canadian energy regulators' experiences with ADR, focusing mainly on the province of Alberta, where the Alberta Energy and Utilities Board (AEUB) has developed and implemented an ADR program over the past several years. The third and final section examines the prospects for ADR in Canadian energy regulation. It discusses the critical challenges and fundamental questions pertaining to the use of ADR in the energy regulatory context.

Opportunities

Of the two main approaches to resolving a dispute – adjudication and joint decision making alternative dispute resolution generally encompasses dispute resolution processes falling into the latter category. The main processes include *negotiation*, where the parties resolve their own differences without assistance from a third party, *mediation*, where a neutral third party helps the disputants negotiate a solution, and – in the energy regulatory milieu – *facilitation*, which falls somewhere in between these two processes, and refers to regulatory board staff assisting disputing parties to resolve their differences. The term 'appropriate dispute resolution,' which is favoured in Alberta and used also by the National Energy Board (NEB), refers to using the most efficient and effective means of resolving a dispute with the greatest probability of success (Savage, 2001). As such, it extends the three-point continuum of negotiation–facilitation–mediation discussed earlier to include processes in the adjudicative category of dispute resolution, notably *arbitration*, where the disputing parties empower a third party to assess the evidence and impose a binding decision on the parties, and *adjudication*, where a person or tribunal empowered by legislated authority makes decisions that are binding on the parties. This results in the following five-point continuum:

Negotiation → Facilitation → Mediation → Arbitration → Adjudication

Moving from the left-hand to the right-hand side of the continuum involves concomitant moves from informal to formal methods of decision making, from less costly to more expensive forms of making decisions, from private to public forums, and from voluntary to involuntary processes, as well as shifting from processes in which parties have more control over outcomes toward those in which they have less control (NEB, 2002). Given this chapter's focus on joint decision making in dispute resolution, it employs the term 'alternative' (rather than appropriate) dispute resolution, which will be used to refer to negotiation, facilitation, and mediation. This chapter's emphasis is on energy regulators' creation of formal ADR programs that offer energy disputants the opportunity to use mediation to resolve their differences.

Proponents of ADR note that it enjoys both procedural and substantive advantages over adjudicated forms of decision making. It can be less costly and more expeditious than its adjudicative counterpart; it can also be more democratic than adjudicative processes because it empowers disputing parties to resolve their differences in a process akin to direct democracy (Stephenson and Pops, 1991). ADR is an approach to solving problems based on social interaction that 'encourages reflective understanding by the relevant parties who codetermine the content of social consensus' (Protasal, 1991, 194). Indeed, the main reasons the NEB gives for its use of ADR are to meet the public's evolving need for greater involvement in energy regulatory decision making, and to save time and money (NEB, 2002). Industry actors have voiced similar reasons for using ADR, including a reduction in costs, a shortening of time lines, the maintenance of energy stakeholder control of decision making in conflict resolution, a reduction in demands on government, and improved communications and relationships among parties in the energy industry (Savage, 2001).

Experiences

A number of Canadian energy regulators have developed and implemented (or are in the process of developing and implementing) formal ADR programs. A full examination of all current and forthcoming programs is beyond the scope of this chapter. This section focuses predominantly on the use of ADR by the AEUB. It begins with a brief overview of current ADR initiatives at the NEB and the British Columbia Oil and Gas Commission (the Commission).[3]

The National Energy Board

The NEB is currently developing a formal ADR program. It has stated for some time that it wants to be more open in its regulatory processes and that it wishes to conduct its business differently. Indeed, in 1998, the acting chairman of the NEB, Kenneth Vollman (currently the chair of the NEB), identified ADR mechanisms as a means of addressing the contemporary challenges of physical regulation of pipelines (Vollman, 1998). In 2001, the NEB adopted its Mediation Practice Direction for resolving landowner objections during detailed route hearings for oil and natural gas pipelines and power lines (NEB, 2001). This voluntary process provides an opportunity for landowners and industry to resolve disputes using mediation at the stage when the details of routes are being decided. NEB staff serve as mediators in a voluntary, informal, and confidential process, the intent of which is to settle the issues pertaining to the objection, with a view to eliminating the need for a formal public hearing.

Staff are bound by the confidentiality of the proceedings and are forbidden to reveal anything the disputing parties say in a mediation outside the mediation process except as agreed to by the parties. Moreover, mediation sessions are only open to the parties to the mediation and their representatives. They are not open to the public unless the parties to the mediation consent. Parties to the mediation are responsible for the costs of their own representatives and advisers, but the NEB does not charge for the mediation services of its staff or for the facilities used in a mediation session. If the parties reach an agreement, that agreement is not normally filed with the NEB, nor is it subject to the NEB's approval. Furthermore, the NEB has no duty to enforce the negotiated outcome.

The NEB is currently developing a formal ADR Program to extend the use of ADR to other types of regulatory decisions and processes.

These include industry–public disputes such as landowner and en-croachment issues, industry-industry disputes such as toll-related is-sues, and regulatory development processes, for which ADR could be used to empower energy stakeholders in developing regulation. At the time of writing the NEB was consulting with stakeholders in the creation of an ADR Pilot program.

The British Columbia Oil and Gas Commission

The B.C. Oil and Gas Commission has statutory authority over most aspects of the regulation of the upstream oil and gas sector in the province and is intended 'to provide an efficient, integrated approach to the management and regulation of the oil and gas industry to meet economic, environmental and social objectives' (B.C. Oil and Gas Com-mission, 1998). The Commission is somewhat unique in the field of Canadian energy regulation in that it is legislatively required to utilize ADR in its operations. Section 8(1) of the Oil and Gas Commission Act stipulates that the Commission 'must encourage the use of consensual alternative dispute resolution methods for the purpose of resolving disputes relating to the commission's discretion, functions and duties.' This includes both the use of ADR in resolving conflicting interests in the application process, and the use of ADR in the Commission's re-consideration process, during which energy stakeholders can request a review of Commission decisions.

   In the summer of 2002, the Commission released its Public Involve-ment Guideline (B.C. Oil and Gas Commission, 2002), which outlined the roles, responsibilities, strategies, and processes for industry to un-dertake public involvement. This guideline notes that when a dispute arises between an energy industry applicant and an affected party, the Commission will attempt to encourage and facilitate the use of ADR. Furthermore, when energy stakeholders believe that the Oil and Gas Commission failed to consider a concern in its decision-making pro-cess, they can submit a 'Request for Reconsideration' and use ADR to resolve the dispute. The Commission is currently developing and imple-menting its formal ADR program in ways that will involve third-party mediators in conflict resolution. Up to this point, Commission staff have used facilitation to help energy stakeholders resolve energy dis-putes, or stakeholders have negotiated directly with one another to reach agreement. In addition, the Commission has undertaken a two-year ADR process at the community level using a well-known mediator.

The Alberta Energy and Utilities Board

The AEUB is an independent, quasi-judicial agency of the Government of Alberta. Established on 15 February 1995 by the Alberta Energy and Utilities Board Act, the AEUB joins two previously separate energy regulators, the Energy Resources Conservation Board and the Public Utilities Board.[4] The regulator is responsible for the 'safe, responsible, and efficient development of Alberta's energy resources' (oil, natural gas, oil sands, coal and electrical energy) as well as for the pipelines and transmission lines that move energy resources to market. The AEUB also regulates investor-owned gas, electric, and water utilities with a view to safe and reliable service at just and reasonable rates.[5]

The AEUB developed its ADR system in the late 1990s in response to a number of factors, including increased industry–landowner conflict, concern about the number and duration of AEUB public hearings, public distrust of industry and the AEUB, and industry and stakeholder support (Kruk, 2000). The Board assembled a multistakeholder steering committee that included representatives from the Canadian Association of Petroleum Landmen, the Canadian Association of Petroleum Producers, the Small Explorers and Producers Association of Canada, the Department of Agriculture, Food and Rural Development, and the environmental and agricultural communities. The committee, chaired by an AEUB staff member and supported by a private consulting firm, sought to 'design a system to improve EUB facilitation and to introduce mediation and other collaborative options into the EUB application process' (Canadian Dispute Resolution Corporation, 2000, 3).

The AEUB's Appropriate Dispute Resolution Program was formally introduced in January 2001 with Informational Letter 2001–01. The AEUB uses the term 'appropriate' rather than the more common term 'alternative' to recognize the range of dispute resolution options available and to underscore the facilitation role played by AEUB staff in the process (some mediators do not consider facilitation a means of formal ADR). Dispute resolution options range from informal negotiations, where the parties deal directly with one another with no outside involvement, to facilitation, where board staff help parties resolve conflict, to mediation, where independent mediators assist the parties.

At the heart of the new system is industry's responsibility to address public concerns through public consultation.[6] When disputes arise, the ADR program offers an additional means for landowners and industry to resolve disputes through direct interaction rather than through AEUB hearings. Although the ADR Program and guidelines are intended for use primarily in disputes about proposed facilities or modifications to existing facilities, ADR can also be used for disputes over the operation of facilities under AEUB jurisdiction. The program's goals include improved landowner–industry relations, better use of public and private resources and time, and reductions in the number of AEUB hearings (AEUB, 2001, 2).

The process begins with a Preliminary ADR (PADR) meeting, where the disputing parties discuss the nature and extent of their conflict and plan potential means of resolving their dispute. A mediator attends this meeting and helps the parties address issues such as how to resolve the dispute, who will participate in its resolution, how a mediator (if desired) will be selected,[7] the role of advisers (e.g., AEUB staff or lawyers), the use of confidentiality, and the means of handling any costs and payments arising from the dispute's resolution. In industry–landowner disputes, the industry applicant generally covers the costs of this preliminary meeting. If the conflicting parties opt to mediate their dispute, they reach agreement at the PADR meeting as to how they will handle issues related to confidentiality, deadlines, and the acquisition of technical, scientific, and other information, as well as the binding nature of a final agreement and its enforcement. An ADR multiparty stakeholder committee maintains a roster of qualified service providers (experienced ADR professionals who can help the parties understand mediation and the role of the PADR and who can help the parties select an initial mediator) and mediators on the AEUB website.

The role of AEUB staff ranges from facilitation to involvement in the PADR meeting to mediation. Staff can attend the disputing parties' negotiations (if requested), facilitate their communications, and assist with technical issues. If parties decide to have a PADR meeting, they can request and are encouraged to accept the presence of AEUB staff to provide regulatory and other information; however, there is no requirement for AEUB representation. To develop staff capacity to provide facilitation and other ADR-related support to disputing parties, the AEUB has increased staff training in these areas.

The program introduces a number of important new features into the energy application process in Alberta. First, where conflicts over energy developments occur, the onus now rests with the disputing parties to resolve the disagreement. Participation in the ADR Program is voluntary and does not preclude access to an AEUB hearing; that said, the AEUB 'strongly encourages the parties to at least attend a Preliminary ADR Meeting to discuss options and procedures to deal with the disputes' (AEUB, 2001, 2). The AEUB aims to hold hearings only when disputes are protracted or involve multiple stakeholders (e.g., an entire community).

Second, confidentiality can now be applied to the resolution of disputes. When disputes are dealt with at AEUB hearings, proceedings and decisions are a matter of public record. Agreements reached through ADR must conform with energy regulatory and statutory requirements, and therefore 'certain technical, scientific and other information or components of an agreement may have to be disclosed to the EUB or other regulatory authorities' (ibid., 7), but in an ADR process, parties to a dispute can undertake in confidence certain aspects of their proceedings (e.g., compensation). The chapter's next section returns to the issue of confidentiality in ADR proceedings.

Third, in contrast to an AEUB hearing, participants in the ADR Program can address issues beyond the AEUB's jurisdiction. For example, the authority to order compensation rests not with the AEUB, but with the Surface Rights Board. Where parties wish to include compensation in the resolution of their dispute, the AEUB can arrange for the Surface Rights Board to attend a mediation; in this way, the parties can comprehensively address their dispute.

The AEUB's first Annual Report for its ADR Program (AEUB, 2002a) noted that in 2001, roughly 3,000 of the almost 30,000 oil and gas facility projects proposed in Alberta generated significant concerns on the part of landowners who might be affected. Although industry applicants resolved most of these disputes without the assistance of AEUB staff or mediators, there were 161 staff facilitations (115 had been completed by the end of the year, with 98 resolved) and 30 mediations (23 completed by the end of the year, with 19 resolved and 4 going to a public hearing).[8] The average time taken to conduct a mediation from date of referral to mediation until the end of the process was 28 days, with the duration of the PADR meetings and mediations themselves averaging 2.5 hours and 7 hours, respectively.

The average cost of a mediation for both the PADR meeting and the mediation (including the service provider, mediator, and facility rental) was $4,300. This figure excludes legal counsel and other experts, but it is noteworthy that the percentage of mediation cases involving lawyers and third-party experts was very low in comparison to AEUB hearings. Overall, participants (including the disputing parties, AEUB staff, mediators, and lawyers) expressed satisfaction with the ADR process, with 33 out of 34 respondents indicating they would participate again.

Prospects for the Use of ADR in Energy Regulatory Processes

Given the opportunities ADR affords energy regulators for more expeditious, economical, and stakeholder-empowered decision making, it is perhaps not surprising that Canadian regulators are increasingly incorporating ADR into their decision-making processes. This shift in the process of energy regulatory decision making merits deliberate reflection by energy regulators, energy stakeholders, and the academic community alike. As Stephenson and Pops (1991, 13) note in an examination of negotiated conflict resolution techniques in public administration, 'history suggests that optimism about new decision modes in public administration has invariably been followed by a set of cautionary judgments enunciated after some experimentation and reflection.' Given that the development and implementation of formal ADR programs in Canada are still in their infancy, this chapter's examination of the prospects for ADR in energy regulation includes a discussion of current challenges in the design and execution of ADR programs as well as a number of cautionary judgments (which at this time are perhaps better termed 'pre-cautionary judgments'). The paragraphs below examine some of the key design and process issues respecting the use of ADR in energy regulation, and then raise some fundamental questions regarding the implications of the shift that ADR represents from third-party adjudicative to stakeholder-negotiated decision making. Sustainable development does not anchor this chapter's analysis as it does many of the other contributions to this volume; that said, the foregoing analysis identifies some potential implications of ADR for notions of sustainable development. These pertain chiefly to the fundamental questions raised in the latter portion of this section of the chapter.

The current and future prospects for the use of ADR will depend first and foremost on energy regulators' design of ADR programs that respond to the needs, interests, and responsibilities of the actors and institutions in the energy regulatory policy domain. These considerations are primarily process-related and, as discussed below, pertain chiefly to stakeholder-to-stakeholder relations, multiparty disputes, the relationship of ADR to the broader regulatory process, enforcement, and evaluation. The prospects for ADR will also depend, however, on the capacity of this form of conflict resolution to respond to fundamental questions pertaining to administrative law and democracy. As the following paragraphs discuss, these broader issues pertain to the implications of ADR for essential concerns such as natural justice and procedural fairness, democratic considerations for openness and transparency in decision making, and the pursuit of the public interest. The first set of considerations respecting process noted at the outset of this paragraph identify specific challenges in the design and execution of ADR programs; the second set of considerations raises some cautionary flags as to the broader implications of ADR for energy regulatory decision making.

Process Considerations

Regulators face a number of challenges and issues respecting the design and execution of ADR programs. First, parties to a dispute may exhibit considerable asymmetries in the financial, organizational, and technical resources they possess (Stephenson and Pops, 1991). This is perhaps most apparent in industry–landowner disputes, where energy companies tend to possess considerable financial, organizational, and technical resources vis-à-vis landowners. Energy companies can generally bring more financial and organizational resources to bear on ADR processes than landowners, and are also likely to possess relatively more knowledge about the energy project that has given rise to the dispute. When companies have considerable experience managing landowner relations, they may also be relatively better informed about the rights of landowners and the content of agreements the company has reached with landowners in the past.

In order to address financial asymmetries, the practice in Alberta has been for energy companies to pay for the ADR process (energy applicants underwrite the costs of intervenor funding in the public hearing process in Alberta). In British Columbia, there is no explicit requirement for industry or the B.C. Oil and Gas Commission to level the financial playing field between energy disputants, although it is implicitly understood that industry applicants will incorporate the costs of third-party mediation into their application costs. The Commission does not provide direct financial assistance to either party to a dispute. At the NEB, the means of addressing financial asymmetries are perhaps less apparent, as the board does not have legislative authority to require industry to fund intervenors in public hearings.[9] With respect to informational asymmetries, in Alberta, landowners can retain legal counsel for ADR proceedings, can request scientific study of the potential implications of the energy project in question, and may invite the Farmers' Advocate of Alberta to attend ADR meetings.[10] The Farmers' Advocate has recommended that the AEUB include more mediators with agricultural expertise on its mediator roster.

Second, there can be considerable design issues challenging the use of ADR in multiparty disputes. When a proposed energy project affects multiple parties with diverse interests, designing an ADR proceeding capable of resolving such a multifaceted dispute can be an exceedingly complex task. In Alberta, for example, a large application that covered a geographical area of some twenty square miles with the potential to affect multiple landowners confronted the AEUB with a complex design challenge. The number and diversity of landowner interests rendered infeasible a single ADR undertaking. Although the company undertook a series of separate ADR processes with individual landowners, the process involved significant logistical complexities and financial and organizational costs. The company held individual PADR meetings with close to a dozen landowners, but there remained a number of outstanding objections, and the application eventually went to a public hearing. The complexity involved in designing multiparty ADR processes does not mean that they are infeasible, but it does suggest that in some circumstances, an adjudicative process might be preferable.

A third issue deserving reflection is the relationship of ADR to the broader regulatory process – in particular, its relationship to energy company public involvement or consultation processes. ADR is related in two main respects to the public consultation process. In the first instance, the need for an energy company to engage in the ADR process can result from inadequate public consultation. When a firm has poorly managed its stakeholder relations in the public consultation process, conflicts that could have been resolved at the consultation stage can escalate into disputes requiring an ADR process. When the applicant–stakeholder relationship has degenerated and there is little trust remaining between the parties, it is often too late to resolve contested issues through public consultation. The matter must then be dealt with in an ADR proceeding. In this sense, the ADR stage of energy applications may be related to the consultation stage in an undesirable sense, serving as a substitute for public consultation or as a symptom of consultation processes gone awry. This can lead to higher costs in terms of time and financial resources when disputes could have been dealt with earlier and more readily in public consultation.

One means of reducing the likelihood of ADR becoming a substitute for adequately conducted public consultation is to create a closer relationship between public involvement and ADR processes – in effect, to integrate the use of ADR into public consultation. This is the second and more proactive sense in which ADR can relate to public consultation. Incorporating ADR into public involvement processes in the preapplication stage permits energy companies and affected stakeholders to address conflict 'hot spots' as they arise rather than at later stages in the regulatory process (e.g., at the post-application/pre-decision or post-decision stages). Introducing ADR earlier in the regulatory process may also reduce the quantity and duration of ADR processes. Experience in Alberta suggests that ADR should be introduced as quickly as possible, before parties become polarized and stop listening to one another (AEUB, 2002b, 15). The proactive use of ADR may also decrease the degree to which conflict between energy company applicants and affected stakeholders is protracted, as there may be more goodwill and trust between the parties when intervention takes place earlier.

Fourth, ADR can challenge energy regulators in the enforcement of agreements reached through the ADR process. ADR agreements can include arrangements between the parties regarding issues outside the jurisdiction of the regulator, such as compensation, private road speeds, fencing, and dust control. The NEB is currently examining its eventual role with respect to enforcing the terms of an agreement beyond its jurisdiction. In Alberta, affected parties can request that the AEUB review cases in which companies have breached commitments made in an ADR agreement, even if these commitments lie beyond the board's jurisdiction. Stakeholders would use the same process as they would if a company had breached a commitment made in the public hearing process that lay outside the AEUB's jurisdiction (a Section 40 Review).

Fifth, evaluating ADR processes may prove challenging, as many of the potential benefits associated with ADR may be difficult to measure and quantify. Although the results of mediation (e.g., the percentage of disputes resolved through ADR) and the financial aspects of ADR programs – Board and industry expenditures, savings where public hearings deal with a smaller range of issues or are averted altogether, industry savings through more rapid approvals, and so on – will provide useful measures of the relative success of ADR, other considerations may not lend themselves as readily to measurement. The AEUB's Annual Report on its ADR program focused on mediation results, and on timelines and costs; through feedback from participants, it also assessed parties' levels of satisfaction with the process.[11] Going beyond these sorts of measures may prove difficult. For example, as described in the first section of this chapter, the NEB identifies one of ADR's key benefits as improved stakeholder relations. It will be challenging to develop indicators to measure changes in stakeholder relations that are directly attributable to ADR. Moreover, to the extent that these changes can be measured, identifying tangible benefits associated with these changes will also challenge evaluation.

Broad Implications

ADR involves a shift in the decision-making process in energy regulation away from an adjudicative, board-led process toward one of joint stakeholder resolution of issues. There are a number of fundamental questions pertaining to this shift that merit careful reflection. Does the adoption of ADR impair the pursuit of core principles in energy regulation such as natural justice and procedural fairness? Does it bear implications for democratic considerations for openness and transparency in public decision making? And does it negatively affect the public interest? A comprehensive analysis of any of these issues lies beyond the scope of this chapter; the aim herein is to sound a cautionary bell with a view to stimulating further inquiry, reflection, and debate.

Natural justice and procedural fairness have been among the primary concerns of administrative law (Mullan, 2001, 147–8). Claims to procedural fairness of those affected by government decisions have resulted in the incorporation of procedural norms into the administrative process. The central provisions of natural justice and fairness hold that if and when an administrative decision affects the rights, duties, and interests of an individual, group, or firm, the party generally has a right to a government hearing. This right encompasses notification of and legal representation at the hearing, the appointment of a fair and impartial adjudicator to conduct the hearing, and written reasons that explain the adjudicator's final decision (Johnson, 2002). As noted earlier, a complete assessment of the extent to which ADR might challenge these administrative law principles is beyond the scope of this chapter; that said, one main issue stands out as meriting further scrutiny: does an ADR process limit the right to be heard of all parties to a dispute?

ADR processes generally take place between an energy industry applicant and the party (or parties) directly affected by the proposed energy facility. A fundamental question follows from this characteristic of ADR processes: Does the shift from a public hearing procedure to an ADR proceeding reduce the capacity for other parties with broader concerns pertaining to the application to be heard? For example, in Alberta, when an energy company proposes a facility on a piece of agricultural land, the landowner and energy firm could utilize an ADR process in the event of a dispute between them. If a third party, such as an environmental group or a community group, were to object to the application, does the use of an ADR proceeding (i.e., instead of a public hearing process) reduce the opportunity for these parties to be heard in the case? Current practice suggests that it might. In Alberta, at the Preliminary ADR meeting, the key parties to a dispute (in the preceding example, the energy company and the landowner) decide who the parties to the ADR proceeding will be. If they decide to exclude other parties (which they sometimes do), to the extent that this differs from the opportunity for these other parties to be heard as intervenors in a public hearing, the ADR process may impair the pursuit of natural justice and procedural fairness. This is a fundamental issue deserving greater attention and one that may bear directly on notions of sustainable development. If the use of ADR results in reduced access for environmental groups to represent their interests in the energy regulatory decision-making process, this may weaken the capacity of environmental NGOs to challenge energy developments they oppose, and it may lead to conflict in business–government–society relations in the energy sector if environmental groups perceive that they are being 'shut out' of the regulatory process.

The potentially thorny issue of ADR and natural justice and fairness just described relates to the second issue: democratic considerations for openness. In a democratic society, there are expectations that conflict resolution in the public sector will feature a certain degree of openness (Mills, 1991, 9). Yet one of the crucial features of ADR programs is the confidentiality of the proceedings. Confidentiality enables more frank and open dialogue between the disputing parties, and in some instances it catalyzes the resolution of disputes, because disputing parties may reveal more information respecting their underlying interests to one another than they would if the discussions were to form part of the public record. Aspects of an agreement beyond the jurisdiction of the regulator can remain strictly confidential. As noted earlier, in the NEB's Mediation Practice Direction, agreements are not normally filed with the board or subject to board approval.

With a public hearing, there is a written record of proceedings and a written explanation of a regulatory board's decision on the public record; in contrast, ADR processes do not take place in the public domain, and some of the information respecting negotiation processes or outcomes may not be publicly available. The regulator generally must approve those aspects of the agreement under its jurisdiction, but the substance of discussions leading to the agreement can remain confidential.[12] The potential implications of this feature of ADR warrants closer scrutiny. Does the confidentiality of ADR agreements stymie the establishment of precedent and thereby challenge the transmission of decisions?[13] Mills (1991) argues that it does. And perhaps more importantly, to the extent that there is less information on the public record of proceedings and their outcomes, does this result in a real (or perceived) lack of transparency in energy regulatory decision making for the general public and for other energy stakeholders (e.g., community groups, other interest groups, and industry stakeholders)? When these 'other energy stakeholders' are individuals, groups, or organizations with concerns respecting sustainability, ADR processes may harm notions of sustainable development. In a similar manner to the earlier discussion of natural justice and procedural fairness, if policy actors with sustainable development objectives perceive that there is a lack of openness and transparency in energy regulation, this may weaken their (real or perceived) capacity to access information concerning energy development and bear undesirable consequences for business–government–society relations in energy regulation in the sustainable development era. These are complex issues that regulators will need to confront in order to preserve the real and perceived democratic legitimacy of their decision-making processes.

The final question concerns the public interest. As Rounthwaite (1998, 513) notes in an analysis of ADR in the public sector: 'ADR has a lengthy history of use in attempting to resolve "private" disputes and a somewhat shorter history in addressing disputes that involve broader questions of public interest and policy.' Given the relatively recent adoption of ADR in the field of energy regulation, it is essential to query the nature and extent of ADR's implications for the public interest. Does ADR, by empowering energy stakeholders to resolve disputes themselves, hamper the pursuit of the public interest?

This seemingly counterintuitive question pertains ultimately to the *process* of ADR as opposed to its *outcomes*. The process of ADR derives its legitimacy because it empowers affected parties to resolve disputes in direct interaction with one another, and in this respect, ADR implicitly defines the public interest as the negotiated compromise among the various affected stakeholders (Stephenson and Pops, 1991, 21). But are there weaknesses in this implicit definition of the public interest? ADR may result in more expeditious, less costly energy regulatory decision making, but do the agreements negotiated necessarily do more to pursue the public interest than those arrived at by energy regulatory board members? As Duke notes in a review of ADR in the energy regulatory sector, board staff 'are the only party concerned exclusively with the broad public interest' (Duke, 1995, 5). To the extent that board staff or board members do not participate (or participate less) in ADR processes, does this hamper the pursuit of the public interest in mediations? The relationship to sustainable development on this last point may arguably be one of paradox. Sustainable development is often associated with devolved and decentralized forms of decision-making involving citizen participation (Juillet and Andrew, 1999), and yet this analysis suggests that ADR processes – which by their very nature devolve power to disputing parties – may hinder the pursuit of the broad public interest if they focus on the more narrow interests of the disputing parties themselves. These are challenging theoretical and empirical questions, but their contemplation is of vital importance to the application of ADR in energy regulatory milieus.

Conclusion

In May 2000, U.S. Federal Energy Regulatory Commissioner Linda K. Breathitt addressed the World Forum on Energy Regulation in Montreal. The focus of Commissioner Breathitt's remarks was that alternative dispute resolution would 'play a key role in addressing the needs of today's increasingly competitive marketplace'; she noted that 'ADR processes help ensure that disputes are resolved more quickly, effectively and economically than under traditional [adjudicative] approaches' and that they can result in better business relationships between energy stakeholders (2000, 1, 5). As Canadian energy regulators increasingly design and implement ADR programs to capitalize on the opportunities ADR affords, it will be crucial to address a range of key issues related to ADR's use. This review has argued that energy regulators will need to resolve crucial program issues pertaining to stakeholder-to-stakeholder relations, multiparty disputes, the relationship of ADR to the broader regulatory process, enforcement of agreements reached through ADR, and evaluation of ADR programs. While there is good reason to be optimistic that many of these challenges can be met – information, financial, and other asymmetries between disputing parties can be addressed through equitable funding arrangements; the integration of ADR into industry's public consultation processes can attend to conflicts as they arise rather than at later stages in the regulatory decision-making process; and survey instruments could be developed to track and evaluate the impact of ADR on such nebulous qualitative variables as stakeholder relations – it will be imperative to recognize and identify the potential limitations of ADR. Ascertaining the circumstances or situations under which ADR is infeasible, inadvisable, or inappropriate will be a critical step in the continued adoption of ADR in the energy regulatory sector.

ADR raises fundamental questions respecting natural justice and procedural fairness, openness and transparency in regulatory decision-making, and the pursuit of the public interest. As argued in this chapter, ADR processes may bear negatively on natural justice and procedural fairness if they limit the right to be heard of an individual, group, or firm in the making of administrative decisions that affect them. In addition, ADR may lead to real or perceived reductions in openness and transparency in regulatory decision making when the use of confidentiality results in lower levels of public disclosure of information respecting regulatory decision-making processes or outcomes. Finally, the reduction or elimination of regulatory board or staff members' participation in ADR processes may impede the pursuit of the public interest in energy regulatory decision making – a pursuit that constitutes the central and defining purpose of energy regulators. In light of the risks that ADR might pose for this trio of fundamental interests, it is of utmost importance that energy regulators reflect carefully and proceed cautiously as they design and adopt ADR programs. ADR holds considerable potential as a 'first' or 'complementary' resort for the resolution of energy disputes, but it is essential that energy regulators, energy stakeholders, and academics alike constantly reflect on the procedural and substantive implications of shifting energy regulatory decision making for alternative, stakeholder-led forms of energy regulation.

NOTES

1 Canadian energy regulators also facilitate joint decision-making by energy disputants (as described further on in this chapter).
2 I would like to thank the many individuals who generously gave of their time and effort to discuss Canadian energy regulators' use of alternative dispute resolution processes. In particular, I would like to extend my appreciation to Philip Dack, Coordinator, Planning and Mediation Program, City of Calgary; Karla Reesor, Alternative Dispute Resolution Coordinator, National Energy Board, and Bill Remmer, Alternative Dispute Resolution Coordinator, Alberta Energy and Utilities Board. I am also grateful to Bruce Doern and Glen Toner for their helpful comments. Any errors of fact or interpretation are mine alone.
3 The Ontario Energy Board also utilizes ADR in its regulatory decision-making processes, but given space limitations, this chapter examines only the work of the AEUB, the NEB, and the B.C. Oil and Gas Commission.
4 On 1 April 1996, the Alberta Geological Survey (AGS) also joined the organization.
5 The board is also responsible for regulating fluid milk rates within the province, but this chapter focuses on the Board's energy regulatory authority.
6 Although the ADR program is also applicable to industry-to-industry disputes, given space limitations, this chapter focuses on its use for industry–landowner conflicts.
7 The mediator who attends the PADR is not necessarily the final mediator who assists the parties to resolve their dispute.
8 In the first eight months of 2002, thirty-two mediations were undertaken through the ADR Program. Of the twenty-four cases closed in this period, eighteen were resolved, and at the time of writing, four of the unresolved cases had gone to a public hearing. (Data provided by the AEUB. Statistics are for 1 January 2002 to 31 August 2002.)
9 Except in the matter of landowner costs of participating in hearings on the detailed routing of a pipeline.

10 The Alberta government appoints the Farmers' Advocate of Alberta to deal with problems and concerns of farmers. One of the functions of the Office of the Farmers' Advocate is to provide information on subjects such as surface rights, seismic activity, mineral leasing, and other topics related to the operation of the oil and gas industry in Alberta. The Farmers' Advocate is an individual with an agricultural background and experience in farming.

11 Due to relatively low survey response rates from landowners, the AEUB has modified its data collection processes to conduct participant surveys immediately after the completion of an ADR process. Participants are now asked to complete the surveys before they leave their final ADR meeting.

12 In Alberta, this has resulted in a new dynamic in board–staff relations, as staff members who have participated in confidential ADR proceedings are not able to share with board members those aspects of the negotiations undertaken confidentially.

13 It is interesting to note that in an industry–industry dispute at the AEUB in 2002, the parties opted for a public hearing rather than an ADR process because the circumstances giving rise to the dispute were unprecedented. Given the degree of uncertainty surrounding the case, the disputants wanted to seek clarity from the board through a public hearing and create precedent for future cases of its kind.

REFERENCES

AEUB (Alberta Energy and Utilities Board). 2001. *Informational Letter (IL) 2001-1 Appropriate Dispute Resolution (ADR) Program and Guidelines for Energy Industry Disputes*. Released 8 January. Calgary: AEUB.
– 2002a. *EUB Appropriate Dispute Resolution: Annual Report, January–December 2001*. Calgary: AEUB.
– 2002b. *Making Synergy Real: Conference Proceedings, February 25 and 26, 2002*. Calgary: AEUB.
Breathitt, Linda K. 2000. 'Alternative Dispute Resolution (ADR) – An Invaluable Tool For Today's Evolving Energy Markets.' Remarks of Commissioner Linda K. Breathitt, Federal Energy Regulatory Commission, to the World Forum on Energy Regulation, Montreal. 24 May.
British Columbia Oil and Gas Commission (BCOGC). 1998. 'Information on the Formation and Intent of the Oil and Gas Commission.' 31 October. See www.ogc.gov.bc.ca/documents/misc/formationandintent.doc[.]

– 2002. *Public Involvement Guideline: A Guideline to Involve the Public in Oil and Gas Operational Planning.* British Columbia: BCOGC: July.

Canadian Dispute Resolution Corporation. 2000. *Report for Implementation of an Appropriate Dispute Resolution System for Alberta's Upstream Petroleum Applications.* Calgary: CDRC.

Duke, Kenneth M. 1995. *Alternative Dispute Resolution (ADR) and the B.C. Utilities Commission Regulatory Process.* British Columbia: BCUC.

Johnson, David. 2002. *Thinking Government: Public Sector Management in Canada.* Scarborough: Broadview.

Juillet, Luc, and Caroline Andrew. 1999. 'Développement durable et nouveaux modes de gouvernance locale: le cas de la ville d'Ottawa.' *Économie et Solidarités* 30, no. 2: 75–94.

Kheel, Ted. 1985. 'Where Will ADR Be in the Year 2000.' *Dispute Resolution Forum.* Washington: National Institute for Dispute Resolution.

Kruk, Gerry. 2000. 'The Appropriate Dispute Resolution Initiative of Alberta's Energy and Utilities Board: Restoring Trust and Co-operation in Industry-Landowner Relations in Alberta's Petroleum Industry.' *Canadian Journal of Administrative Law and Practice*, 14: 293–322.

Mills, Miriam K., ed. 1991. Introduction to *Alternative Dispute Resolution in the Public Sector.* Chicago: Nelson-Hall.

Mullan, David J. 2001. *Administrative Law.* Toronto: Irwin Law.

NEB (National Energy Board). 2001. *Practice Direction: Mediation of Detailed Route Objections.* Calgary: NEB.

– 2002. 'Appropriate Dispute Resolution at the National Energy Board.' Presentation by Karla Reesor, ADR Coordinator. See www.neb-one.gc.ca/safety/aw02_kreesor_neb_e.ppt[.]

Protasal, Greg J. 1991. 'Resolving Environmental Conflicts: Neocorporatism, Negotiated Rule-Making, and the Timer/Fish/Wildlife Coalition in the State of Washington.' Pp. 188–204 in Miriam K. Mills, ed., *Alternative Dispute Resolution in the Public Sector.* Chicago: Nelson-Hall.

Rounthwaite, H. Ian. 1998. 'Alternative Dispute Resolution in Environmental Law: Uses, Limitations, and Potentials.' Pp. 513–49 in Elaine L. Hughes, Alistair R. Lucas, and William A. Tilleman, eds, *Environmental Law and Policy*, 2nd. ed., Toronto: Edmond Montgomery.

Savage, David B. 2001. 'Appropriate Dispute Resolution in the Canadian Petroleum Industry.' Presentation to the Canadian Institute Conference on *Managing Community Consultation and Stakeholder Relations.* 3 December. Calgary.

Stephenson Jr, Max O., and Gerald M. Pops. 1991. 'Public Administrators and

Conflict Resolution: Democratic Theory, Administrative Capacity, and the Case of Negotiated Rule-Making.' Pp. 13–25 in Miriam K. Mills, ed., *Alternative Dispute Resolution in the Public Sector*. Chicago: Nelson-Hall.

Vollman, Kenneth W. 1998. 'The Emerging Context for the Physical Regulation of Pipelines.' Presentation of the Acting Chairman of the National Energy Board to the International Pipeline Conference. 9 June. Calgary.

Chapter 12

The Alberta Energy Sector's Voluntary Approach to Climate Change: Context, Prospects, and Limits

ALASTAIR LUCAS

Voluntary action is a key element of the climate change strategy proposed by Alberta and, to a lesser degree, of the plan developed by the federal government. Both governments intend to use voluntary sectoral agreements to establish greenhouse gas (GHG) emission targets that will serve as a basis for domestic emissions-trading schemes. Although questions have been raised about the efficacy and reliability of purely voluntary, industry-driven approaches (Sax, 1999; Hornung, 1999), there is positive energy-sector experience with voluntary measures.

The thesis of this chapter is that Alberta has adopted this voluntary, sectoral-agreement approach in addressing provincial GHG emissions, especially energy-sector emissions, for three reasons. First, the emission reductions required are relatively undemanding. The provincial GHG emission target is expressed in terms of emissions intensity – GHG emissions relative to GDP – not absolute reduction. Thus, it becomes clear in the review below that the Alberta Plan is not likely to reduce emissions; it will merely to reduce the rate of increase in a rapidly growing provincial economy. Second, voluntary compliance in the energy sector is not new, but is reflected in the long-standing government–industry collaboration in the regulation of air emissions and, more generally, in the economic, social, and environmental management of energy resource development in Alberta. Third, Alberta's proposed sectoral agreements are not purely voluntary. There is an explicit regulatory backstop that ensures a firm legal basis for enforcement should voluntary arrangements fail in particular cases. From this perspective, the voluntary sectoral agreements are a valuable adjunct to legal requirements.

As Chapter 1 noted, climate change became a major Canadian public policy issue in 2002. Previously, the debate had been in the context of planning to meet long-term international obligations to reduce GHG emissions. But 2002 saw the parameters of the debate change: Kyoto Protocol ratification became a focus, and the usual debate arose between Ottawa and the provinces over federal and provincial roles and obligations and the issue of equity. What emerged was broader recognition of the impact of energy and energy policy on climate change; from this, in turn, federalism issues emerged that recalled the fierce energy battles of the late 1970s and early 1980s and that, especially for Alberta, raised the spectre of the hated and never to be forgotten National Energy Program (NEP).[1]

In the next section, I assess the fundamental elements of the Climate Change Conventions, which are the drivers behind these voluntary GHG reduction initiatives. After this, I will consider the potential impact on the energy sector of GHG reduction.

This leads to Alberta's climate change strategy, which, because it is based on emissions intensity – GHG emissions relative to GDP – rather than on absolute reduction, does not address the quantitative reduction obligations of the Kyoto Protocol obligations of the Conventions. I then consider the role of voluntary measures as a set of GHG reduction instruments. To that end, I critically review the nature of voluntary instruments. Then I address the legal context for such voluntary measures. I underline the significance of a legal framework for voluntary measures and assess the legal implications of voluntary programs – implications that must be considered in program design.

The Climate Change Conventions

Although Canada played a significant role in the early development of international climate change policy and law – it hosted a landmark conference in Toronto in 1988[2] – this country's commitment to climate change action began with its signing, along with 153 other countries, of the United Nations Framework Convention on Climate Change (UNFCCC) (UN, 1994) at the Earth Summit in Rio de Janeiro in June 1992. In 1994, this commitment was made binding in international law by federal Cabinet ratification. The central commitment of the parties to the Framework Convention was to adopt national policies and take corresponding measures with the 'aim' (ibid., Art. 4.2 (a)(b)) of reducing GHG emissions to 1990 levels. Although the developed countries were required to 'take the lead' (ibid., Art. 3.1; 4.2(a)) by estimating emissions and reporting these through emissions inventories forming part of 'national communications' (ibid., Art. 12), no specific emission limitations for parties to the convention were established. What was established – and this is characteristic of complex modern international conventions – was a process and a set of institutions to refine and implement the convention. These institutions now include a secretariat to manage the ongoing operations under the convention (ibid., Art. 8), especially to facilitate the convention's main decision-making body, the Conference of Parties (COP) (ibid., Art. 11). Also, expert review teams have been established to assess national communications and to coordinate and support the COP.

Beginning with the April 1995 Berlin Conference (COP1), COPs began to work toward strengthening the general GHG emission reduction commitments by developing quantified limits and targets as well as by establishing specific time frames.[3] The Kyoto Protocol (UN, 1997) was a product of the third COP (COP3), convened after parties had agreed[4] to work toward a protocol or other legal instrument to address emissions in the post-2000 period. The Kyoto Protocol is thus a legal instrument that is subsidiary or adjunct to the Framework Convention.

For Canada, the protocol requires a 6 per cent emission reduction relative to 1990 levels by the 2008–12 period specified. For the protocol to become operative as a matter of international law, it must be ratified (as specified in the protocol) by at least fifty-five countries representing 55 per cent of 1990 GHG emissions.[5] In line with the Framework Convention, the Kyoto Protocol has established the Convention of the Parties to the Framework Convention as its decision-making institution (UN, 1997, Art. 1.1). Since the 1997 Kyoto Conference, a series of COPs[6] have been working toward establishing operating rules and guidelines, especially for carbon accounting, measurement and monitoring, and implementation of the Kyoto mechanisms of joint implementation: the Clean Development Mechanism and emissions trading (Grimeaud, 2001). These mechanisms will provide the basis for international emissions trading as well as for offsets that would be credited to countries in calculating emission reductions to meet commitments under the protocol.

Canada signed the protocol in 1997, but federal Cabinet ratification was required to make it binding in international law on Canada as a nation-state. This ratification decision, which became the focus of the climate change debate, culminated in ratification in December 2002.[7]

Energy Sector Impacts

The Canadian energy sector, and especially the Alberta-centred oil and gas and coal-fired electricity-generating industries, have expressed concern about the economic impact of the GHG emission reductions required to fulfil Kyoto. They point to heavy financial burdens relative to other economic sectors, to regulatory uncertainties, and to the disadvantage it places them in regarding the American export market, given that the United States has declared its intention not to ratify the protocol (Hyndman, 2002). The industry also underlines the mismatch between the protocol's apparent underlying assumptions and mechanisms on the one hand, and an industry and regional economy heavily based on primary energy resource development, on the other. This regional economy is growing significantly, particularly in response to rising energy demand in the United States. Large, long-planned new facilities to develop Alberta's oil sands are likely to be developed during the Kyoto Protocol's time frame for emission reductions (McCarthy, 2001).

Alberta, with its critical economic interest in energy resource development, has similar concerns. At issue are future provincial energy resource revenues, especially those resulting over the longer term from continued oil sands development, since oil sands facilities are already major sources of emissions. This concern was underlined by reports in 2002 that Alberta oil production from oil sands had for the first time exceeded production of conventional crude (Alberta Energy and Utilities Board, 2002b).

The upstream oil and gas sector produces 30 per cent of Alberta GHG emissions, and the electricity sector adds 22 per cent (Donner, 2002). However, two additional factors are at the core of the current debate. First, of the 30 per cent of upstream oil and gas emissions, 23 per cent are attributable to hydrocarbons exported to the United States (ibid.). This has sparked Canada's push, in Kyoto Protocol Conference of the Parties implementation forums, for credit against national obligations for export of this 'clean' natural gas to the United States.[8] A second factor is apparent when Alberta GHG emission sources are weighed against emissions from the rest of Canada. Alberta fossil fuel – primarily coal-fired power generation – accounts for 51 per cent of its total, whereas in the rest of Canada these sources produce only 21 per cent of emissions (ibid.). It is clear that the Alberta energy sector would bear a disproportionate emission reduction burden. This points to the key issue of burden sharing among governments and industrial sectors.

A Made-in-Alberta Climate Change Strategy

Alberta's analysis begins with the emissions 'gap' of over 30 per cent identified between the Kyoto target reduction and a business-as-usual emissions forecast.[9] The response is based on an emissions intensity objective rather than on an absolute reduction. Actions are proposed to reduce emissions relative to GDP by 50 per cent of 1990 levels by 2020. These actions include emissions reductions, government leadership, energy conservation, carbon management, conservation and technological advance, the enhancement of agriculture and forest sinks, and adaptation (Alberta, 2002a).[10] Core objectives of the made-in-Alberta approach include investment in new energy and environmental technologies with an eye to potential economic benefits and energy conservation (ibid.).

Clean coal technology is one example of available technology into which the Alberta government and the electricity sector have already put considerable effort. This is consistent with the province's emphasis on addressing the emission intensity of energy development, rather than quantified GHG reduction.[11] Other technologies will target carbon management; these will include underground CO_2 sequestration and use for enhanced oil recovery, and CO_2 enhanced production of 'clean' coal bed methane. Research will include investigating the effectiveness of agriculture and forestry sinks in addressing climate change. Another fundamental objective is to ensure that the province's actions are compatible with those of the United States, its largest trading partner. Alberta officials have underlined the need to maintain competitiveness, noting that much of the work of quantifying Kyoto Protocol implementation costs was based on the assumption that the United States would be a party. American withdrawal has created the need for new studies of options and costs (ibid.).

Techniques proposed include sector-oriented emission reduction programs based on voluntary government–industry sectoral agreements that will incorporate GHG emission targets and reporting protocols. Cited examples of existing public–private partnerships are Alberta's Climate Change Central, whose mandate includes facilitating climate changes measures, educating the public, and operating a provincial energy efficiency office, and the Clean Air Strategic Alliance (CASA), which is developing an emissions management approach for the Alberta electricity sector (CASA, 2000).

Bill 37, the Climate Change and Emissions Management Act (Alberta, 2003), which replaced its substantially similar 2002 predecessor, Bill 32 (Alberta, 2002c), provides the statutory framework for the Alberta plan. It embeds the emission intensity approach by specifying the provincial emission reduction target relative to GDP as 50 per cent of 1990 levels by 2020. This act authorizes the responsible minister, with Cabinet approval, to enter into voluntary sectoral agreements. It also specifies elements of agreements, including maximum emission levels per unit of energy input or output.

The Role of Voluntary Measures

Voluntary measures are a major element of the Alberta strategy. The cornerstone initiative will be negotiation of sectoral agreements for reducing GHG emissions (Alberta, 2002). Sectors prominently identified are electricity, oil and gas, and transportation. Another core action will be to develop an offset emissions trading approach that will 'reflect Alberta's unique needs and circumstances [and] complement the negotiated sectoral agreements' (ibid., 18). This will also involve voluntary elements since, although eligibility rules for emission credits to meet GHG offset requirements will be established, the reduction commitments for sectors will be determined through the sectoral agreements.

The negotiated sectoral agreements of the kind proposed will be classic voluntary measures. These are best illustrated by the voluntary environmental sectoral agreements negotiated in European Union countries. Assessment and monitoring of these agreements suggests that they have had considerable but by no means universal success (Torvanger and Skodvin, 2002; Albrecht and François, 2002). But the model and principles for Alberta are in fact much closer to home. The model is the government–industry–NGO partnership adopted by Alberta's CASA (CASA, 2000). This partnership, with its multistakeholder, consensus-based process, has facilitated reductions in refinery emissions. Most recently, it has developed an approach and framework for reducing flaring at petroleum wells. The flaring initiative, which produced a 50 per cent reduction in one year, involved the voluntary development and acceptance of performance standards backed by potential coercive compliance action and a clear AEUB enforcement policy.[12] The principles likely to provide guidance are those developed by a project team of the Alberta-based New Directions Group, an industry-government–NGO–academic environmental policy concept group (New Directions Group, 2001).

Voluntary action has also been a significant component of federal GHG reduction strategy since the initial National Action Program on Climate Change was developed to implement the obligations of the Framework Convention on Climate Change. The Voluntary Challenge and Registry (VCR Inc.) – originally conceived as a government–industry partnership based on petroleum and natural gas industry initiatives, and now operating as an incorporated not-for-profit entity – has also been an element of the national program. More than 900 organizations have developed voluntary GHG reduction plans and registered these with VCR Inc. Voluntary measures, especially industry–government 'covenants,' along with emissions trading that involves an element of voluntariness, as well as VCR Inc., are mentioned in the May 2002 Federal Climate Change options paper (Canada, 2002a, 26) and in the November 2002 federal Climate Change Plan (Canada, 2002c, 29, 30).

Assessment of Voluntary Initiatives

Voluntary initiatives to achieve environmental protection emerged during the 1990s as a promising approach, one that was promoted by both industry and government. In part, they were a response to concerns about invasive and inflexible command-and-control regulation (Hahn and Stavins, 1991; Stewart, 1985; OECD, 1994) in the form of requirements established by regulation and backed by quasi-criminal penalties. Other factors include shifting societal norms that seemed to support market-based approaches and light-handed governance, with which voluntary action is consistent (Muldoon and Nadarajah, 1999; Sunstein, 1996). Cost cutting has shorn government agencies of the resources to maintain regulatory roles and sometimes even to act effectively as policy leaders (Muldoon and Nadarajah, 1999).

Voluntary initiatives have been supported by the theory of reflexive law. According to Teubner (1983), legal control is 'indirect and abstract, since the legal system only determines the organizational and procedural premises of future action.' As applied to environmental management for sustainability, the idea is that instead of imposing direct regulation, reflexive law encourages institutions such as corporations to establish self-reflective processes, including communications with other institutions (such as government and NGOs) regarding how to achieve environmentally responsible management (Orts, 1995, 1254; Gaines and Kimber, 2001, 161). The results may involve internal environmental management systems or external voluntary initiatives such as sectoral agreements and emissions trading.

Canadian voluntary programs are still either under development or not yet at stages where effectiveness relative to regulatory instruments can be definitively measured. But a picture is beginning to emerge, and as a result, voluntary initiatives have been criticized on a number of grounds. First, it is argued that closed industry–government negotiation of voluntary arrangements results in the exclusion of interested and affected members of the public. This removes the discipline of having to address issues promoted by third-party interests (VanNijnatten, 1999). Second, voluntary initiatives cannot be effectively 'enforced' against non-performing 'free rider' companies; the result is a lack of accountability (Muldoon and Nadarajah, 1999). The Pembina Institute's assessment of VCR Inc. – registered companies suggests that only a small percentage of companies submitting 'action plans' met basic criteria, including the taking of emissions inventories and the commitment to take at least one future action to reduce GHG emissions (Pembina Institute, 1997; Hornung, 1999) Few companies that met this action plan test provided sufficient information and clear evidence that actions taken exceeded business as usual. Between 1990 and 1998, emissions from VCR Inc. submitter companies in the electricity generation and oil and gas production sectors rose much more quickly than Canada's total emissions, and pipeline sector emissions increased four times more quickly (Bramley, 2000, 8). This led to the conclusion that mandatory reporting requirements, essential technical support for companies participating in VCR, and stronger incentives for GHG emission reductions will be needed to make the VCR Inc. program credible and effective in achieving additional GHG reductions.

Part of the incentive issue has been addressed by the Baseline Protection Initiative (BPI), which will provide credit for early action in voluntary GHG reduction, either in future emissions trading or in other federal programs that may be implemented (Canada, 2002b). Notwithstanding this refinement, the role of VCR Inc. in the federal Climate Change Strategy has waned somewhat: from prominence in the 1998 national ministerial response to the Kyoto Protocol, when a climate change policy development process was established (Energy and Environment Ministers, 1998) to barely being mentioned in the 2000 Climate Change Strategy (Canada, 2000) and in the May 2002 federal Climate Change Options Paper; to mere reference as one of several important supporting mechanisms in the November 2002 federal plan (Canada, 2002c).

A third criticism is that successful regulatory programs may be undermined by less stringent voluntary initiatives and that regulatory strengthening may be pre-empted. These problems may arise when regulators' authority is based on broad, open-textured discretionary statutory powers such that resources for compliance actions are limited. A final criticism is that sectoral inequities may result from the presence of non-participating free rider companies (Muldoon and Nadarajah, 1999). This may challenge the resolve of the industry's volunteer leaders. Another form of inequity may be felt by smaller companies with fewer resources and less access to government; these companies may be unable to achieve voluntary agreements.

These criticisms have led to a reassessment of the role of voluntary initiatives. Rather than being viewed as alternatives to command-and-control regulation, they are recognized as valuable adjuncts to regulatory systems, and their effectiveness is seen as critically dependent on linkage to clear, appropriate, and effective policy and legal frameworks (Danier and VanNijnatten, 2001; Muldoon and Nadarajah, 1999; New Directions Group, 1997). If this assessment, regarding a limited role for voluntary initiatives in emission reduction, is correct, why have the government of Alberta and the energy sector continued to place so much heavy reliance on voluntary instruments for reducing GHG emissions? There are in fact strong reasons, which are discussed in the next section.

Alberta's Cooperative Energy Sector Regulation

One reason why voluntary initiatives, including voluntary sectoral agreements, are so prominent in the Alberta strategy for reducing energy-sector GHG emissions is that they are consistent with a regulatory system with which the Alberta-based industry is already familiar and to which it has adapted. The industry is comfortable with a system based on collaboration and consensus, in which the energy sector has considerable influence and substantive involvement in both policy and decisions. It is a system in which the results of this collaboration are incorporated into regulatory approvals and in which compliance is similarly collaborative and iterative, responding to particular conditions and circumstances. This regulatory system, which in Alberta is administered in part by the Energy and Utilities Board (AEUB) and in part by the Department of the Environment (AENV), includes few directly enforceable ambient or emission standards. It is fundamentally a regime of reflexive law into which voluntary initiatives also fit, as outlined earlier. But it does include regulation of air emissions generally; and GHG emissions are air emissions that the environmental regulatory legislation encompasses, but for which limits have not been specifically imposed. This is discussed in the next section.

Alberta Environment Emissions Regulation

Although there are basic numerical standards for particulate emissions and for several specific hydrocarbon contaminants (Alberta, 1993), none exist for major contaminants, including SO_2 and NO_x. For the latter, there are non-statutory guidelines only (Alberta Environment, 1997). There are no limits for CO_2. Alberta Environment can enforce these guidelines when it is issuing approvals for energy facilities by incorporating them as terms and conditions of approvals. But during this approval process, there is room for dialogue and negotiation regarding facility processes, emission control technology, dispersion modelling, and emission timing (Alberta Environment, 1997b).[13]

Recent AENV initiatives have underlined and extended this cooperative regulatory approach by incorporating into a pilot phase an explicit voluntary program. The Leaders Environmental Approval Document (LEAD) program enables demonstrated 'good environmental performers' to develop and commit to environmental performance goals aimed at reducing environmental effects and at improving environmental quality (Alberta Environment, 2001). Participants commit to an environmental management system (EMS), be it in effect or in preparation; to performance goals or measures for achieving reductions in emissions or environmental effects; to monitoring and reporting systems, enhanced public involvement, and continuous improvement; and to participation in relevant voluntary programs such as CASA or VCR. The program benefits offered by this program include flexible requirements such as those relating to facilitywide emission limits, as well as streamlined approval and approval amendment processes. The program document states confidently that 'all participants [industry, government, NGOs] will benefit from the environmental partnership approach fostered under the ... program' (ibid., 3).

EUB Emissions Regulation

Similarly, on the AEUB side, the board has discretionary powers and guidelines. The energy industry has long played an important consultative role in guideline development. More recently, the AEUB's industry consultative process has broadened to include stakeholders among the public; even so, industry input remains significant. Since 1999, the AEUB has applied this multistakeholder approach to achieve major voluntary reductions in petroleum industry flaring. This has taken the form of performance 'requirements' based on a 'General Bulletin' requesting voluntary evaluation and reporting by specified dates (AEUB, 2002), as well as the issuance of a Flaring Guide (AEUB, 2002) followed by annual reports (ibid., 2002d). An important factor in the reduction of gas flaring was the participation of a project team under the CASA, a voluntary industry–government–NGO partnership to reduce energy industry emissions (ibid., 2002c).

Other collaborative and ultimately consensual initiatives include the AEUB's review and revision of the Sulphur Recovery Guidelines for natural gas processing facilities (ibid., 2001a) and the development of an 'appropriate dispute resolution' facilitation/mediation system for major energy facility approval applications (ibid., 2001b).

The EUB's predecessor, the Oil and Gas Conservation Board (later the Energy Resources Conservation Board), was established in the 1930s to implement measures to control widespread flaring of natural gas by oil producers and thus to achieve energy resource physical and economic conservation. From the beginning, this board's approach was to promote energy resource conservation in the context of minimal direct industry intervention (Breen, 1993). This cooperative and consensual approach was strongly promoted by the Social Credit government of Ernest Manning during the formative years of Alberta's energy sector in the 1950s and 1960s.[14] The Alberta government has maintained the independence of the AEUB and has focused on its position as resource owner – a role more commercial than regulatory.

For example, there has never been mandatory unitization of petroleum reservoirs in Alberta in order to achieve conservation by maximizing recovery from reservoirs. Instead, the board has played a persuasive and facilitative role by conducting reservoir studies and pointing when necessary to its powers to impose production penalties (Kennett, 2002). The Oil and Gas Conservation Act was amended in 1971 to include provisions for mandatory unitization of reservoirs (Alberta, 1971), but these sections were never proclaimed in force. Even so, their existence and the possibility of proclamation and implementation constituted a strong incentive for well owners to voluntarily negotiate unit and unit operating agreements. Another example of government–industry research and technological collaboration and consensual regulation is the development of the Athabasca oil sands. This includes the government–industry initiative to establish the Alberta Oil Sands Technology and Research Authority (AOSTRA).

Alberta's Proposed Sectoral Agreements

Sectoral agreements for GHG reduction are a central component of Alberta's climate change plan and strategy. It is expected that the government 'will negotiate binding agreements with specific sectors, including electricity, petroleum, transportation, forestry [and other industries] to set measurable goals for reducing greenhouse gas emissions' (Alberta, 2002a, 16). This contemplates consensual agreements that include 'commitments.' These may take the form of emissions intensity improvements, absolute emission reductions, step changes that reflect capital stock turnover, and new technology development (Alberta, 2002b, 13). Bill 37 specifies that sectoral agreements may include provisions for such matters as sectoral objectives, baselines, schedules, monitoring and reporting, offsets and emissions trading, and enforcement and compliance, as well as energy intensity factors (through the establishment of maximum emission levels per unit of energy input or output, or material input, or product output) (Alberta, 2003).

Regarding electricity, the existing sectoral approach through government partnership in the CASA is incorporated. The Alberta plan notes that the CASA is currently developing a broader emissions management approach for the sector, one that will include performance expectations for GHG emissions. In the case of the oil and gas sector, the government will 'build on recent trends' to achieve continued emission reductions per unit of production. A petroleum sector agreement will 'reflect the realities of the Alberta industry in terms of capital stock, the nature of Alberta's energy resources, technological change, best industry practices and the desire for a level playing field both internationally and with US-based industry' (Alberta, 2002b, 13). Specifically targeted for 'investigation with industry' are upstream energy efficiency actions and potential gas processing plant rationalization. Also noted are industry–government technology collaboration, as well as carbon capture and storage and CO_2-enhanced coal bed methane development.

The emissions trading approach is intended to 'complement' the sectoral agreements. It is expected that facilitation of emissions market participation will precede negotiation of the agreements.[15] An emission reduction registry will be established to ensure secure title to emission units as well as transparent verification.

Clearly, these proposed negotiated agreements with energy industry sectors are consistent with the cooperative, partnership approach to energy sector regulation generally, and in particular, with the similar approach to regulation of energy sector emissions by environmental and energy regulatory bodies. Sectoral agreements will also fit with government–industry–public stakeholder partnership programs such as the CASA. However, although the strategy document speaks of 'stakeholders,' it pays little attention to the general public or to NGOs. This means that transparency may prove to be an issue.

There is no doubt that the Alberta government recognizes the importance of linking its voluntary agreements to clear policy objectives and to an effective and enforceable regulatory system (Muldoon and Nadarajah, 1999; VanNijnatten, 1999). This was underlined by the New Dimensions Group's government–industry–NGO project team in its template for the development of effective covenants to manage GHG emissions (New Dimensions Group, 2001). In the Alberta strategy document, this recognition is expressed in an example that outlines the CASA's successful development of a framework for reducing petroleum industry flaring through voluntary actions. These voluntary flaring performance standards, the strategy document notes, 'were "*backstopped*" by clear government statements regarding the consequences of not achieving the sector-wide objectives' (Alberta, 2002b, 13). Voluntary standards could then be accepted by regulators without risk that this could be judicially challenged as action without legal authority.[16] The Alberta plan specifies that voluntary agreements will 'include a regulatory backstop to ensure a level playing field within each sector' (Alberta, 2002a, 17). Bill 37 implements this backstop approach by specifying enforcement of and compliance with the terms of agreements, including 'financial and non-financial penalties,' among the matters to be included in sectoral agreements (Alberta, 2003, s. 4(1)(m)). It also gives the provincial Cabinet the power to make regulations regarding the enforcement of rights, obligations, and liabilities under sectoral agreements. The bill goes further by enabling Cabinet to apply its regulatory powers to fill gaps in the sectoral agreement scheme by making the terms of agreements – with necessary modifications – applicable to persons not party to agreements, by making the agreements binding on those parties, and by establishing parallel regulatory obligations for sectors without voluntary agreements (ibid., s. 18(1)(l)(n)(o)).

Conclusions

Alberta's emissions intensity–based strategy is not likely to produce energy-sector GHG reductions in a time frame or in absolute volumes necessary to contribute to meeting Canada's Kyoto Protocol obligations. It is a weak commitment and a relatively undemanding emission target for what is expected to be a rapidly growing, energy-based provincial economy. In this context, a voluntary approach is attractive because it is easily achievable. A second reason why Alberta has adopted the voluntary, sectoral-agreement approach is that it fits comfortably into the historic Alberta partnership model of energy sector regulation, including regulation of emissions. Finally, the regulatory 'backstop' that has been confirmed by Bill 37, the Climate Change and Emissions Management Act, addresses the need for explicit legal authority and enforceability to promote the ultimate accountability of both government and industry. From this perspective, the voluntary sectoral agreements are an instrument for implementing these legal requirements.

This voluntary approach based on emission intensity targets leaves unresolved the fundamental question of absolute emission reductions to meet Canadian Kyoto Protocol obligations. How this Alberta strategy fits with the federal Climate Change Plan remains unclear. As of mid-2003, negotiations have not advanced on the critical national issue of allocating GHG emission targets to governments and industrial sectors.

NOTES

1 See Canada, Department of Energy, Mines and Resources, Energy Policy Sector, The National Energy Program, 1980, Report EP 80-4E; 'Klein

Compares Protocol to Trudeau-era Policy,' *Calgary Herald*, 14 June, 2002:
A4.

2 J. Bruce and D. Russell, 'Canada's Role and Actions Since 1980.' In H.
Coward and A. Weaver, eds., *Climate Change in Canada* (Montreal: McGill-
Queen's University Press, 2003).

3 The process or 'Berlin Mandate' was established by Decision 1/CP.1.

4 Through the Ad Hoc Group on the Berlin Mandate, established at COP. 1.

5 Fifty-five countries party to the UNFCCC accounting in total for at lease
55 per cent of 1990 emissions of Annex 1 parties: Art. 25.

6 COP. 1 to COP. 7, the latter held in Marrakech, November 2001.

7 Parliamentary debate on a ratification resolution, though not formally
necessary, began in November 2002 and was completed in December 2002.

8 Based on emissions displaced in the United States, less emissions in
Canada.

9 As noted in Alberta (2002) (Assessment of Economic Impacts of the Kyoto
Protocol), p. 3, the gap is growing and predictions of its size are uncertain
because this depends on economic activity and government policy.

10 In contrast, the federal Climate Change Plan (Canada, 2002c) aims to meet
the Kyoto Protocol reduction target of 6 per cent of 1990 levels by 2008–12
through a 240 megatonne national emission reduction.

11 The federal Climate Change Plan also proposes an emissions intensity
approach for large industrial emitters with a 55-megatonne sectoral
reduction target: Canada, 2002c, 30, 31.

12 The Alberta Flaring Guidelines are discussed below.

13 The AEUB's Guide 56 states at p. 12 that application for energy facility
approvals must submit dispersion modelling data for assessment. AEUB
applications that are likely to affect the environment are referred to AENV
for review and recommendations, which must be incorporated into
approvals.

14 Breen (1993, 502–3) recounts Manning's relatively successful 'court
proofing' of the Alberta oil and gas legislation.

15 Specific statutory powers to establish an emissions trading system in Bill
32 do not appear in Bill 37. The latter contains only references to the
exchange, trade, or sale of 'emission offsets, credits and sink rights' in the
context of emission offsets, as well as regulation-making powers in
relation to 'economic and financial instruments and market-based
approaches' to GHG reduction. The reason for this statutory de-emphasis
of emissions trading, that creates uncertainty as to whether Bill 37 is
specific enough to authorize the full range of measures required to
support an emissions trading system, is unclear.

16 In *Environmental Resource Centre v. Canada (Minister of the Environment,*
[2001] FCT 1423 the Federal Court found that the minister acted without
jurisdiction in deciding under the Canadian Environmental Assessment
Act that a proposed oil sands project was not likely to cause significant
adverse environmental effects, because the minister relied on Alberta's
Regional Sustainable Development Strategy (RSDS), a voluntary
multistakeholder, consensus-based planning process as a mechanism to
respond to uncertainties associated with cumulative effects although the
minister had no legal authority to act should this mechanism not deliver.

REFERENCES

Aalders, M. 1993. 'Regulation and In-Company Environmental Management
in the Netherlands.' *Environmental Law and Policy,* vol. 15.
Alberta. 2002a. *Albertans Climate Change: Taking Action.* October.
– 2002b. *Albertans and Climate Change: A Plan for Action (Draft for Discussion).*
July.
– 2002c. *The Climate Change and Emissions Management Act,* Bill 32. Alberta
Legislature first reading, 18 November.
– 2003. *The Climate Change and Emissions Management Act.* Bill 37, Alberta
Legislature.
Alberta Energy and Utilities Board (AEUB). 2001a. *Guide 60: Upstream
Petroleum Industry Flaring Guide, 1999 and Update.* Calgary: AEUB.
– 2001b. *Interim Directive 2001–03, Sulphur Recover Guidelines for the Province of
Alberta.* 29 August. Calgary: AEUB.
– 2001c. *Information Letter 2001–1. Appropriate Dispute Resolution Program and
Guidelines for Energy Industry Disputes.* January. Calgary: AEUB.
– 2002a. *General Bulletin 2002–05, Requirements for Evaluation of Solution Gas
Conservation.* Calgary: AEUB.
– 2002b. 'Alberta's Resources 2001 and Supply and Demand Outlook 2002–
2011.' 30 May. Calgary: AEUB.
– 2002c. 'EUB Releases 2001 Flaring and Venting Industry Performance
Report.' September.
– 2002d. *Statistical Services 2002–60B, Upstream Petroleum Industry
Venting Report, for year ending December 31, 2001.* 19 July. Calgary:
AEUB.
Alberta Environment. 1997. *Alberta Ambient Air Quality Guidelines.* January.
See www.gov.ab.ca/env/dept/facts/airqualt.htm[.]
– 1997b. *Approval Process, January 1997: 'Stage 3 – Review of Application.'*
Edmonton: Alberta Environment.

- 2001a. *Leaders Environmental Approval Document (LEAD) Program: Pilot Phase, Overview.* June. Edmonton: Alberta Environment.
- 2001b. *LEAD Program Guide.* April. Edmonton: Alberta Environment.
Albrecht, J., and D. Francois. 2002. 'Negotiated Environmental Agreements in CO₂ Emissions Trading.' In P. ten Brink, ed., *Voluntary Environmental Agreements.* Sheffield: Greenleaf Publishing.
Bramley, M. 2000. *Greenhouse Gas Emissions from Industrial Companies in Canada: 1998.* October. Calgary: Pembina Institute.
Breen, D. 1993. *Alberta's Petroleum Industry and the Conservation Board.* Edmonton: University of Alberta Press.
Canada. 2000. *Canada's National Implementation Strategy on Climate Change.* Ottawa: Public Works and Government Services Canada. October.
- 2002a. *A Discussion Paper on Canada's Contribution to Addressing Climate Change,* May.
- 2002b. *Canada's National Climate Change Process: Baseline Protection Initiative.* 27 August. www.nccp.ca/nccp/baseline_pro/indie_e.html[.]
- 2002c. *Climate Change Plan for Canada.* November. www.climatechange.gc.ca[.]
Clean Air Strategic Alliance (CASA). 2000. *2000 Annual Report.* See www.casahome.org[.]
Danier, E., and D. VanNijnatten. 2001. 'Voluntary Instruments.' In W. Leiss, ed., *In the Chamber of Risks.* Montreal and Kingston: McGill-Queen's University Press.
Donner, J. 2002. 'Alberta Environment Strategic Directions, Alberta Emissions.' Edmonton: Alberta Environment. 5 February.
Energy and Environment Ministers. 1998. Joint Meeting of Energy and Environment Ministers, Halifax, 19–20 October. *Record of Decision, Summary of Decisions* No. 8, Voluntary Challenge and Registry Inc.
Gaines, S., and C. Kimber. 2001. 'Redirecting Self-Regulation' *Journal of Environmental Law and Policy* 13: 151–63.
Grimeaud, D. 2001. 'An Overview of the Policy and Legal Aspects of the International Climate Change Régime.' 2 *Environmental Liability* 39 (Pt. I), 95 (Pt. II).
Hahn, R., and R. Stavins. 1991. 'Incentive-Based Environmental Regulation: A New Era from an Old Idea.' *Ecology Law Quarterly* 18: 1–13.
Hornung, R. 1999. 'The VCR Is Broken.' In R. Gibson, ed. *Voluntary Initiatives: The New Politics of Corporate Greening.* Peterborough: Broadview Press.
Hyndman, R. 2002. 'Competitiveness of Industry Cannot be Undermined.' C^3 *Views* (Alberta Climate Change Central Newsletter). February.
Kennett, S., ed. 2002. Canada Energy Law Service, Alberta, para. 249. Toronto: Carswell, Continuing Service.

McCarthy, S. 2001. 'Greenhouse Gas Concerns Not Seen Halting Oil Projects.' *Globe and Mail*. 7 June: B-7.

Muldoon, P., and R. Nadarajah. 1999. 'A Sober Second Look.' In R. Gibson, ed. *Voluntary Initiatives: The New Politics of Corporate Greening*. Toronto: Broadview.

New Directions Group. 2001. *Developing Credible and Effective Covenants for the Management of Greenhouse Gas Emissions*. www.newdirectionsgroup.org[.]

– 1997. *Criteria and Principles for the Use of Voluntary or Non-Regulatory Initiatives to Achieve Environmental Policy Objectives*. Canmore, AB: NDG.

Organization for Economic Cooperation and Development (OECD). 1994. *Meeting on Alternatives to Traditional Regulation*. Paris: OECD.

Orts, E. 1995, 'Reflexive Environmental Law. *Northwestern University Law Review* 89: 1227.

Pembina Institute. 1997. *Corporate Action on Climate Change, 1996: An Independent Review*. Drayton Valley: Pembina Institute.

Sax, D. 1999. 'Voluntary Initiatives in Canada: Developing Principles.' *Environmental Liability* 4: 3.

Stewart, R. 1985. 'Economics, Environment and the Limits of Legal Control.' *Harvard Environmental Law Review* 9: 5.

Sunstein, C. 1996. 'Social Norms and Social Roles.' *Columbia Law Review* 96, 914–15.

Teubner, G. 1983. 'Substantive and Reflexive Elements in Modern Law.' *Law and Society Review* 17: 239.

Torvanger, A., and T. Skodvin. 2002. 'Environmental Agreements in Climate Politics.' In ten Brink, ed., *Voluntary Environmental Agreements*. Sheffield: Greenleaf Publishing.

United Nations. 1994. *Framework Convention on Climate Change, 1992* (UNFCCC) (1994). 9 May 1992, in force 21 March 1994. www:unfcc.int/resource/conv/index.html

– 1997. *Kyoto Protocol to the United Nations Convention on Climate Change*. 11 December. UN Doc. FCCC/CP/1997/L.7/Add.1.

VanNijnatten, D. 1999. 'The Day the NGOs Walked Out.' In R. Gibson, ed., *Voluntary Initiatives: The New Politics of Corporate Greening*. Toronto: Broadview Press.

Voluntary Challenge and Registry (VCR Inc.). 2002. www.vcr-mvr.ca[.]

Chapter 13

Conclusions and Related Energy Policy Challenges for a Martin Liberal Government

G. BRUCE DOERN

The purpose of this book has been to examine key energy policy issues and challenges for Canadians over the past twenty years and into the early 2000s. Rooted in a broad interdisciplinary analysis by both academics and policy practitioners, it has explored and explained how energy policy has evolved over the past twenty years and also how and why energy policy ideas, interests, and governance approaches have changed. Drawing on the contributing authors and on other literature, chapter 1 set the context for change by introducing key political-economic factors and forces such as the following: the current overall federal energy policy in the context of key international developments, such as free trade and the emergence and varied meanings of sustainable development; energy supply and use, and the core barriers and opportunities for conservation and for movement toward a low-carbon economy; the Bush Administration's National Energy Policy and its alternative to the Kyoto Protocol; the climate change debate and Canada's overall federal-provincial process for dealing with the Kyoto Protocol; the basic federal–provincial energy regulatory system; and broad changes in the configuration of energy policy interests.

In this final chapter, we consider, and offer concluding observations about, six analytical and practical energy policy and governance challenges facing a Paul Martin-led Liberal government in the short to medium term: (1) Kyoto Protocol implementation challenges; (2) energy security; (3) northern pipelines, Aboriginal peoples, and sustainable northern development; (4) electricity restructuring and the limits of regulatory-market design; (5) energy science and technology (S&T) and innovation policy links; and (6) prospects for turning the struggle for sustainable development in the energy policy field into something closer to an actual achievement. Each of these policy and governance challenges is important, in that each reflects concerns and ways of framing energy policy that, although increasingly influenced by the broader politics and economics of Kyoto implementation, are nonetheless also driven by producer and energy supply interests, by still varied views of energy as a economic development engine for Canada's provinces and regions, and by governments of various partisan and party persuasions, each of which is seeking to make progress in sustainable development. In every province, the sustainable development agenda is a struggle more than a reality and is broader than energy, and thus is subject to choices about priorities and budgetary resources, not to mention wide variations in degrees of regulatory vigour.

The Next Kyoto Implementation Stages

Chapter 1 set out the overall federal-provincial politics and policy processes of Kyoto that led up to the crucial decision by Prime Minister Jean Chrétien to sign the Kyoto Protocol. The contents of the Kyoto Protocol encompassed the principles of the federal Climate Change Plan for Canada (Canada, 2002a). Other chapters have dealt with various aspects of Kyoto or Kyoto-related impacts. For example, chapter 3 discussed the North American energy and electricity trade, and chapter 8 analysed Alberta's response to the Kyoto Protocol and its implications for Alberta's core economic engine – its oil and gas industry, including the oil sands. The signing of the Kyoto Protocol is an important political and economic decision, but its implementation is still to come under a Paul Martin-led Liberal government and in the changing configuration of federal–provincial and regional politics, not to mention the pressures and policies of the Bush Administration.

The implementation issues relating to Kyoto centre on the precise extent to which the mix of regulatory, incentive, and voluntary instruments and approaches to energy policy change will be put into effect, and the impact of these on different provinces, on different industrial sectors, and on Canadians as individual energy users. Much will depend on whether the rest of the Kyoto signatories are going to accept some of Canada's extra demands for credits because of its so-called 'cleaner' exports of energy to the United States.

The raw political economy of implementation decisions is partly revealed by the basic breakdown of greenhouse gas (GHG) emissions by province. Alberta has per capita emissions of 72.5 tonnes, which is

30.8 per cent of the total for Canada. Ontario has only 17.0 per cent emissions per capita but 28.0 per cent of the total. The figures for Quebec are 12.0 per cent per capita and 12.7 per cent of the total. Saskatchewan has a high per capita figure of 59.8 but a small percentage of the total, at 8.8 per cent (Environment Canada, 2002; Environmental Studies Program, 2002). In federal-provincial terms, there is little doubt about where the burden-sharing fault lines are. They lead inevitably to a focus on Alberta and Ontario, with the Liberal federal government of Paul Martin as Kyoto advocate, energy development salesman and promoter, and campaigner to overcome Western Canadian alienation. But there are also particular issues for every province in the context of how each sees energy development as well as environmental policy, and the balance between these.

Kyoto implementation will also be strongly affected by the emission distributions among industrial and other sectors of the economy and society. The current distributions are as follows: transportation 27 per cent, public electricity and heat production 19 per cent, manufacturing industries and construction 10 per cent, petroleum refining and other energy industries 9 per cent, residential use 6 per cent, land use change and forestry 0.3 per cent, and solvent and other product use 0.1 per cent (Environment Canada, 2002; Environmental Studies Program, 2002).

Although important as aggregates, these sectoral categorizations of emissions do not fully coincide with the structure of business interest groups within and across these realms; and, of course, ultimately they cascade down to involve thousands of firms and institutions, including state-owned entities, as well as Canadians as home owners, residents, and users of transportation systems and vehicles. Clearly a lot of stakeholders, firms, and individuals will have to be persuaded, induced, and compelled to change their behaviour if targeted reductions are to be achieved.

Because of these complexities of both burden and benefit sharing, there is undoubtedly room, as governing provincial regimes change, for many forms of foot dragging, special pleading, and other practised arts of regulatory inertia. Thus Kyoto implementation will occur in some overall important way; however, like policy implementation in many or most complex policy fields, it will not be a pretty sight. The federal and provincial governments do not function in a one-policy world, not even in a very big one-policy world such as energy policy in the context of Kyoto. Obviously, there are many demands on overall public agendas and on the various public purses at the federal, provincial, and international levels.

Despite these constraints, climate change advocates are right to remind Canadians and their elected governments that these first Kyoto Protocol implementation steps are merely the first in a coming half-century march to deal with climate change, its sources and its effects.

The Re-emergence of Energy Security

Energy security was a key and explicit goal of federal energy policy in the late 1970s and early 1980s, but then faded somewhat as an 'upfront' or emphasized energy goal. Recent developments have undoubtedly enhanced and deepened the ways in which energy security may be viewed, in both rhetorical and practical terms. This includes security of supply for Canada and for North America as a whole. Canada is now seen as a partial guarantor of supply for the United States vis-à-vis the Middle East. Hence, the earlier discussion of energy supply and demand (in chapters 1, 2, and 3), and of the political economy of forecasts and of the possible low-carbon economy, re-enters the analysis here.

Security also means security from terrorist attack. And, of course, security can easily be parlayed into a debate about the security of the planet and hence the rebalancing of energy sources to reduce GHGs and to deal with global warming. Wrapped up in these views of security are also views and theories about the extent to which governments or markets are the best or primary guarantors of security, be it present or future, real or perceived. More simply, what combination of state and market decision making is needed?

The first issue is obviously that the Americans have developed a strong interest, for security and economic reasons, in Canadian oil and gas supplies, including long-term supplies. The 11 September terrorist attacks have assigned a double-meaning to notions of energy security for both Canada and the United States. The recent impetus has been to provide extra physical security for pipelines, power grids, and nuclear power facilities in the context of overall critical infrastructure in Canada, the United States, and Mexico. These new security concerns have so far centred on a series of governmentwide meetings that the National Energy Board (NEB) and Natural Resources Canada (NRCan) have been involved in concerning such infrastructure, and also many meetings with the United States and FERC regulators to discuss American concerns that Canadian pipelines may be targeted to disrupt American supply. The NEB library has had key kinds of information about pipelines removed or made secret because of heightened security concerns.

This sense of security vigilance is added to earlier notions of energy security, which have generally focused on reducing dependence on Middle Eastern oil supplies. For Canada, energy security has also meant that this country would be able to tap its own petroleum reserves sufficient for its long-term needs. In any such set of concerns, the Alberta oil sands loom large, even given their higher costs relative to traditional reserves and their environmental disadvantages.

It is likely, therefore, that security of supply within energy policy will resurface on the agenda in more overt institutional ways. It does not seem likely that Canada will revisit the NAFTA energy provisions about sharing supply in emergency contexts, but it *is* likely that more overt political attention will be paid to how regulators such as the NEB deal with supply and demand estimations and scenarios. It is likely that market processes will continue to determine such supply concerns, but it must be remembered that American energy actions under the Bush plan are not all market driven. There are significant elements of state intervention and political power to remove regulatory delays so as to ensure production and supply.

Also linked is the great economic opportunity that has arisen for Canada to sell more natural gas and also more oil to American markets. The United States has always been crucial to the economics of the Canadian oil and gas industry (and hence also to Canada's ultimate security of supply), and of course the prosperity of Alberta and other oil and gas producing areas such as Atlantic Canada is enhanced greatly by these expanded sales. There is also a political reason for this optimum-sales position approach: the federal Liberals can thereby ensure that Alberta sees a more supportive federal policy than was the case in the early 1980s, under Trudeau's National Energy Program (NEP). But benefits will also accrue to Atlantic Canada's now maturing energy production industry. As we have seen, after the 2000 election the Chrétien Liberals wanted to turn federal energy policy into something that was conducive to national unity and not a replay of the energy wars of the early 1980s. This seemed a decent prospect, but Chrétien's decision to ratify Kyoto means that national unity may well be a serious victim again of energy policy. The Martin Liberals also have ambitions to woo Alberta with energy policy favours and to dent the political power base of the opposition Canadian Alliance in Alberta and in other parts of Western Canada. The merger of the Canadian Alliance and the Progressive Conservatives will also change energy politics, both regionally and nationally.

In this security-cum-regional context, brief mention must also be made of the processes for reviewing and approving energy exports, especially natural gas. The NEB Act requires the NEB to ensure that long-term exports of natural gas will be surplus to reasonably foresee-able Canadian requirements. Oil exports are not a problem in this respect, because crude oil is only bought and sold on a short-term basis.

As mentioned earlier, political concerns about security of supply have been so sensitive that prior to 1987, this aspect of the NEB's mandate was backed by the legal requirement to ensure that there would always be proven reserves for twenty-five years (NEB, 1996). There were several reasons for eliminating this provision. Among them was the view in Western Canada that this was a subsidy cost paid by Western producers to support Eastern consumers and indus-trial users of gas. Under Mulroney, the NEB in 1987 moved to a mar-ket test and review process to ensure long-term supply (the 'market-based procedure').

It is important to emphasize that this export approval function is still anchored by the NEB's own estimating and monitoring of Canada's energy reserves. But the export licence process is now a far simpler two-step process involving assessment (in effect the monitoring func-tion noted earlier) and a challenge mechanism. When proposed export contracts are filed publicly with the NEB, any Canadian industrial user can use the challenge process if it believes – and can show in a public hearing – that it cannot obtain the gas from a supplier on simi-lar terms and conditions. This mechanism has not been used very much, and thus the NEB is satisfied after fifteen years of gas deregula-tion that the market-based approach is working and is more efficient than the pre-1987 export regime (ibid.; NEB, 2001). The NEB's 2000 report on natural gas market dynamics and pricing concluded that the natural gas market had been functioning so that Canadian require-ments for natural gas were being satisfied at fair market prices (ibid., 2001), with fairness being judged by equivalence or convergence in domestic versus export prices.

The relatively routine and quiet operation of this monitoring func-tion may as a result of the Bush Administration's desire to be able to rely even more than at present on Canadian natural gas supplies and eventually on sources such as the vast Alberta oil sands. This is because Canadians may become more politically aware again of longer-term supply issues. So far, private producers and users in Canada are satisfied with the market-based monitoring process; however, some provincial governments in Atlantic Canada such as New Brunswick have been raising concerns about whether they will get economic access to Sable Island gas. In a recent decision, the NEB ruled against the concerns of the New Brunswick government, arguing that free North American energy markets were still the best policy (Seskus and Cattaneo, 2002). However, the NEB's own forecasting review studies are now having to take into account more complex multiple scenarios, including an extreme-case Bush NEP scenario in which American demand is forecast at very high levels. These scenarios, when published, may well require quite elaborate hearings by the NEB, because concerns may arise as to whether the Canadians still have access to their own sources of energy supply.

Ultimately, this security debate will necessarily involve renewed debate about exactly which combination of state and market role is the best guarantor of long-term supply and of the supply mix. In this regard, it is useful to recall a less well-known Mulroney era policy event that reflected the intellectual underpinnings for the promarket focus of the current security-of-supply regime. This was the Energy Options report, published in 1988 by the Minister of Energy's Energy Options Advisory Committee (Canada, 1988). After an elaborate public consultation exercise, it concluded that energy policy participants had rejected the 'hoarding' approach for a 'development' approach. By a development approach, it meant an approach that relied on free markets. By a hoarding approach, it meant policies to slow the rate of development below what is economic under prevailing conditions in order to ensure that future generations would be left with an adequate supply. The committee concluded that these hoarding policies were fundamentally flawed for four reasons. First, they presumed that policymakers had the wisdom to forecast the future. Second, they frustrated the very mechanism – namely, market pricing – most likely to foster the growth of needed oil and gas reserves. Third, they divided the nation by frustrating the needs and aspirations of the producing regions. And finally, they assigned to governments the responsibility for prescribing choices as opposed to allowing Canadian producers and consumers to generate the needed solutions through their diverse market interactions (ibid.). Although the implicit and explicit claims for the development model are somewhat overstated in the above critique, they nonetheless capture the real changes in energy markets and in views about how past policy worked or failed to work.

Northern Pipelines, Aboriginal Peoples, and Sustainable Northern Development

The chapters by Abele and by Bankes and Wenig focused in different ways on the energy and sustainable development issues facing territorial and Aboriginal governments in the North, and facing the federal government in the North and on the frontiers. We offer further observations on energy policy in the North, noting not only the new configurations of territorial governance, Aboriginal governance, and pipeline proposals for new natural gas supply (which Abele and Bankes and Wenig focused on) but also sustainable development links to the 1997 federal Oceans Act and to northern S&T.

The *North* often means the non-provincial North. However, definitions of the North in the new energy policy–sustainable development context can also include northern development within key provinces and can encompass, as well, contending definitions centred on key energy-sustainable development links. For example, a recent review process on federal 'Northern S&T Strategy' has related its view of the North to the permafrost and other criteria rather than to political boundary definitions of the North, because key aspects of supportive ecosystem S&T require a physical/spatial definition rather than a political/jurisdictional definition.

Official energy federal policy on the North is still the 1985 Mulroney government's *Canada's Energy Frontiers: A Framework for Investment and Jobs* (Canada, 1985). The Conservative policy on the frontiers was intended to move away from the previous Liberal NEP regime, which the Mulroney government argued was 'very strongly criticized by the oil and gas industry, Canadian business in general, and by our trading partners. It impaired Canada's energy and economic performance [and needed new policies] that encourage rather than smother initiative' (ibid., 2). Thus, the main thrust of the energy policy on the frontiers would be to enable the frontiers to 'make an important contribution to Canada's long term energy security' (ibid.). A second major theme in the 1985 policy was 'shared management based upon the principle of equality of governments,' which the Mulroney government had already put in place with the Western and Atlantic Accords, and which it then wanted to apply to the North as well (ibid.).

The rest of the 1985 policy then dealt with the following: a new legislative framework under a then proposed new petroleum resources bill; some principles of resource management; fiscal regime changes regarding royalties and an exploration tax credit; and a 50 per cent Canadian ownership requirement at the production stage. Only in the resource management section of the policy was there an oblique reference to environmental issues, despite relatively fresh memories of the 1970s Berger Commission debate. Another key institutional feature of this policy was that the frontiers energy policy would come from the Department of Indian Affairs and Northern Development (DIAND), which was at the time, as well as historically, seen as a strong pro-energy development department and a much more influential player in federal energy policy than it seems to be so far in the early 2000s debate.

The 1985 policy is still the official policy on Canada's energy frontiers. In many respects, it is now out of date, because much has changed in the North since the mid-1980s. The key impetus for change is the need for a new north-south gas pipeline to bring Alaska gas and/or Delta gas south. As Bankes and Wenig show, the multibillion-dollar pipeline could run down the Alaska Highway into Alberta and then to North American markets, or it could run down a largely Canadian northern pipeline route. These huge investments and the intense politics surrounding the pipeline route and its environmental assessment have been brought to the fore by the Bush Administration's NEP and by the re-emergence of energy security issues.

A second crucial change – as Abele stresses in chapter 10 – is that the northern territorial governments, including the new government of Nunuvut, have all been given greater self-government powers, including regulatory powers, on both the economic and environmental sides of the regulatory coin. Aboriginal self-governance has conferred direct powers on Aboriginal peoples, and this has been accompanied by a quite different set of views about resource development compared to the Berger era. This time, by and large, Aboriginal peoples tend to favour development provided it is managed in a northern democratic context.

Some of these issues of basic environmental policy and sustainable development, in the context of renewed concerns about energy security, will undoubtedly arise in the applications for, and eventual building of, a new northern frontier pipeline for natural gas. The regulatory process will be much more complex than in the Berger era. Several federal, territorial, and First Nations authorities will be involved. And, of course, heavy-duty cross-border politics and economics – including possible subsidies from the United States – will be central to the eventual choice of the pipeline route.

The NEB cannot take a position on any particular route for a pipeline, but as a lead regulator, it has responsibilities to ensure that the multiple-board processes of the new governance structure in the North function efficiently and effectively. An initial manifestation of this need surfaced when the several boards involved released in January 2002 their joint Cooperation Plan for public comment. The larger prodevelopment push for regulatory coordination was also revealed by the federal government's decision to energize the Northern Pipeline Agency (NPA). This came in late November 2002 when the NPA, established twenty-five years ago, was again given its own administrator (Nguyen, 2002). In recent years the head of the NPA had also been the head of the NEB.

Layered over these changes in the North (and elsewhere in Canada) is the challenge involved in handling in practice the impacts of concepts of sustainable development. Bankes and Wenig use the sustainable development provisions in the Auditor General's Act as their analytical touchstone in the North. Another key change here is the passage of the 1997 Oceans Act, which is administered by the Department of Fisheries and Oceans (DFO). Northern energy development is now partly governed by laws governing Canada's 'third' ocean and all the complex ecosystem linkages among coastal waters and estuaries, fish habitat, energy development, and sustainable development. For example, the Mackenzie Delta is a unique ecosystem with both offshore and onshore dimensions.

The legislation contains references to and provisions for the *precautionary principle, sustainable development* per se, and *integrated management*. But the interpretation and practical meanings of these concepts are not clear and are open to different interpretations by departments and agencies such as DFO, Environment Canada, Parks Canada, and DIAND. The Oceans Act is a significant piece of legislation, and developed out of criticisms that DFO had mismanaged the east coast cod fishery. However, it does not explicitly recognize any concepts of economic development such as through provisions for performance-based approaches to regulation.

A further change is also crucial in a northern context – namely, the need noted earlier for a Northern S&T Strategy. S&T activity in the North, never strong to start with, had been seriously harmed by federal program-review budget cuts in 1994–5. Federal science-based departments with S&T roles in the North cut their northern activities in the mid-1990s largely because there were no voices at the table to defend these activities. However, in 2001 a major federal government-wide review of northern S&T activities occurred premised not only on the need to restore cuts and reinvest in the North but also on the recognition that many of the key harmful effects of climate change and energy development would be in the North, if not already occurring there. The review also recognized that in contrast to the south, the northern 'S&T and Innovation System' was not a public–private system but largely a public–government system (see more on overall energy S&T below). The proposed Northern S&T Strategy was developed at a time when its planners thought they could take advantage of the Chrétien government's emphasis on innovation (as reflected in the 2000 Throne Speech). Initial Cabinet support seemed highly likely until the events of 11 September 2001 strongly altered federal spending and other priorities.

Electricity Restructuring and the Limits of Market Design

Even though electricity is but one subsector of energy policy, and even though prior to the 1990s it had not been an area of major federal concern (it falls within provincial jurisdiction), the emergence of electricity restructuring and the August 2003 North American electricity blackout have elevated it to a major national and North American energy issue. As we have seen, the 1990s developments in the United States and Britain and then in Alberta and Ontario brought electricity to the forefront of energy politics, economics, and policy (Canadian Electricity Association, 2000; Cameron, 2001; Czamanski, 1999). Electricity restructuring, as the chapters by Dewees and Schott have shown, involved efforts to recognize and operationalize the fact that not all aspects of electricity are natural monopolies and that electricity can, to some extent, be treated like a normal product or service. At the same time, electricity is not like other normal products in that it cannot be stored and involves instant transmission and use according to the laws of physics. Moreover, it is an essential service for Canadians, just as for the citizens of any modern country (Doern and Gattinger, 2003;

Palast et al., 2003). Restructuring therefore has involved aspects of the following: deregulation, to allow new producers of electricity supply to enter the market; new or expanded regulation to coordinate market operations and ensure the reliability of electricity grids and that anticompetitive behaviour does not arise; and privatization and/or the breaking up of monopoly companies. And all of these varied potential acts of change are occurring at a time of environmental and sustainable development debates and pressures.

The three chapters on electricity restructuring focus on different aspects of recent Canadian and North American developments. They reach different but always highly cautionary conclusions about recent efforts to design freer but still managed or regulated markets. Dewees in chapter 5 broadly supports restructuring and concludes as well that the more market-oriented aspects of these changes are more likely to produce environmental gains as well as better sustainability. Dewees, however, also sees as a serious problem the apparent unwillingness of some governments to let markets function. In Ontario, the Conservative government's decision in November 2002 to freeze electricity prices for several years, less than six months after the new electricity market opened, is seen by Dewees and other experts as ill advised. The province's new Liberal government, which was elected two months after the August 2003 electricity blackout, judged that this price freeze was unsustainable on both energy and fiscal grounds, and announced in October 2003 that it would let prices rise. However, in other respects the Ontario Liberal policies are vague and poorly considered.

The analysis in chapter 6 by Vaughan, Carpentier, Patterson, and Miller takes electricity restructuring generally as a given but then examines possible scenarios regarding the likely effects of electricity restructuring in North America on Canada's ability to meet its Kyoto Protocol commitments to reduce GHG emissions. Their overall conclusions – necessarily qualified by limitations in data and assumptions – are that restructuring is likely on balance to make Kyoto Protocol commitments more difficult to achieve because of stronger shifts toward GHG-emitting fuel sources either in the United States and Canada, including decisions to locate some source plants south of the border. These authors qualify their negative findings by also showing other potentially more positive developments in North American environmental policy, including cooperative initiatives that are being taken and that are analytically separate from restructuring per se. Chapter 6 also discusses the growing policy and institutional importance for Canada's utilities and electricity producers of the regional transmission organizations (RTOs) in the United States, which have recently been mandated by the U.S. Federal Energy Regulatory Commission (FERC).

In chapter 7, Stephan Schott offered an overview of electricity restructuring in Ontario and elsewhere but through the broader analytical prism of *socially efficient* electricity production and related criteria for sustainable production. Schott is very sceptical of restructuring developments in Ontario (and elsewhere) and argues for a much broader social cost–benefit analysis of the two polar models: state monopolies, and market-centred electricity systems. The hybrid nature of the Ontario system is deemed by Schott to have produced something closer to the worst of both systems rather than the best.

Despite the different conclusions reached in these examinations of electricity restructuring as a macro energy issue, these authors are quite cautious and nuanced in their conclusions. In different ways, each sees electricity as different from oil and gas; with the latter, market-oriented approaches have dominated for the past two decades. And each sees 'market design' – which in essence means still-regulated managed markets – as being highly complex and therefore problematic. They also all show how particular restructurings depend on complex local–regional situations and circumstances, politically, economically, and institutionally. Unlike in oil and natural gas, there is no continentwide sense of a Canada–U.S. market in electricity; there are only contingent cross-border grids whose management as grids is only beginning to be faced up to.

The interim joint U.S.–Canada report on the August 2003 blackout did not assign any blame to Ontario or Canada for the blackout. It focused blame on First-Energy Corp, an Ohio power company (Tuck, 2003). Clearly, though, the blackout and its aftermath have pointed to serious issues regarding complex grids and how they are regulated and managed in the public interest on both sides of the border.

Federal S&T Policies and Energy Innovation

Canadian energy policy is influenced by, and increasingly embedded in, federal S&T and innovation policies. Virtually all participants in the energy policy debate are calling for some kind of expanded use of S&T and innovation as a complement or alternative to regulation. Private firms, especially the ones that are interested in sustainable development and environmental industries, are heavily engaged in such research and innovation (Toner, 2004). Also, governments require new forms of S&T that are 'regulation-relevant' – in short, which offer the right kind of technical knowledge at the right times and in the right places to facilitate compliance and changes in behaviour that are relevant both to the corporate bottom line and to sustainable energy use. As Jarvis's analysis in chapter 4 shows, energy and sustainable development policy is especially in need of data, as well as ongoing energy and environmental reporting that will allow governments and society as a whole to come closer to reaching the Holy Grail of internalizing the external costs of different energy sources and of ensuring that the resulting prices and costs are transparent.

Energy S&T and innovation must be placed, analytically and institutionally, in the context of the broader transformation of federal S&T policy that has occurred over the past decade. This transformation has seen the emergence of change under the innovation paradigm and under the concepts of national and regional–local systems of innovation (Wolfe, 2002; de la Mothe, 2000; Doern and Levesque, 2002). This overall area of energy policy also brings us more explicitly into the realm of energy spending, especially by the federal government. Unlike other aspects of energy policy, S&T policy has been mainly a federal preserve, largely because historically Ottawa had the money. Federal S&T policy for the energy-sustainable development sector over the past twenty years can be cast as a series of spending spurts and reductions, with each having some intended and unintended impacts on the energy sector.

The 1980 NEP was a well-funded initiative that included S&T funding support for measures to improve energy conservation both in production and in end use (e.g., in homes and buildings). On their own, high energy prices during this period forced a search for energy-saving technologies and processes. But even in the heyday of the NEP, the largest part of federal energy S&T actually went to nuclear energy, largely through support for Atomic Energy of Canada Ltd. (Doern and Toner, 1985). This was true even though nuclear energy was mainly an Ontario-centred power source.

A second 'burst' of S&T support occurred under the Mulroney government's Green Plan of 1989–90 (Doern and Conway, 1994). This included some funding for alternative energy technologies. However, the Green Plan ended quickly in the mid-1990s, soon after the Chrétien Liberals launched their Program Review (Swimmer, 1996). Program

Review was the third change with a strong impact on S&T budgets. In the name of deficit reduction, all federal departments took heavy cuts. This included, in particular, cuts of up to 40 per cent in the S&T budgets of federal science-based departments and agencies, including energy-related departments such as NRCan and Environment Canada.

Another, perhaps more continuous, thread of change running through the period from the mid-1980s to the present has been the gradual adoption of the above-mentioned innovation paradigm as the preferred way of thinking about and acting on federal S&T policy. An early manifestation of this was in the late 1980s, when the Mulroney government took steps to force some federal S&T laboratories – such as in the resource and energy sectors – to become more commercially relevant by requiring them to raise revenues from the industries they were serving. Revenue raising would be an initial surrogate for commercial relevance and would be supportive of the view that more federal S&T should be conducted in or with the private sector (Doern and Kinder, 2002).

The Mulroney government certainly spoke of competitiveness and innovation, but it was the Chrétien government that made innovation the centrepiece of its main microeconomic policy paper, *Building a More Innovative Economy* (Industry Canada, 1994). This document reflected the need for a government role in the knowledge economy, but it was also very eclectic about just what this role would be, and about what was meant by innovation. The dominant view inherent in innovation policies – a view that evolved out of free trade, the globalization of production, and the revolution in telecommunications, computers, and capital and financial mobility – was that market liberalization was the best overall policy for governments to follow. The Liberals' emphasis on innovation crystallized further in 2001, when it became the top agenda item in the Throne Speech following Chrétien's third electoral victory in November 2000, and in 2002, when that government's innovation strategy paper, *Achieving Excellence* (Industry Canada, 2002) was made public. This ascendancy of the innovation agenda occurred just as the Kyoto Protocol debate was intensifying – specifically, around how much of the Canadian approach should be regulation based as opposed to incentive, S&T, and innovation based (Macdonald et al., 2003).

A further key debate that made room for an innovation policy paradigm arose from the partial breakdown of the earlier postwar model, which had been centred on the belief that there was a spectrum of scientific activity (de la Mothe, 2000). The broad presumption of this model was that basic or *pure* research drove the later *applied* research and development, and that this is what led to innovative products. For at least the past fifteen years, this assumption has been challenged by other evidence and experience which shows that interactions are much more complex – indeed, the causal links are often reversed and much more subtle. In short, the pathways to real innovation, in energy and other economic and production realms, are multiple, interactive, and complex rather than linear.

Thus, the overall federal institutional system for innovation has evolved in recent years in the context of changing views about the nature of S&T and R&D, the need for Canada to be globally competitive in a knowledge-based economy, and experimentation with new organizations and networks for delivering R&D and innovation support for both national and regional–local systems of innovation. This system has been built on long-standing bodies and agencies such as the National Research Council (NRC), as well as on the federal granting bodies and federal labs, but also on a set of newer bodies, programs, and policy funds, which have been organized in various ways. These include the Canada Foundation for Innovation (CFI) and the Sustainable Development Technology Fund (SDTF). Many of these newer instruments and vehicles have been referred to as third-party delivery mechanisms, and themselves constitute a crucial and important effort to foster innovation in how things are done.

In its 2000 survey of federal energy policy, NRCan summed up its challenges in energy research and technology development as twofold, namely, 'making existing energy supplies and technologies cleaner and more efficient, and developing energy technologies that are climate-friendly' (NRCan, 2000, 141). It also emphasized that NRCan through various programs and labs 'is involved in almost every facet of energy research and development' (ibid., 143).

A core program fund is the interdepartmental Program on Energy Research and Development (PERD). PERD is the federal government's principal means for funding non-nuclear energy R&D. PERD, through NRCan's Office of Energy R&D, administers a $58 million fund (it was almost $200 million in the mid-1980s). This fund is allocated through an extensive interdepartmental planning process that is managed by NRCan and that is closely linked to NRCan's energy policy through an annually updated document called the 'Energy Priority Framework' (EPF) and its associated S&T Companion Document (S&TCD), which frames the priorities into the various S&T realms. The PERD component of NRCan's energy S&T is delivered through eleven federal departments and agencies, with about 50 per cent going to NRCan's Energy Technologies Branch and the balance to other departments such as Environment Canada, Transport Canada, and the National Research Council to support energy-related R&D. At present, there are six 'strategic intents' in the PERD program. These six deal respectively with oil and gas; transportation; buildings and communities; industry; electricity; and the minimizing of the negative impacts of climate change on the Canadian energy sector.

As emphasized earlier, another key change was the re-emergence of the climate change issue in the late 1990s and early 2000s, with all its S&T and innovation implications. As we have seen, climate change funding had emerged in the 1990 Green Plan; however, by the late 1990s it was being linked much more closely to the Kyoto Protocol. The late 1990s funding included new, related funds and pools of money to develop new technologies. In principle, this brought back into the policy and mandate domain some of the same areas of S&T that had been wound down over the preceding few years. However, it brought them back with different kinds of funding and institutional mechanisms in which NRCan's labs (and federal labs as a whole) could not participate directly. For example, regarding major S&T and innovation funds such as CFI and the new Sustainable Development Technology Fund (SDTF), federal labs were not eligible. Another example was the Technology Early Action Measures (TEAM) component of the Climate Change Action Fund.

The above reference to the climate change issue and the emergence of new funds does not alter the fact that oil and gas as an energy source still underpins federal energy S&T policy and S&T funding in the energy sector per se. This includes crucial support for oil sands research linked to the growth and maturation of the oil sands as a national and Alberta energy resource (CANMET, 1994; 1995; CONRAD, 1998). The oil sands were already benefiting from federal and Alberta S&T in the 1980s, and this had helped reduce production costs from about $30 a barrel in the late 1980s to future estimated costs by the mid-2000s of around $15. Hence, it was, by the late 1980s, already assuming an increasingly large role as a source of Canada's oil supply (15 per cent, even in 1988). But a further related and crucial example of stakeholder and combined governmental S&T impetus was the work of the National Task Force on Oil Sands Technology (NTFOSS). This task force issued its major report in May 1995, in which was proposed a development strategy to triple oil sands production to over 50 per cent of Canada's domestic supply by 2020 (CANMET, 1995, 12). NTFOSS recommended changes to the Alberta and federal fiscal regimes, but it also contained recommendations for both S&T and sustainable development. In its S&T components, the task force recommended five strategies to 'ensure that the incremental improvements and step-out or breakthrough technologies are identified, developed, demonstrated and commercialized' (ibid., 12). The sections of the report on sustainable development contained recommendations regarding improvements in energy conservation, GHG emissions, land use and reclamation, air quality, water conservation and quality, and biodiversity. All of these aspects were technology driven. In the wake of this stakeholder impetus and for other reasons, S&T investment and innovation had increased massively by the early 2000s (CONRAD, 1998). NRCan's lab, the CANMET Western Research Centre, focuses almost totally on the oil sands in close concert with the Government of Alberta, key energy firms, and universities (CANMET, 2001).

However, despite these S&T activities, it is crucial to reiterate that a still very high portion of federal energy S&T goes to nuclear energy – a larger proportion than to alternative energy. This is partly because of simple institutional inertia and partly because the nuclear industry in Canada does not emit GHG emissions and is lobbying hard among federal ministers for new investments in its next-generation research facilities, whose costs will be in the $400 million range. But the as yet unknown environmental S&T and related costs of long-term nuclear waste storage are also queuing up in the federal budgetary line, so nuclear energy's future in Canada is still very precarious (Doern, Dorman, and Morrison, 2001).

These levels of S&T support for nuclear energy, compared to alternative sources, may be on the verge of changing as the new S&T funds mentioned above kick in and take effect and as funding for fuel cell technology expands. Nonetheless, some of the S&T funding priorities seem badly out of step in the matter of preparing for the full array of future needs and energy alternatives.

These are by no means the only issues to touch on the links between S&T and innovation policy and energy policy in a sustainable development context. We referred earlier to the real needs of northern S&T strategy. The provinces also contribute to energy research and to industrial innovation incentives; for example, they support environmental industries that are being 'grown' around the need for new alternative technologies. The Americans' huge investment on such technologies under the Bush Administration's energy plan is also likely to lead to both funding and partnership opportunities for Canadian firms. But in the final analysis, it is still the federal government that must ensure that sensible links are forged between S&T funding and viable alternative energy futures for Canadians.

Energy Policy and Sustainable Development: From Struggle to Achievement?

Last but not least among Canada's related energy policy and governance challenges is the basic issue of how both federal and provincial governments might further 'institutionalize' and entrench the concept of sustainable development in energy policy decision processes. The analysis in this book has cast the issue of energy and sustainable development more as a struggle than as an achievement. In an overall sense, this conclusion rests on the fact that Canada's per capita energy consumption has not improved over the past two decades. Sustainable development ideas and some conservation measures and new technologies have undoubtedly prevented results from being even worse, but the net energy record in this aspect of energy policy is not a good one.

In this final section we comment briefly on some final aspects of this question. Other chapters have already zeroed in on key aspects of sustainable development. The origin and central features of the sustainable development paradigm were set out in chapter 1, as were current provincial energy policies. This analysis indicated that all governments endorse the concept in some overt manner but without necessarily practising it. Sustainable development was also central to earlier analyses of the climate change and Kyoto debates, and it is also inherently a feature of discussions about the North, the Oceans Act, and federal S&T and innovation policy.

Sustainable development is now a formal part of policymaking in many Western countries, albeit, as in Canada, with widely varied degrees and forms of practice and also wide varieties of criticism (Lafferty and Meadowcroft, 2000). Most often, sustainable development is used in the 'triple bottom line' meaning of the term – namely, a balanced consideration of economic, social, and environmental factors and values in policy development. As we have emphasized, this is a much looser notion than one centred on sustainable ecosystems. At the federal level, the triple-bottom-line notion of the concept is meant to inform and guide policy in many policy fields such as forestry (a renewable resource for which greater sustainability has been achieved), as well as in the areas of health and education. It must be stressed that this book has dealt only with the energy-related aspects of sustainable development and thus cannot pronounce on its effectiveness in other areas of policy (Toner and Frey, 2003).

But federal policy statements have elaborated further on what sustainable development means for the energy economy. It opens with the familiar starting point that it is a policy paradigm that 'requires that Canada's present energy needs be satisfied without compromising the ability of future generations to meet their needs. Sustainable development means that the energy economy performs well economically and environmentally, i.e. that sound economic performance is balanced with appropriate consideration of the environmental effects of producing and consuming energy' (NRCan, 2000, 29). But then federal policy asserts that 'in the case of energy, sustainable development *does not imply preserving one particular source of energy over another*. The challenge of sustainable development is not to guarantee future generations with specific reserve levels for any particular form of energy. Rather the challenge is to provide secure, safe, efficient, reasonably priced and increasingly environmentally friendly access to energy services' (ibid., 31).

Federal energy policy is certainly not at present this intergenerational in nature, nor is it this neutral among fuels and sources of energy. Nor has it resulted in core conservation improvements when expressed as energy use per capita. Thus, a key practical concern is how this concept of sustainable development plays out among the core regulatory institutions of the federal government and their provincial counterparts, as well as internationally. One question, for example, is whether the federal National Energy Board Act should be changed to make sustainable development a statutory responsibility of the NEB (Doern and Gattinger, 2003). After all, sustainable development is a part of the Oceans Act and also the act governing Natural Resources Canada and the Auditor General Act.

Sustainable development as an idea also means that there is an even broader set of governmentwide sustainable development players, simply because all federal ministries are expected to develop and implement sustainable development strategies (Toner and Frey, 2003; Toner, 2000). Hence, it is a policy that is much broader than energy policy per se and is also likely to produce resource allocation and regulatory choices that are not all focused on energy per se, or on conservation, or GHG reductions. Some progress is now likely as Kyoto commitments are implemented, but there is still a very long way to go to implement a difficult but crucial component of Canadian energy policy in the next decade and the decades thereafter.

Concluding Observations

Each of the energy policy and governance challenges drawn together in this final chapter reveals areas of both contested priorities and institutional change facing a Liberal Martin government but also some areas of continuity with the last twenty years of energy policy as a whole under the Mulroney Conservative government and the Chrétien Liberals.

Although our broader survey of provincial energy developments has not included all provinces, it does show the variety of provincial energy policy circumstances and changes. The greater importance of North American electricity markets is a central feature of change. There are certainly strong indications of promarket approaches overall, but at the same time growing concerns about sustainable development and about exactly how to practise such precepts. Central to this on the national stage has been the national debate over the Kyoto Protocol commitments, but there are also, crucially, many provincial and interregional aspects to the now pending implementation challenges, including not only Alberta's oil sands–fuelled energy prosperity but also the fact that the Atlantic provinces with offshore oil and gas reserves are now poised for expansion and export growth, largely into an energy-hungry American market. British Columbia also has aggressive plans for its offshore resources as an engine for economic growth.

With regard to energy and sustainable development in the North and with respect to pipeline development there, the analysis has emphasized the much changed situation in the North relative to two decades ago and relative to the Berger Commission era. Territorial and Aboriginal governance structures may be more propipeline and prodevelopment than before, but there are still very serious issues concerning whether and how local benefits for northerners will be secured through strengthened democratic institutions. We have shown how laws and views of sustainable development have changed in the North. These changes include the new Ocean Act and other concerns about the already existing adverse impacts of climate change in the North. These changes suggest that federal policy statements such as the 1985 statement on energy in the North and in the frontier areas are out of date and require a significant reappraisal. The same applies to S&T policy for the North, where Program Review and its aftermath severely cut S&T resources at the very time when sustainable development issues were most becoming newly evident and most needed good science to underpin them and deal with them.

The analysis of federal S&T and innovation policy in an energy and sustainable development context has brought out a mixed picture. Bursts of S&T support have been followed by deep cuts and then, in recent years, by renewed funding, including the provision of third-party delivered funds. Federal energy S&T policy has certainly also moved in a market-oriented direction with regard to the role of federal energy labs, through partnerships and levered funding. But at the same time, a quite high proportion of federal R&D goes to nuclear research, even though this is not officially in line with the broader declared thrust of energy policy. Nuclear energy does not produce GHG emissions, yet it still lacks wide support as an energy source alternative because of public concerns about the long-term management of nuclear wastes.

Many sections of this book examined aspects of sustainable development. This final section has drawn concluding overall attention to the continuing need for more concerted efforts to institutionalize and actually implement sustainable development in federal and provincial energy policy thinking and practice. For many, climate change is the acid test for sustainable development in energy policy, but it is evident that sustainable development issues go well beyond this, and well beyond energy policy, and that it will take a great deal of institutional and NGO pressure to manage and further operationalize this crucial aspect of Canada's and the world's energy future. Businesses will also play a key role, because so many Canadian and foreign firms are already engaged in sustainable development production practices.

REFERENCES

Cameron, Peter. 2001. *Competition in Energy Markets*. Oxford: Oxford University Press.

Canada. 1988. *Energy and Canadians into the 21st Century*. Ottawa: Minister of Supply and Services.

– 2002a. *A Discussion Paper on Canada's Contribution to Addressing Climate Change*. Ottawa: Public Works and Government Services Canada.

– 2002b. *Climate Change Plan for Canada*. Ottawa: Government of Canada.

CWRC (CANMET Western Research Centre). 1994. *Western Research Centre Business Plan 1994–1997*. Ottawa: CANMET, Natural Resources Canada.

– 1995. 'Briefing Materials for Opening of Froth Treatment Facility.' Devon, Alberta. 6 October.

– 2001. *Western Research Centre Business Plan 2001–2004*. Ottawa: CANMET, Natural Resources Canada.

Canadian Electricity Association. 2000. 'Canadian Electricity Association Brief to Energy Ministers.' September.

Canadian Oil Sands Network for Research and Development (CONRAD). 1998. 'Canadian Oil Sands Network for Research and Development.' Briefing Deck. October. Ottawa: CANMET, Natural Resources Canada.

Czamanski, D.Z. 1999. *Privatization and Restructuring of Electricity Provision*. London: Praeger.

de la Mothe, John. 2000. 'Government Science and the Public Interest.' In Bruce Doern and Ted Reed, eds., *Risky Business: Canada's Changing Science-Based Regulatory Regime*. Toronto: University of Toronto Press.

Department of Indian Affairs and Northern Development. 1985. *Canada's Energy Frontiers: A Framework For Investment and Jobs*. Ottawa: DIAND.

Doern, G. Bruce, and Tom Conway. 1994. *The Greening of Canada*. Toronto: University of Toronto Press.

Doern, G. Bruce, Arslan Dorman, and Robert Morrison, eds. 2001. *Canadian Nuclear Energy Policy: Changing Ideas, Institutions and Interests*. Toronto: University of Toronto Press.

Doern, G. Bruce, and Monica Gattinger. 2003. *Power Switch: Energy Regulatory Governance in the 21st Century*. Toronto: University of Toronto Press.

Doern, G. Bruce, and Jeff Kinder. 2002. 'The Roles of Federal S&T Labs: Institutional Change and Future Challenges.' A Report on the CRUISE Workshop on the Roles of Federal S&T Labs: Institutional Change and Future Challenges. April. Ottawa: Carleton Research Unit on Innovation, Science and Environment (CRUISE).

Doern, G. Bruce, and Richard Levesque. 2002. *The National Research Council in the Innovation Policy Era: Changing Hierarchies, Networks, and Markets.* Toronto: University of Toronto Press.

Doern, G. Bruce, and Ted Reed, eds. 2000. *Risky Business: Canada's Changing Science-Based Policy and Regulatory Regime.* Toronto: University of Toronto Press.

Doern, G. Bruce, and Glen Toner. 1985. *The Politics of Energy.* Toronto: Methuen.

Environmental Studies Program. 2003. *Ratification of the Kyoto Protocol: A Citizen's Guide to the Canadian Climate Change Policy Process.* Toronto: Environmental Studies Program, University of Toronto.

Environment Canada. 2002. *The Costs of Kyoto – What We Know.* Ottawa: Environment Canada.

Industry Canada. 2002. *Achieving Excellence.* Ottawa: Industry Canada.

– 1994. *Building a More Innovative Economy.* Ottawa: Minister of Supply and Services.

Lafferty, William M., and James Meadowcroft, eds. 2000. *Implementing Sustainable Development.* Oxford: Oxford University Press, 2000.

Macdonald, Douglas. 2003. 'The Business Campaign to Prevent Kyoto Ratification.' Paper presented to the Canadian Political Science Association Meeting, Dalhousie University, 31 May.

Macdonald, Douglas, Debora VanNijnatten, and Andrew Bjorn. 2003. 'Implementing Kyoto: Why Spending is Not Enough', Paper presented to Conference on New Prime Minister ... New Era, School of Public Policy and Administration, Carleton University, Ottawa, 29–30 October.

National Energy Board (NEB). 2001. *2001–2002 Estimates: Part III – Report on Plans and Priorities.* Ottawa: Public Works and Government Services Canada.

– 1996. *Ten Years After Deregulation.* Ottawa: National Energy Board.

Natural Resources Canada. 2000. *Energy in Canada 2000.* Ottawa: Natural Resources Canada.

Nguyen, Lily. 2002. 'Ottawa Resurrects Pipeline Agency.' *Globe and Mail.* 29 November: B5.

Palast, Greg, J. Oppenheim, and T. MacGregor. 2003. *Democracy and Regulation: How the Public Can Govern Essential Services.* Oxford: Pluto Press.

Seskus, Tony, and Claudia Cattaneo. 2002. 'Gas Giants Applaud NEB Ruling.' *Financial Post.* 20 September, 1.

Swimmer, Gene, ed. 1996. *How Ottawa Spends, 1996–97: Life Under the Knife.* Ottawa: Carleton University Press.

Trebilcock, Michael, and Ronald Daniels. 1995. 'The Future of Ontario Hydro.' *Utilities Law Review*, Winter.

Toner, Glen. 2000. 'Canada: From Early Frontrunner to Plodding Anchorman.' In William M. Lafferty and James Meadowcroft, eds. (2000), *Implementing Sustainable Development* (Oxford University Press) Chapter 3.

Toner, Glen, ed. 2004. *Building Canadian Capacity: Sustainable Development and the Knowledge Economy*. Vancouver: UBC Press (in press).

Toner, Glen, and Carey Frey. 2004. 'Governance for Sustainable Development: Next Steps and Policy Innovations.' Paper presented to the Conference on New Prime Minister ... New Era, School of Public Policy and Administration, Carleton University, Ottawa, 29–30 October.

Tuck, Simon. 2003. 'Canada Off the Hook for Power Blackout.' *Globe and Mail*. 20 November: A8.

Wolfe, David. 2002. 'Innovation for the Knowledge-Based Economy: From the Red Book to the White Paper.' In Bruce Doern, ed., *How Ottawa Spends 2002–2003: The Security Aftermath and National Priorities*. Toronto: Oxford University Press.

Contributors

Frances Abele teaches in the School of Public Policy and Administration at Carleton University. She has been studying northern political and economic development for the past twenty-five years and is the author of *Gathering Strength: Training Programs for Native People in the Northwest Territories*, and (with Katherine Graham and Carolyn Dittburner), *Soliloquy and Dialogue: Overview of Major Trends in Public Policy Relating to Aboriginal Peoples*. Dr Abele is president of the Association of Canadian Universities for Northern Studies.

Nigel Bankes is a professor of law at the University of Calgary where he teaches resources law, Aboriginal law, and international environmental law. He is the co-author of *Canadian Oil and Gas* and a former chair of the Canadian Arctic Resources Committee.

Keith Brownsey teaches political science at Mount Royal College in Calgary. He has written extensively on Canadian provincial politics as well as Canadian political parties. His current research centres on the politics of Alberta's oil and gas industry.

C. Line Carpentier heads the Environment, Economy and Trade program at the North American Commission for Environmental Cooperation (CEC) in Montreal. Her recent publications include *Environmental Challenges and Opportunities of the Evolving North American Electricity Market*, 'Carbon Sequestration in Agro-Forestry: Supporting Sustainable Agriculture?' in the *American Journal of Alternative Agriculture*, and (with S.A. Vosti, and J. Witcover) *Small-Scale Farms in the Western Brazilian Amazon: Can They Benefit From Carbon Trade?*

Donald N. Dewees is a professor of economics and professor of law at the University of Toronto. He is the author (with David Duff and Michael Trebilcock) of *Exploring the Domain of Accident Law: Taking the Facts Seriously* (1996) and (with M. J. Hare) *Reducing, Reusing, and Recycling: Packaging Waste Policy in Canada* (1999). In 1998 he served as vice-chair of the Ontario Market Design Committee, which advised the government on introducing competition into the province's electricity market.

G. Bruce Doern is a professor in the School of Public Policy and Administration at Carleton University. He is also the director of the Carleton Research Unit on Innovation, Science, and Environment (CRUISE), and holds a Research Chair in Public Policy in the Politics Department at the University of Exeter. His recent books on energy and environmental policy include *Canadian Nuclear Energy Policy: Changing Ideas, Institutions, and Interests* (co-edited with Robert Morrison and Arlsan Dorman, 2001); *Power Switch: Energy Regulatory Governance in the Twenty-First Century* (co-authored with Monica Gattinger, 2003); and *Risky Business: Canada's Changing Science-Based Policy and Regulatory Regime* (co-edited with Ted Reed, 2000).

Monica Gattinger is assistant professor in the Public Administration Program at the University of Ottawa. Her principal areas of research inquiry are public policy, public administration, and governance. Her main areas of research are policy consultation, business–government–society relations, and the influence of globalization on domestic policy and administration. She is the co-author (with Bruce Doern) of *Power Switch: Energy Regulatory Governance in the Twenty-First Century* (2003).

Bill Jarvis is the director general of the Policy Research Directorate at Environment Canada. He is responsible for providing the knowledge tools that can guide the department and the government's environmental and sustainable development strategies and priorities. He spent fifteen years in energy policy development, analysis, and implementation with Natural Resources Canada. Recent published works include 'A Question of Balance: New Approaches for Science Based Regulations,' in *Risky Business* (ed. Doern and Reed) (2000); *Helping Prometheus: A Summary of Discussions and Recommendations from a Workshop on Science, Government and the Media* (1999); *The Role and Responsibilities of the Scientist in Public Policy* (1998); and *Blood, Fish, and Tears: A Summary of Round Table Discussions on the Credibility and Acceptability of Science Advice for Decision-Making* (1998).

Alastair Lucas is professor of law and chair of natural resources law at the Faculty of Law and adjunct professor of environmental science at the University of Calgary. He is also director of the University of Calgary–Latin American Energy Organization Energy and Environmental Law Project. Recent publications include *Human Rights in Natural Resource Development: Public Participation in the Sustainable Development of Mining and Energy Resources* (co-edited with Donald Zillman and George Pring (2002). His research is in domestic and international energy and environmental law. He is co-editor of Butterworths' *Canadian Environmental Law* and Emond-Montgomery's *Environmental Law and Policy*, co-author of *Oil and Gas Law in Canada*, and author of various articles on energy, environmental, and natural resources law. He is a special legal advisor to the North American Commission for Environmental Cooperation.

Paul Miller is the program manager for air quality at the North American Commission for Environmental Cooperation in Montreal. He is actively involved in coordinating efforts among the North American countries to promote cooperative efforts in addressing transborder air-quality problems. Dr Miller has also worked with the Northeast States for Coordinated Air Use Management (NESCAUM) in Boston, where he provided technical and policy coordination on air pollution issues among the air-quality agencies of eight northeastern states. He has been a visiting fellow at Princeton University's Center for Energy and Environmental Studies, and a National Research Council associate at the Joint Institute for Laboratory Astrophysics, University of Colorado at Boulder.

Robert W. Morrison is a senior research associate in the CRUISE Program at the School of Public Administration at Carleton University and an adjunct research professor in technology, society, environment studies at Carleton. A physicist by training, he is a former director general of Uranium and Nuclear Energy at Natural Resources Canada. Since leaving the government in 1997, he has consulted on energy, security, and sustainable development issues with Natural Resources, Foreign Affairs and International Trade, Ontario Power Generation, the Belgian government, and the OECD in Paris. One of his recent publications is *Canadian Nuclear Energy Policy: Changing Ideas, Institutions and Interests* (co-edited with Bruce Doern and Arlsan Dorman) (2001). He served on the Nuclear Working Group of the Canada–U.S. Power System Outage Task Force and is a member of the Expert Group on Multilateral Approaches to the Nuclear Fuel Cycle at the International Atomic Energy Agency in Vienna.

Zachary Patterson is a PhD candidate in the department of geography at McGill University in Montreal. For his dissertation he is working on a statistical model that will be able to predict freight mode split for the Montreal–Toronto corridor, as well as test the emissions implications for the transportation sector of different GHG reduction policy scenarios in this corridor.

André Plourde is an associate professor and chair, Department of Economics, University of Alberta, where he is closely involved with the specialized MBA program in natural resources and energy. His research interests have centred on energy economics, Canadian energy policy and trade, and the environmental aspects of energy exploitation and use. He is the co-author of two books, and his work has also appeared in a number of academic journals, including *Energy Journal, Journal of Finance, Natural Resources Journal, Canadian Public Policy, Resources and Energy Economics, Economic Modelling, Journal of World Trade, Osgoode Hall Law Journal, Quarterly Review of Economics and Finance,* and *Journal of Energy and Development.* In addition to his academic work, he has also acted as consultant to industry and government on energy and environmental issues. He was recently elected vice-president and treasurer of the International Association for Energy Economics.

Stephan Schott is an assistant professor in the School of Public Policy and Administration at Carleton University. He is actively involved with the Carleton Research Unit on Innovation, Science and Environment (CRUISE) and with the student and alumni network SIGNALS. He recently published an article on energy and environment policy in *Policy Options* (2002) titled 'Are There Any Convincing Economic Reasons for Electricity Privatization and Deregulation in Ontario?' He currently is working on a joint paper with Pierre-Olivier Pineau on 'Time of Use Pricing and Electricity Demand Transfer: A Long Run Analysis of Capacity and Prices' with an application to Ontario. His other related research focuses on natural resource management, particularly fishery management in Atlantic Canada, and theoretical and experimental evaluation of behaviour in common pool resource and public goods environments.

Scott Vaughan is director of the sustainable development and environment division at the Organization of American States, and previously, visiting scholar, Carnegie Endowment for International Peace. Recent publications include 'North American Integration and Limits to Environmental Cooperation' (August 2004); 'The Greenest Trade Agreement Ever: NAFTA's Promise and Reality?' (March 2004), and 'Measuring the Environmental Effects of Agricultural Liberalization' (November 2003).

Michael M. Wenig is a research associate with the Canadian Institute of Resources Law and an adjunct professor of law at the University of Calgary. His primary focus is on the integration of environmental and natural resources law. Mr Wenig's publications have been in the areas of energy policy, sustainable development theory, ecosystem and watershed-based regulatory approaches, cumulative effects management, and pollution liability.